A Hunger
for
Home

Louisa May Alcott
and *Little Women*

Sarah Elbert

TEMPLE UNIVERSITY PRESS
PHILADELPHIA

Temple University Press, Philadelphia 19122
© 1984 by Temple University. All rights reserved
Published 1984
Printed in the United States of America

Library of Congress Cataloging in Publication Data

Elbert, Sarah.
    A Hunger for Home.

    Bibliography: p.
    Includes index.
    1. Alcott, Louisa May, 1832–1888. 2. Women in litera-
ture. 3. Feminism and literature. 4. Novelists,
American—19th century—Biography. I. Title.
PS1018.E4 1984   813'.4 [B]   83-4824
ISBN 0-87722-317-3

Contents

Acknowledgments

David Brion Davis and the late Walter Simon initially encouraged me in the study of intellectual and cultural history; their exemplary scholarship and friendship remain important influences in my life and work. Michael Colacurcio, Jonathan Bishop, and Cushing Strout communicated their distinguished sensitivities to American literature and history. Michael Kammen kindly helped me to "get on with it" as I began my doctoral dissertation. Mary Beth Norton directed "Louisa May Alcott and the Woman Problem," giving generously of her time and wisdom.

William Riley Leach counselled, edited and stimulated my efforts to treat Alcott's work and life in their largest context; his generous help greatly enriched this study. Barbara Brenzel, Anne and Ira Brous, Cynthia and Gould Colman, Wendy Chimielewski, Ann Douglas, Ellen DuBois, Linda Gordon, Heidi Hartmann, Alice Kessler-Harris, Laurie Nisonoff, Mary Ryan, Susan Reverby, Anne Klejment, Kitty Sklar, and Ellie Leiman read various stages of this study. Their constructive criticisms greatly aided the completion of this book. Anna Davin, Sally Alexander, and Lee Davidoff provided both scholarly encouragement and sisterhood. Howard and Roz Feinstein shared psycho-historical perspectives with me and stimulated new approaches to Louisa and May Alcott's relationship, as did Rebecca Allerton.

Marian Ferguson, Elizabeth Fox-Genovese, and Harold Livesay took the time to read and constructively comment on a first draft of this work.

Susan Jacobs typed, read, and commiserated with this manuscript, as did Scott Heyman and Sally Wessel at an earlier stage. Both Ken

Arnold and Michael Ames from Temple University Press provided committed, lively editorial supervision. I am grateful to the staff of Houghton Library, Harvard University, and to the late Mr. William Bond and Mrs. F. Wolsey Pratt for access to Alcott materials and also for permission to quote them. Marcia Moss, curator of the Concord Free Public Library, shared illustrative materials and her impressive knowledge of the Alcott's "set." Madeleine B. Stern is an Alcott scholar of enviable delicacy and erudition; I am grateful for her many kindnesses and the example of her works. Madelon Bedell has enriched the store of materials and analysis of the Alcott family and kindly shared insights and information with me. Gerda Lerner encouraged this study and edited my introduction to Alcott's novel, *Work* (New York, 1977). Leslie Parr of Arno Press directed the task of publishing Louisa May Alcott's untitled manuscript *Diana and Persis* (New York, 1978). Professor Catherine Covert of Syracuse University shared insights into the career of Samuel J. May.

The staff of Manuscripts and Archives at Olin Library (Cornell University) and the faculty and staff of the Department of History (SUNY, Binghamton) provided generous encouragement and stimulation. The English Institute (Aarhus University, Denmark) offered sensitive criticism and wonderful hospitality in 1978. I remain forever indebted to Hanne Anderson, Kirsten Drotner, Hanne Tang Grodahl, Kirsten Mellor, Stephanie Olsen, and Erik Arne Hansen in particular.

To my students in history and literature I owe many happy hours of mutual criticism and stimulation. Thank you.

This book is dedicated to Sander Kelman and to Adam and Carrie Kartman. Without them it would have been neither necessary nor possible.

Preface

Louisa May Alcott's lifelong heroine was her father's friend and contemporary, Margaret Fuller. In the early 1840s, like many Romantic reformers of her generation, Fuller celebrated the "tides of life" flowing within herself and every unique individual being.[1] She also rebelled against current social and literary conventions. Her growing pains had a sexually specific ache: nineteenth-century society insisted that "one should be either private or public." Fuller, however, refused to choose between womanhood and individuality.[2] She used her powerful intellect to carve out a brilliant, public role at the center of the "American Renaissance," but also longed for ordinary domestic warmth, crying out, "The life, the life! O, my God! shall the life never be sweet?"[3]

Louisa May Alcott, a feminist of the next generation, helped make those two demands inseparable. Her contemporaries took up Fuller's cry in behalf of egalitarian households and a public role for women in rational democratic society. Unlike Fuller, however, Alcott was not an original thinker. Her great gift lay in reaching ordinary women with the broad-ranging program of nineteenth-century feminists. She wrote out of her own experiences, struggling to make her stories "true."

Margaret Fuller once called Louisa May Alcott and her sisters "model children," prototypes of a new generation of Americans who might shape a more democratic Eden.[4] Born into New England's reform movement, Louisa chose to remain at its center all her life—the famous author of *Little Women*, commonly signed her letters "Yours for reform of all kinds, L.M.A."[5] Readers found it natural that Bronson Alcott's daughter should write with unusual empathy for juvenile audiences. Her father, after all, had canonized childhood in meticulous observations of his daughters' early development.⁶ In fact, he and Abigail May Alcott were in the forefront of Romantic efforts to reform domestic life and thereby transform society at large, and they achieved immortality in these roles as the model parents in *Little Women*. Yet Louisa herself never equated individual self-culture with universal reform. Contemporary reviewers judged her a "benefactor of households" partly because she seemed to "enter into the lives and feelings of children," but also because she made an explicit connection between domestic equality, woman's rights, and democracy at large.⁷ Not only Sarah J. Hale, the influential editor of *Godey's Lady's Book*, but also Lucy Stone, Susan B. Anthony and Julia Ward Howe, valued Alcott's works.

Between the publication of *Little Women* in 1868 and her death in 1888, through several novels and dozens of short stories, Louisa Alcott chronicled an entire history of nineteenth-century woman's life and work. The March family trilogy of *Little Women, Little Men* (1871) and *Jo's Boys* (1886), which has never been out of print, has been translated into twenty-seven languages. In addition, Alcott wrote four popular adult novels—*Moods* (1865, rev. ed. 1882), *Work* (1872), *A Modern Mephistopheles* and *A Whisper in the Dark* (1888)—and a series of pseudonymous romantic thrillers as well as reviews, poems and articles for major periodicals such as *Atlantic Monthly*, Putnam's Magazine, *Harper's New Monthly, Commonwealth*, and *The Independent*.⁸

Her name remains a household charm invoked by writers from Betty Smith (*A Tree Grows in Brooklyn*) to Gertrude Stein (*Everybody's Autobiography*). Within a generation after Alcott's death, however, Ednah Dow Cheney, a family friend and her first biographer, felt it necessary to remind young readers that "Miss Alcott was very much interested in the question of woman's suffrage." Although she was a shy woman, "Miss Alcott" spoke publicly in behalf of woman's rights when the subject was "very unpopular," Cheney reports.⁹ The author of *Little Women* attended a meeting of the Woman's Congress in Syracuse, New York (1875), proudly counting herself a delegate from Massachusetts.

In 1926 Thomas Beer amused a new generation of twentieth-century readers with the Alcott family's nineteenth-century eccentricities. Although he expressed sympathy for Miss Alcott's hard life as a working woman, he nevertheless denounced her as the first "titanness."¹⁰ The Romantic adventures of nineteenth-century American men like Bronson Alcott, it seems, had aroused the ire of petticoat tyrants. According to Beer the mothers of America preferred a cloying diet of domestic tranquility gleaned from the pages of *Little Women*. They were turning their husbands, brothers, and sons into "Miss Alcott's boys," thereby castrating all that was vital and masculine in American society.¹¹ Beer's diatribe,

The Mauve Decade, represents a long wave of antifeminism that tended to equate woman's rights with repression and sentimentality.[12] Deaf to Alcott's plea for an abundant and adventurous life, Beer, like many succeeding critics, saw Alcott's domestic realism as a challenge to the natural world presented in *Huckleberry Finn*.

Yet female readers in particular have always been attracted to Jo March, the heroine of *Little Women*. Overs the years a new feminist contingent gathered. Suspicious of the appeal in Alcott's fiction, younger feminists feared that their susceptibilities were false consciousness; after all, Jo, a warmhearted tomboy, seems doomed to wander forever in the secret garden of female adolescence, never becoming an adult. It is the central argument of this study, however, that Alcott's works appeal to generations of female readers precisely because "little women" still face involuntary choices between domestic life and individual identity. That social choice remains a personal, painful part of growing up, much as Jo March felt it. Jo, like Margaret Fuller, and like Alcott herself, wanted both domesticity and individuality—her predicament was part of the "woman problem"—and her refusal to yield either part of herself lies at the heart of the woman's rights struggle. In this sense, all of Alcott's writings are feminist polemics that insist on woman's right both to homelife and individuality.

Domesticity and feminism have veered apart and careened together many times since the first woman's rights movement. Perhaps this explains why readers have all but forgotten that a generation of liberal feminists, including Alcott, linked their demand for democratic households to demands for woman's suffrage and a democratic society. Although a reading of Alcott's life and works in their contemporary context will not elevate her fiction to high art, it will enable us to see the nineteenth-century woman problem as Alcott presented it to her popular audience. She was the most autobiographical of authors, and her contemporary readers knew about her Romantic inheritance and her feminist sympathies. This study of her fiction and feminism is therefore structured within the narrative chronology of her life.

Louisa tested the limits of Romantic individualism both in her life and in her early fiction. Increasingly she doubted the universality of Emerson's prescriptive pathways to self-reliance, love, and individual identity. Women, she found, simply could not maintain unique relationships to nature, prescribed and bound as they were to private households. She painfully concluded that the communal experiments of her childhood years had not altered the sexual division of labor.

Her family's desperate poverty and her father's belief in individual perfectability as a model for society led him to found "Fruitlands," a short-lived, communal farm near Harvard, Massachusetts. He attempted to reaffirm agrarian patriarchy as a way to escape the new industrial capitalist order. Domestic tragedy was the result, but the Alcotts emerged from it a more democratic household.

The problem of determining the right relationship between woman, labor, property, and the family is most strikingly evident in the working out of dietary restrictions at Fruitlands, and at all other nineteenth-century intentional communities. Louisa never forgot her mother's frustrations at Fruitlands; she presents a bountiful harvest table laid out by women in all her fiction. Louisa also satirized men's fearful retreat from female abundance in "Transcendental Wild Oats."[13] Indeed, feminism and household democracy emerged together both in Louisa's adolescent life and in the contemporary woman's movement of the 1850s.

The Civil War played an enormous part in moving Alcott and her generation from Romantic perfectionism to rational realism. Her involvement in local and then national organizations espousing antislavery, Sanitary Commission work, woman's rights, and temperance were representative of many liberal reformers' experiences. Alcott's *Hospital Sketches*, the record of her own brief Civil War nursing experience, was her earliest popular success.[14]

After the Civil War, Louisa's fiction reflected this changing reform perspective. Using homelife as a metaphor for social order, she argued for a corporate rational world. Postwar feminists valued true love over Romantic passion, household democracy over patriarchy, and viewed coeducation as a model for institutional change. Romantic individualism seemed painfully impossible in a world of huge social problems. Significantly, Louisa revised her first published novel, *Moods*; she also edited and commented upon her early diaries. The issues she addressed remained the same in her own mind: individual rights and responsibilities, the search for democratic access to American abundance, and woman's right to both individuality and domesticity. However, her revisions tended to soften the hardships she and her family endured in their struggle for individual security. She had, of course, achieved security for all the Alcotts with the publication of *Little Women*.

Louisa never felt comfortable outside her native-born, genteel circle of liberal reformers. She never doubted the absolute sanctity of the individual soul, and yet she promoted a program of indoctrination and assimilation for the urban working classes, embattled farmers, blacks, and immigrants. She generally overlooked contradictions between individuality and social control, assuming that everyone wanted to be just like the people she knew and loved. Equality of opportunity, she argued, meant enabling the less privileged to gain the values, tastes, habits, and skills of Louisa May Alcott's "regular set." With a little institutional help, the less fortunate would be free to sell their labor power and rise to the middle class, where there was room for all.

At the end of her life Louisa wrote about a home for poor newsboys in New York City. The working boys paid a small sum for dormitory space and a hot meal, but Louisa was particularly attracted by the boys' opportunity to save their pennies. In the dormitory stood a great table "full of slits, each one leading to a little place below and numbered outside, so each boy knew his own. Once a month the bank is opened, and the lads take out what they like, or have it invested in a big bank for them to have when they find homes out West, as many do," she wrote, and "they make good farmers." The overseer told her how "that every day," a young man came in to report that he was a newsboy who had gone west and now owned "eighty acres of land and a good house." He had come back to New York to find his sister and "take her away to live with him."[15]

Alcott and her circle imagined a new Garden of Eden in America, one in which sexual relationship was purged of conflict and betrayal. They had complete faith in America's ever-expanding economy; progress came from unimpeded growth. Alcott presented positive portraits of abundance; feminists' social influence would resolve social conflicts through coeducation and helpful sheltering institutions. In *Jo's Boys*, her last novel, she presented a model university community presided over by the heroines of *Little Women*. She did not live long enough to develop the careers of the social housekeepers she was educating at Laurence University. We do not know if the new generation would have joined Edward Bellamy's nationalist clubs or the Fabian Socialists, as did Elizabeth Cady Stanton's daughter, Harriet Stanton Blatch, and Francis Willard, President of the Women's Christian Temperance Union. Certainly Alcott's heroines did not withdraw from the world; they went forth to clean it up.

Alcott's life and her works demonstrate the full range of feminist concerns in the nineteenth century. Above all, she cared about woman's "hunger for home" and "the cry for bread," central facts of an ordinary woman's life.[16] She moved from Romanticism to rationalism, from a near mystical union with nature to faith in social science. Yet her allegiance to a liberal woman's rights program never wavered, and her fiction made an important contribution to popular acceptance of liberal reform institutions. Of course, the woman problem remains. Perhaps we may gauge the success of feminism by the appearance of a future generation of "little women" who will not recognize Jo March's dilemma as their own.

A Hunger
for
Home

Louisa May Alcott
and *Little Women*

CHAPTER I

Something to Love and Live For

It is too true that love is a mere episode
in the life of a man. It is a whole history
in the life of a woman.

Abigail May to Amos Bronson Alcott,
June 10, 1829

In the twilight of a snowy Christmas Eve during the Civil War, four sisters sit before a crackling fire, knitting quietly. Their poverty is softened by the "comfortable old room," graced with books, pictures, and Christmas roses blooming in the window. But Jo March, the heroine of *Little Women*, darkens the atmosphere:

It's bad enough to be a girl anyway, when I like boys' games and work and manners: I can't get over my disappointment in not being a boy; and it's worse than ever now, for I'm dying to go and fight with papa, and I can only stay at home and knit like a poky old woman.[1]

Contemporary female readers of *Little Women* understood Jo's rebellion. One hundred years later, however, the relationship between Alcott's fiction and what her friends called the "woman problem" appears oddly unexplored. Although her biographers sympathetically identified many of the real people and incidents that Alcott fictionalized, the vivid way in which her life and work exemplify the conflicts specific to the "woman problem" remains to be reconstructed and examined.

To grow into manhood in Alcott's time meant the possibility of individual achievement and recognition, accompanied by the chance of failure. It was harder for women. Like most of her readers, Alcott accepted woman's traditional commitment to family and homelife; yet she also demanded individuality as her "natural right." It was precisely her ability to communicate this tension between domesticity and feminism that explains her enduring popularity as a writer for women.

The Connecticut Yankee

Louisa's perspective on womanhood in American society began with a notable family legacy. She was both a May and an Alcott. Her mother, Abigail May, descended from distinguished colonial gentry; her contemporary relations were members of Boston's elite: prosperous and influential ministers, bankers, lawyers, and merchant capitalists.[2] Had Abigail May married in her class, Louisa's literary talents might have remained a graceful avocation. But her father, Bronson Alcott, was the son of an impoverished farmer.[3] His grandfather, Captain John Alcocke, a Revolutionary soldier, settled in Wolcott, Connecticut and accumulated nearly one thousand acres of Spindle Hill before he died. Amos Bronson Alcox, his grandson, was one of eight surviving children born to Joseph and Anna Bronson Alcox in an unpainted, three-room frame house, cobbed together from two older cabins on the eighty acres that constituted the family's total holdings. Although his mother was barely literate herself, the money she earned from spinning and weaving helped send her brother Tillotson to Yale.

Amos Bronson Alcock, however, never attended college. At the age of thirteen he left a small common school in Wolcott, ending his formal education. His experience was not an isolated one. Horace Mann, another Massachusetts school reformer, labored in his father's fields while spending less than ten weeks at school per year; he too left school at thirteen. Raised on his family's own meat, corn, grain, and milk, Bronson wore homemade clothes that were spun, woven, and sewn by his mother. His father supplemented the family's income by making baskets and plow handles in the evening, using the light supplied by their own moulded tallow candles.

Theirs was a hard, meager life without the good pictures or books that later softened Louisa's fictional portraits of genteel poverty. Bronson's Uncle Tillotson, on the other hand, became the headmaster of Cheshire Academy and owned a home filled with books that entranced his nephew. Bronson spent a month with his uncle as a charity student at the academy, but the painful experience of being a poor, rural bumpkin at an elite Episcopalian boys' school proved humiliating. He returned to Spindle Hill and began his own lifelong experiment in self-education. With his cousin, William, he gathered a small store of books from neighbors and friends. The most influential and comforting was *The Pilgrim's Progress*.

Bronson's journals record many readings of Bunyan's nonconformist text, and later he re-created its adventures for his daughters, encouraging them to play-act the odyssey. Louisa prefaced *Little Women* with her own adaptation of the second half of the book, in which the Pilgrim's wife, Christiana, accompanied by her children and her friend, Mercy, finds her own way to Heaven. Emphasizing that girls take up women's burdens early, she wrote:

> Tell them of Mercy: she is one who early hath her pilgrimage begun. Yea, let young damsels learn of her to prize the world which is to come, and so be wise; for little tripping maids may follow God along the ways which saintly feet have trod.[4]

His brothers and sisters found work in local factories, but Bronson, ambitious and adventurous, joined the new throng of Yankee pedlars travelling the South to sell American manufactures stimulated by the War of 1812. His stock, three hundred dollars worth of combs, jewelry, thimbles, spectacles, sewing silks and cottons, needles, purses, playing cards, and puzzles for children was taken on consignment from a Norfolk dealer. His biographer, Odell Shepard, calculated that the young pedlar walked a hundred miles, tin trunks in hand.[5]

Bronson quickly found himself a commercial and social success. He talked to gentry, brought them news of the road, visited their libraries, and slept in their outbuildings. He had begun just after New Year, by April, 1819 he made one hundred dollars, enough to travel to New York, buy himself a new suit, and still give his father eighty dollars with which to frame a new house.

On a second peddling trip, accompanied by his cousin William, he walked twenty miles a day in the company of Dutch drivers who drank rum and swore a great deal. Hoping to gain temporary teaching jobs in South Carolina, both men walked another six hundred miles through swamps and forests to Norfolk, Virginia. There Bronson caught "typhus fever" and William nursed him through it. The experience cured sober William of itinerancy and may have inspired him to take the medical course at Yale, thence to become a well-known physician and author of one hundred and eight popular advice pamphlets. But Bronson, fond of cider and good company, forged on with another cousin, experiencing what he later called a jolly easygoing time. This hopeful start at recouping the family's fortunes, however, ended bleakly when his father had to sell a portion of the small homestead to pay debts accumulated by unsold and consigned goods from Bronson's later trips.

Perhaps to escape crude jokes that plagued them because of the original family name, the cousins changed their name from Alcock to Alcott. Amos Bronson Alcock became A. Bronson Alcott and his cousin became William Andrus Alcott, but their genteel new names brought no commensurate prosperity. In 1819 a severe depression struck the East. Bronson disregarded the hard times and his debt to his father and merchant suppliers, and spent the small cash reserves from his third trip in a flourish of vanity. He bought a "black coat, and a white cravat of daintiest tie, crimped ruffles, gleaming amethystine pin.'"[6] This mild extravagance quickly became a token of immoral material ambitions to the young man himself and to his family.

Bronson was determined to earn enough cash to free the family from debt before he was twenty-one. Yet by twenty-three he had merely reinforced his family's indigence. Nevertheless, he had set a path consistent with the contemporary belief in individual responsibility and entrepeneurial drive that supposedly benefitted both the individual and society as a whole. This secular belief, aided by the older Protestant faith in individual responsibility and freedom of will, added fuel to Bronson's sense of failure. He might have joined the swelling urban migration and become an industrial wage earner; but he never became a factory worker.

For a brief time, however precariously, he had escaped the chilling, dour atmosphere of his childhood in a rural backwater. He had learned to enjoy convivial visits with men of property and taste. Yet his relatively small commercial failure effected a larger, subjective impoverishment; much that was spontaneous and vivid in his personality was repressed. The self-conscious capacity for charming others remained with Bronson, enlarged and refined, but he was henceforth reserved, even calculating, in his effect. Father Isaac Hecker, who shared Bronson's desire for spiritual community many years later, recalled his personality in a kindly but skeptical fashion: "Alcott was a man of great intellectual gifts or acquirements. His knowledge came chiefly from experience and instinct. He had an insinuating and persuasive way with him."[7]

What Louisa made of her father's youth is instructive. In her early works, including both juvenile and adult fiction, itinerants appear as impoverished and homeless male orphans or disappointed lovers. Taken in by warmhearted surrogate mothers, their dangerous habits are changed by the love and security of proper family life. Once grown, they require careful monitoring and must prove themselves by stable useful employment. Later, Louisa Alcott colored her father's youthful experience to reflect his gentle reputation as the father of the "Little Women." "Eli's Education," which she published in the popular children's magazine, St. Nicholas[8] features a young man, Eli, who spends his small peddling profits on a fancy broadcloth suit and ruffled shirt, hoping to attract the attentions of a pretty girl. His extravagances are so beyond his means, however, that his father, who reproaches his son for "shiftless dreaming," is forced to mortgage part of the family farm. Properly ashamed and repentant, Eli works hard as a pedlar and endures many hardships to repay his father and recover his sense of modesty and decorum. Eli learns wisdom and virtue, and later, like Bronson Alcott, becomes a famous teacher, "diffusing good thoughts now as he had peddled small wares when a boy."[9] A gentle tale that locates a young man's minor vanity and selfishness in puppy love, it was also a sympathetic tribute to Bronson from Louisa. "This is a true tale," she wrote, "of a man becoming famous for his wisdom, as well as much loved and honored for his virtue and interest in all good things."[10]

What is missing from this story, however, and perhaps from Bronson's awareness as well, was his fierce, youthful vanity and ambition, his need to be the center of attention. Instead, he turned his feelings of rejection and his quest for gentility into a moral imperative to self-sacrifice and goodness.

Bronson's mother, Anna Bronson Alcox, undoubtedly admired her oldest son; she marveled at his intellectual attainment in light of her own meager education: "If he is my son, his mind is great it goes up and spreads far and broad."[11] She conveys in a terse but vivid way that his aspirations and struggles were a fulfillment of her own dreams. Bronson treasured her encouragement and memorialized their relationship:

> I was diffident,—you never mortified me; I was quiet,—you never excited me; I loved my books,—you encouraged me to read, and stored my mind with knowledge. You helped me when I needed help, were glad at any success of mine, never frowned upon me when I failed. You knew my love for neatness of appearance, my sense of the beautiful,—and you cherished it. These things I have not forgotten.[12]

A grateful tribute to be sure, but one written to a mother whose approval, as he recalled it, was for an ideal son whose successes and failures replicated those of Bunyan's Pilgrim. She loved him as he loved to be good. His ordinary desire to preen a bit, to escape from farm drudgery and homemade clothes into a larger society that valued drawing-room conversation and elegant attire was translated into "a love of neatness" and innate aesthetic sensibility. She knew, or Bronson felt she knew, that he meant to be good, altruistic, saintly.

But was Bronson a saint? His wife and children were never wholly sure whether they lived with a saint or merely with an unusually unrealistic man. One friend of the family recalled that he knew of only two occasions in which Bronson's wife, Abigail May, manifested impatience with Bronson's "saintly" behavior. On one of these she exclaimed, "I do wish people who carry their heads in the clouds would occasionally take their bodies with them.[13] This rare critique points to the larger truth about Bronson's "saintliness:" he refused to accept his own weaknesses as a human being, preferring to assume the mask of idealized goodness. Bronson never felt that his own commercial failure or dandyism were ordinary lapses to be accepted and forgiven; his need to achieve and his committment to an ideal self could be sustained only by constant affirmation from his parents and friends, and later from his children. Louisa, though often confused about her feelings towards Bronson, sensed his need for that affirmation and confirmed much of his idealized self in her fiction.

In Louisa's short story, Eli turns to teaching to repay his debts, with the help of his Uncle Tillotson. Bronson took the same path, and for the same reason. With his uncle's help he gained a position as master of the Center District School in Cheshire, Connecticut. It was a new start, a new way to prove his goodness, and an auspicious moment to win respectability, even influence in the community. The state's schools were in sorry shape by the time Bronson began teaching. Despite the legacy of public generosity—Connecticut appropriated over $1,000,000 as a permanent education fund in 1795—the school population had outgrown the state budget. The number of children in public schools had doubled in thirty years and funds were inadequate to equip schools or pay teachers a living wage. Male schoolmasters earned twelve dollars a month; and female teachers, who only taught in the summer, made six dollars a month. Pupils sat on backless benches in twenty-foot schoolrooms that might house fifty or sixty students, as Bronson's schoolroom did. They had few books or slates, and little motivation to learn under the traditional recitation method.[14]

Bronson and his cousin William Alcott, who also taught school, joined once again in a new venture. They read, talked, and felt themselves part of a new educational reform movement upon which the fate of the republic seemed to rest. A new view of childhood and education was sweeping America in the aftermath of eighteenth-century philosophical and republican reform. Enlightenment science provided grounds for optimism about progress and order in human society. All matter shared certain observable properties, making possible the discovery and application of physical laws. The heavens and the earth were not only ordered but comprehensible to educated people. Scientific laws properly applied contributed to a technological and industrial revolution. It seemed to many eager witnesses of these changes that human beings themselves could be scientifically educated to perfect human consciousness and behavior.

Bronson Alcott forged his own educational ideas in this new intellectual context. Just as he chose to nourish his own "goodness," so too he thought that proper family nurturance and enlightened education would produce a virtuous and harmonious society of "good" individuals. He read *The American Journal of Education*, which spread the gospel that supervised recitation or even the rational presentation of instructional materials was not enough. Rather, proper education depended upon the arts of emotional persuasion. These new methods, pioneered in Bronson's time by the Swiss educator, Petalozzi, among others, stressed what are often called "modernizing principles:" the mastery over one's own passions, a belief in objective order, the value of work as an end in itself, and the ability to postpone gratification. Bronson also read and re-read John Locke, finding further confirmation for a progressive reform of education. Locke's notion that the mind itself is a "tabula rasa", a blank slate that simply receives impressions about the material world through sensory organs, ran counter to older ideas of children's inborn depravity. Old New England primers, like those Bronson had read as a child, instructed children that the most they could hope for, if they died in infancy, was "the easiest room in hell." Puritan theology assumed that even a newborn babe was doomed by the original sin of Adam and Eve in the Garden of Eden; only stern adult discipline and the suppression of children's naturally craven tastes could overcome innate depravity.

Along with many other reforming schoolmen, Bronson rejected these beliefs, arguing instead that childhood was an innocent state and that children might delight in learning if gently led by loving parents and teachers. Bronson also drew his ideas from Robert Owen's *New View of Society*. Human beings, Owen maintained, were not nasty, brutish, and competitive at all, but naturally cooperative if they could escape the constraining institutions of private property and individualism. While Locke supported a society of enlightened individualists, Owen supported an enlightened society of socialists. For the time being, Bronson was content to follow Locke in the schoolroom.

He had notable success in wooing pupils to think for themselves and to develop their capacities to learn, inducing the *Boston Recorder* to commend his school.[15] Bronson himself helped pay for these improvements, putting backs on the benches, buying one hundred and sixty-five books as a lending library for the whole community, and hanging inspiring pictures. He encouraged singing and dancing at a time when playgrounds were unknown. But he did not, perhaps could not, save enough to pay back his six hundred dollar debt to his father.

Bronson was able to express all the warmth and physical affection for his small pupils that his own childhood lacked. He was gratified by their admiration.

Some parents resented Bronson's charismatic influence over their children, despite his election to the new Connecticut Society for the Improvement of Common Schools. To add to Bronson's troubles, a second public school opened, and with renewed competition from a nearby academy, he found himself back on the road to his parents' home.

This time, however, he was not a tired poverty-stricken Pilgrim, but the Pied Piper of a new generation of children whom he intended to lead to the Promised Land. Bronson's success still lay before him.

The May Character

In March of 1826, Reverend Samuel May, a young Unitarian minister, member of the local school board, and the brother of Bronson's future wife, organized a series of common school reform conventions in Brooklyn, Connecticut. In response to an invitation circulated the following year, William Alcott sent in a report of his cousin's school, accompanied by Bronson's descriptions of children, the "idea books" he encouraged them to keep, and his innovative practice of democratic self-government in the schoolroom. Reverend May was impressed, generously hospitable, and full of energy for the great task of reform. He invited Bronson to visit him in Brooklyn.

A gentleman with strong democratic leanings, May welcomed his poor country colleague, Bronson Alcott, as one of the reform brethren. He and Bronson shared an important belief; that education was an inalienable right. As May declared, "No one shall be compelled by the poverty of his parents to live in darkness and sin."[16] Although their backgrounds could hardly have been more different, theirs was more than a chance meeting of minds. It was the curious historical conjunction of diverse social reformers dedicated, for very different reasons, both to changing and conserving the relationship between American society and culture. For both of them the intellectual and moral culture of the whole people was the key to individual success and to the harmonious well-being of the republic.[17]

In July 1827, Bronson called upon the Reverend May and his wife at the May home. By chance the minister was out, his wife resting upstairs, recovering from the birth of their first child. Bronson was greeted by Abigail May, the Reverend's sister, visiting from Boston. She was a twenty-seven year old spinster, tall, amply proportioned, with heavy features and dark complexion. Though scarcely pretty, Abba May possessed a force of personality and a vivacity that animated her face and lightened her stately figure.[18] She loved music and dancing and moved with a graceful assurance the Bronson had rarely seen in the rural girls of his own class. He recorded his initial impression of Abigail May in his journal: "An interesting woman we had often portrayed in our imagination. In her we thought we saw its reality."[19] Abigail May also described this first meeting, but in a manner more shrewd and less inhibited: "I found . . . an intelligent, philosophic modest man," she said, "whose reserved deportment authorized my showing many attentions."[20]

Bronson was only a year older than his hostess; and by all accounts unusually tall, blond, and handsome. As a friend observed, Bronson's "glance was bright and eager, though not deep, which sparkled upon you."[21] Less physically attractive than her visitor, Abigail was a gently reared, well-educated young woman, unprepared for the dislocation that followed her mother's death and the remarriage of her father, Colonel Joseph May, a year later. As the youngest child in her family, with sisters already married and established in their own households, she had expected to assume her place as hostess of her father's gracious Federal Street home. But her stepmother, Mary Ann Clary May, was not inclined to share those pleasant responsibilities. Still, Abigail found much to do in her brother Sam's parsonage, helping his wife, Lucretia Coffin May, with the duties of a parson's wife and the care of a one-month-old infant. She also helped maintain the genteel tone of the household with a tact that appealed to Bronson. Indeed, on his first visit to the family, he stayed for almost a week.

It may be true, as Madelon Bedell argues in her rich history of the Alcott family, that "for both it was clearly a case of love at first sight." But it is more certain that Bronson was powerfully drawn to the genteel, comfortable atmosphere of the May household. He found the "May character" lovable, and spoke of the whole family enthusiastically as "distinguished for their urbanity, benevolence—their native manners—and nobleness of soul—moral purity and general beneficences."[22]

The Mays possessed considerable means to "influence public opinion," as Bronson put it.[23] They were also untouched by the rigors of deprivation. Neither brother or sister had ever attended a public school nor faced the hard facts of rural poverty. In fact, Sam's recollections of their education were of "my generous father, who thought the best patrimony he could give his children was a good education—so we were sent to the private schools in Boston that enjoyed the highest reputation."[24]

Sam May was properly grateful for the education appropriate to gentlemen. After attending what he called "ma'am school," run by respectable ladies for small gentry, he left his sisters with their schoolmistresses to attend a series of private preparatory schools for boys. At the age of thirteen, when Bronson left formal schooling forever, Sam was being readied for Harvard by Master Elisha Clapp. Sam, along with sons from other distinguished Bostonian families—the Otises, Elliots, and Parkers—received instruction in Latin, Greek rhetoric, and mathematics at a cost of one hundred dollars per pupil. He entered the Harvard class of 1817, along with his cousin, Samuel Sewall and his friend George Emerson, brother of Ralph Waldo Emerson. Classwork was mostly recitation, even at the university. At that time the library owned fewer than 20,000 books, though an infusion of European-trained scholars and an expanded program of library acquisitions lay in the near future.[25]

At twenty, Sam May entered Harvard Divinity School and studied the philosophy of John Locke, along with Biblical criticism and theology. When he completed his training in 1820, he possessed, as his father put it, "an education that will enable you to go anywhere, stand up among your fellow men and by serving them in one department of usefulness or another, make yourself worthy of a comfortable livelihood, if no more."[26] Bronson Alcott could scarcely have disagreed with the pronouncement, but he knew that such an education was far more likely for young men with family connections and substantial material resources.

"Usefulness" for the Mays meant reform activity in a broad range of social institutions; these included anti-slavery, education, prisons, charity relief, and politics. Bronson had slept in slave quarters and sold goods to slave owners on his peddling trips. Like many early nineteenth-century citizens of enlightenment, he hoped and expected that slavery would die a natural death. Having observed what he took to be cordial, even friendly relationships between masters and slaves, the actual deprivations of slave life went unremarked in his journals. But Sam May's first glimpse of the "peculiar situation" was quite different. In his memoirs he recalled a trip South to celebrate his approbation as a minister by the Boston Association of Unitarians.

> We saw, standing by the roadside, a row of Negro men, 20 or 30 in number, and soon perceived that they were all handcuffed, and that the irons about their wrists were fastened around a very heavy chain that was passed between them attached to the tail of a large wagon in which were bundles, apparently of clothes, and some young children lying upon straw, 4 or 5 black women were passing along the line and giving to each man a thick slice of coarse bread . . . we had heard of the abomination of slavery and the internal slave trade, but had not seen it before . . . But here the monstrous wrong stood palpably before us . . . I never before felt so grateful, as I do now, that I was not born where human beings can be bought and sold, and treated like cattle. . . . I am ashamed of my country and my race.[27]

By the time Bronson Alcott and Abigail May's friendship ripened into marriage, Sam was an antislavery agent. He had defended Prudence Crandall, a Quaker schoolteacher in Connecticut who accepted black pupils only to be arrested by the local sheriff. Sam May's ideals were no less admirable than his courage in carrying them out. Although his sister lacked the formal education and civic opportunities afforded a male citizen of her class, she was of one mind and heart with her brother.

Abigail May's coming of age did not include a graduation ceremony that released her into a world rich with possibility. Even as children, only Sam was free to explore Boston's wharves, engage in snowball fights on the Commons, and race his sled with playmates down Beacon Hill. His sisters' domestic roles were shaped by their mother's lessons in baking, scrubbing and washing. Like other notable housewives, Mrs. May thought that the mistress of a proper household should possess the skills to supervise her staff's daily chores. She also had Abigail trained in the customary French, music, and dancing. Beyond the practice of these skills, Abigail's life was circumscribed. She travelled only in the company of family or close friends. At home she learned what she could of the outside world from Sam, who brought Harvard friends home to visit.

Her education was "finished off" by a year of study with one Miss Allyn of Duxbury, an educated spinster who undertook such work for the daughters of family friends. Abba Alcott later told her daughter Louisa that as a young girl she studied "French, Latin and botany, had read history extensively, and made notes of many books such as David Hume, Edward Gibbon, Hallman's *Middle Ages* and Robertson's *Charles V*."[28] Her reading followed the pattern later recommended by her close girlhood friend, Lydia Maria Child, in *The Mother's Book* (1831). Mrs. Child advised girls to read history, biography, and even current novels, providing that they respected woman's ability to reason. One of Child's favorite novelists was Catherine Maria Sedgwick, whose books Abigail read as a young woman. Sedgwick allowed her female heroines an innovative independence and a strong desire for education. She pioneered a new fiction that Abigail's daughter, Louisa, would later develop and deepen in her own books for girls.

By the time Abigail May met Bronson Alcott she was a well-educated, active woman by the standards of her generation. After Bronson returned to Cheshire following his visit with the Mays, Abba toured Boston schools, talked with teachers, and even read a biography of Pestalozzi. She and Sam not only urged Bronson to move to Boston, Abigail declared herself ready to become his assistant. She found a school on Salem Street that would welcome Bronson as master and herself as his assistant. Sam, taken aback by this unexpected assertiveness, strenuously objected to the impropriety of his unmarried sister teaching with a single man for whom she felt such obvious attraction. He wrote to her:

I will frankly say that I see no other objection than the remarks and opinions of the world. A man may bid defiance to these, a woman cannot, without incurring the greatest danger. The circumstances of our acquaintance with Mr. Alcott, and his having gone to Boston at my suggestion and with my recommendation, would lead a censorious world to ascribe selfish views both to myself and you if you were to unite with him in his school. For this reason, and for this alone, I decidedly advise you to relinquish the plan altogether.[29]

Acceding to Sam's wishes, Abba chose merely to introduce Bronson to the May circle of influence. Bronson accepted the position of master at the Salem Street primary school.

"We Love Her . . . She Loves Us"

The Boston so familiar to Abigail May was still a small city of no more than 58,000 residents in 1828. But even the critical English visitor, Harriet Martineau, found it unique in Young America, a place, she believed, that compared only to London in the richness of its population. The Common greens provided constant entertainment and recreations, including July 4 fairs and a variety of open stalls for outdoor refreshments. Children could sail their boats on the frog pond in fine weather and sled down the Common's snowy slopes in winter. Nearby, two walks served such citizens as Colonel May, Ralph Waldo Emerson, and now, Abigail May and Bronson Alcott.

Bronson thoroughly savored his move to Boston, grateful for the introductions provided by Sam and Abigail May to the city's most influential citizens and its most edifying cultural activities. He heard Emerson preach, and approved mildly of the liberal Unitarian. He also listened to Lyman Beecher, whom he found too intent on building one particular faith. His reading of Robert Owen's socialist, freethinking philosophy had already moved him into an idealistic frame of mind beyond both rational Unitarianism and enthusiastic evangelsim. He and his friend Miss May were more drawn to circles of universal reform that included the abolitionist William Lloyd Garrison and Frances Wright, an Owenite speaker and champion of free love (though that doctrine proved a bit advanced for the young couple). They also met William Russell, editor of the *American Journal of Education*, and Elizabeth Peabody, a disciple of William Ellery Channing who had opened an infant school in Roxbury.

In this stimulating world, Bronson and Abigail's friendship blossomed into romance. Yet it was romance plagued by serious problems, ranging from his poverty and fears of committment to her understanding that "it is too true that love is a mere episode in the life of a man. It is a whole history in the life of a woman."[30] Her recognition of how much depended upon this momentous event in a woman's life reflected her personal experience of the social realities in antebellum America.

By her own account, Abigail May was "much indulged—allowed to read a great deal—fed nice food and had many indulgences not given my brothers and sisters. I was a good child—but wilful."[31] While she certainly had little direct knowledge of her father's public responsibilities, his departure and return each day were major events in her domestic world. She watched for him at the front window and at seventeen wrote him that he was her "morning song and evening lullaby." But by her late twenties the privileges and pleasant intimacies a favored girl enjoyed with her father were supposed to be transferred to her husband. In early nineteenth-century America the guardians of public welfare agreed with the prescriptions of William Alcott, Abigail's future cousin by marriage, who wrote several popular books on marriage and family life. In *The Young Wife* Alcott wrote that only modern times have revealed the "silent" power

> which woman has in governing the world. She is to wield the sceptre, first over her husband, and next over the children whom God may give her . . . It is in vain, or almost in vain, to hope for any single amelioration of our race, through family influence, til this point is secured—til woman's life, amid her household, is one uninterrupted series of kind actions, words, tones and gestures, and til she has overcome and transformed her husband.[32]

With a characteristic bustle of energy and enthusiasm, Abigail May hurried to fulfill her mission. Feeling unworthy, however, Bronson drew back, perhaps remembering his days as a peddler and his unsuccessful efforts to support his family. In his eyes their's was an "ambiguous relationship." After spending much time with Abigail, he shared his journal with her, but he mystified her by praising her "character" without mentioning his very real emotional and physical attraction to her.[33] It was Abigail who finally threw caution to the winds, perhaps sensing how constrained Bronson was by feelings of social inferiority. "I told him my feelings," she wrote, "They were innocent and only needed explanation to be cherished or rejected by him."[34]

Bronson chose to cherish Abigail, and she wrote delightedly to her brother Sam of her engagement:

> I am engaged to Mr. Alcott not in a school, but in the momentous capacity of friend and wife . . . I do think him in every respect qualified to make me happy. He is moderate, I am impetuous—He is prudent and humble—I am forward and arbitrary. He is poor—but we are both industrious—why may we not be happy? . . . I never felt so happy in my life—I feel already an increase of moral energy—I have something to love—to live for—I have felt a loneliness in this world that was making a misanthrope of me in spite of everything I could do to overcome it.

She signed her letter to "the most affectionate and tender of brothers," as "your sister Abba."[35]

Their engagement lasted for two-and-a-half years. Bronson now felt relaxed enough to use the family's pet names for his betrothed, calling her Abba or Abby. Initially, Colonel May was not pleased at the match and even more displeased at his daughter's engagement without "asking my permission or advice." But he wanted peace in the family, and above all peace in his old age when "the shadows of evening are advancing." He invited Mr. Alcott to visit and took the trouble to "draw him out."[36] Bronson expressed his deepening feelings in his journal, which bore more than a little resemblance to the sentiments in Abigail's favorite romances: "I do love this good woman," he wrote, "and I love her because she is good—I love her because she loves me. She has done and continues to do much for me. How can I reciprocate her goodness?"[37]

A quick succession of family tragedies contributed to the delay of the marriage. In November of 1829 Abba was crushed by the death of her sister, Louisa Greele, and a month later by the death of little Joseph, the son of Sam and Lucretia. Bronson, emotionally and physically distant, failed to express his sympathies. The distraught Abba needed comfort and material help, but he was able only to intellectualize the meaning of "sorrow." Abba was left with the care of her sister's two small children; she took them to Sam's parsonage, where her brother and sister-in-law shared in the anguish and consequent responsibilities. Bereaved and more than a little shaken by Bronson's behavior, Abba struggled to understand a man whose life seemed so different from her own. In an earlier time, she would have become engaged to someone of her own class and background, possibly to a man of more suitable temperament. In 1829, Abba's engagement to Bronson led her to think seriously about her future. She could not take for granted the status and role enjoyed by her mother's generation of privileged ladies.

Slowly she began to assert her needs and convictions, communicating to Bronson her own romantic vision of companionate marriage. She argued that women were no longer the servants of men. As a daughter of the American Revolution she further claimed that woman's place was at man's side and in his heart, refining and civilizing him, "compelling him by the irresistable force of merit to accept her as an intelligent companion." Inchoately, Abba was working out the beginnings of her own domestic feminism, trying to forge a union between an older and a newer perspective. On the one hand, she believed that woman's first priority was the care of her home and family; on the other, she argued that sexual equality in marriage and outside it would rescue "one half the world laboring under conscious and almost contented inferiority."[38]

What she meant by equality was something quite different from

Louisa's understanding of that word a generation later. Abba wanted to become Bronson's companion in a deeply romantic sense—"in his heart." She tenderly—almost sentimentally, at this point in her life—placed being, rather than doing at the center of loving marriage. Abba was also inclined to believe that a union of true hearts could not admit impediments to happiness; she invited and expected Bronson's correction of her faults. But she wanted to be loved as much for herself as for her possibilities. Bronson, on the other hand, loved her because she loved him.

If, upon occasion, Bronson seemed distant, Abba never really accepted emotional distance in her suitor. His cool, lofty presentation of himself was certainly a good deal softened by an almost homely simplicity in his personal tastes. The American reverence for the founding fathers, at that point in time, found more to admire in Franklin-like simplicity than in upper-class elegance. Bronson, for example, loved New England apples and cider, cold spring water and cottage bread. Above all, his dignified reserve, which quite possibly concealed fears of rejection and humiliation, seemed familiar to Abba. His serenity, his air of moral rectitude, his acceptance of her unstinted love, all reminded her of her father. It never occurred to Abba that her husband would be less than an adequate provider, though he lacked Colonel May's position in the world. Nor did she suspect that Bronson could and would reject the role of provider altogether. He was her Connecticut Knight. His emotional armor had protected him in the many battles she saw him waging on his way from Spindle Hill to Boston, and Abba assumed that he would battle even more bravely for the honor of his lady.

Abba's halting efforts to understand Bronson and to prepare herself for an unconventional marriage reflected the uncertainty and confusion that many Americans felt over the relations between the sexes in the 1820s. Traditional grounds for marriage—similarity of birth, class, social status, the subordination of women, and the obligation of men to support their wives and children—were increasingly challenged by a new generation of men and women.

Thanks largely to circumstances which neither controlled, Abba and Bronson were among those who labored to create a new basis for marriage; unlike many of their contemporaries, they chose the most Romantic of grounds. Ideally, they would marry to perfect their individual lives and to produce children who would contribute to the perfection of the human race. In the forefront of romantic reform, Abba and Bronson agreed that to fashion a perfect society through perfect domesticity.

This approach to marriage seemed unrealistic, even foolish, to Abba's relatives in particular. Still wedded to older patriarchal principles, and concerned with the couple's "housekeeping" and financial prospects, Colonel May viewed Bronson as a possibly dangerous marital choice. He believed that men and women from different backgrounds should not marry. Moreover, men should possess sufficient material resources to support their wives and children. Romantics premised a unique spiritual and creative force present in every individual human being at birth. A growing recognition of woman's spiritual equality concurrently led some prescriptors to accept the notion of household democracy as promoting domestic harmony. Serious doubts and misgivings over the virtues of courtships such as Abba's and Bronson's nevertheless resonated throughout the remainder of the nineteenth century. People remained troubled because Romantic relationships so clearly failed to create a firm foundation for the relations between the sexes. Women, above all, were disturbed by the dangers of romantic love, even as they were drawn to its liberating potential.

Insistence upon the ultimate integrity of the individual soul, in the absence of the older corporate community, commonly led to conflict with social conventions and prescriptive norms. One might transcend ordinary economic and social barriers to personal achievment, to be sure; for this reason Romanticism had a strong attraction for laissez-faire Jacksonians. Romantic love might also join two people of more than usual enterprise and adventure, helping them to overleap the barriers of their social system. Wedded in defiance of family and custom, a couple could deepen and enrich their courageous union. On the other hand, when individuals listen only to an inner voice, ordinary human selfishness could bloom into domestic tyranny. Furthermore, a denial of the outside world's constraints could result in spiritual anarchism.

A cooperative awareness of domestic problems, Louisa Alcott observed, was more likely to lead to democratic solutions. Individuality might otherwise be lost in an orgy of possessive individualism. She argued that true love, not Romantic passion, guaranteed mutual concern for the needs of everyday life, and she offered a liberal, rational alternative to Romantic relationships through the fictional courtships and marriage portrayed in her novels.

Louisa believed that Romantic marriages also undercut possibilities for genuine female self-reliance. In all her fiction she challenged the romantic belief that differences of temperament, class, and culture constitute the essence of constructive challenge and growth within domestic unions. Yet she was all too conscious of the thrill, the passionate attraction of such differences. In fact, her underlying admiration for her parents' romance kept that passionate impulse alive in her fiction, and made the rational alternative she demanded more difficult for her readers to accept.

On May 22, 1830, at King's Chapel, a reform Unitarian church that Colonel May helped establish, Abba and Bronson declared their bonds. Neither reported the attendance of any Alcott relatives, but Colonel and Mrs. May, faithful to the gentility that so marked their circle, gave the young couple a gracious reception. Soon thereafter, the Alcotts took up residence in one room of a nearby boarding house. This living arrangement, a product of the couple's penury, was not unusual for many young couples. It was, however, a harbinger of Abigail May Alcott's precarious future.

CHAPTER II

Model Children

Our birth is but a sleep and a forgetting:
The Soul that rises with us, our life's Star,
Hath had elsewhere its setting,
And cometh from afar:
Not in entire forgetfulness,
And not in utter nakedness,
But trailing clouds of glory do we come
From God, who is our home:
Heaven lies about us in our infancy:

William Wordsworth,
"Ode: Intimations of Immortality"

To the delight of both herself and Bronson, who looked upon children with a nearly mystical respect, Abba became pregnant within a month after their wedding. Parenting and educating a new generation of nineteenth-century Americans seemed an awesome responsibility to them, as it did to many of their reformist generation. The "rights of children," as they were newly perceived, seemed to follow logically upon the acceptance of the rights of man. If, as Wordsworth wrote, "Heaven lies about us in our infancy," a divinely democratic promise awaited the children of rich and poor alike.

Childhood Hath Saved Me

Romantic premises overturned traditional Calvinist orthodoxy, but they were not the principal causes of nineteenth-century anxiety over child raising. Children's feelings and lives were of concern because structural changes in family life and work, which resulted in the separation and removal of middle-class children from the adult world. By 1830, particularly in cities like Boston, fathers spent little time with their children in domestic activities; mothers, on the other hand, enlarged their sphere to form Maternal Associations and Infant School Societies, including the one whose female board of managers hired Bronson Alcott. As one contemporary observer put it, "The sphere of duty assigned to woman considered singly is limited to one family and one circle of society: but the fulfillment or neglect of those duties are extended almost beyond belief."[1] Accordingly, as households became segregated from the competitive, public world of men, women's identities were redefined. They became associated with goodness, but a goodness that needed cultivation and supervision.

In the 1830s and 1840s a spate of new books, pamphlets, and especially magazines featuring advice and family-oriented fiction and poetry supplanted older domestic authorities.[2] Horace Bushnell, Theodore Dwight, and William Alcott all wrote for *The Mother's Assistant* and *Young Lady's Friend*, and their articles appeared with pieces by new female experts such as Lydia Maria Child, Catherine Sedgwick, and Catherine Beecher. Bronson Alcott contributed from a pedagogical perspective while expecting his first child. By tapping a market for advice materials, in fact, he hoped to guarantee a comfortable living for his family. He published a pamphlet, *Observations on the Principles and Methods of Infant Instruction*, in the fall of 1830.[3] While *Observations* did not win the competition sponsored by Philadelphia's public school system for a proposal on infant education, the work interested two Quaker philanthropists, Robert Vaux and Reuben Haines. Haines offered Bronson Alcott and his friend and colleague, William Russell, the opportunity to implement their ideas at a new school in Germantown, Pennsylvania.

Alcott's educational principles and methodology have often been viewed as "too advanced and experimental . . . for use in a common school," especially by sympathetic biographers.[4] Alcott's ingenuous estimation of himself as an "original" has reinforced this view. Social historians, however, who have analyzed the enormous body of nineteenth-century prescriptive literature, place Bronson Alcott in the mainstream of liberal reformers. Bronson's dogged application of current liberal educational theory to raising the Alcott girls impresses his biographers in large measure because he recorded the experience so thoroughly.[5] Sam May, Henry Barnard, and Horace Mann, as well as Bronson Alcott and Lydia Maria Child read the same Pestalozzian works, which espoused a system of parenting and education in harmony with the development of each child's own instincts and abilities.[6] In particular, Pestalozzi stressed what later became dogma for progressive educators: children were to learn by doing and to experiment with real objects. Louisa's fiction for children was also directed at their parents; she too preached the Pestalozzian method.

Bronson Alcott presented himself as a devoted American disciple in his essay, "Pestalozzi's Principles and Methods of Instruction," published in the *American Journal of Education* in 1829.[7] In that piece he emphasized the most contradictory aspect of Pestalozzi's philosophy and method without observing the contradiction. Developed from Locke's dictum that all knowledge proceeds through sensory perception, the proper nurture and education of children depended upon the cultivation of three faculties: reason, emotion, and will. But Locke's premise depended upon a "tabula rasa," the mind's originally blank slate. Bronson Alcott, however, like so many other educational reformers, presumed the existence of neo-platonic ideal forms. The infant was born not merely innocent, but emerged "trailing clouds of glory;" he possessed an innate moral sense that required a balanced environment to grow up "naturally."

Wordsworth's American devotees managed to combine an appreciation of innate goodness with a fervent trust in environmentalism. They wanted to perfect the socialization process through the senses and the emotions, ultimately evoking the power of the will to do good—even more, to be good.

In a discussion of Romantic theory M. H. Abrams noted that "in any period, the theory of mind and the theory of art tend to be integrally related and to turn upon similar analogues, explicit and submerged."[8] Bronson Alcott was determined to shape his environment in the deepest sense: achieving immortality; he repeatedly invoked Wordsworth's metaphors of the soul as "our life's star," "trailing clouds of glory." Romantics saw an observing mind as one that projected the soul's light upon material reality and then received back something greater than mere reflections of nature. Bronson intended his "Journals" and "Observations" to be both monuments to his own mind and works of art. He trusted Wordsworth's reassurance that, although our sensibilities fade with age "into the light of common day," the mind still retained its supple recollections, the "fountain light of all our day."

Though dedicated to infant education, Bronson was more concerned to validate his mind as a projecting, original force. Both his childlike personna, admired by many of his friends, and his devotion to childhood itself were entirely consistent with a Romantic faith that human nature was everywhere the same and that feeling was the great common denominator. Before social institutions spoiled them, children were the closest to their natural sensibilities—the wellspring of creativity. By preserving his childhood innocence, Bronson felt he possessed a reliable aesthetics and politics. He was all but oblivious to social struggles for the control of childhood going on around him.

A larger battle was going on in the public school movement. Sam May was hotly engaged in this battle throughout his long life. By the 1830s and 1840s people throughout New England—including workers, newly arrived immigrants, and middle class reformers—were debating such questions as state versus local control, school standards and curriculum, and the place of the normal schools in the educational system.[9] Class conflct, for example, underlay a controversy concerning the establishment of normal schools (teacher training schools), a reform championed by Sam May, Henry Barnard, and Horace Mann. The very citizens who were supposed to benefit from professionally trained teachers often suspected that taxpayer's money merely educated the daughters of the rich and provided them extra income while they awaited marriage.[10] Other matters shaped the debate. Some people charged that normal schools would drive up the cost of hiring teachers, while others objected that professional training for teachers was undemocratic. One might have expected Bronson Alcott, a self-taught teacher, to join the fray, but he did not.

His deepest commitment to education was evidenced in the singular intensity he brought to parenting his first two children. Anna Bronson Alcott, the first of four Alcott daughters, was born in Germantown on March 15, 1831. Her father immediately began recording his "Observations on the Phenomena of Life as Developed in the Progressive History of an Infant during the First Year of its Existence."[11] His final manuscript of some 2,500 pages, which records both Anna's and Louisa's earliest years, has been duly celebrated as one of the first American diaries of child development. Inspired by similar diaries kept by Europeans and also anxious to recapture the romantic innocence of his own childhood, Bronson was determined to test the limits of individual perfectability in both himself and his daughters. "Childhood Hath Saved Me," he wrote, thereby revealing his own needs.[12]

Both Bronson and his intellectual mentor, Pestalozzi, believed that children suffered from inherent personal weakness, depravity, and "wildness," but they thought these weaknesses could be controlled without cruelty and excessive discipline.

Bronson's methods, if not their underlying emotional pathology, were shared by a number of prescriptive writers. Lydia Maria Child, for instance, accepted "evil propensities" as perhaps hereditary, but she counted upon gentle nursery influences to keep those propensities from being aroused.[13] Both Alcott and Child agreed that the development of enlightened understanding and the capacity to act from principle rather than passion was at the heart of primary education.

Bronson's recurrent striving for perfectability distinguishes him from the more moderate reformers. "We do not yet know," he wrote, "what favorable influences from birth will do for the infant, from the beginning, and paying due respect to his whole nature, we shall cooperate with it, in due accordance and harmony with the laws of its constitution, and suggest to the world, both by success and failure, what the human being may become."[14] This tendency to indulge in abstractions, expressed in phrases like "his whole nature," set him apart from his wife who had a concrete regard for her first baby, even an awareness of Anna's sexual specificity. More preoccupied with the work of mothering, than the usual preference for a son, Abba Alcott enjoyed holding and nursing her baby. She wrote to her brother Sam and his wife:

> Lucretia, I suppose, is ready with her condolence that it is a girl. I dont need it. My happiness in its existence and the perfection of its person is quite as much as I can well bear. Indeed, I cannot conceive that its being a boy should add there to.[15]

Mother Love: Infant Perfection

Bronson's salary was sufficient to hire a housekeeper and nurse for Anna's first few days. But even at the beginning Abba was determined to care for Anna by herself, a determination vigorously encouraged both by Bronson and contemporary attitudes. In Jacksonian America motherhood was the primary holy responsibility of women, precluding all other duties and interests. Bronson, who accepted this general outlook, observed both mother and infant at a dispassionate distance; this suited him temperamentally and seemed necessary for the task of recording and testing. By July the record of Anna's progress was one hundred pages long, the beginning of a history that Bronson hoped would become a history of human nature.

During Anna's first year, Abba so arranged her life around the infants needs that "the occasions for tears were few," as her father put it.[16] Such "management" of very young babies was not at all unusual. In fact, Anna's first few months, and to a certain extent Louisa's, followed standard, prescriptive advice. What was unusual, perhaps, was the complete committment of both parents to following the prescriptions.[17]

Supported by the views of her friend, Lydia Maria Child, who believed that children should rarely cry if a mother is wholly attentive and caring, Abba nursed her child frequently, on demand. Both parents hoped to maintain the child's "naturally" happy disposition, even at the expense of neglecting to wash or dress her, which might bring on tears. Anna thrived, and at five months slept peacefully through the night without a light. By six months she had a small swing for her amusement and a cart in which she enjoyed daily outings. The child-entered household granted Anna the right to sleep in her parents' bedroom, and more often than not Abba went to sleep with Anna at the infant's bedtime.

While recording Anna's "animal activity," Bronson also reported the presence of a "conscious and intelligent soul" in her at two months.[18]

He was sure she had smiled at a vase of violets, a response to beauty clearly indicating a divine soul. Rocking cradles, sudden noises, or movements were all shunned, as the manuals suggested, to avoid intrusions on infant peace. Bronson, however, occasionally violated these prescriptions by making scary faces that made Anna cry. He wished to prove that she possessed an imagination, could conjure up a vision of what had frightened her, and thus repeat the fear and the tearful response.

Bronson's observations in Anna's early months reflect a blend of earlier Protestantism and the beginnings of "modern" emotional manipulation. They extol the virtues of freedom while insisting upon the internalization of parental ideals:

> The child must be treated as a free, self-guiding, self-controlling being. He must be allowed to feel that he is under his own guidance, and that all external guidance is an injustice which is done to his nature unless his own will is intelligently submissive to it . . . He must be free that he may be truly virtuous, for without freedom there is no such thing as virtue.[19]

Alcott rejected the idea that external rewards or punishments should shape the moral life of children. Instead, he believed that children should be encouraged to choose freely the moral life that pleased their father most. Clearly, he believed that children possessed freedom of the will and that freedom could only be a choice made for morality. The contrast with Abba is striking, for she had no inclination whatever to test her daughter's moral sense at this early stage.

The following incident is typical. Anna, accustomed to falling asleep in her mother's presence, resisted being put to bed alone. Bronson concluded that she missed the light in the parlor. Her father went into the room and spoke kindly but firmly, indicating that he wanted her to go to sleep in the darkened room. She stopped crying and fell asleep, whereupon her father assumed that she had yielded to the tone of his instructions. Anne was seven months old at this time. Bronson was undoubtedly correct in surmising that she did not understand his words, but other explanations of her behavior did not occur to him: first, that she might miss her mother's company, not the light, and second, that her father's voice may have provided reassurance in Abba's absence.[20]

As on so many occasions, Louisa made use of her family history in her fiction. In *Little Women*, for example, she presents a similar situation, though the small son is already several years old. Used to his mother's company until he falls asleep, he also resists going to bed alone. The father goes to the child's room, speaks firmly about going to sleep without demanding his mother's company, and then insists that the mother remain in the parlor while the child cries himself to sleep:

The minute he was put into bed on one side, he rolled out on the other, and made for the door, only to be ignominiously caught up by the tail of his little toga and put back again, which lively perform- ance was kept up till the young man's strength gave out, when he devoted himself to roaring at the top of his voice. The vocal exercise usually conquered Meg; but John sat as unmoved as the post which is popularly believed to be deaf. No coaxing, no sugar, no lullaby, no story, even the light was put out, and only the red glow of the fire enlivened the "big dark" which Demi regarded with curiosity rather than fear. This new order of things disgusted him and he howled dismally for "Marmar" as his angry passions subsided and recollec- tions of his tender bond-woman returned to the captive autocrat.[21]

His "Marmar" tries to yield to her darling, bravely announcing, "He's my child, and I won't have his spirit broken by harshness." But the father insists that the child not be spoiled by indulgence. Father wins out, and assuming that the quieted child is asleep, covers him up. But the child is not asleep, and asks with a penitent hiccough, "Me's dood, now?" The end of the incident finds "Marmar" tenderly watching both husband and son asleep together, the child cuddling "close in the circle of his father's arm and holding his father's finger, as if he felt that justice was tempered with mercy."[22]

Overindulgent mothers and firm but merciful fathers balance one another in the ideal homes Louisa created, but she also identified a thornier problem that surely existed in her own childhood. A good mother might be so wrapped up in maternal duties that she forgot to be a good wife. Domestic reformers like Bronson and Abba Alcott placed equal emphasis on companionate marriage and parental devotion. Nursemaids, like cooks and housemaids, might free up a matron's time so that she could please her husband with attention to details of dress, housewifery, and culture. Too great a reliance on such "help," however, conflicted with domestic democracy and with perfectionist values.

Louisa May: The First Year

In the summer of 1832 Bronson's observations were interrupted by Abba's second pregnancy, a development which tired and occasionally depressed her. Moreover, their living situation was altered by the death in October of the Alcott's patron, Reuben Haines. Bronson's subsidy vanished and the Alcott-Russell school was closed. Bronson opened another school in Philadelphia, with Vaux's help, but it lasted less than a term. Still, Bronson found time to observe Anna, and somehow had the leisure to read. Abigail bore the brunt of increasing domestic chores and diminishing income.

In Germantown, at yet another boarding house, their second daughter was born on November 29, 1832. "Abby May inclines to call the babe Louisa May," Bronson wrote Colonel May, "a name to her full of every association connected with amiable benevolence and exalted worth."[23] It was the name of her deceased sister, Louisa May Greele. Bronson assured his father-in-law that Abba was comfortable and would soon be able to take charge of her domestic and maternal duties. Of her earlier depression and longing for the company of friends, he said nothing, assuring the family that his wife was "formed for domestic sentiment rather than the gaze and heartlessness of what is falsely called society." During her second pregnancy Abby had done most of the housework herself, while at the same time caring for their five small boarders, Bronson's pupils, whose room and board money were necessary to the family income. Abigail found it a "thankless employment to take care of other people's children."[24] The whole situation meant that Louisa May Alcott's first few months were considerably less fortunate than Anna's. Nevertheless, Bronson began a new record of Louisa's progress.

Louisa was as a sturdier, more assertive infant than Anna. "A fair complexion, dark bright eyes, long dark hair, a high forehead, and altogether a countenance of more than usual intelligence," was one friend's description of this second daughter at two months of age. She held her own even when Anna's jealousy showed itself in biting or scratching her little sister. She learned very early to make her needs and dissatisfactions loudly known, whereas Anna had been privileged to have her mother anticipate them. Bronson, who again maintained a scientific detachment, commented on a lack of maternal attention to Anna, who was forced to accompany Bronson to his schoolroom because he could no longer afford a housekeeper. Abigail Alcott interpreted the problem somewhat differently. "Mr. A. aids me in general principles, but nobody can aid me in detail," she said.[25]

Overworked, living in a crowded apartment but still convinced of her obligation to achieve maternal perfection, Abigail blamed herself for the children's suffering. Bronson prescribed a summer vacation, which meant that he left Abigail and the girls with his mother at Spindle Hill while he went to Boston to meet with publishers and seek the means for a new school.

In the fall they returned to another Philadelphia boarding house. In these unsatisfactory, depressing, even monotonous quarters, Bronson found "free uninterrupted thought" almost impossible. The situation was equally oppressive to Abigail, but in the spring of 1834 it was Bronson who took a room of his own across the street from the Philadelphia library in order to read and continue his writing. For Abigail, however, this solution led merely to a more intensified and isolated domesticity. She and the girls moved to a cottage in Germantown. Louisa, less than two years old, had to make do with her mother's distracted care, her sister's resentment, and her father's weekend visits. Bronson was not earning any money and his ascetic furnishings in Philadelphia—a bed, clothes trunk, wash stand, two chairs and books—seemed proof to him of his own self-sacrifice. Dwelling on the hardships of his own childhood and adolescence, he demanded compensations now. "Thrown into the world and left to seek my intellectual pittance for myself, how have I been vainly striving to feed on husks."[26] He congratulated himself on his own "generous heart" and innate tendency to pure ideality," which had produced a man of high purpose despite deprivations. The thought both pleased and pained him, for he was aware of Abba's burdens and the children's dissatisfactions. "I cling too closely to the ideal to take necessary advantage of the practical and my wife and children suffered from this neglect."[27]

They unquestionably suffered. On May 20, Abba nearly died from a miscarriage, saved only because her landlady quickly summoned a physician to the cottage.[28] This incident seemed to confirm Abba's fears about her own health and the survival of the babies. Her eldest sister, Catherine, died at twenty-nine, leaving a small son; her sister, Louisa, died at the age of thirty-six while Bronson and Abigail were engaged; and a brother, Edward, had died when Abigail herself was scarcely two years old. Samuel May was the third son of her parents to receive that name, the only one to survive infancy. Fever, dysentery, and whooping cough were only a few of the contagious diseases that carried off about thirty-five percent of the children born to every mother of Abba's generation.[29]

After Abba's recovery the family reunited and moved back to Boston, where Bronson resumed writing his diary on child development. Friends of the Mays and Alcott's fellow school reformers helped recruit pupils for his new Temple School. Elizabeth Peabody became his chief assistant and helped to gather children from the city's liberal upper-class. The families of his students included Chief Justice Lemuel Shaw (the father-in-law of Herman Melville), Josiah Phillips Quincy (cousin to John Quincy Adams), and George Emerson. Elizabeth and her sisters, Sophia (later Mrs. Nathaniel Hawthorne) and Mary (later Mrs. Horace Mann) were part-time teachers and close friends of the Alcotts.

Bronson embarked on deeper philosophical studies in this new setting. He abandoned his older faith in Lockean ideas, turning instead to such works as Coleridge's *Aids to Reflection*, which synthesized Platonic ideas with Christian precepts. He invented a new motto: "Plato for Thought, Christ for Action," and determined that the "historical" Jesus was no more or less divine than he was himself.[30] Moreover, he interpreted the life of Christ more radically than the religious liberals of his times. For Bronson, Jesus existed as the ideal spirit within each child, and he was determined to commune with that divine spirit in his pupils. If children's minds could be turned inward, if they could become conscious of their own divine spark of truth, then they might become truly good.

Alcott's conversion from Locke's materialism to Plato's idealism was shared by many supporters of the Temple School; it reflected, if radically so, the paradox of Emersonian individualism. Transcendentalism, the philosophic movement that united Bronson Alcott, Emerson, Thoreau, and Margaret Fuller, among others, was both a challenge to the competitive materialist spirit of the Jacksonian age and a reinforcement of its belief in individual enterprise. Placing the locus of true virtue within the individual soul, it fostered self-reliance and also made every citizen his own policeman. Transcendentalism provided a new basis for order in an expansionist age by replacing external, community controls with internalized, individual ones. There was, of course, a strain of antinomian heresy in Transcendental assertions that every person possessed a private pipeline to the Universal Will. But Bronson's education of his own children proved that the bonds of affection and emotional dependency could be strengthened to check selfish individualism. His own "model children" were the vanguard of a new generation whom Bronson hoped to educate.

The Terrible Twos

Creating the models for citizenship within his own family occupied Bronson intensely. He found Anna at three-and-a-half docile, shy, and fearful. Louisa, he thought, was a dangerously independent infant, too stubborn, assertive, and even rude. Bronson reasserted control, imposing a discipline he thought Abba too gentle to supply.

A rigid schedule was set up for the girls, and they were separated to maximize parental supervision and reduce quarrels. Both arose at 6:00 A.M. were dressed and washed by their father, and played until breakfast at 7:00. At 8:00 Louisa was given over to her mother's care, while Anna went to the Temple School with her father. After Louisa's nap, the two girls would lunch with the family and take a walk with Bronson or a servant. Then came playtime in the apartment, a light meal at 6:00, and conversations with their father before a bedtime ritual at 7:30.[31]

Louisa encouraged this firm, structured schedule in her prescriptive stories for children, but she emphasized intimate bedtime chats with mother rather than father. In fact, in *Little Men* Aunt Jo keeps the same kind of careful records and observations of all twelve Plumfield students that her father pioneered. In Louisa's version of the system, however, Jo records the development of each child as a special private interchange between herself and the pupil. She tells one, "I dont show my records to any but the one to whom each belongs. I call this my conscience book: and only you and I will even know what is to be written."[32]

Bronson's schedules allowed a generous amount of bodily freedom. At evening time the girls would romp unclothed in the privacy of their rooms. They were never restrained from exercise, a conditioning that Louisa continued as an adult. She found rugged walks and even scrubbing floors a means of venting frustrations and soothing her temper. In *Little Men* she depicts weekly pillow fights that release the children's pent-up energies at bedtime. The naughtiest pupils are encouraged to run out their passions or dig and hoe in the school's garden.

As the Alcott sisters grew, Louisa became a dominant and frequently aggressive playmate; Bronson observed how Anna's earlier hostility toward her sister slowly abated. He analyzed the situation, and concluded that at two years Louisa was still the prisoner of instinct, undisciplined, "pursuing her purposes by any means that will lead to her attainment."[33] He suspected that eating meat was part of her problem, and that she had also inherited her mother's volatile temperament. "The will is the predominating power," he believed, in both Louisa and Abba, and it must be "broken" by both physical discipline and spiritual encouragement.[34] Louisa preferred to sit in her mother's lap at the table; Bronson insisted that she stay in her own chair. Refusing to "mind father," she shouted, "No, No," a rather ordinary display of behavior we now associate with the "terrible twos." Bronson spanked her, and repeated the spanking until she sat "on the little chair by the side of her mother."[35] He disliked such discipline because it contradicted his belief in the divinely granted individuality of each human being. But it was necessitated, he thought, by her mother's previous indulgence. In fact, today we might judge Louisa's "No" merely a natural assertion of precisely the individuality her father cherished.

Passionate Baby, Stubborn Girl

Louisa competed with her sister for nurturance and attention from the moment of birth, and this fact, no less than her parents' genuinely loving encouragement, provoked her initiative and independence. By the age of three she was a frequent visitor to Temple School. She developed a large vocabulary for her age, supplementing her speech with all sorts of pantomine, and she even played the heroines in impromptu family dramas. Both Bronson and Elizabeth Peabody used literature to develop analytic powers in the children at school, and Bronson found that his smallest pupil, Louisa, appreciated "all the relations of expression, using every part of speech."[36]

Bronson read Wordsworth ("Our birth is but a sleep and a forget-ting") to Louisa and to his other pupils. He wanted to instill in them, even at so young an age, the ideas he had gleaned from his reading of Words-worth and Jesus. The children also learned *The Pilgrim's Progress* by diagramming it and acting it out in little plays. Louisa and her sisters acted out the Pilgrim's journey at home with Abba's help. The storytell-ing and the conversations gave the girls immense pleasure, confirming Elizabeth Peabody's view that Bronson had a way with children beyond any teacher she knew.[37]

Discipline at school was consistent with that at home: self-examination led to the all-important development of self-sacrifice. Since one child's behavior might result in group punishment, the Temple School pupils monitored each other. Peer pressure, as we call it today, frequently checked disobedience. The principle of self-sacrifice was even more intensely instilled at home. When Anna's sprained ankle won her the rocking chair that Louisa coveted, Bronson asked the older girl to give it up to her sister. He reminded her that "very good little girls give up their own wants to the wants of their little sisters, whom they love. Love makes us want to give up our own wants. If you love your little sister, you will give up the chair to her." Anna, almost four years old, insisted that she loved her sister but also wanted to sit in the chair. Finally, Bronson had to reward her with a very material object, an apple, in order to elicit the required sacrifice. When he asked if Anna gave up the chair for love or apple, Anna admitted, "because I wanted the apple . . . and I like sister too."[38]

Apples apparently served both as treat and temptation in the girls' training. Bronson later left an apple on a wardrobe as a temptation to little girls who should not take things without permission. When he left the room, both girls climbed to get it, by Louisa grabbed first and then shared the prize with her sister. Anna confessed first, admitting that her con-science troubled her and would restrain her in the future. Louisa grinned and said, "I wanted it," tardily admitting that she was naughty. The experiment was repeated, and Louisa instructed herself, "No, No, Father's. Me not take Father's apple, Naughty, Naughty." Her own appetite triumphed, however; she ate the apple and then told her mother, "Me could not help it. Me *must* have it."[39]

Years later she recalled a more public demonstration of her educa-tion in self-denial. On her fourth birthday, which was also her father's thirty-seventh, a party was held at Temple School. Louisa remembered that she wore a crown of flowers and

> stood upon the table to dispense cakes to each child as the proces-sion marched past. By some oversight, the cakes fell short, and I saw

that if I gave away the last one I should have none. As I was queen of the revel, I felt that I ought to have it and held on to it tightly til my mother said, 'It is always better to give away than to keep the nice things; so I know my Louy will not let the little friend go without.' The little friend received the dear plummy cake, and I a kiss and my first lesson in the sweetness of self denial, a lesson which my dear mother beautifully illustrated all her long and noble life.[40]

Louisa's written reminiscence did not include a recognition that she shared her birthday with her father, or that the party had been chiefly in his honor. What she still felt was sharp regret at publicly having to sacrifice the "dear plummy cake."

She remembered a good deal more from this time, much of which found its way into her fiction in only slightly altered form, including the fact that "running away was one of the chief delights of my early days."[41] On one occasion, she joined some Irish children in the ash heaps and wastelands of Boston, sharing their cold potatoes and salt fish. Together they trooped to the Commons and had a fine time until nightfall brought them back to Bedford Street; then, to Louisa's astonishment, she heard a towncrier announcing the loss of "a little girl, six years old, in a pink frock, white hat and new green shoes." Her parents had sent the crier, and when Louisa arrived home they disciplined her by tying her to a sofa.[42] This method of punishment was one Louisa's mother may have learned from Lydia Maria Child, who recommended it in her advice books. Louisa clearly approved of it in retrospect, and used it to punish her favorite tomboy, Nan Harding, for straying off in *Little Men*.

The Gospel Lesson

At about the time Louisa began discovering the world on her own, Bronson Alcott was encountering difficulties maintaining the Temple School. Diverse in character, these difficulties led to its collapse in a cloud of heresy and scandal. In the mid-1830s Bronson expanded his conversations with children to include both Sunday School dialogues with adults and Wednesday morning sessions on the new Testament with interested ministers and lay people. Precursors of the more famous "Conversations" by Margaret Fuller, a Temple School associate and the brilliant author of *Women in the 19th Century*, these spirited discussions clearly expounded heretical doctrines. Human beings, Alcott argued, were directly in touch with the Divine Spirit—in touch, moreover, without benefit of institutionalized religion. And Christ, whom Bronson always referred to as Jesus, was a perfect man, but possessed of no more immaculate origins than any other man. Influential clergy of less liberal persuasions, including the powerful Rev. William Ellery Channing, disapproved of these views, and attendance at the Wednesday morning sessions gradually fell off. It was Alcott's publications, however, that drew the most vociferous protest.

In 1837 he published *Conversations with Children on the Gospels*, a relatively inoffensive discussion of human birth which explained that a mother gives her body up to God, who with her aid "brings forth the Child's Spirit in a little body of its own."[43] It created a furor. Never mind that Sophia Peabody, a notably genteel censor, felt elevated by Bronson's *Conversations*. Nor did it matter that Dr. William Alcott, who did not associate himself with heresy of any sort, commended his cousin's work. Dr. Alcott's own *The Physiology of Marriage* delicately presented the issue of sex to readers with the express purpose of restraining sexual passions that led to ill health and madness.[44]

The controversy raged throughout 1836 in the *Courier*, the *Boston Daily Advertiser*, and the *Christian Register*. Friends rallied to Bronson's defense, and even Judge Lemuel Shaw offered advice to save the school. Most of these friends approved of Bronson's influence upon their children, but urged caution and a less public espousal of unpopular notions. Bronson neither yielded nor concealed his views.

The Panic of 1837 further affected his diminishing enrollments and financial credit. A second depression indicated that it was no time for gentry to entrust their children's education to unpopular critics.

The radical agitation that marked Boston politics reinforced Alcott's image as a dangerous figure. As early as 1829 he joined William Lloyd Garrison and Sam May in organizing the Massachusetts Anti-Slavery Society. Abigail May Alcott was already a charter member of the Massachusetts Female Anti-Slavery Society, as was Lydia Maria Child and Elizabeth Peabody. In 1833 Garrison founded the American Antislavery Society, using his abolitionist newspaper, *The Liberator*, to stir up support. A Boston mob attacked Garrison, and during the riot that ensued Abba Alcott hid Garrison's portrait of George Thompson, the English abolitionist. Afterward she visited and comforted Garrison, "the poor man who had been good to the slaves."[45] Abolitionism, Transcendentalism, communitarianism, and women's rights seemed all of a piece and equally dangerous to many people in those years.

The withdrawal of pupils forced Bronson to sell his school equipment. Even then he was still several thousand dollars in debt. He tried to open a smaller school, then a still smaller one on Beach Street. He had plowed his small profits back into his schools, continually purchasing the newest and best books and equipment. In the final year of his last, tiny school (1839), he accepted a black girl as one of his students. Abba and Sam May, who remembered the heroism of Prudence Crandall in Connecticut, supported him in this action. Yet it served as final proof to his few remaining patrons that Alcott was beyond the limits of good sense and caution. By June only a few children, including Anna, Louisa and Elizabeth, along with their black classmate, Susan Robinson, remained as Bronson's students.[46]

The girls' education in self-sacrifice continued in the context of this long cycle of poverty and hard times for the Alcott family. While the recurring business cycles of prosperity and depression certainly contributed to the instability of small experiments like the Temple School, it was also clear that Bronson Alcott lacked practical shrewdness. More opportunistic schoolmasters prospered in the expanded public market for education during that period. Bronson's devotion to democratic opportunities for learning, especially the extension of equal schooling for blacks, was cheered by the expanding reformist circle, but it infuriated potential patrons.

Given the times, Bronson probably warranted the charges that his educational practices were "corrupting" and immoral, although he certainly would have denied this. Yet his methods seem flawed even judged from a modern perspective. That Alcott sought to reconstruct the character of sexual repression, not to eliminate it, raises questions about his entire approach to the education of children. His attitude toward spontaneous sensual activity, for instance seems contradictory. He enjoyed bathing his daughters and allowed them to romp naked before bedtime, yet insisted upon the innocence or non-existence of infantile sexuality. Similarly, his classroom manner appeared almost seductive in character, though he believed steadfastly in his pupil's innocence.

Bronson's pedagogy and his parental practices in general were designed to control even while they appeared to liberate the spontaneity of children. Anna, for example, was encouraged in every way to exhibit only what was expected of her, and she fused completely with Bronson's expectations. He found in Anna the confirmation he sought, but it made her deeply dependent upon her father. Louisa was less satisfying to her father in many respects, a failure that may have saved her from the conformity that tyrannized Anna. Bronson's emotional interrogations, however, evoked a self-consciousness that made Louisa feel greedy, selfish, impulsive, jealous, and aggressive.

Louisa's personal "success" notwithstanding, the self-sacrifice and repression driven into her was taught not only by parents like Bronson, but by society at large. Unselfishness can be explained as a simple Christian virtue, but for women of Louisa's era its meaning was more complex. In mid-nineteenth century New England, female self-sacrifice helped provide emotional and financial "capital" for the "take-off" period of industrial development. To be sure, the cult of domesticity made the home a "refuge in a cruel and heartless" world, but it also reinforced the notion that women should work to feed and nurture their families for love, not money. Female labor in the home could not be reimbursed because such payment would deplete the capital that went to build canals, railroads, mills, and factories. Furthermore, many thought that a man's individual responsibility promoted optimism and entrepeneurial drive. When the fortunes of the marketplace contracted, however, casting working men out, that proud individualism created feelings of personal worthlessness. A good woman was supposed to help her man bear failures; she should and often did keep the family going by a variety of means—sewing for others, taking in boarders, doing laundry, or earning meager wages that were viewed as "pin money" by employers.[47] Certainly Bronson was less than pragmatic about his entrepeneurial ventures, but it was Abba who bore the brunt of the social circumstances attending his personal failures. She could do little after the closing Temple School to support her family, however. They had borrowed again and again from Colonel May, and relations between Abba and her father were strained to the breaking point.

In 1838 Bronson Alcott's misfortunes were exacerbated by family calamity. Abba suffered another miscarriage, and a year later bore a stillborn son. Reform-minded friends came to the Alcotts' aid once again, confirming Louisa's life-long conviction that her personal relationships were more reliable than any institutions. Among those who helped, none was more important than Ralph Waldo Emerson, who had befriended Bronson during the Temple School days. The two men had first met to discuss publishing one of Bronson's manuscripts, *Psyche: The Breath of Childhood*, a record of Elizabeth Alcott's infancy. Emerson was kind but firm. The manuscript, he believed, was pedantic, mannered, and overblown. Still, he felt that Bronson Alcott "unerringly takes the highest moral ground and commands the other's position, and cannot be outgeneralled." He saw courage and nobility in Bronson's emotional distance from the opinion of others. On March 31, 1840, the Alcott family left Boston for a small house in Concord, about a mile from the Emersons.

CHAPTER III

Armies of Reform

It is said to be the age of the first person singular.

Ralph Waldo Emerson, 1827

One of Louisa May Alcott's biographers observes that the young Louisa never knew anyone who was less than a general in the armies of reform.[1] She grew up in the company of triumphant individualists, some of whom believed in competitive enterprise, while others, like Emerson, proclaimed the natural moral order complete in each individual soul. "Trust thyself," Emerson wrote, "Every heart vibrates to that iron string."[2] Louisa's parents believed, along with most of their reformist generation, that Americans stood on the edge of a new Eden even as the spirit of laissez-faire laid waste to the very wilderness that promised them prosperity, liberty, and happiness.

The spiritual equality guaranteed by new beliefs conflicted with deepening social stratification emerging both in Eastern cities and in the more sparsely settled West. Working men demanded an end to the "aristocracy of talent and place" and a political guarantee of their free enterprise through reforms providing "equal education, equal property and equal privileges." Antislavery advocates challenged slaves' bondage as a barrier to all liberty. The welfare of the blind was championed by Dr. Howe, and the care of the insane by Dorothea Dix. The rights of children were championed by Bronson Alcott himself.[3] The moral equality (some said superiority) of women did not in itself change their subordinate status in society. But Mary Wollestonecraft's *Vindication of the Rights of Women*, which Abba and then Louisa read, resonated to Emerson's "iron string:" "If woman be allowed to have an immortal soul, she must have, as the employment of life, an understanding to improve."[4]

Spiritual self-improvement as the means to a perfect society gradually created a terrible contradiction in the Alcotts' family life. Wollestonecraft had quoted Lord Bacon in a passage that defines Bronson's growing conflict with his wife and daughters: "He that hath a wife and children hath given hostages to fortune; for they are impediments to great enterprises, either of virtue or mischief." Private property was the basis of family life for the Alcotts as for most Americans; yet, as the reformers said, the drive to gain property led men to sell their souls.

If private property was the barrier to family harmony and spiritual perfection, perhaps (Bronson was coming to believe) communality was a proper basis for society. In the meantime, the children found much to enjoy in Concord. The Hosmer cottage stood near the Old South Bridge of the town. Only a few open fields separated it from the Concord River where willows and cattails sheltered children and small wildlife; its banks became a playground for the Alcott girls. The house itself was large compared to the rented rooms and cottages of Louisa's earlier years. At seven and a half, she now had the run of a suburban cottage which offered a maze of small rooms available for hide-and-seek and play-acting of all sorts. Outside there were barns, sheds, and almost two acres of land on which Bronson planned to cultivate vegetables and fruits.

Behind them eighteen miles away in Boston, were six thousand dollars in debts and memories of failure and despair. In the midst of anxieties over the closing of Temple School, mounting debts and reduced income, Lydia Maria Child became a friend in need. She took care of Abba daily for five weeks after the stillbirth in 1838. In the following autumn forty-year old Abba became pregnant again, and this time the outcome was a tragedy she never failed to mourn in later years. A son was born in April, 1839; he survived for a few minutes only to be buried in the May family vault.[5]

The move to Concord temporarily revived Abba's spirits and physical energies. Bronson repaired the house and barns, plowed and planted a large garden. Anna attended a Concord private school run by Henry and John Thoreau—her father was content with their progressive educational practices—and Elizabeth and Louisa enjoyed an infant school in Emerson's home, taught by Mary Russell. It was a bustling, crowded but hopeful time again. Yet the Alcott household allowed little privacy. Contemporary reformers, called for the separation of innocents from the marketplace, but Louisa enjoyed no such tranquility. The years between her sixth and tenth birthdays were precarious and insecure, and she matured beyond the innocent trustfulness encouraged by prescriptive literature.

The children in Louisa's fiction share their families' privations, if any, and even very young boys and girls are conscious of their material and emotional environment. Over many years she came to divide her literary children into three categories: the naive, gentle-hearted dependents of secure homes, often a bit selfish in their removal from the larger society; the self-sacrificing and self-conscious offspring of fallen gentry; and the tough skeptical urchins who survived in the streets by a premature self-sufficiency. In many ways her parents were the privileged innocents of the Transcendental period, while she herself developed the perspective of an urchin. Her awareness of her family's fragility and the contradictions between self-reliant individualism and woman's dependency made her a very practical little girl. Anxious, responsible, and increasingly self-critical, she felt protective even as a child of the parents who could not protect her or themselves from the insecurities of the larger world.

The move from the center of Boston's commercial disarray to the reform activities in Concord represented far more than a journey of eighteen miles. To appreciate the enormous social distance the Alcotts traveled in Louisa's childhood, we must begin with the peculiarly American flowering of Romantic reform that called itself Transcendentalism.[6] The Transcendentalists criticized the dominant materialist ideology, but remained optimistic about human perfectability. They believed that the transformation of human consciousness marked a first step toward creating an earthly paradise. Often less interested in the struggles of democratic politics than in the creation of a social community supporting "instinctive selfhood," they envisaged a free society made up of self-reliant, natural men and women. In a sense the Alcotts saw themselves and their country outside of history and politics, born again into a unique relationship with their environment and each other.

The Transcendentalist Club met for the first time in September 1836, and included such men as George Ripley, Ralph Waldo Emerson, James Freeman Clarke, Orestes Brownson, and Bronson Alcott. With the exception of Alcott all were ministers or former ministers, and graduates of Harvard College. Emerson urged his friend Bronson's admittance to the group on the grounds that he was a "God-made Priest." The group grew to include Cyrus Bartol, Theodore Parker, Jones Ripley, and Margaret Fuller.[7] Although an impressive sampling of what historians have called the "American Renaissance,"[8] it did not encompass the entire spectrum of those concerned with America's "manifest destiny."[9]

Universal Being

Nevertheless, Louisa experienced the full range of the Age of Reform. Her childhood reverberated with conflicts between the social pillars of established order and the various outcasts who struggled to shape a new order. Yet reform and material success were not wholly incompatible. Horace Mann and Sam May, for example, both prospered, confident that the expansion of business and educational opportunities would benefit workers as well as owners. Bronson Alcott, however, was an outcast. The failure of Temple School drew him outside the circle of genteel reformers. The whole family shared Bronson's feelings of despair and alienation. Abba tried to defend him to her father, who had always thought Bronson irresponsible. Why had Alcott failed? Because he refused to "cut his suit to fit the cloth," as Colonel May had advised.

In his own mind, Bronson had no choice but to join those who "came out" of sin to fashion a "community" to fit their intentions. As Bronson filled his journal with nostalgic evocations of Spindle Hill, he began to imagine an ideal, organic community of simple values. He even planned to become a pedlar again, this time distributing ideas instead of Yankee goods. He was not alone in dreaming of a Utopian alternative, nor was he alone in looking both backward and forward at the same time. One could "come out" from the sins of materialist avarice and join the growing band of universal reformers in communities like Brook Farm, Hopedale, and Oneida. In such places one could build an environment conducive to spiritual perfection.

Bronson took heart from his friendship with Ralph Waldo Emerson and set about exploring opportunities to engage "a band of valiant souls gathering for conflict with the hosts of ancient and honorable errors and sins."[10] After settling on the Hosmer estate, Bronson's friendship with Emerson deepened through prolonged visits, and conversations.

Emerson's friendship opened doors to Bronson in nearby Watertown and Newton as well as Concord, where he once again delivered his Conversations. For her part, Louisa delighted in the friendship both of the Emerson children and their father, whose hospitality included a distinguished library open to the Alcotts. Throughout her life she acknowledged the friendship and influence of Emerson on her life and work.

Indeed, during her childhood, Emerson's esteem and affection for the Alcotts filled an emotional vacuum left by Colonel May's withdrawal. Still a faithful ally of his sister, Sam had strong reservations about Bronson's growing dissociation from liberal institutional reforms. Emerson's social status, however, more than matched that of the lofty Mays and Sewalls. Moreover, Emerson viewed the Alcotts' "family straits" as part of a general affliction visited upon the purest, most enlightened souls of his generation. Their trials were ultimate proof of the corruption infesting an American society that failed to appreciate its noblest hearts.

Like Bronson, Emerson proclaimed a new age in which "a nation of men will for the first time exist, because each believes himself inspired by the Divine Soul which also inspires all men."[11]

Echoing the fervor of the Puritan Jeremiah Emerson implored

Americans to withdraw from corrupt social institutions. In August 1837, he stated that the existing society was such that it alienated man from himself and nature. "The tradesman," he declared, "scarcely ever gives an ideal worth to his work, but is hidden by the routine of his craft, and the soul is subject to dollars."[12]

In "Nature," Emerson expressed the heart of Transcendentalism. "There is a property in the horizon," he asserted, "which no man has but he whose eye can integrate all the parts, that is, the poet. This is the best part of these mens' farms, yet to this their warranty—deeds give not title."[13] The philosopher and the poet were one in experiencing nature as the emblem of the spirit, in seeing natural law as the twin to moral law, divinely given and intuitively felt by all free men.

"Nature always wears the color of the spirit," Emerson said, discarding the older Lockean notion that the material world shapes our perceptions. The incandescent spirit within man shines forth and illuminates the world. Indeed, the spirit alone sees and constructs the world. "I become a transparent Eye Ball. I am nothing. I see all. The currents of Universal Being circulate through me: I am part of particle of God."[14]

In both Europe and America this kind of antinomian belief inspired a transformation of literature and art. Nature became an emblem of the spirit and the human viewer a creative artist through his perception alone. Wordsworth and Coleridge exemplified the Romantic Revolution in England, and they inspired Hawthorne, Whitman, Thoreau, and Emerson. A whole reform generation matured at the feet of these Romantics, among them Bronson and Abba Alcott. Louisa Alcott also drew on this legacy, as did many women who saw real feminist potential in Romanticism. They believed that women no less than men shaped the world about them through their perception of it. Like the Christian perfectionists and evangelicals they resembled, Romantic idealists cherished each human being's original, unmediated relationship to the universe.

Louisa May Alcott explored these views both in her life and in her fiction. Though a girl, she imagined herself to be the son in her family. Her temper and her active body made her feel alien to the gentle, submissive character her father and even the most radical male reformers thought natural for little girls. At eight she wrote her first poem, "The Robin," and her mother was convinced that she would "grow up a Shakespeare."[15] Poems, impromptu plays with her sisters, and storytelling became acceptable outlets for her independent fantasies. In these she could be anybody, an adventurous boy or a daring, romantic heroine. Her mother's warm encouragement, however, was balanced by her father's constant admonitions. Both parents left notes on the children's pillows. In one, Bronson gave Louisa two pictures, one of a child playing the harp and the second of an arrow. He wrote, "Two passions strong divide our life—meek, gentle, love, or boisterous strife." Below the harp he printed, "Love, Music, Concord," and beneath the arrow, "Anger, Sorrow, Discord." Years later Louisa wrote above his note, "Louisa began early, it seems, to wrestle with her conscience."[16] Bronson's prescribed struggles for self-effacement were matched by her own stubborn demand for experience in the world. She accepted Emerson's essays as if their titles were signposts on a woman's pilgrimage; later she preached the importance of friendship as a preface to love in the lives of women, thereby integrating the best Romantic dicta with feminist goals.

To Bronson Alcott and his friends, then, Emerson's essays seemed to light a path to a better world. But unlike Emerson, who had wealth at his disposal, Alcott suffered from poverty that prevented him from pursuing his utopian dreams. He hired out as a day laborer, mowing fields and chopping wood for his neighbors at one dollar a day. He found some employment in his precious "Conversations;" there was more demand for them as the Lyceum movement swept the nation. More successful lecturers, like Emerson, were booked into towns, cities, and villages to provide cultural stimulation for a nation hungry for specifically American genius. Growing more leery of any commercialization of his efforts, however, Bronson charged no fixed fees, depending instead upon the generosity of his hosts and their guests. He might give two or three talks in series on "Self Culture" or "Human Life," walking to his sponsors' homes and relying upon their hospitality if the distance required an overnight stay. There might be twenty of thirty persons, old New England citizens, of cultivated minds interested in hearing this prophet of "newness."[17]

The differences between reformers who confronted political and religious institutions directly and those who withdrew from society to seek personal salvation were great. But both groups often shared general principles and goals. Garrison communicated with John Humphrey Noyes, for example, the founder of the Christian perfectionist community at Oneida; the two agreed in their criticism of the relationship between private property and the state. Both men, along with Bronson and his closest friends, increasingly saw slavery as the incarnation of sinful private property which they viewed as the most important obstacle to achieving Christian perfection in America.

Emerson and Alcott were supportive of George Ripley, who lost the pulpit of Boston's Purchase Street Church in 1841 by declaring that "the purpose of Christianity is to redeem society, as well as the individual."[18] Bronson sat in Emerson's house and listened to Ripley's plans for a new society. The result was Brook Farm, and the new model community was soon joined by Margaret Fuller and Nathaniel Hawthorne. The Alcotts were invited to participate, but the group was not spiritually-minded enough to suit Bronson. The Brook Farm members were to receive ten cents an hour for their work, physical and mental; also, they ate meat, and sold their produce for butter and other animal products.[19] As Bronson attended more discussions about intentional communities, his particular needs assumed specific dimensions. There must be no money involved in the community's sustenance, no meat, no stimulants of any kind, and the spiritual enlightenment of members must be paramount. Bronson could not subsume his personality, or what he saw as his unique principles, to Brook Farm's leadership.

He agreed with Emerson that the ways of trade had become theft, and commerce so abused that it was unfit for any man's livelihood. The cotton worn by New Englanders was drenched in the blood of slaves; one man in ten died every year in Cuba so that Americans might have their sugar. As long as some men lacked property, Emerson thundered, the title of those who owned their own land was tainted. Emerson's solution was an end to the division of labor. Only when men refused to engage in trade and rejected wages could social institutions be reformed and all men be "equally restored to selecting the fittest employment of their individual talents."[20]

Bronson, Abba, and their daughters were moving farther from the moderate stance taken by Colonel May. Partly to effect a reconciliation, Louisa was sent to visit her grandfather in Boston. Her father soon forwarded her a short note with a sketch of the Hosmer cottage and an admonition to "step lightly and speak softly about the house. Grandpa loves quiet, as well as your sober father and other grown people."[21] If the Colonel was impressed by a quiet granddaughter, her behavior did not compensate for the reports he heard of her father's activities. Joseph May was an antislavery man, and his son was a passionate spokesman for the Abolitionist cause, but Bronson's friends were now disrupting public order with their demonstrations, and they were increasingly met with violent opposition.

The political situation was growing more heated. Some of the Alcotts' friends set up small alternative stores where customers could be sure of purchasing goods made only by free labor. William Lloyd Garrison was refused a platform in every Boston church when he preached not only boycotts of slave-produced goods, but civil disobedience to prevent the return of fugitive slaves. After an angry mob threatened Garrison, he was put in the Leverett Street Jail, ostensibly for his own safety. Bronson was his first visitor, and he also went regularly to the office of Garrison's paper, *The Liberator*. In those pages Garrison had declared, "I am in earnest, I will not equivocate; I will not excuse; I will not retreat a single inch, and I will be heard."[22]

While Garrison agitated and courted imprisonment, and Emerson preached and wrote, Bronson Alcott seemed determined to live the ideals he shared with his friends. He neither owned land nor engaged in trade, and by January 1841 the Alcotts financial situation was hopeless. The Temple School creditors were still unpaid, and by now the family owed money to Concord tradesmen as well.

In February Colonel Joseph May died, attended by Sam and his only surviving daughter, Abba. Colonel May left a total of $17,627 by the executors' first reckoning, and a substantial amount of household goods.[23] He divided his money in equal shares, not only to Abba and her two surviving brothers, Sam and Charles, but also to his adopted daughter, Louisa Caroline Greenwood, and to his dead daughters' surviving children in trust with their legal guardians.

The residual legacies finally amounted to only $1,150 each, scarcely enough to meet the Alcotts' debts in any event. But Colonel May had treated Abba, in her view, like her orphaned, dependent nephews and nieces, who were unable to administer their own affairs. Certainly the Colonel was tough-minded and specific in his will, giving "to my daughter Mrs. Abigail Alcott, one hundred dollars and the silver teapot, which belonged to her dear mother," in addition to her share of the estate. Sam received one hundred dollars, all his father's books, and his "wardrobe," and Louisa Caroline Greenwood was given one hundred dollars, the Colonel's gold watch, and his "pew no. 20 in King's Chapel." On the face of it this seemed fair, but Abba was crushed by a further restriction he placed upon her share of the cash monies. "I direct that the share of my daughter Abigail," he declared, "as well as the hundred dollars before given to her be secured by my executors to her sole and separate use, without the control of her husband or liability for his debts in such manner as they judge best."

Love and Property

The inventory of Joseph May's estate revealed that Bronson owed his father-in-law $1,729.[24] Joseph May had kept careful track of the money he lent his children, and entered the sums (with interest) in his books along with business credits and debts. But he forgave his son, Charles May, "all whatever sums of money which may be found charged against him in my books, amounting now to more than two thousand dollars besides interests." And he also left him, in addition to his share in the residual estate, "fifty dollars and also my silver watch." Bronson's debts were not forgiven. In fact, when the will went into Probate Court the executors "prayed Allowance" for certain charges made against the estate, including a payment to William Minot for the costs of defending suit against Amos Bronson Alcott for $2,400, April 29, 1841. Another $75 went to W. Minot "for defence of suit of blank assignee of A.B. Alcott vs. Executors."[25]

In the fall of 1841 the final accounting by the executors still listed $1,729.02 due from Bronson Alcott to his father-in-law's estate. By the time the will was out of probate, all debts having been collected and proper disbursements made to those with claims upon Colonel May's property, there was about $15,000 left. No record indicates that Bronson ever paid off his debt. But Bronson's creditors sued May's estate, and the legal fees for defending the properties had to be substracted from the residue, paid by heirs.[26] It was just as the prudent Colonel May had feared.

Certainly Abba's father had given ample warning to Bronson of his concern for his daughter's financial security. In 1834 he had written to her expressing his concern, and bluntly stated her indebtedness;

> You have made several mistakes since you began to manage for yourself, and without or against the advice of your friends—marrying without possessing the needful to keep a house—and without having tried the success of your Friend's pursuits to obtain a support—changing your places of residence—removing to Germantown—furnishing a large house there to accomodate boarding scholars—selling your furniture at auction—removing to Philadelphia—all which have consumed four and a half years of the best part of your life—nearly all your property—and left you burdened with a debt of $1,000 or more.[27]

Abba replied that her husband was not a "spendthrift" and that neither of them were self-indulgent. She ended with a blow to the family status: "Would you have me take in washing?" she asked.[28] By the time her father made his will, his lack of faith in her had indeed forced Abba to dismiss her laundress and take in sewing, if not washing.

In fact, the careful terms of Colonel May's will reflected Abba's social and legal status as a married woman in 1841. Before the reformed married women's property act was passed in Massachusetts in 1845, a wife's inheritance from a benefactor, as well as her wages and any property not guaranteed to her use by a premarital agreement or trusteeship, belonged to her husband. She was not a legal person in her own right; her husband had legal right to her body, her property, even the custody of her children should she seek a separation or divorce. As a Suffolk County trustee of poor widows and orphans, Colonel May knew their fate well. He was determined to protect his bequest to his daughter from Bronson's creditors, Bronson's idealism, and from Abba herself.

She did not appreciate his stewardship. "I had supposed," she wrote with some sadness, "that time was mellowing his severe judgement of my motives, and that my husband and children were becoming objects of care and regard to him . . . he did not love me."[29]

The predicament of a nineteenth-century married woman who could not shape the laws of the democratic society that governed her, nor use her resources in a way that suited herself, was doubly tragic. Obliged by honor, and in Abba's case with ties of love, to follow her husband's fortunes, she was also "protected" from lifting the financial burdens she legally shared. Louisa did not overlook the pressing grievances endured by married women. Nor did other feminists, who campaigned successfully in state after state to reform the property laws governing the rights of married women. It was a radical reform enlisting many conservative men who opposed granting wider political rights to women. Elizabeth Cady Stanton, however, claimed that legislative victories for married womens' property rights really reflected the needs of middle-class businessmen who sought to secure portions of their property from creditors (like Bronson's) by passing property over to their wives for safekeeping.[30] In any case, the redress of this particular inequality came too late to help the Alcotts, though they participated in the petition drive for legislative reform.

The year of 1841 passed leaving their debts unsettled and the inheritance still entangled in inventories, property management, and sales. In the following winter, Bronson's despair and stalemated efforts to earn a living by itinerant "Conversations" frightened Abba enough to write her brother that she feared for her husband's sanity. "If his body dont fail his mind will—he experiences at times the most dreadful nervous excitation—his mind distorting every act however simple into the most complicated and adverse form—I am terror-stricken at this."[31] There was other bad news. Emerson's son, Waldo, died early in 1842. One of the Alcott girls, inquiring after her playmate, brought the news home to Abba.

Emerson bore his pain stoically, however, and two weeks after his own tragedy he offered such a generous gift to Bronson that it promised to transform his future. Emerson would raise the money for Bronson's passage to England, where Alcott at least might be cheered and restored to health by congenial society. Bronson had a small reputation in England and even some friends, including an English disciple of Pestalozzi named James Pierrepont Greaves, who had corresponded with Alcott. Harriet Martineau had also taken news of Bronson's Temple School to England, though she had serious reservations about the romanticization of childhood. Alcott had forwarded signed copies of *Conversations with Children on the Gospels* and *Record of a School* to Greaves. By 1842, in company with the like-minded reformers Henry Wright and Charles Lane, Greaves established a communitarian experiment at Ham Common near Richmond, England. They named it "Alcott House" and invited their American preceptor to visit and even preside over the experiment.[32]

After persuading his brother Junius to take "my place in the family during my absence," Alcott sailed for England on May 8, 1842 with ten sovereigns and a bill of exchange for twenty pounds in his pocket, courtesy of Emerson's fund-raising efforts.[33] Although mildly worried about Bronson's journey alone, Abba accepted it without complaint. She wrote Sam that marital affections were still warm, but that "our diversity of opinion has at times led us far and wide of a quiet and contented frame of mind—I have been looking for rest—he for principle and salvation—I have been striving for justice and peace—he for truth and righteousness."[34]

Cottage life during the months of Bronson's English visit was peaceful, if impoverished. The executors released small sums for Abba's subsistence, Emerson was quietly generous as usual, and the reduced family managed with visits from friends who rarely came without contributions of food, clothing or tiny comforts for all. Abba and the girls sent warm, affectionate messages of local news to Bronson, intermixed with reassurances of their own fidelity and longing for him. It was an interlude of harmony and self-sufficiency for the female family, although Louisa felt the burdens keenly. Her lifetime of service in behalf of Marmee and her sisters begins at this period.

On her tenth birthday Abba gave Louisa a pencil case accompanied by a tender note. She had observed that Louisa was "fond of writing" and wished to encourage the habit. A year later Louisa received a picture of a mother and daughter with the words, "I imagined that you might be just such an industrious daughter and I such a feeble but loving mother, looking to your labor for my daily bread." Louisa was not yet eleven years old, but she put the picture in her journal and wrote a poem to her mother under it:

To Mother

I hope that soon, dear mother,
    You and I may be
In the quiet room my fancy
    Has so often made for thee,

The pleasant, sunny chamber,
    The cushioned easy-chair,
The book laid for your reading,
    The vase of flowers fair;

The desk beside the window
    Where the sun shines warm and bright:
And there in ease and quiet
    The promised book you write;

While I sit close beside you,
    Content at last to see
That you can rest, dear mother,
    And I can cherish thee.[35]

Meanwhile, Bronson was enjoying a stimulating trip. He went to the Anti-Corn Law Conference at Westminister, where he heard fiery denunciations of the burdens of taxation, low wages, and disenfranchisement. He predicted an imminent revolution in England to his correspondents at home. He tried to tell George Thompson, the abolitionist and radical political reformer whose portrait Abba had saved, that "it was not bread or wages . . . but property, gain and the lust of gain—these are parents of the ills they suffer." "Thompson," according to Alcott, was "too busy to hear, and the people too hungry to believe."[36] Nor would Robert Owen hear Alcott's arguments, especially his Transcendental message of individual withdrawal, self-denial, and purification. Owen, like Thompson, was appealing to Parliament in behalf of reform legislation that would shape a new response to English working people's demands. Bronson concluded that the Transcendental Club was wiser by far than these English radicals, who welcomed him as an American reformer and a bearer of Garrison's letter of introduction, but who rejected his favorite philosophical formulas. Even Carlyle, Emerson's preeminent man of genius, seemed uncongenial to Bronson. The two found each other impossible after Bronson, invited to breakfast, innocently mixed the strawberries and potatoes on his plate until the juices ran together.[37] Carlyle was convinced that Alcott was eccentric beyond hope.

But Bronson did find sympathetic souls, especially Charles Lane and Henry Wright, men who would play a great and troubling role in Alcott's life. Greaves had died suddenly, just before Bronson's visit, but his library and his principles were intact at "Alcott House" in the care of Lane and Wright. The "friends of human progress" met there, some twenty of them, to hear Alcott and his two new comrades argue that the laws of man, which "inculcate and command slaughter," were not to be obeyed. They propounded "no government" theories, and proposed a New Eden in New England, where temptations might be avoided. For his part, Bronson exhorted his listeners to adopt Emersonian "politics." Quoting the Concord Sage, he declared that "character is the true theocracy," and that natural law must be based on the simple ground of man's innately moral nature. Flushed with a new excitement, Bronson appeared to his audience as a man capable of transforming Emerson's abstract principles into concrete reality.

In the autumn of 1842 Charles Lane, his son William, and Henry G. Wright returned with Bronson to Concord, where they intended to "plant Paradise." They brought with them Greaves' library of 1,000 books as well as several hundred additional volumes on philosophy, mysticism, vegetarianism, health reforms and astrology which they purchased with cash gifts from English admirers. Lane had $1,888, savings accrued from his former career in business as the editor of the *London Mercantile Price Current*.[38]

Abba and the girls were delighted to have Bronson home and they welcomed his new friends. Walking together after their arrival, Louisa asked Abba, "Mother why am I so happy?" to which her mother replied, "Kind friends, Dear Husband."[39] The model family was reunited and enlarged with Bronson's friends. They were happily unaware that their pleasure would be shortlived, for Bronson brought back from England a set of utopian ideas that would throw his domestic life into turmoil. He had heard much in England that made him suspect that his miseries were largely due to the contradictions inherent in a family's simultaneous pursuit of spiritual perfection and genteel domesticity. It was not the first time he had considered this problem, but he had always cast aside his doubts and tried harder to combine the two goals. His new friends led him to question anew the meaning of "husband," "father," and "friend." A New Eden must have an innocent family life, they argued, one that removed "selfish" maternal and paternal obstacles to perfect union. To transcend those obstacles, Bronson might have to construct an association free of special, biological bonds.

Ralph Waldo Emerson would never have gone this far. In his introductory lecture on "The Times," he warned against those "perfectionists and come-outers," who possessed only a portion of the truth and who proposed utopian social improvements that would violate the sanctity of private life.[40] In a sense, Emerson was describing Alcott, a man he valued as a companion, but who he also found intellectually unreliable and narrow. "He is not careful to understand you," Emerson said of the "reformer." "If he gets half a meaning that serves his purpose, it is enough. He hardly needs an antagonist, he needs only an intelligent ear." Emerson did not know it, but Bronson had found willing ears and allies in Charles Lane and Henry Wright.[41] Abba Alcott innocently confided her bewilderment about Bronson's new reformist friends to her diary. Aware of her own abilities to manage the household and maintain a peaceful nursery she wrote,

What a union of these dear English friends will effect, is an interest-ing problem now before us to solve—can Mr. Wright do what this dear Father can not do? At present the children are doing very well furnished with few simple and harmless materials, they manufac-ture their own employment and recreation, and seem to derive more satisfaction and pleasure, than they have ever done by suggestion.[42]

CHAPTER IV

Transcendental Wild Oats

Give me one day of practical philosophy.
It is worth a century of speculation.

Abigail May Alcott, Journals, 1842

Daily rehearsal for the New Eden began at Hosmer cottage in the fall of 1842. The household's diet grew still more spartan: breakfast plates became unnecessary as each resident put a portion of cottage bread, apples, and potatoes on a napkin, washing the food down with a mug of water. Presumably the absence of plates meant less work for the women, although Abba and her daughters continued to do the general cleaning, laundry, and sewing for the household.[1] The sexual division of labor, in fact, became more rigid, as did the educational regime established for the children.

At the heart of these changes was Charles Lane, benign but unrelenting. He helped carve out the sphere of public activity as the proper domain for men's work. While the women worked at home, Lane, Bronson, and Wright visited other New England radicals and wrote articles for the *Dial*, *The Liberators*, and various other reform periodicals. The men, not the women, cast about for a new location for their experiment.

The children were involved in the "newness" not only through their curtailed diet, but also because parental authority was now shared equally with Charles Lane, who undermined the authority Abba exercised in her own sphere. He became the children's primary teacher in morning and afternoon lessons; diary-keeping, spelling, conversations, grammar, and arithmetic followed the old Temple School model with even stricter emphasis on self-criticism. After lunch there were more lessons with Lane in geography, drawing, geometry, French, and Latin. It was only after four o'clock that the children were turned out to sew with Abba or play. Then came a frugal supper, similar to breakfast, followed by spiritually uplifting conversations with all the residents. The entire household was asleep by nine.[2]

The Alcotts sought to transcend the problems of the larger society by intentionally shaping a community where relationships could be uncontaminated, spiritually committed, and free from selfish power struggles. Yet an enormous power struggle ensued within the new household itself. For the first ten years of her life, Louisa's father had been the undisputed "head of the house." His right to exercise that role remained unquestioned so long as Abba and her daughters felt themselves part of a natural domestic order. Certainly there was volatile conflict in the household; Abba's complaints were common knowledge, but they centered around financial difficulties and loss of status. Believing her marriage to be ideal, Abba attributed her privations to external forces buffeting the family. The business world was both unprincipled and unpredictable, which meant that doing good and doing well were often contradictory. Perhaps Bronson was too good for that world. On the other hand, she knew that her brother Sam and others who practiced what they preached were able support to their families.

Bronson's decision to challenge the traditional structure of the conjugal family put terrible pressure on Abba, pressure she was ill-equipped to handle and less disposed to accept. Poverty, diminished social status, even the disapproval of her father and stepmother, were hard enough to bear. This revolution in family life, however, Abba found intolerable. Lane and her husband had struck at her influence in the home, which according to contemporary norms provided compensation for the exclusion of women from public decision-making. Louisa understood her mother's unhappiness at the loss of her domestic influence, and she supported Abba's search for power within the consociate family.

Bronson had invaded the female domains of nursery and kitchen many times before, but his assaults had been sporadic. This time he and Lane proposed to dissolve the privileged bonds joining a married couple and their children, and to forge a larger union of perfect love with no privileged, special relations. Any number of like-minded people might join, and everyone, according to Lane, would have to adjust their habits to the new "industrious order." Lane perceived, however, that Abba was not adjusting well. He wrote to a friend, "Her pride is not yet eradicated and her peculiar maternal love blinds her to all else."[3]

Abba had welcomed friends and kin into her home before. Elizabeth Peabody boarded with the Alcotts in the Temple School period, and William Alcott and his wife had shared the Alcott home at Cottage Place and helped meet the rent. But on each occasion Abba viewed herself as a generous matron, extending temporary hospitality to help others and make ends meet. This time, worn out and oppressed by the new changes, she fled the Hosmer cottage on Christmas Eve of 1842. "Circumstances," she wrote in her journal, most cruelly drive me from the enjoyment of my domestic life. I am prone to indulge in occasional hilarity but I seem frowned down into stiff quiet and peace-less order. I am almost suffocated in this atmosphere of restriction and form . . . a desire to stop short and rest, recognizing no care buy myself seems to be my duty.

I hope the experiment will not bereave me of my mind. The enduring powers of the body have been well tried. The mind yields, falters and falls . . . They all seem most stupidly obtuse on the causes of this occasional protraction of my judgment and faculties. I hope the solution of the problem will not be revealed to them too late for my recovery or their atonement of this invasion of my rights as a woman and a mother. Give me one day of practical philosophy. It is worth a century of speculation.[4]

Like many other women of her day, Abba accepted the sexual division of labor. Her voluntary assumption of the larger burden of domestic work and responsibility, she felt, should command man's respect for woman's rights in her own sphere. Thus she was willing to be her own mistress and maid, but would not be maid to Master Lane. Nor could she accept a token equality as one among others to be consulted by Lane and Bronson on domestic arrangements. To Abba, democratic domestic management meant that household workers controlled household affairs; she and her daughters were the principal domestic workers.

Unsure how to deal with this usurpation of power, Abba fled to her May and Sewall relations, and took Louisa and William Lane along to enjoy a traditional Boston Christmas of good food, social visits, church services, and even a public lighting of the Christmas tree at Amory Hall. She came back to Concord soothed and refreshed, but hardly more amenable. Again, Lane tried to convert her with a vision of the exalted and expanded domestic role she might enjoy as mother of all humanity. He referred to himself as "thy brother, Charles," and said that he had not overlooked her "excellences." Her approval of "any important step was highly desireable." He offered her the opportunity to be a "warming, shining light . . . in which you may rise above all annoyances and crosses whatever, and shed a benign lustre on husband, children, friends, and the world."[5] Some writers have concluded that Abba was briefly pacified, but there is substantial evidence to the contrary. Indeed, there is evidence that each member of the new consociate family viewed this utopian experiment differently; each hoped to realize very individual, disparate goals in the venture.

Confusion of Hopes

Deep but hidden differences about sexual mores and property rights surfaced almost immediately. Henry Wright deserted the consociates. He had married in England and fathered a child (not in that order) without the approval of his celibate brethren. Having left wife at home, he fell in love in the new world with Mary Sargeant Gove, who, after eleven years with a brutal husband, had run away with her young daughter. Their brief love affair ended sadly when Wright died, penniless and outcast in Mary Gove's arms. She eventually remarried another reformer and published her recollections of the consociates as part of her novel, *Mary Lyndon*.[6] In this work, both Alcott and Lane are charged with abandoning Wright. Lane, moreover, is depicted as cheating Wright out of his share of a valuable cargo of English books. Whatever the true circumstances, it seems certain that Wright's sexual behaviour lay outside the limits of the consociates' admittedly confused sexual plans. Scholars disagree, in fact, on whether the Alcott House group in England was celibate, homosexual, or merely intent on regulating and controlling sexuality in the same intense way they organized their social lives. Certainly the Alcott House and Fruitlands had distinctive, even eccentric practices, but their emphasis on socially controlled and proscribed sexual relations, subject to spiritual justification, is typical of many intentional communities in the 1840–1870 period.

The defection of Wright unsettled everyone, distracting them from the necessity of finding a permanent place for their community. Emerson noted that Bronson had a genuine revulsion for hiring out his labor, and an equally sincere belief that beautiful, rich farmland "should be purchased and given" to him. Emerson refused to raise the money for Bronson's one-hundred-acre farm, but there were other potential benefactors. Isaac Hecker, partner with his brothers in a New York grain mill and bakery, was living at Brook Farm. Like many other communitarians, he visited various settlements, weighed and compared the merits of each, and even lived in several successive communities. Bronson invited Hecker to join the consociates and in a letter outlined rather abstract plans for the proposed venture. Hecker was too cautious to invest his money in such an indeterminate scheme, but he did live with the group once the "free use of a spot of land" was obtained. Later he recalled that Alcott received him at Fruitlands "very kindly but from mixed and selfish motives, I suspect he wanted me because he thought I would bring money to the community. Lane was entirely unselfish."[7]

Charles Lane's unselfishness was genuine in that he welcomed like-minded communitarians regardless of their ability to invest money. Confident of his own capacity to earn a living, he did not feel a need for wealthy benefactors. In fact, he believed that abundant and relatively cheap American land removed the major material obstacle to living out perfectionist ideals. Furthermore, there is no evidence that he ever shared Bronson's confusion about dependency and spirituality. It was never clear, for instance, whether Bronson was unable to make money or simply refused to do so (perhaps feeling that charity bestowed by more worldly friends was evidence of his own saintliness). But if Lane was comfortable about sharing his capital, he was also possessive of Bronson's friendship, at least from Abba Alcott's point of view. Nor, as we mentioned, did he accept the priority of a married couple's bonds.

Bronson never grasped the deep conflict between Abba's priorities and Lane's dogmatic vision. Odell Shepard comes closest to explaining why. He observes that Bronson did not like England because "he did not see it."[8] The landscape was of no interest to him; consequently he failed to realize what underlay English reformist demands: a large population long since thrown off the land, a rigid class system, and virtually no possibilities for small freeholds. While Bronson could not earn money to buy land either for his own family or a consociate community, Lane saw earning the necessary capital as an ignoble means to a noble end; he impatiently took up the burden of financing their venture. "I do not see," he said, "any one to act the money part but myself."[9] He wrote to Junius Alcott, as part of his new family, and asked his advice. "I hope the little cash I have collected will suffice to redeem a small spot on the planet . . . Please put your best worldly thought to the subject and favor me with your view as to how and where we could best lay out $1,800 or $2,000 in land, with orchard, wood and house."[10] Lane was bent on escaping the historical burdens of old England in New England.

Emerson suggested they locate at "The Cliffs," near Walden Pond. Alcott was receptive, but Lane "came home first" bringing news of a farm at Harvard, Massachusetts, fourteen miles from Concord. The next morning Lane and Bronson walked there, talked with the owner, Wyman, and viewed the "90 acres, 14 of them wood, a few apple and other fruit trees, plenty of nuts and berries, much of the land very good, the highest part very sublime. The house and barn were very poor, but the water excellent and plentiful." Wyman wanted $2,700, but agreed to sell the land for $1,800 and to lease the buildings rent-free for a year. They had found Fruitlands.[11]

An American Kitchen Garden

In forming "the basis for something really progressive, call it family or community or what you will," Lane was not only sowing "Transcendental Wild Oats," but hungrily planning an English kitchen garden in the wilderness. This garden had "90 acres much of it first rate; some worth 100 dollars per acre, the whole 20 dollars per acre; would that some of the English half starved were on it."[12] As he wrote an English friend, "This I think you will admit, looks like an attempt at something which will entitle transcendentalism to some respect for its practicality."[13]

Sam May was also involved in financing Fruitlands, although in a somewhat confused fashion that augured badly for the future. He and Abba apparently shared one view of the May contribution toward ownership and property rights, Lane quite another, while Bronson felt himself above such petty issues. To Bronson, Fruitlands was "universally owned," but he could not leave Concord without paying his family's debts. Lane wryly noted, "I need not tell you on whom that falls."[14] He paid the debts, leaving himself five hundred dollars poorer. Bronson, however, also asked Sam May to sign a promissory note for three hundred dollars needed to complete the purchase price of the farm. This sum was payable to Wyman's agent over two years in biannual installments of seventy-five dollars each, the first payment due in November of 1843.[15]

The confusion over who was responsible for those payments is further indication of the serious disagreements among the settlers. Abba saw Lane's payment of the Alcotts' Concord debts as reimbursement for her housekeeping chores. In other words, she saw her family as conventional householders who had taken Lane in as a paying boarder. Lane's understanding was that Sam May was lending money from the May estate to reimburse him for settling Bronson's debts. Hence it seemed proper that May money would go towards the November payment for a communal homestead. Sam's version indicates some contradictions in his own views of communitarian versus conventional family life:

> When Mr. Lane purchased the farm in Harvard, without consulting me, he had the Deed made to me as his agent, and came to me with it, ready to be delivered into my hands, so soon as I would sign with him a joint promissory note to Mr. Wyman for three hundred dollars. After some hesitancy, I consented to sign the note, and to accept the trust. I did this hoping, as I told him, by doing so to secure to my sister a house for herself and family.[16]

If Sam May really assumed he was merely acting as his sister's trustee in the purchase of her home, one wonders why he took up a similar trusteeship on November 1, 1843 for a Skaneateles, New York communal experiment. Along with seven other individuals, he agreed to hold that property deed ("to be enjoyed in common henceforth and forever") for seventeen residents and nineteen others who would work the land. His signature generously guaranteed conveyance to "all other persons upon the globe who might wish to join." These signatories also agreed that exclusive and individual property holding was wrong, that governments based on force were destructive, and that "all buying and selling is wrong."[17]

Such an avowal put May in close agreement with Charles Lane, who said about the Fruitlands deed: "Let my privation be ever so great, I will never make any property claim on this effort. It is an offering to the Eternal Spirit, and I consider that I have not more right than any other person; and I have arranged the title deeds, as well as I could to meet that end."[18] Lane was clear in his mind on the issue of property, but May remained uncertainly committed both to entrepeneurship and Christian socialism. He was for "newness."

In any case, with the help of Sam May Bronson and Lane finally had their property. In early June they arrived at Fruitlands to greet their new recruits; they settled on the floor for the night, "having no time to put up the bedsteads."[19] Within a short time newcomers joined the group, including two men from Brook Farm: Samuel Larned, aged twenty, described by Lane as "a counting house man and . . . what the world calls genteel,"[20] and Isaac Hecker. The others included Abraham Everett, known as "the Plain Man," a forty-two year-old cooper whose "rather deep experience" entailed being shut up in an insane asylum by some relatives who hoped to get his money. Wood Abram (or as he was originally called, Abram Wood), was a friend of Thoreau's and led the children on nature walks. Samuel Bower, a nudist, came from Alcott House in England. Beside Bronson, only one member of the group, Joseph Palmer, possessed any real knowledge of farming. He was known as the "man with the beard," or the "Old Jew," as his full beard was unusual in those parts before the Civil War.[21] Heckled, persecuted, even fined and imprisoned when he refused to shave, Palmer stuck to his principles. He was an Abolitionist, a temperance man, and fully subscribed to Fruitlands' goals. Yet he never accepted its impractical agricultural notions. Although hired laborers and beasts of burden were outlawed as being inharmonious with natural freedom, Joseph Palmer brought his plow and team to supplement the spade work. He never actually lived at Fruitlands during the consociate experience, but he had property nearby and was a daily mainstay.

Finally, there was one venturesome woman, Ann Page, who arrived from Providence, Rhode Island. She shared in the domestic chores and childcare as her contribution to spiritual perfectionism. A spinster of about forty years, she left after a stormy scene with Abba, the specifics of which were never made clear.[22]

The June migration to Fruitlands began a golden summer. The consociates' simple crop of vegetables and grains prospered while Anna conducted school for her sisters and William Lane. They sang, did their sums, wrote in diaries, walked and played in the woods. Their diary entries that summer make Fruitlands seem simply another family home, one more delightfully situated in the country.

The older girls helped their mother bake, cook, sew and wash dishes, while the men "planted corn, and cut wood, and fixed round about the house out of doors."[23] Less isolated from friends and playmates than the lack of a public road might have indicated, Abba at first had outside help with the laundry and sewing. Anna recorded that she and Louisa walked home with a "Mrs. Willard," who came to help their mother with the washing and took home some sewing to do for the Alcotts. The sisters visited with Mrs. Willard's daughter and were invited to come again. Catching a lift with Mr. Wyman, who was driving over to visit Fruitlands, they found more company—"two ladies and a girl who came to see us."[24]

Even lessons, when they centered on simple reading, writing, arithmetic, or singing, were pleasant. Anna did "some sums with fractions with Mr. Lane" and seemed more self-confident than usual. "I think," she said happily, "I have learned more lately than I ever did before. I think I understand what I learn too." She also wrote out a French fable in "very good French."[25] By September, however, a slight chill fell on Anna's faithful journals. Shutting out the "ugly" things, arming herself with books, placating dissenters in the community with small gifts of flowers and with her own poems, Anna tried to make everything appear "beautiful." "Beautiful is my favorite word," she said, "If I like anything I always say it is beautiful. It is a beautiful word. I can't tell the color of it . . . I wrote down all the beautiful names we could think of, and in the evening wrote the colors of them."[26] Anna made other, sadder entries, but Bronson's notations show that he had read them and chose to remove them.

Louisa felt less inclined to stress the "beautiful" in their life together. Her favorite pastimes included roaming the woods and fields and playing at being a horse.[27] She also recorded a number of times that she "felt sad because I have been cross today." Crying made her feel better, as did reciting poetry, which also put her to sleep. She was a faithful recorder of visits from grownups, who included Parker Pillsbury (who "came and talked about the poor slaves"), Emerson, Thoreau, Willaim Russell and Lydia Maria Child.[28] Louisa continued to love acting, but she hated music lessons with Miss Page.

When her father and Mr. Lane went "preaching" in far-off cities like Boston or New York, Louisa was happiest. Then, she said, with striking honesty, "it was very lovely."[29] She hated to be without her mother and sister Lizzie. When Abba and Lizzie visited Boston without her, she mournfully declared, "Nobody is as good to me as dear Marmee."[30] Often feeling cross, she made promises to herself and Mother to be better. "If only I kept all I make," she sighed, "I should be the best girl in the world, but I don't, and so am very bad."[31] Forty years later she reread the smudged lines and appended: "Poor little sinner! She says the same at fifty."[32]

A Barren Harvest

It is hard to imagine how much better she might have been at age ten—what with ironing, husking corn well into the night, cooking, minding baby Abba (Abigail May, the youngest daughter), and still finding time to read Plutarch, as well as Byron, Dickens, Maria Edgeworth, and Goldsmith's *The Vicar of Wakefield*.[33] She eventually bestowed the same feelings and the same literary tastes on "Jo March," her alter ego in *Little Women*.[34]

After reading a story about "Contentment," Louisa wrote, "I wish we were all rich, I was good and we were all a happy family this day."[35] Clearly she wavered between feeling that the family's miseries were due to poverty and the suspicion that her own failings made her parents unhappy. She also wrote poetry, and in a four stanza rhyme entitled "Despondency" expressed her fears about the future, hoping that God, who fed the birds and flowers, would also take care of the Alcotts.[36] Anna thought her sister's poems were fine, but Louisa "didn't like them so well."[37] She was much less sure than Anna of her ability to please critics, a feeling Lane reinforced by pressing both girls to work harder. He exhausted them with long, demanding, often unrewarding lessons which they soon learned to resent. Convinced, like Bronson, of the great profundity lying dormant in a child's mind, Lane was apt to ask the girls questions like, "What is man?" After much Socratic coaching, they learned to reply (by rote), "A human being is an animal with a mind, a creature; a body; a soul and a mind."[38]

Most of the recruits to Fruitlands came and went after brief encounters with the rigid life. Isaac Hecker left Brook Farm partly because he wanted even more spartan simplicity in daily life, but also because he had seen directly into the heart of Fruitlands' dissonance. He had brought "three pairs of coarse pants and a coat,"[39] the better to begin hard work for his simple diet at once. A humble man, he doubted whether "the light is light." Hardly lacking the "will to follow or light to see,"[40] Hecker merely wondered if the "perfect" life could be achieved at all on an earth beset by worldly temptations. Nevertheless, he thought the Fruitlands people had much to recommend them. "I desire Mr. Alcott's strength of self-denial and the unselfishness of Mr. Lane in money matters."[41] He was certain that he could not go back to his own family, much as he loved them, because he could not engage in the family business or indulge himself in their luxuries. Alcott and Lane encouraged Hecker to stay, but he was candid about his reservations, which he communicated directly to Bronson. He observed Bronson's "want of frankness, his disposition to separateness rather than win cooperation with the aims in his own mind; his family who prevent his immediate plans of reformation; the fact that his place has very little fruit on it, when it was and is their desire that fruit should be the principle part of their diet; my feeling that they have too decided a tendency towards literature and writing for the prosperity and success of their enterprise."[42]

Isaac Hecker was as close to the reasons for Fruitlands' rapid deterioration as participant-observer could be, although he failed at that time to include the most important. Later he put his finger on it. "Somebody once described Fruitlands," he declared, "as a place where Mr. Alcott looked benign and talked philosophy while Mrs. Alcott and the children did the work."[43] Indeed, as Lane and Alcott grew increasingly averse to the daily imperatives of subsistence farming, more of the work fell to Abba and the children. A visitor to the farm inquired if they had any beasts of burden, and Abba bitterly replied, "Yes, one woman."[44] In the late fall, while Bronson and Lane were preaching the consociate gospel in the salons of Boston and New York, Abba and the girls were forced to harvest a substantial barley crop by themselves. Dashing about in a rising windstorm, they filled laundry baskets and sheets with cut barley, and dragged them to the barn in hopes of salvaging this staple of their diet. They were utterly exhausted when the men returned. Moreover, an early winter brought unusually cold weather. The house was drafty, the woodpile insufficient to keep the main fireplaces going, and everyone suffered from colds and fever.

At about this time Bronson and Lane began to discuss new communal arrangements in earnest. They considered alternative communities that might offer them shelter, and most important, broached the feasibility of separating Abba and the girls from Bronson. Bronson had taken Anna on a summer trip to the Oneida Community in upstate New York. But he quickly concluded that "complex marriage," another means of avoiding exclusivity in love and providing for children's support, was no more acceptable to Abba than the Shakers' celibacy. Moreover, Oneida already had one securely dominant patriarch, John Humphrey Noyes. Louisa wrote tersely in her diary, "Father and Mr. Lane had a talk, and father asked us if *we* saw any reason for us to separate. Mother wanted to, she is so tired, I like it, but not the school part with Mr. Lane."[45]

Abba had been writing pathetic letters to her brother describing her plight and entreating his aid in saving her family. Sam was outraged at her portrait of their situation, one confirmed by Lydia Maria Child, who entertained Bronson and Lane on one of their trips to New York and wondered if they were quite sane.[46] Sam refused to make the November payment on the money owed to the Wyman creditors. In a letter written in January, he justified his wish to be "exonerated from the liability to pay the 300 hundred dollar note," because "Mr. Lane and Mr. Alcott have separated and my sister and her family have left the place."[47] In fact, Sam had already given notice to Lane in November (when the consociate family was still together) that he would not meet the note.

Mrs. Alcott informed the others that she would heed the advice of her brother and friends. As Lane reported to an English friend, Abba planned to

> withdraw to a house which they will provide for herself and her four children. As she will take all the furniture with her, the proceeding necessarily leaves me alone and naked in a new world. Of course Mr. A. and I could not remain together without her. To be 'that devil comes from Old England to separate husband and wife,' I will not be, though it might gratify New England to be able to say it. So that you will perceive a separation is possible. Indeed I believe that under the circumstances it is now inevitable.[48]

So Abba fled Fruitlands once again, this time for good. Her rebellion brought the experiment to an abrupt end.

Although the reasons for Abba's rebellion and for the crisis at Fruitlands should already be clear, the various explanations offered by the major participants are worth exploring. They not only illuminate the conflicts between the sexes in the nineteenth century, but go far to explain the emergence of a feminist movement. They show, in part, why Louisa Alcott's novels have been so appealing to so many women for so long a time.

Celibacy and the Sexual Division of Labor

In a long letter written at Concord shortly before the move to Fruitlands and published in *The Herald of Freedom*, Lane and Alcott laid out their plans for a purer family as the means to spiritual perfection.[49] Significantly, Abba did not sign it, although she was not averse to putting her name on numerous public statements and reform petitions. Several key motifs in that long letter reveal the sources of communal conflict as well as the issues that led many mid-nineteenth-century Americans to try alternatives to traditional arrangements for sexuality, family, labor, property, and community. Lane wrote,

> The Holy Family, in its highest, divinest sense is our true position, our sacred earthly destiny. It comprehends every divine, every human relation consistent with universal good, and all others it rejects, as it disdains all animal sensualities.[50]

He comes dangerously close here to embracing the virtues of celibacy and eliminating traditional family relations, as did the Shakers. He claimed he did not wholly agree with the Shakers," but saw them as entitled to "deeper consideration." Such serious attention was warranted in part because

> we witness in this people the bringing together of the two sexes in a new relation, or rather with a new idea of the old relation. This had led to results more harmonic than anyone seriously believes attainable for the human race, either in isolation or association, so long as divided, conflicted family arrangements are permitted. The great secular success of the Shakers; their order, cleanliness, intelligence and serenity are so eminent, that it is worthy of enquiry how far these are attributable to an adherence to their peculiar doctrine.[51]

Certainly the Shaker model had much to recommend it as far as many women were concerned. Its female members found relief from the burdens of pregnancy, and those already with children were made welcome. Shaker work patterns reflected less of a sexual division of labor than that found in the larger society, and all work was equally valued. Further, women had an equal vote in the common government. The Shakers understood that the traditional family relations, which rendered women dependents of the men who "owned" them, was an obstacle to the salvation of both sexes.[52]

The point, however, is that Lane as well as Bronson wanted to impose on Abba something approaching this Shaker model. Even more than Alcott, Lane insisted (in principle) that Abba should be consulted about consociate life, that her support of every aspect of the venture was vital to its success. At the same time he fully understood that "Mrs. Alcott has no spontaneous inclination towards a larger family than her natural one; of spiritual ties she knows nothing though keep all together she does and would go through a great deal of exterior and interior toil."[53] Yet Lane, ordinarily so sensitive, wanted his own way. He saw no hypocrisy in men imposing celibacy, dietary regulations, household schedules, and a host of other restrictions on Abigail May Alcott.

Both men assumed that domestic activities were natural to women. Neither dreamed that there was anything artificial about the sexual division of labor at Fruitlands; nor did they see anything wrong with telling Abba and the girls how to manage their work. Lane sympathized with Abba's burdens as the only woman resident, but he thought her work could be lightened by recruiting more women for domestic chores.

Bronson, of course, had his own special perspective on the Fruitlands' experience. For years he had wanted to escape the burdens of supporting a large family; he wanted "spiritual," not material, responsibilities. He wanted to free the body and human relationships from all imperfections, everything that constrained the "free" pure spirit.[54] The consociate family gave him a temporary solution to his problems—an unsatisfactory one to be sure, from Abba's point of view—for it freed him from his duty to support the family while ironically strengthening the sexual division of labor.

The Trouble Was Women

In the end both men blamed the women for the crisis at Fruitlands. The obstacles to harmony and community were females, who seemed irrationally committed to the exclusive love of their own biological family. Lane went further in pointing to the "maternal instinct" itself as the source of the difficulty. Both the "maternal instinct" and the family, he wrote Emerson, "are selfish and oppose the establishment of the community which stands for universal love."[55]

After the breakup, Lane authorized Sam May to transfer the deed to the property to Emerson. Both Abba and Sam later claimed, rather incorrectly, that Lane had turned Abba, Bronson, and the children into the cold, that he retained ownership of the land, and that he tried to break up the Alcott family. However, Lane was deeply committed to avoiding the ownership of private property. Emerson accepted the trust, and eventually the property was bought by Joseph Palmer in installments. Lane returned to England with his son, began another school, and married an English matron whose commitment to communal life had been tested by previous residence in another intentional community. He continued writing in a friendly way to Joseph Palmer, expressing his "hope that you will have prosperity enough in the culture to release yourself gradually from my encumbrance whereby I may be enabled just to pay the rent on an acre or two to cultivate with my own hands."[56] The mortgage was finally paid off in 1851.

Dedicated and persevering, unshaken in his beliefs, sure that his male perspective was universal, Lane cherished the best of his American experience. "I am differently employed now," he wrote, "but I still desire the field and the garden. If I had such a spot here as Fruitlands I should not quit it, but enjoy a life fruitful in all good."[57]

Bronson responded differently to the troubles at Fruitlands. Not only did the outcome of the venture leave him seriously ill for a time (a sign, perhaps, of his temperamental dislike of conflict), but he also learned to temper his view of the family and sexual relations. As he wrote many years later,

> I have long since questioned the fitness of any considerable number of persons for community life. A school is a possibility. Yet any separation from parents for any long time, seems undesirable unless in the case of their unfitness to have charge of their children.

The family is *the unit* around which all social endeavors should organize if we would succeed in educating men for the true ends of existence. And the cooperation of women in the practical working out is indispensable.[58]

Bronson also relented a little in regard to food consumption, although he would always feel ambivalence toward matters of the flesh and self-indulgence. He dined often with Emerson, who had refused to invite Charles Lane to dinner for fear that Lane's lectures on the evils of meat, yeast breads, and wine would "destroy the appetite of his guests." On one occasion, when Emerson was carving up an expensive roast, and discussing the horrors of cannibalism at the same time, Alcott remarked, "If we are to eat meat at all, why should we not eat the best?"[59]

Bronson Alcott changed his views about the family in large measure because Abba had declared her independence. Abba's conception of Fruitlands diverged sharply from the men's. She felt that the men neither understood nor acknowledged the value of female self-sacrifice. Women's domestic duties, she said, were simply taken for granted:

A woman may perform the most disinterested duties. She may 'die daily' in the cause of truth and righteousness. She lives neglected, dies forgotten. But a man who never performed in his whole life one self denying act, but who has accidental gifts of genius, is celebrated by his contemporaries, while his name and his works live on from age to age. A man passes a few years in self denial and simple life, and he says, "Behold A God."[60]

Visiting the Shaker community with the men, Abba observed on the spot that the model was not for her. "There is servitude somewhere," she declared, "I have no doubt. There is a fat, sleek, comfortable look about the men and among the women there is a stiff, awkward reserve that belongs to neither sublime resignation nor divine love."[61]

More important, Abigail resisted the larger consociate unit planned by the men because she believed it threatened her legitimate power in the family and therefore her personal identity. The roles she found thrust upon her were those of "universal mother" and maid of all work; both of which appeared to her as a mockery. Almost immediately she was thrown into an overt struggle with Bronson to save the family she cherished. And in the process of trying to preserve domesticity, Abba painfully asserted her equal right to make decisions affecting herself and her daughters. In so doing she radicalized a feminist perspective she had been developing since her courtship.

Empowered by the money left to her exclusive use by her father (which Bronson and his creditors vainly tried to get), Abba removed herself from the consociates, thereby forcing her husband to choose between his family and his experiment. She acted with exhilarating independence, and arranged to rent four rooms in a nearby Still River farmhouse. She was joined by the children and later by Bronson, where the family lived cheaply and practically.

Domesticity and Feminism

Abba realized that she, Louisa, and Anna would have to earn a living for the family if they expected to determine the character of their domestic life. Ironically, Abba's desire to preserve the forms of the past led her to develop a stronger version of domestic feminism. Abba's chief ally was Louisa, who refined and passed on that feminist legacy to all women and men who read her books. Her fiction gives us perhaps the fullest picture of the struggles over sexual relations and domestic life at Fruitlands—and for that matter, at other intentional communities in which reformist, middle-class men tried to impress their values upon community life as a whole.

In her amusing short story, "Transcendental Wild Oats," Louisa depicts practically everyone who lived at Fruitlands. The story is often sarcastic at the expense of the "brethren." For instance Louisa describes the garden at Fruitlands as a riot of confusion because each of the brethren has sown his chosen grain in the common field; barley, rye and oats wave companionably together in the summer sun. The members also plant an orchard in the expectation of autumn harvest, though the trees need at least three years to mature and bear edible fruits.

The humor of the story, however, often yields to grim reflection, particularly in Louisa's version of the conflict between Charles Lane ("Dictator Lion") and her mother ("Sister Hope"). She casts her father as "Abel Lamb," a docile, sweet, and passive man, who accedes to the wishes of Dictator Lion but who later accepts the wise management of his wife. By making Bronson the innocent victim of Lane's alleged plot against women and the family (when Bronson was hardly innocent at all), Louisa preserves the image of a benign father while elevating her practical mother to a dominant position in domestic life.

The struggle between Lane and Abba takes place over every important aspect of the domestic and communal economy. Dictator Lion seeks to control women by making them subservient drones in the new order. At the very moment he is preaching about the "truth" that "lies at the bottom of the well," Sister Hope is slaving in the kitchen to prepare meals for eleven people. Later, after the Dictator decides to retire to a Shaker community, Sister Hope is left to starve in the old house, bereft of money and friends. "You talk to me about justice," she declares, "let us have a little since there is nothing else left."[62]

Louisa's portrait of Lane's attitude towards women is darkened by her contention that he intended to found a colony of Mormons, who "under his patriarchal sway, could regenerate the world and glorify his name forever." Why did Louisa make such a sensational claim when she must have known that Fruitlands, whatever its faults, had little in common with the Mormon's tightly organized capitalism and patriarchal polygamy? She probably chose this analogy because she wanted to show how far Fruitlands diverged from a feminist democracy. Fruitlands was not only far from a feminist democracy, it was a community where male values substituted for male property holding as the patriarchal basis for control.

In her other fiction, and particularly in *Work*, Louisa refined her view of women's domestic labor, implicitly arguing against the position stated by Lane and her father; "Of all the traffic in which civilized society is involved, that of human labor is perhaps the most detrimental, from the state of serfdom to the receipt of wages may be a step in human progress, but it is certainly full time for taking a new step out of the hiring system."[63] In Louisa's view, the male boarders at Fruitlands wanted to build a community around household production and "humble exchange . . . without the interval of money."[64] They also wanted to withdraw from the existing industrial capitalist order, which led them to reaffirm agrarian patriarchy as "newness."

. Louisa had little sympathy with these notions. Wage earnings for women, she believed, made escape possible from the tyranny of patriarchal families and equally patriarchal communal ventures. Of course, wages were often exploitative; cooperative, small endeavors were better, but essentially women needed wages to command respect from others in the nineteenth century. For Louisa, the new order offered genuine possibilities for freeing women from household drudgery, not by bread and apple picnics, but through coeducational public schooling and through remunerative work for women outside and inside their homes.

In "Transcendental Wild Oats" as well as other works, Louisa, shows how food and diet and also domestic labor become concrete vehicles for the expression of sexual conflict. In their broadside announcing Fruitlands, Bronson and Lane had this to say about animal foods:

It is calculated that if no animal food were consumed, one fourth of the land now used would suffice for human sustenance . . . The sty and the stable too often secure more of the farmer's regard than he bestows on the garden and the children. No hope is there for humanity while Woman is withdrawn from the tender assiduities which adorn her and her household to the servitudes of the family and the flesh pots.[65]

They went further. They equated the spread of manure on the field with the infusion of diseases into the human body. The diseases resulting from consumption of meat or vegetables grown in manured fields required cure by "stimulants and medicines . . . which ended in a precipitation of the original evil to more distances and depth."[66] Ominously, they suggested that the body's befoulment, its excrement and dirt, might infect the soul. This perfectionist, antisensual approach to food and diet did not sit well with Louisa. In the thirty-five pages of "Transcendental Wild Oats" she devotes eleven paragraphs, scattered throughout the work, to the subject of food. The men are portrayed as ascetic and self-denying; they forbid the consumption of "sugar, molasses, milk, butter, cheese and flesh."[67] The women, however, offer abundance and comfort, "the bread and wine of a new communion."

Louisa, like her mother, was unpersuaded by Lane's contention that a kitchen without animal food and pastries would be a better, freer place for women. On the contrary, she realized that the men were, in their desire to purify their behavior and master their own drives, attempting to invade and eliminate women's right to dispense the abundance they themselves created. Louisa even suggests that the men were seeking refuge from the sensual lives of women. Certainly she felt deprived as a child of the small treats to which mothers try to dispense from the leanest larders. Years later in her fiction she presented kind nursies dispensing "warm sweet stuff" to soothe children's throats, and mothers cheerfully providing gingerbread and milk to little women and men.[68]

Louisa was a thoughtful, self-critical girl at Fruitlands. Openly partisan, she grew intensely conscious of the life-sustaining character of women's domestic work. In addition, she accepted the work as inescapable; men would not or could not do it. But having grasped the meaning of her mother's experience, she began to realize that women who lacked a voice in community government were powerless to extend their spheres of activity beyond the household.

Louisa was awakened to a new link between domestic reform and women's rights. She grasped the personal necessity of feminism. While opponents cried out that feminists destroyed sacred family bonds, she learned at Fruitlands that feminism could provide a new basis for family survival even as it challenged the traditional structure of households and society.

Louisa did not mention sex directly in "Wild Oats," but she quoted her father and Lane: "Pledged to the spirit alone, the founders anticipate no hasty or numerous addition to their numbers. The kingdom of peace is entered only through the gates of self-denial; and felicity is the test and the reward of loyalty to the unswerving law of Love."[69] Lane and Bronson might have meant that the colony should not become a refuge for the poor and homeless, at least not in its initial stages. On the other hand, Bronson believed that future parents must be free of all selfish lust if the spiritual seed with which God Himself impregnates human beings was to reach fulfillment. There must be no unplanned babies and no physical love-making between parents who were not perfected to nurture the divine seed.

Abba was forty-two years old at Fruitlands, and she had survived eight pregnancies in ten years. She was scarcely hoping for another pregnancy, but she found involuntary celibacy dictated by strangers' beliefs distasteful. Perhaps more threatening, Bronson clearly intended family ties to be no stronger than the generalized spiritual bonds that connected him to Lane and other kindred spirits.

Throughout her writing career Lousia insisted that women's domestic work was important and that women's voices be heard in the larger world. She learned at Fruitlands that these demands were insepa-rable. Her experiences there shaped her fierce loyalty to the "natural" family and also her perception that the burdens of motherhood were inescapable.

CHAPTER V

The Trials of Life Began

The trials of life began about this time,
and happy childhood ended. One of the most
memorable days of my life is a certain gloomy
November afternoon, when we had been holding
a family council as to ways and means.

Louisa May Alcott, Journals, 1847

"The bright days of summer" came once more to Louisa and her sisters in Still River, where the Alcotts moved after a bleak winter in rented rooms at the Lovejoy farm in Harvard village. Their playmate, Annie Clark, recalled the "happiness of the little people" on rides and picnics with Mrs. Alcott and Miss Chase, the village schoolteacher.[1] It was the summer of 1844. "Hay carts would be provided with seats and trimmed with evergreen and carefully stowing away our luncheon baskets, we one by one would take our seats in the rustic omnibuses, and start away, singing and laughing for a long day's pleasure."[2] Louisa's Still River schoolmates remembered those months thirty years later as seeming "very much like a chapter from one of Miss Alcott's stories."[3]

At twelve years, Louisa's most serious crime was speaking disrespectfully to her mother and then escaping punishment by sneaking out with her best friend Sophie Gardner. The two friends ran into the pasture, past Bronson serenely hoeing in the garden, to visit the grave of a spider Louisa had accidentally crushed the day before.[4]

In a short while the Alcotts found themselves on the road to a new home in Concord. And it was Abigail Alcott, having asserted her authority at Fruitlands, who continued to initiate plans that would determine the future life of the family. In May she filed a request with the Suffolk County Probate Court for appointment of her cousin, Samuel E. Sewall, and her brother, Samuel J. May, as "trustees for my benefit under the will of my father."[5] William Minot and the elder Samuel May relinquished their trusteeship, and in August Abba's new guardians received "one thousand and fifty dollars, being Mrs. Alcott's share of the residue and remainder" of her father's estate, "to be held in trust for her separate use according to said will."[6]

While Abba secured her inheritance, Sam May and Bronson talked seriously about ways to provide both for May's conception of conventional material security and Alcott's spiritual needs. Sam wrote to Emerson in December that he had "spent time with Mr. And Mrs. Alcott in consultation upon their plans for the future." He noted, delicately, that "Mr. A. must have something to do." "For a while," however, "it seemed difficult to so arrange the proposed purchase of a place—house and land—that my sister and her family might have a shelter secured to them, without implicating him in the sin of living upon soil appropriated to his exclusive use."[7] The plan they devised was that May and Sewall, as Abba's trustees, would expend $1,000 of her legacy in buying the old Coggswell house in Concord and a small amount of its land "to be secured to her and her children." It is not clear that Abba Alcott would have chosen Concord without its particular advantage of congenial society for Bronson. Emerson's presence was the most important, for he would "keep a rational view in sight, and there will be less of ultraism and yet perfect freedom of action," as Sam May saw it.[8]

Emerson in fact donated money to purchase the remainder of the Coggswell estate so that as Sam May said "all the children of men, if they could get upon the land, might feel welcome there as to a common inheritance."[9] For emphasis, Sam restated his sister's property rights: "As it respects the rest Mr. Sewall and myself are bound as trustees to see that whatever may be bought with Abba's money is secured to her and her children so far as any legal protection can secure it."[10]

Sam May never doubted his sister's hospitality ("every one who knows her, knows that like her heart her door will be wide open to any of the human race who may need a home"), nor did he doubt Bronson's sincerity.[11] But he treated Bronson as if he were suffering a prolonged adolescence. May assured his partner in benevolence, Emerson, that he would, if possible, "give to Mr. Alcott as large a portion of the earth as he might need, to gather about him as many as he could draw to him. Not that I fully apprehend his thought—nor think the plan practicable so far as I do understand it. But he is so sincere, so devout, so full of faith that I long to have him try his experiment to his own entire satisfaction."[12]

They moved back to Concord under those arrangements. Secure for the moment in her property rights, Abba was hospitable to all who needed a home, as her brother predicted. She even invited Charles Lane to live with them in Concord. He visited for a time and helped with the children's lessons, much to Lousisa's chagrin. But he did not remain long, because he perceived Emerson's gift as one made in individual friendship, not in genuine commitment to a communal dream.

Bronson also invited a young teacher, Sophia Ford, to share their home, hoping to secure a school for himself in Concord, and an assistant in Miss Ford. Louisa took her lessons with Miss Ford, and for a while with Mr. Lane. But she yearned for the fun of Still River, writing a friend that she did not "have half so good a time as I did at Miss Chase's school, the summer I went there was the happiest summer I ever spent in the country, there was such a lot of jolly girls to play and blab with."[13] Sensitive about the donated baskets of clothing and food that everyone knew had sustained her family in the Still River months, she now referred to Sophia Ford as "my governess" and talked about wading through ponds and climbing apple trees "tearing our clothes off our backs, luckily they were old and breaking our bones (!); playing tag and all sorts of strange things. We are dreadful wild people here in Concord, we do all the sinful things you can think of."[14] Louisa had learned to translate Alcott eccentricities into normal high jinks, Alcott poverty into a kind of genial respectability. Her friends tenderly noted the contradiction. "To one who knows the destitute circumstances of the Alcott family in this period," wrote Annie Clark, in retrospect, "the little Louisa's somewhat airy references to summers in the country and 'my governess' may afford innocent mirth."[15]

Louisa entered a new phase of her life in Concord. She was no longer simply an observer of woman's troubles (her mother's) for she had embarked upon her adolescence—although in those days no one thought "little women" went through such a stage. Protected from worldly experience, their innocence preserved, little women presumably experienced nothing of the turmoil and stress that we now associate with female adolescence. Destined for marriage and motherhood, young women supposedly knew only a chaste, confined domesticity between girlhood and true womanhood.

On the other hand, male adolescence was viewed as frightening and dangerous. Men such as Bronson and William Alcott, Sylvester Graham, and Samuel Fowler, who feared the demands of their own bodies, were among those who warned against the dangers of male adolescence. These reformers "chose the body as the focus of their reform effort," and the male adolescent body in particular.[16] Cut off from an older moral system with clear lines of authority and subordination, young men in Jacksonian America constituted threats to the established order. Their behavior could be controlled through individual restraint and through permanent, domesticating relationships with women. "Boys," wrote William Alcott,

> in their fancied wisdom and strength, grow impatient of parental restraints and are more or less ungovernable. The passions become strong, or at least active; and so do the appetites. . . . At this very

period—this stormy period—this Tierra Del Fuego of human life, the young in the usual course of things are to be scattered abroad. . . . This separation of the sexes, occurring at the time when it does what shall prevent a most inevitable and fatal shipwreck? At this critical period . . . it is wisely ordered that a new passion spring up. . . . It is love of the opposite sex.[17]

Ideally, the May-Alcott marriage should have calmed Bronson's fears. American girls were still pure, and their civilizing influence was supposed to save men. The problem, as Smith-Rosenberg describes it, was that

> In return for this grant of sexual power, a woman was to limit her own sexual desires even more stringently than she did her husband's. She was expected, as well, to remain subservient to him and to her children in all other areas of life; she must narrow her horizons to the hearth and the nursery, be obedient, self effacing and nurturant within that sphere.[18]

Nevertheless, Bronson found Eve's temptations even in rural Fourth of July picnics; holiday food, apparently could trigger the destructive power of male sexuality. Nurturant women prepared the "doughnuts, cold meat, pickles, cakes and pies" that Bronson brusquely declined at Still River. "Vanity," he said, "and worse than vanity." Yet his daughters were not "averse from sharing more varied foods" at outings and at the tables of their friends. They had been raised on the blandest of vegetarian menus, but even this proved no protection against their sexual maturation.

The contradictions between female restraint and female abundance were nowhere more apparent than in contemporary assessments of youth. Male adolescent passions were supposedly domesticated by youthful love matches with innocent girls, but this reassuring view ignored the fact that girls, even when fiercely constrained by social conventions, did pass through an adolescent stage marked by sexual and emotional turmoil. Louisa May Alcott has given us ample evidence of this volatility both in her domestic fiction and in her life. She was aware of her own superabundant energies, and equally conscious of the need for self-restraint.

It is commonly assumed that Louisa May Alcott's most popular novels, like most nineteenth-century domestic works by women, evaded the problem of adolescent female sexuality by separating it from the safer subject of domesticity. A number of explanations have been offered for this evasion: first, that sexual awakening in young women was inappropriate material for genteel, young female readers. A more probing explanation is that female writers were reinforcing attitudes already established in the lives of their female readers, who at that time were asserting increasing control over their fertility. This explanation receives support from other analyses that focus on a growing separation of the sexual spheres in a dynamic, capitalist marketplace; this separation encouraged both a female distaste for male sexuality, and a male fear of individual excess. Yet these views, although interesting, do not particularly enhance our understanding of why nineteenth-century women writers treated domesticity and sexuality as they did.

Madeleine Stern's rediscovery and publication of Louisa's "tales of passion" suggest a third explanation for Alcott's supposed failure to deal with adolescent and adult female sexuality.[19] That Louisa produced many of these stories under a pseudonym seems to suggest a dichotomy in her mind (and possibly in the minds of her readers) between a fiction that is genteel and sanitized; and one that is gothic and passionate. It is certainly true that in these pseudonymous tales Alcott writes of fallen women who express sexual desire, but only with disastrous consequences. Yet this theory ignores a central theme in all of Alcott's fiction: the problem of presenting domesticity and female adolescent sexuality at the same time. As Madelon Bedell points out, Alcott's writings repeatedly portray a

> romance between a child-woman and an older man; the latter often a guardian, an uncle, or an older male friends; in short, a displaced father. The theme is constant. It runs like a thread through her works, from the early sentimental short stories she published in her twenties, to the pseudonymous thrillers she wrote in her thirties, the children's novels of her mature period, and the later melodramatic works she began to revive as she grew old.[20]

In the domestic novels Alcott proposes safe marriages to kind, protective father-like figures who will channel the energies of their young wives to good works. In the "gothic" tales and the fully romantic novels, heroines reject "fathers" as too powerful and threatening, precisely because they awaken women's sexual passions. Preoccupied with the motif of the father-lover, Alcott had clearly linked the volatile relationship between the domestic and sexual elements of a young woman's life. But she was doing more. As Bedell remarks of the romantic and gothic stories, Alcott was warning women against marriages based on a love that would destroy their "independence and power."[21]

The Most Beautiful Girl Runner

It is not necessary, however, to turn to Alcott's fiction for evidence of a passionate adolescence. Her life is proof enough. As a young woman,

Louisa enjoyed sexual role-playing and romping with boys, however briefly or circumscribed from our point of view. In that short, golden summer at Still River, she "married" a boy in a mock gypsy ceremony attended by family and friends in the woodshed.[22] The bride and groom even jumped over a broomstick. But bliss was shortlived. The couple had a tiff, the bride slapped the groom, and the marriage was "annulled." Against her mother's strong objections Louisa later participated in "kissing games."[23] On one occasion, out of sight of Abba, she "commandeered a neighbor's horse and sleigh and took a friend, Clara Gowing, for a short drive, returning the team to where she found it. Remembering the incident years later, she wrote to her old friend, with enjoyment, that "Bart kissed me when I got out." Gowing annotated this confidence with the reminder that "promiscuous kissing was under a ban in their family."[24]

Her awakening at first took physical forms conventionally permitted only to boys in the 1840s. She ran and played with fierce energy. Her journal entries reveal an unusual freedom to run outdoors, to enjoy nature, and to express herself generally. One entry in particular survived the cautious editing and deletions of later years:

> I had an early run in the woods before the dew was off the grass. The moss was like velvet, and as I ran under the arches of yellow and red leaves, I sang for joy, my heart was so bright and the world so beautiful. I stopped at the end of the walk and saw the sunshine out over the wide "virginia meadows." It seemed like going through a dark life or grave into heaven beyond. A very strange and solemn feeling came over me as I stood there, with no sound but the rustle of the pines, no one near me, and the sun so glorious, as for me alone. It seemed as if I *felt* God as I never did before, and I prayed in my heart that I might keep that happy sense of nearness all my life.[25]

She left this entry intact (after rereading it in 1885) because it marked the day "that little girl got religion . . . in the wood when dear Mother Nature led her to God."[26] Just as other women gained a sense of power from evangelical religion, Louisa found hers in a romantic union with Nature. These experiences laid the goundwork for her feminism. "Dear Mother Nature" presided over a reassuring personal conversion; the sun shone "as for me alone," and she experienced a solemn feeling of female autonomy that she had acquired outside conventional paternal religious structures.

Louisa's friends observed the emergence of her adolescent passions and energies. Llewellyn Willis described her in that period as a girl with

> a clear, olive brown complexion, and brown hair and eyes, she answered perfectly to the ideal of 'the nut brown maid.' She was full of spirit and life, impulsive and moody and at times irritable and

nervous. She could run like a gazelle. She was the most beautiful girl runner I ever saw. She could leap a fence or climb a tree as well as any boy and clearly loved a good romp. She was passionately fond of nature, loved the fields and forests, and was in special harmony with animal life. Her brief description of herself in the opening chapter of *Little Women* is most accurately true.[27]

Willis gave similarly detailed and romantic portraits of Louisa's sisters. Anna was an "ox-eyed Juno," amiable, quiet, and possessed of a dignified sense of humor. Beth looked very like her counterpart in *Little Women*; sweet and sunny, she played the piano "with something of a real appreciation, and behaved like Cinderella in the kitchen." Abba May, who decided early to call herself May, was "the baby of the family and much petted." "Inclined to be childishly tyrannical at times," she had the clear blue eyes and golden curls of her counterpart "Amy" in Louisa's fiction.[28]

Strange Feelings

In September of 1845 the two oldest girls acknowledged "strange feelings, a longing after something. I don't know what it is." (as Anna put it for both of them).[29] They talked about "how we should like to live and dress." Louisa dreamed of becoming a writer as a way to escape poverty. Her mother encouraged this dream because she saw it as a refuge for her daughter's "troubled spirit," while Anna announced that Louisa would "write something great one of these days." Both girls took the romantic devotion to creativity seriously. Anna, however, regretted her lack of special talent. "As for me," she said,

> I am perfect in nothing. I have no genius, I know a little music, a little of French, German, and Drawing, but none of them well. I have a foolish wish to be something great and I shall probably spend my life in a kitchen and die in the poor house. I want to be Jenny Lind or Mrs. Seguin and I can't and so I cry.[30]

The girls' longing represented a dramatic change in female expectations from those of Abba's youth. Being a model wife and mother in behalf of a model Republic meant little to them. Abba knew this, and hoped to help them sort out their feelings. In particular, she urged Louisa to continue expressing herself in notes and journal entries.

Abba was busy desperately trying to make ends meet in Concord. Bronson had not gotten his school after all, but he reconstructed their house and cultivated and harvested most of their food. Finally, in March of 1846 his carpentry allowed Louisa the privacy of her own room, which she had "wanted so long,"[31] She confessed that "it does me good to be alone, and Mother has made it pretty and neat for me. My work basket and desk are by the window, and my closet is full of dried herbs that smell very nice. The door that opens into the garden will be very pretty in summer, and I can run off to the woods when I like."[32]

This early phase of Louisa's romantic adolescence corresponded with the rise of feminism in America. Abba, herself committed to this new movement, aimed at giving her girls comfortable dress, healthy diet, exercise, and intellectual stimulation; these goals were gaining ground among educators, homeopathic physicians, by 1890 the most popular ladies magazines agreed with the reformers. Important family friends, above all Harriet K. Hunt, set new models for female advancement, stirring the imagination of young girls like Louisa.

Harriot K. Hunt demanded that "every girl see to it that she has the means of her own support," a demand already abundantly clear to the Alcott women.[33] "When labor becomes honorable and elevating," Hunt continued, "then will every woman prepare herself for useful occupation and follow it. Then will man see that industrial avenues are open to women—that they can follow any business or profession to which they are qualified without being exposed to contemptible insults which are heaped upon those who have independence enough to step out of the beaten track."[34]

When Louisa was fifteen years old, "fretted by the restraints and restrictions which were deemed essential to the proper girls," Harriot Hunt was applying to Dr. Oliver Wendell Holmes for permission to attend medical lectures at Massachusetts Medical College. She buttressed her application by referring to her own medical experience and by invoking Elizabeth Blackwell, who was already attending medical classes at Geneva Medical College. Dr. Holmes and the President and Fellows of Harvard found it "inexpedient" that Harriot Hunt should receive the "scientific light" she requested from her male colleagues at the Medical College.[35] Unshaken, she continued practicing medicine and preaching women's rights. Eventually she received an honorary M.D. from the Female Medical College of Philadelphia in 1853.

In her autobiography, *Glances and Glimpses*, Hunt cast off the widespread notion that the treatment of adolescent girls and boys should be different. Like her romantic contemporary, Margaret Fuller, she argued for a more fluid, even androgynous educational regimen, in which "boys should be taught every pleasant kind of handwork that girls are," and girls freed to "run, and walk, and play with hoop and ball." "Parents," she said spiritedly, "in the development of your children it is for you to beautify all uses, not to sexualize them: giving it to a feminine boy, manhood; and to a masculine girl, womanhood."[36]

Louisa's youthful journals mirrored Hunt's prescriptions:

I have made a plan for my life, as I am in my teens, and no more a
child. I am old for my age, and dont care much for girls things.
People think I'm wild and queer; but Mother understands and helps
me. I have not told anyone about my plan; but I'm going to *be* good.
I've made so many resolutions and written sad notes, and cried over
my sins, and it doesnt seem to do any good! Now I'm going to *work
really*, for I feel a true desire to improve, and be a help and comfort,
not a care and sorrow, to my dear mother.[37]

If her resolution to "work really" deepened, so did her inclination
toward romantic attachments. In fact, her fifteenth year marked the
beginning of "my romantic period . . . when I fell to writing poetry,
keeping a heart journal and wandering by moonlight instead of sleeping
quietly." She started to read romantic writers, including Hawthorne and
Charlotte Bronte. "*The Scarlet Letter*, she wrote, "is my favorite. Mother
likes Miss B. [Frederika Bremmer] better, as more wholesome. I fancy
'lurid things' if true and strong also."[38] In both *The Scarlet Letter* and *Jane
Eyre*, a young heroine barely out of childhood meets her fate in the person
of a much older man. Louisa would later reflect critically on such relationships, but now she was fascinated by their possibilities.

Louisa developed attractions for her own "older men" during this
period, above all for Thoreau and Emerson. They were safe objects for her
adolescent fantasies, and later the father-lovers of her fiction. Louisa had
already known Thoreau through the Thoreau brothers' school in Concord, a successful enterprise that preceeded the Fruitlands experiment.
Through Sophia Ford, who suffered an unrequited passion for Henry
Thoreau, Louisa herself drew close to Thoreau; he soon became her idol
and friend.[39] Thoreau's "prejudice for Adamhood," which led him to
experiment in rustic semiseclusion at Walden Pond, made him a hero for
Louisa. He had briefly courted her distant cousin, Ellen Sewall.

Henry eventually boarded with the Emersons on Lexington Street,
although he worried about "dangerous prosperity" and "success without
identity" in such a comfortable home. He was searching for his own
home and perspective within the Transcendental model. In 1842, John
Thoreau accidentally cut his finger while sharpening a razor. The cut
developed into a painful, fatal case of lockjaw. Henry nursed his brother
and held him in his arms as he died. John's death, coupled with that of
Emerson's son, deeply affected everyone in the Concord circle, including
Louisa. Henry's loss and his struggles for self-realization struck a sympathetic chord in Louisa. In two of her novels, *Moods* and *Work*, fictional
replicas of Henry become fit lovers for her forthright, strong heroines. In
fact, she demanded masculine rights for her heroines, and stretched the
limits of domesticity to include a right to adventure for women.

The Concord world of Louisa's adolescence was a tight circle, the friendships intertwining. It was Emerson who bought land at Walden Pond, enabling Thoreau to cut his wood (with Bronson's help), and to build a cabin in the spring of 1845. The first draft of *Walden* and *A Week on the Concord and Merrimack Rivers* were written by Thoreau at the cabin and read aloud to Bronson as the two men walked in the woods, Louisa often trailing behind them. The Alcotts brought picnic refreshments to their friend, who regularly emerged from isolation to dine with the Emersons and his mother.[40]

Henry took the Alcott girls and Lewellyn Willis in his boat to see the reflections of heaven and earth on the water. He played his flute for them. He told them more about Indian history and legends than anyone Louisa knew, and she found his combination of idealistic philosophy, biology, and culture far more entrancing than the abstract authoritarianism of Charles Lane or the fussy recitation style of Misses Page and Ford. More than anything, his youthful journey down a river (both real and emblematic) sparked Louisa's own determination to find herself and make a living for her family. It was a task deeply complicated by her sex.

To forego domesticity in favor of individual freedom was unthinkable for a woman unless, like Margaret Fuller, she possessed remarkable genuis and strength of character. Of course, even Fuller suffered, perhaps more so because she was so exceptional. She noted sorrowfully that the wives of her friends—Sophia Peabody Hawthorne, Lidian Emerson, perhaps even Abigail May Alcott—"don't see the whole truth about one like me."[41] By "truth" she meant the social consequence of her powerful bid for individuality. Transcendentalism had crowned her its queen, but she reigned alone, without the domestic hostages or nurturance that usually sustained men's quest for individual realization. Yet if women saw her true circumstances, she wrote,

> they would understand why the brow of Muse or Priestess must wear a shade of sadness. . . . They have so much that I have not, I can't conceive of their wishing for what I have. (Enjoying is not the word: these I know are too generous for that.) But when Waldo's wife, and the mother of that child that is gone thinks me the most privileged of women, and that Elizabeth Hoar was happy because her love was snatched away . . . and thus she can know none but ideal love: it does seem a little too insulting at first blush. And yet they are not altogether wrong.[42]

Fuller was not an everyday presence in Louisa's life. Her regular visits were nevertheless impressive, and would bear fruit in Louisa's first romantic novel, *Moods*. By 1845 Fuller lived in New York City, and Louisa's closest connection to her was through Ellen Fuller Channing. Margaret's sister, married to Ellery Channing and living in Concord, was unable to take her older sister's dispassionate distance from married men's romantic friendships. Henry Thoreau, like Emerson and Margaret Fuller, sympathized with poor Ellen, but also validated Ellery's right to "freedom" despite his marital ties.[43] Transcendentalism found the domination of one human spirit by another to be the greatest sin. Louisa felt the effects of such dominance, fought it in the next few years, and later described the experience in stories.

Louisa's early writings give little hint of the strong challenge she would mount against the conventional ideal of genteel womanhood. She wrote poems and fairy tales for her family and Ellen Emerson in a style considered appropriate to her sex: the language of flowers, which was both a Romantic convention and a sentimentalized means of joining prescriptive homilies with appealing fantasies. But she also tapped her passionate imagination by writing blood and thunder melodramas for amateur theatricals in the barn. Later her family and friends encouraged this "safe" outlet for passionate fantasy. One of her characters, Rudolpho, was often played by Louisa herself in magnificent boots, which "Jo March" was to wear in *Little Women's* home theatricals. "The Mysterious Page" and "Norma or the Witches Curse" thrilled the Emerson family, the Ellery Channings, and the Hosmers as much as did Louisa's subsequent "Captive of Castile," "The Unloved Wife," and the "Prince and the Peasant."[44]

The Alcott girls and Willis formed their own Pickwick Club and acted out Dickens. During this time Emerson, the most available candidate for Louisa's adolescent affections, gave her books by Goethe, Shakespeare, and Dickens. After reading a translation of Goethe's romantic correspondence with the fifteen-year-old Bettina Von Armin, Louisa played "Bettina" to Emerson's "Goethe" in her fantasies. She was fourteen. The Transcendentalists had sanctioned Goethe's and Bettina's relationship as "pure and poetic," so Louisa felt free to substitute the forty-three year old Emerson for Goethe. She wrote him poems, dropped wild flowers at his door, and sighed melodramatically "in a tall cherry tree at midnight, singing to the moon till the owls scared to bed."[45] Emerson remained happily ignorant of "Bettina's" mooning, but he later heard of the unrequited romance from Louisa herself. He was, "much amused," she said, "and begged for his letters, kindly saying he felt honored to be so worshipped." Louisa admitted to having burned the evidence, but she never lost affection for her "master who did a great deal for this admirer by the simple beauty of his life, and the truth and wisdom of his books, the example of a great, good man, untempted and unspoiled by the world which he made better while in it and left richer and nobler when he went."[46]

As Louisa developed safe infatuations for Thoreau and Emerson, she moved away from her father. Troubled in an undefined way by his sexual presence—a discomfort which was sharpened in her teens when Abba replaced Bronson as the dominant figure in the Alcott household—Louisa began treating her father as a harmless eccentric as a form of self-defense.

At a party during her early twenties Louisa met a young Massachusetts artist named C. W. Reed. She invited him to sketch their second Concord home, "Orchard House," which he began to do the very next morning. "When Louisa spied him," a friend later remembered, "she bounded down the path across the road and at a hand vault cleared the bars of the gateway and entered the field where he drew." Looking over his shoulder, she inquired about the details of his drawing technique: "Where is your line of sight . . . point of sight . . . vanishing points, etc.?" she asked. Reed replied that he simply drew the lines as he saw them.[47]

Louisa watched the completion of the work, then asked him in to meet her father. Bronson looked at Reed's sketch, placed his hand on the young man's head and remarked, "Young man, you are a child of light, a child of God." Reed did not understand, so Bronson elaborated while taking him round the flower garden. "These are God-like," he told Reed. "They represent all that is good, but the nightshade, bella donna and others of like nature are of darkness, of evil." Before Reed could venture any comment, Louisa "gave him a poke with her toe as a hint for him to keep silent and let her father ramble on in his own deep faraway manner, which he did for a time . . . then Mr. Alcott retired to his study and the young people chatted after their own manner."[48] When she went over the journals in later years, Louisa was likely to add references to her father as "Plato." Her manner, not quite disrespectful, suggests a fond mother, tolerant of an adolescent son's vagaries and pretensions.

City Lights

At the very time Louisa's Romantic period was reaching full flower, she was drawn away from it through the influence of her mother. During the 1840s Louisa was still grappling with Romantic "self-culture," the reform of self through introspection, self-discipline, and moral self-improvement. But increasing ties with northeastern feminists and their male reformist allies were leading Louisa to question the capacity of transcendental individualism to fully liberate women. It had failed for the Alcotts in Fruitlands and Concord. Now personalist solutions seemed ever less adequate in the face of newly emerging industrial and urban conditions—conditions which Abba had come to understand better than Bronson Alcott ever would.

In 1847 the Alcotts were still in financial trouble. That year they earned or received less than five hundred dollars, and when that was gone they were still two hundred dollars in debt to local merchants. That fall a water-cure hotel in Waterford, Maine offered employment to Abba and Bronson; Abba would serve as its matron and Bronson could assume a vague appointment as resident "preacher and teacher."[49] Bronson would not accept the move, but Abba broke loose. She left Concord with her youngest daughter, Abigail May, and Eliza Stearns, a young girl whose parents had boarded her out with the Alcotts in hopes of curing her mental and emotional retardation. Since Anna was teaching in Walpole, New Hampshire, only Bronson, Elizabeth, and Louisa remained home in Concord.

Abba was a thorough success at organizing institutional structures. In a whirlwind of activity she supervised the housekeeping at Waterford, consulted on "the best methods of diet," tried out the baths, wet-packs, and took vigorous walks to cure Eliza.[50] Above all, she earned a living. She also enjoyed the fact that the guests at Waterford were New England gentry, including artists, writers, and reformers like Elizabeth Peabody.

But successful employment away from her husband and family evoked intense anxieties. She returned to Concord that summer after suffering a series of nightmares, including one in which Lizzie needed her mother's help in practicing the piano (she could not find the right not), and Louisa, "running in the lane," screamed out for her mother. Dominating her dreams was the struggle with Bronson over domestic responsibilities. One night she dreamt of a conversation in Concord between herself and Bronson. Bronson declared he was "planning an observatory," while she replied that she "had other purposes." "Don't do anything to make this place more attractive," she said to her husband, "I want to find a different home for the girls." Bronson replied, very cheerily, "don't be anxious, young people are very apt to find homes for themselves."[51] Abba clearly felt that her adolescent girls still needed a mother's guidance, and that Bronson, assuming his usual idealistic distance from their real needs, was merely anticipating his own freedom when his children disappeared to find homes of their own. Young women, she believed, needed to move gradually toward full independence; the home provided for by mothers (and increasingly, by maternal networks) offerred the best protection en route to self-reliance.

In the fall of 1848, Mrs. James Savage, wife of a prominent Boston merchant and a long-time friend of the Mays, urged Abba to move to Boston, where a circle of wealthy female philanthropists planned to privately subsidize a "missionary to the poor." Emerson's personal charity to the Alcotts, even when supplemented by the income from the residue of Abba's inheritance, had already proved insufficient; both

Anna and Bronson needed more remunerative work. Bronson happily imagined possibilities for a school, "a reading room, a Journal, a press, a Club," in Boston.[52] Louisa would supervise the household while her younger sisters attended school; Anna would work as a governess to Louisa Greenwood Bond's children; and Abba would become a missionary. This opportunity pleased Abba immensely because it meant she could watch over her children. It also meant she could combine domestic reform, which emphasized the role of mothers in ameliorating the lives of poor girls and boys, with earning a living.

Abba's participation in Boston's voluntary associations marked her entrance into public life. Louisa eagerly approved. Like many of her friends, including Emerson, she had become engaged with the pressing social changes occurring around her. Perfectionist aspirations of the transcendentalist period were left behind. By then Margaret Fuller herself was travelling in Europe meeting with Parisian workers. In England she found Giuseppe Mazzini, who helped her to cast off the individualistic ethic whose High Priestess she had been. He offered instead a collective social movement led by himself and Saint Simon. Fuller also met George Sand and discovered, as Bell Gale Chevigny puts it, "her own androgynous ideal."[53] In one blazing historical moment Margaret Fuller realized the possibilities of combining feminism, political change, and personal growth.

While Fuller was becoming a citizen of the world, Louisa May Alcott was becoming one of Boston's 161,400 residents in 1850. The country had grown. The American population had increased from thirteen million inhabitants in the year of her birth to twenty-three million by the Civil War. But population growth was only one of many changes. In Abba's childhood farmers outnumbered city dwellers by fifteen to one, but by Louisa's girlhood the ratio was five to one. Moreover, the Bostonians of Louisa's generation were twice as mobile residentially as Americans today, with one household out of three moving each year. Although their constant uprootings in search of a livelihood was representative, the Alcotts felt their mobility was exceptional. Like other contemporary native-born Americans, they cherished domestic stability and blamed hard luck for their constant moving.

During Louisa's Temple School years, Boston's residents were 95 percent native-born Americans. When the Alcotts took up residence there in the 1850's the foreign-born inhabitants constituted half the city's population. In particular, the large Irish immigration of the 1840s strained the institutions designed to contain and assimilate the laboring classes. Middle-class residents, including reformers of all persuasions, were alarmed by the immigrants' observable ethnic differences from "American Victorianism as a culture."[54] Progressive, "modern" values, such as "rationality, specialization, efficiency, cosmopolitanism and an interest in a future that can be better than the present in material and social terms,"[55] seemed threatened by "the dangerous classes," as they were increasingly called.[56] Acculturating this European rabble to middle-class values and behavior was precisely the "missionary work" that Abba Alcott embarked on.

Abba's initial backers numbered only twenty-one well-to-do liberal philanthropists who believed that their city's problems should be handled through traditional voluntary relief work. Later, a sewing circle of church ladies subsidized other work for her. She distributed Bibles and baskets of clothing and food. She gave lectures on the dangers of unchecked fertility, the advantages of cleanliness, frugality, and sexual continence, as well as advice on domestic economy. In addition, she took in homeless children and adolescent girls, in order to protect them "from the sharks and lusts that wait." With the enthusiastic help of Louisa and Anna, she struggled against racism in Boston by teaching literacy classes to black adults. Like her fellow missionaries, who belonged to the countless private and independent charity endeavors of the antebellum period, Abba tried to place young and mature women as domestic servants and to find farm work for males.[57]

Historian Eric Schneider estimates that by 1860, the Boston Employment Society found jobs for "21,839 females, 1,859 of them 15 or younger, and for 2,540 males; of the 24,379 persons involved, 55% (13,460) had been placed in the country."[58] He concludes that "instead of organizing the charities, the society organized an employment service for its sponsors."[59] That was exactly the conclusion drawn by Louisa when she fictionalized her own and her mother's experience with such agencies. Abba found work for her clients in middle-class homes; at one point she even found a job for Louisa as a domestic servant. Her daughter bitterly described the details of such "service" in *Work: A Story of Experience* and in a short story, "How I Went Out Into Service."[60]

Since the exploitation and degradation of children was a major concern to the public at large and to charity workers in particular, Abba visited poor families, "investigating their wants and merits."[61] She also surveyed the pattern of welfare dispensation and solicitation of funds in the city. In her thorough, practical way she sought out the causes of the misery she encountered daily among the poor. Her conclusions brought her into direct conflict with the guardians of public welfare, including her distant cousin, Joseph Tuckerman. As a founder of the Society for the Prevention of Pauperism, he represented mainstream liberal Brahmin reformers as well as any individual could. In his published report of 1874, the summary of many years work as "minister at large in Boston," Tuckerman warned against the reproduction of the "dangerous classes" through the infection of children with the lewdness, dishonesty, and profanity of their parents.[62] He argued that poor children did not really have a family life as the middle classes knew it. Poor children lived their lives alone or in bands on the streets where "every child who is a beggar, almost without exception, will become a vagrant and probably a thief."[63] For Tuckerman, the expansion of the public schools, the employment of truant officers, and the establishment of reform schools and other institutions were the only viable solutions to the problem.

Louisa's uncle, Sam May, thought he faced a microcosm of the same situation in Syracuse, New York, and he vigorously championed the same school of thought as Joseph Tuckerman. The building of the Erie Canal in the 1820s had stimulated rapid commercial growth and brought the first influx of Irish immigrants to the city. There were 1600 children in Syracuse by 1855, 600 of whom had never attended school at all. Middle-class distress may be further gauged by the fact that one common school in the 1850s lay in the basement of a tavern, and its pupils were subject to "the brawl and confusion of dram drinking, arrival and departure of noisy travelers and their lumbering vehicles."[64] Syracuse was still small enough for May to think reform possible through a vigorous common school association and the leadership of his own Unitarian congregation. May's record was impressive. He led the expansion of the public schools, campaigned for "idiot asylums," and demanded that the New York State legislature provide a "house of refuge" designed as a reform school for "canal boys" and other juvenile delinquents. He introduced the work of Eduard Seguin, a pioneer educator in training inmates of "idiot asylums," to Syracuse.[65]

May argued for women's rights as another necessary step toward sane society. He urged Andrew Dickson White, later president of Cornell University, to "have both sexes educated equally."[66] May made clear his position that education was the cure for social ills, and that women were the best pupils and eventually the best teachers of the unenlightened masses.

Margaret Fuller's belief that the Old World's social problems required radical solutions (perhaps even wars of national liberation that generated social revolution) reached her American friends through her letters and newspaper articles. The sons and daughters of the American revolution, however, her compatriots and the mainstay of nineteenth-century American reform movements, saw few parallels between down-trodden masses of Europe and the "dangerous classes" of New York or Boston. After all, this was the New World, the land of social mobility for all hard-working folk. Some American novels of the 1840s and 1850s argued that well-intentioned but misplaced philanthropy actually encouraged beggary, pauperism, and vagrancy. The root cause of pauperism, in this analysis, was a lack of proper entrepeneurial spirit. Generally the heroes of these novels—plucky native-born, country-bred young Americans—proved themselves superior to the lowly immigrants.

Abba and her contemporaries were convinced of the propriety of their own civic virtues, and deeply concerned with acculturation and reform. At what age, they asked, could social deviants be most effectively integrated into society? Did that age differ for males and females? At what point should reformers try to separate, contain, and punish miscreants, rather than reform them? Conventionally, boys of the "dangerous classes" were treated differently than girls. Although they might commit the most heinous offenses, society still believed that boys were amenable to reform, that their characters might be restored by hard work, education, and the faith of their middle-class saviors. On the other hand, crimes were a threat to moral order. Primarily defined by their sexual nature, these crimes threatened the family, that institution most responsible for preserving and reproducing social order and harmony.

A Single Standard

Abba at last broke ranks with many of the male reformers because of the double sexual standard. With other feminist reformers, she came to reject the conventional wisdom; the real solution to the problem was a society based on sexual equality, with high standards for morality, companionship, education, and industry. Institutional and individual efforts at charity and reform, however, lagged behind such an ideal. The best that conventional reform could achieve was to avoid financing "schools for scandal," which meant ignoring sexually active girls and concentrating reform efforts, eventually, on institutions for boys. In the 1870s and 1880s "girls over thirteen and colored girls" were still considered unplaceable and unsupervisable by the Boston Children's Aid Society.[67]

Exhausted, Abba gave up her job as a paid social worker in 1850. The experience had taught her a great deal. Her contact with Boston's growing poverty, and above all with the exploitation of poor girls and women, set her own struggles in perspective. She no longer viewed the Alcott family's distress as unique; nor did Louisa. Their sympathies expanded as they identified with the people they tried to help. Abba also developed a deeper understanding of the social and economic causes of poverty. She could no longer blame the victims, nor hope that broader education and stricter supervision would solve the problems. After handling two hundred cases a month, working after hours and bringing some of the most desperate cases home to the Alcott apartment, she had become exasperated with her employers, who she claimed addressed the symptoms rather than the real causes of poverty. "My position among them," she wrote, "has been uncomfortable from the simple reason that while they are sympathizing in the details of wretchedness and want I am busy with the *causes* of so much poverty and crime. Why it is so is a better question than what shall we do. The former implies prevention, the latter signifies the need of cure."[68]

Abba went even further: her radical assessment of the causes of poverty joined her maturing feminism. Unlike the ladies of the South Friendly Society, her last employers, she knew at first hand the poor women who earned $1.50 a day sewing for their betters, and she understood the cause of their exploitation:

> Incompetent wages for labor performed, is the cruel tyranny of capitalist power over the laborers' necessities. The capitalist speculates on their bones and sinews. Will not this cause Poverty— Crime—Despair? Employment is needed but just compensation is more needed. Is it not inhuman to tax a man's strength to the uttermost by all sorts of competition that a certain result may be accomplished in a given time. Alas! for the laborer too often proved an Infernal machine, so he finds himself bankrupt in health and energy, and woman too, how often I am told as an apology for exquisite and extra stitches, that it furnishes employment, for the poor; this hackneyed reply can no longer shield the miserable vanity that can only find gratification in the servitude of numerous fellow beings.[69]

Abba had stretched her own domestic feminism to include the lives of other oppressed women. Her need for a broader interpretation of woman's condition drew her increasingly into the most advanced feminist ranks.

Just as Abba changed in this new environment, so too did Louisa. Except for a brief sojourn at her great-uncle Samuel May's house, she had lost a room of her own. She had also lost the privilege of running freely in the woods and acting out amateur theatricals with family and friends. She had even lost the full-time companionship of Anna and Abba, both of whom were working. Louisa herself had begun to work, teaching with Anna in a small primary school a block away from their cramped South End rooms. The family's hard times were intensified by Bronson's emotional fragility. Hardly recovered from his miseries at Fruitlands and his transitional period in Concord, Bronson found the women's survival skills both comforting and threatening. Yet Boston did supply congenial listeners for his conversations. Perhaps the most rewarding member of this group was Ednah Littlehale. A young, brunette devotee, Ednah apparently sparked anew Bronson's capacity for romantic friendship; he was almost fifty years old when they met in 1848. According to Madelon

Bedell, however, Ednah's name never appears in Bronson's *Journals* after her marriage to Seth Cheney in 1853.[70]

Whether or not Abba and the Alcott girls knew of Bronson's flirtation, they included Ednah Cheney in their circle of friends for many years. Ednah, like Lousia, adored Margaret Fuller and grieved deeply when Fuller died in a shipwreck off Fire Island in 1850. Returning to America with her Italian husband and young son, Fuller was about to face the mixed reactions of Americans who admired her courage and feared her influence. Her New England friends were moving from romantic idealism to positivist social science as they tried to keep their faith both in individualism and democracy. She had chosen a more radical path in the Old World, and perhaps she might have brought it to the New World had she landed safely in New York.

At eighteen, Louisa stood between two worlds. Aware of the active feminist movement, though too busy to attend the first women's rights conventions in Seneca Falls, New York and then at Syracuse, she avidly sought news of them. She heard reports of the meetings directly from her Uncle Sam, who was a member of a central committee for the conventions that also included Harriot Hunt, Lucretia Mott, and Elizabeth Cady Stanton. He sent her copies of the *Proceedings* of the Syracuse Convention, meanwhile, under her mother's influence, Louisa taught literacy and Sunday School classes in Boston's South End.[71] What she learned in this period—about the need for a single sexual standard, the conflict between heredity and environment, between city and country, familial versus institutional responsibility for oneself—she would later integrate into her novels.

For the moment her own passage from adolescence to young adulthood was her most pressing problem; it took place within a broader, intellectual transition from Romantic beliefs in individual salvation to positivist faith in social environmentalism. Like many of her contemporaries, she did not give up the old Romantic faith easily, but she went beyond nostalgia to explore causality. In what ways did a young person's inherent strengths and weaknesses "harden" into character? How much of human society was the result of inherited personal and social history, and how much could be changed in the character of one person? In one lifetime could both the individual and society be redeemed? Louisa began to explore these questions in *Moods*, the book which marked the end of her "Romantic period." Years later Abba wrote that women should assert their right "to think, feel, and live individually . . . be something in yourself."[72] Testing the Emersonian path to individuality on behalf of her sex, Louisa would try to find the relationship between womanhood and human identity. She would pit the heroes and heroines of her girlhood against one another in her first novel, testing their analyses and their solutions to her dilemma. Margaret Fuller had named the problem Louisa tried to explore fully:

> Ye cannot believe it, men; but the only reason why women ever assume what is more appropriate to you, is because you prevent them from finding out what is fit for themselves. Were they free, were they wise fully to develop the strength and beauty of woman, they would never wish to be men.[73]

CHAPTER VI

Outward Bound

Seventeen years have I lived, and yet so little do I know, and so much remains to be done before I begin to be what I desire—a truly good and useful woman.

Louisa May Alcott, Journals, May, 1850

Louisa found every day a battle against Boston's bustle and dirt. Moreover, the city mocked her pride as it tempted her youthful vanity, daring her to do the things she longed to do and could not, because she was both an Alcott and a girl. She felt that family portraits of Hancock, Quincy, and the Sewalls, ghosts of the city fathers, looked askance upon her. It was seven years after her arrival, when she wore her first new silk dress (the gift of a kind aunt) on New Year's Eve in 1857, before she felt the family portraits smiled approvingly on her.[1] The "wilfull, moody" girl believed herself at last to be a "truly good and useful woman."[2]

Care and Woe

In the years between poverty-stricken annonymity and the first evidence of literary talent, Louisa's self-doubts and unwelcome passions often seemed to tire her to death. The mother who had so often comforted her was desperately busy, preoccupied with earning a living for them all. Louisa was all alone in a crowded city. It was not in her character to sit passively at home, waiting for adulthood. She triumphed over her own self-doubts and the restrictions of poverty and sex by going into "service." Her experiences as a working woman during the 1850s permanently shaped the way she thought and wrote about the world. Although working would not resolve her own delicate, inner battle, it gradually prepared her for an active role in the social ferment around her.

Still, inner turmoil at the age of seventeen seemed more threatening to Louisa than the "exile, danger, and trouble" her family faced during

Boston's smallpox epidemic that summer.[3] Moving twice in one year (first from Dedham Street to Temple Place) provided no relief from the "bustle and dirt" that Louisa hated in Boston's South End. When they moved that spring to Samuel May's house in Atkinson Street, she hoped for some leisure, privacy and a few small comforts to lift the "care and woe" she felt.[4] Her hopes were not realized. Sensitive and proud like her mother, she cherished the "romantic tastes" which her cousins thought presumptuous in poor relations. She had asserted the importance of her need for "solitude and out-of-door life," and she resented the loss of both when she had to sew, launder, and clean for well-to-do families at two dollars a week. The contrast between Atkinson Street and scrubbing for a living only exacerbated Louisa's "moodiness."

Abba had her own troubles, importuning her relatives for funds while resisting their advice to separate from Bronson. The whole family caught smallpox, possibly from an immigrant family whom Abba had taken into the garden and fed.[5] Poverty felt doubly humiliating, even terrifying, as the Alcott's endured illness in Boston while their wealthier friends and relatives fled the city's heat and contagion. Bronson was ill enough to frighten them all but he finally recovered with the help of their homeopathic treatment of rest, plain food, and isolation. In August Abba started her own "Intelligence Service" on High Street. Birth and education, she felt, should have made her a philanthropic employer of domestic workers in her own home. Instead, she was the proprietor of an employment agency which daughter Louisa later described as the "purgatory of the poor."[6] For the next three years, the Alcott women teetered between providing "cooks, good parlor and chamber maids, seamstresses, toilette women and dressmakers" for the rich, and taking such jobs themselves.[7] Mrs. Anna Alcott, Bronson's mother, stayed with them briefly during that period and saw firsthand the hopeless, fetid circumstances of the immigrant women. "Oh the poor women," she wrote. "How I pity them."[8]

Yet Abba still found time to write encouraging notes in Louisa's journal. Louisa, in turn, fantasized a time when she could provide "a lovely quiet home" for her mother with "no debts or troubles to burden her."[9] Stretching her imaginary bounty further, Louisa also installed Anna, who was away working as a nursemaid, in a "nice little home of her own."[10] Having established everyone else in comfortable domesticity, she also hoped to find her own inner peace, "a happy kingdom in myself," as she put it.[11] But such a poor young woman scarcely had the time or energy for voyages of self-discovery. Nevertheless, she blamed her own restless mind for some of her troubles. It was a sort of "confused and dusty room that needed sweeping out," but she found herself lacking a housewifely temperament to do it.[12]

She also thought about being an actress with "plenty of money and a very gay life."[13] Instead she entered into domestic service when the Reverend James Richardson called at the Intelligence Service to find a light housekeeping companion for his elderly father and spinster sister.[14] Richardson lived in nearby Dedham; he was not unfamiliar to the Alcotts, having attended Bronson's Conversations. Abba sent him her second daughter. May family pride was partly salvaged by remembering that an earlier generation of honest rural folk sent daughters into service in their neighbors' households. So far Louisa and Anna had earned their keep among friends and relatives. These were humbling circumstances to be sure, but hardly comparable to the exploitation endured by Irish girls, and certainly light-years away from involuntary servitude. Slavery, in fact, the most heinous blot on American independence, was attacked more and more frequently by the Alcotts and other abolitionists in meetings all over New England.

Granted the existing range of servitudes, Louisa viewed her prospective employment in the Reverend James Richardson's household as a harmless adventure. She was wrong. Louisa spent a total of six weeks as maid-of-all-work in his home. She found herself cooking, cleaning, making fires, and running errands; as if these chores were not enough, she was called upon to serve as a one-woman audience for Reverend Richardson's philosophical discourses. She described the experience twenty years later in "How I Went Out Into Service." Even after all those years she was furious with an employer who thought he had bought her self-hood when he hired her labor.[15] "I was not to read, but to be read to . . . to be a passive bucket into which he was to pour all manner of philosophic metaphysical and sentimental rubbish. I was to serve his needs, soothe his sufferings and sympathize with all his sorrow . . . to be a galley slave in fact.[16] When she refused to perform according to Richardson's ideal of female companionship, he treated her like a man-of-all-work. She shovelled snow, hauled wood and water, and generally exhausted herself. When she finally quit she discovered that the purse containing her six weeks' wages held only four dollars. However empty their larder, the Alcotts kept their pride. Louisa sent back the insulting sum.[17]

Ednah Cheney recommended Louisa's "How I Went Out Into Service" to those "who condemn severely the young girls who prefer the more independent life of the factory or shop to what is considered the safety and comfort of service in families."[18] She meant that domestic service in her time was often considered safe, even privileged work for young women. Well-to-do employers felt that their "girls" were elevated by the discreet gentility of the homes they served. Even reformers argued that young maids in their service were learning domestic economy.

Ideally the young women would serve their time, give their employers proper notice, and then marry enterprising young workmen or farmers, their improved habits and skills serving as a sort of dowry. Cheney felt that Louisa's experience of exploitation, the denial of her privacy and her identity as well, exploded this myth. Her story explained why most girls preferred factory work, which at least allowed them to struggle for more of their own "free" time.[19]

One year later, in 1859, Nathaniel and Sophia Peabody Hawthorne bought Hillside, the Alcott home in Concord. The payment was carefully divided to reimburse Emerson for his initial gift of five hundred dollars and to return one thousand dollars to Abba.[20] Emerson promptly established a small trust fund for Bronson, and Sam Sewall secured Abba's portion in the same discreet manner. Once again the Alcotts moved, this time to Pinckney Street in Beacon Hill, where the rent was three hundred and fifty dollars—as much as Abba, Louisa, and Anna had earned the entire previous year.[21]

In the spring of 1859, Louisa sold a "romantic" story she had written at sixteen to *Olive Branch*, a popular weekly that the Alcott girls read avidly. (Years later, when she made the incident a part of *Little Women*, she described reading her "great rubbish," as she called it, to her family.)[22] In the same year Harriet Beecher Stowe's *Uncle Tom's Cabin* became the publishing success of the nation, selling 300,000 copies. Louisa listed it as one of her favorite "best novels," and one she hoped to emulate.[23] By this time Abba was fifty-one and exhausted, no longer with enough strength to be the family's chief breadwinner. Louisa began to teach herself to write in order to support the family. Encouraged by her modest start and by the success of other women's fiction, she felt it could be done and must be done.

Ever since the failure of at Fruitlands, the Alcotts had lived from day to day, unable to make long-range plans and implement them. Louisa, "grubbing away as usual," combined teaching in the family parlor with sewing at night and writing stories whenever she could snatch the precious solitude.[24] Abba took in boarders and sewing to help make ends meet. Anna was in Syracuse during 1854, where Sam May had found her a job teaching school, and May was a pupil in a Boston school. Elizabeth was the family housekeeper. She vaguely considered attending normal school to become a "certified" teacher, and also had a suitor at this time. Aside from indefinite references in family correspondence, however, there is no real evidence of Elizabeth's marital plans. Bronson had engaged on a financially unremunerative series of "Conversations" in the West. Arriving home in February, he opened his purse and showed his wife and daughters one dollar. "Only that!" he said. "My overcoat was stolen, and I had to buy a shawl." "Real love," Louisa decided, was her mother's forbearance and gratitude that her husband was safely home, and her father's comfort in his faithful wife and children.[25]

For Louisa at twenty-two, love was not enough, and she frantically devised schemes to increase her earnings. She considered her progress: "I have eleven dollars, all my own earnings—five for a story and four for the pile of sewing I did for the ladies of Dr. Gray's society, to give him as a present."[26] She decided that this sounded funny, but begged Anna in her letter not to "laugh at my plans; I'll carry them out, if I go to service to do it. Seeing so much money flying about, I long to honestly get a little and make my dear family more comfortable, I feel weak-minded when I think of all they need and the little I can do."[27] Having confessed a moment of frailty, she returned to her increasingly boyish tone; she called Anna "my good little lass," but also admitted that she had privately shed her "quart" of tears over their lot.[28] In public she showed greater strength. When a cousin delivered her story to an editor and brought her the five dollar payment, she seemed to relish his treatment of her as a tough breadwinner. "Now, Lu," he said, "the door is open, go in and win." "So I shall try to do it," Louisa replied.[29]

Practical plans were important to Louisa, because they signalled her ability to control the circumstances of her life. She began by plotting out the stories she would write for popular magazines. By exploiting the issues enunciated by Woman's Rights advocates, which were also the everyday problems of her own life, she created stories for women like herself and her mother. There was now a large reading audience of women who wanted to see their own experiences described in the fiction they read.

Pens and Needles

Still a literary novice, Louisa had to supplement her writing income by needlework for several more years. But she was fortunate in having literary connections, and she was able to justify her own need for independence because it coincided with efforts to support her family. Slowly her fiction trickled into the stream of contemporary passionate thrillers, children's stories, and domestic novels. Undiscouraged by her long apprenticeship, family pride and fierce determination to "*live* and have no time for sentimental musings" kept her planning and writing.[30] In 1855 she finally saw the publication of a complete volume under her own name, *Flower Fables*, a revised version of the fairy tales she had created in Concord for younger friends like Ellen Emerson.[31]

Louisa felt she had learned a good deal about publishers, financing, and marketing, and she put an advance copy of *Flower Fables* into Abba's Christmas stocking. She called it her "first born," but hoped to "pass in time from fairies and fables to men and realities."[32] George Briggs and Co. planned to market the book as a Christmas gift selection. They had little to lose, since the first run was subsidized by Miss Wealthy Stevens, an Alcott family friend. The dedication to Ellen Emerson by "her friend the author" should have added to its marketability. It did not, however, make its author rich; Louisa received only thirty-two dollars from the sales.[33] Nevertheless, looking back in 1886 at her carefully saved "notices," she commented that she was "prouder over the thirty-two dollars than the eight-thousand dollars" she received for six months of receipts thirty-one years later.[34]

The opening fable, "The Frost King, or The Power of Love," seems only a sentimental reminder to children of the necessity for self-sacrifice and faithful work.[35] If the stories had any pretensions to emblematic meaning in the Romantic convention of nineteenth-century flower language, no critic noticed it. But there is one striking theme in "The Frost King:" the complete separation of sexual spheres. In fact, the warm, sun-filled abundant kingdom of the Fairy Queen is engaged in a life-and-death struggle with the cold, windy, frigid domain of the Frost King.

The Frost King, slowly expanding his territory, seeks to kill the tender blossoms in other lands with his cold wind. Violet, "the weakest fairy" in the Queen's band, offers herself as a messenger to the Frost King, hoping to warm his heart. She flies off, brings a garland of fresh flowers for him, and sheds her own golden light upon his "cold dark gardens." He tries to send her back, but Violet, even though she has seen her garland freeze and die around his neck, insists on staying. She accepts one low, dark cell and then another, even deeper and darker. She turns her prison into a sunny little room and tames spiders, teaching them to weave sunshiny golden webs rather to imprison flies. She shares her crumbs with moles and expends her own precious warmth to heat the earth and generate moss, flowers, and vines. At length the Frost King, slightly thawed by Violet's unselfish gardening, promises not to harm flowers in the Fairy Queen's own realm. He will only kill those outside her domain. Why, he asks, should Violet "care about what happens to the flowers in another land, if your own are safe?" Violet sadly replies that within each flower on earth, "there beats a little heart that loves and sorrows like our own." She will save all the flowers everywhere or perish in the attempt.

Nearly dead from her self-sacrificing labors, Violet accepts the king's final challenge to build him a palace fairer than his own icy castle. If she can do this, he will never freeze another flower. Violet manages to create a New Eden in the Frost King's sterile, icy land with the help of all her loving friends. The spiders, flies, moles, birds, and blossoms she had revived and taught to live cooperatively help her create a paradise. In the end, the Frost King's own spirits, "casting off their dark mantles," kneel "before him and beseech him not so send them forth to blight the things the gentle Fairies love so much." The Frost King chooses a Flower Crown, pays homage to Violet and watches his icy castle melt away.

This tale is remarkable, given the Fruitlands experience. Unable to produce life, the Frost King is bent upon destroying it. The Fairy Queen does not battle him directly, but allows her "weakest" fairy to tame the enemy through love. The king's own male spirits desert him, won over to the warmth and abundance of domesticity by busy spinster spiders, breadcrumb-sharing fairies, and monastic cells transformed into country kitchens. It was Louisa's first effort in fiction to save the people she loved by blending domesticity and feminism.

In the summer of 1855 Anna's and Louisa's series of jobs, together with the small income from trust funds, sufficed to send Louisa, Anna, Bronson, Abba, Elizabeth and May to Walpole, New Hampshire. Eliza Wells, the married daughter of Abba's dead sister, Catherine, provided a house rent-free. To the Alcott's anxious relatives, the move seemed sensible. Walpole's quiet hills invoked memories of Spindle Hill, and a diet of vegetables and fruit from the garden Bronson immediately planted would conserve cash. Abba and the girls made tallow candles, soap, and lye from ashes, and rendered sheep fat.

Lousia recorded happily that Walpole was not just a sleepy village. It was also a fashionable summer encampment for artistic, unconventional visitors. Besides gardening, fresh air, and rest, Louisa and Anna enjoyed "plays, picnics, and pleasant people," such as "Fanny Kemble, Mrs. Kirkland, and Dr. Bellows," all of whom joined in creating impromptu theatricals, including one of Louisa's blood and thunder plays.[36]

Louisa found time to write as well as to act. She finished a second book of fairy tales, "Christmas Elves," enlisting May's talents as illustrator.[37] In October she set out for Boston to sell her book. By November, her birth month, which she called "the dullest month of the year," she found out it was much too late to publish a book for Christmas shoppers. Nevertheless, having earned twenty dollars with stories for the *Saturday Evening Gazette*, and with two book-length manuscripts to her credit, she was ready to seek her fortune through writing.[38]

Louisa frequently mentioned acting as a career possibility in her journal, and friends and family members remembered the Alcotts' semi-professional performances years later. Perhaps she could comfortably admit to being "stage struck" because she shared its delights with Anna, who appears to have been the truly gifted actress in the family.[39] More than likely the theater also interested Louisa as a vehicle for her own plays and as an outlet for her fiercely personal sense of comedy and tragedy. She was particularly fond of improvising eccentric old ladies, Dickensian widows and spinsters, and even, on occasion, "Mrs. Malaprop." Among her most popular parlor sketches were satirical imitations of reformers and their critics, including both women's rights advocates and anti-feminists.

Yet her true calling was always literary. Many times over the years she had recorded her passionate determination to achieve success as an author. In 1860, the year she called "A Year of Good Luck," she finally admitted that she had been working on her first serious novel, *Moods*.[40] She belittled her efforts: "Daresay nothing will ever come of it."[41] Yet she added, "But it *had* to be done, and I'm richer for the experience."[42] The feeling that she had been "possessed" by her work made it easier to justify her writing. She half jokingly used the expression, "genius burned," in the belief (also held by her Romantic contemporaries) that all artists acted as instruments in the expression of inspiration.[43]

The Year of Good Luck

Like many gifted women of her day, Louisa was troubled by her ambitions to become an independent artist. As early as October 1856 she confided, "I was born with a boy's spirit under my bib and tucker, I can't wait when I can work so I took my little talent in my hand and forced the world again, braver than before and wiser for my failures."[44] Born with a boy's spirit, she was also clearly a young woman at the age of twenty-four. The conflict made her vacillate between two paths: she could combine marriage with writing, or remain single. Married women might take to writing in order to support their loved ones. Harriet Beecher Stowe and Lydia Maria Child had done so, but they also accepted domesticity as a woman's primary role—insofar as fictional heroines can be trusted to reflect their authors' values.

The second path, a common topic in Louisa's journal and fiction, was spinsterhood. Though she had several "adorers," she disparaged them all as "queer."[45] She clung to the privileges of "boyhood" as long as she could, salvaging the best memories of childhood for her fairy tales. She continued to describe herself and her sisters as the Alcott "girls," a verbal tactic that excused their work as non-threatening girlish fancies and emphasized their sisterhood. Yet the events in her life dispelled the illusion of perpetual childhood. Soon Louisa would follow her chosen path of a single life with a clearer sense of herself.

The changing character of her sisters' lives had much to do with this transformation. Anna found her future husband, John, and increasingly spent her leisure time with him. May, "fortune's favored child," traveled back and forth between Walpole and Boston seeking the best art training available for women at that time. Louisa found small sums from her own earnings to give her, while May and Sewall relations also enjoyed helping the bright, outgoing May. But it was Beth, the homebody, who gave her family the most concern.

Elizabeth, who enjoyed the family's pet names for her, Lizzie and Beth, never moved beyond the pious passivity prescribed for girls in mid-nineteenth century. She was seriously ill, partly as a result of scarlet fever contracted from one of Abba's charity visits to a poor family. She declined rapidly. Even a visit to the seashore failed to restore her wasted body, which weighed less than ninety pounds. Her case was a "critical one," though the actual physical malady remained unknown. The Sewalls offered land in Walden to build a suburban house for Bronson, Abba, and the invalid girl. But both Bronson and his dearest girl, Beth, wanted to move back to Concord.

Her father found a farmhouse with over ten acres of land and an orchard of apple trees for nine hundred and fifty dollars. Emerson once more contributed the largest share of the capital, and other friends put up the difference. Abba's income from the sale of Hillside remained safely invested. Yet Bronson too had become more pragmatic. This time he found no fault with property ownership, and when Beth seemed a bit better he set off an another western tour to earn money. But Beth did not live to enjoy "Orchard House."[46] Waiting in another rented cottage for renovations of Orchard House to be completed, she faded into fitful unconsciousness, dosed against pain with opium, ether, and finally morphine.

The entire family hovered anxiously about her. Abba, the competent nurse of so many other invalids, wrote, "I watched her with jealous care—and I think the cold and perhaps want of more cheerful society—as well as the absence of certain nutritive diet may have caused this sad wrench of her frame."[47] By Christmas she would allow only Louisa to carry her downstairs. Soon Beth could not leave her room at all or sew the little comforts she loved to give as gifts to family and friends. Torn between guilt and misery at her sister's cruel reward for being so selfless and submissive, Louisa would use Beth's death as the model for the most moving episode in *Little Women*.

Bronson was called back home in January because Beth was dying. Louisa wrote that it was "a hard thing to bear, but if she is only to suffer, I pray she may go soon."[48] When Bronson arrived he asked Beth if she knew how serious her condition was, that she might not get well? She replied that she could "best be spared of the four," and that her family would have her still in death as in life. Finally she asked to sit in her father's lap and kissed her mother and sisters. Her last audible words were, "Well now mother, I go, I go. How beautiful everything is tonight."[49] She was only twenty-three. Her emaciated body was like a small child's but her hair had entirely fallen out as if she were a very old woman. Emerson, Henry Thoreau, Frank Sanborn (Bronson's disciple and biographer), and John Pratt (Anna's fiance) bore her coffin to Sleepy Hollow Cemetery in Concord.

Still in mourning, the Alcotts moved to Orchard House that spring. In April Anna told the family she wanted to marry John Pratt. His father, Minot Pratt, had been a director of Brook Farm, and like the Alcotts the family moved to Concord after their communal experiment ended. John and Anna shared a love of home drama productions and a reverence for Bronson's character and philosophy. John worked in an insurance company and he offered his fiance a loving, secure home. However, it was too soon after Beth's death for the Alcotts to contemplate another daughter's leaving the house, even for such an acceptable union. The young couple agreed to wait for a while.

Louisa was deeply distressed by Anna's love affair. In the midst of Elizabeth's final sufferings, she wrote that "I'll keep my lamentations over Nan's affairs till this duty is over."[50] In May she admitted that John Pratt was a "true man," but still likened Anna's engagement to Beth's death. "So another sister is gone," Louisa said.[51] She had only one sister left and vowed to "turn to little May for comfort."[52] The two did indeed draw closer, but it was more than obvious, even to Louisa, that May was the prettiest Alcott daughter, the liveliest, most sociable, and surest to follow Anna's example. Being a daughter and a sister were no longer enough. Louisa increasingly felt forced to be herself.

In the fall she was back in Boston. "The only bread winner just now,"[53] more alone and depressed than ever, she walked the familiar streets thinking about her sister's death and her own relentless struggle to earn a living. She came to Mill Dam. The Great Bay of the Charles River was on one side, alive with commerce, and the stagnant waters of Back Bay spilled out from the other. Impulsively she thought of suicide, but drew back. "There is work for me and I'll have it," she wrote afterwards about her despair and recovery.[54]

Reverend Theodore Parker helped her regain faith and energy when he preached on "Laborious Young Women:" "Trust your fellow beings and let them help you. Don't be too proud to ask, and accept the humblest work till you can find the task you want."[55] Louisa said it was just what she needed to hear.[56] "A test of character and courage," she called the alternate periods of employment and distress she had endured.[57] At twenty-six she looked back and felt that "the past year has brought us the first death and the first betrothal, two events that change my life. I can see that these experiences have taken a deep hold and changed or developed me."[58] Once before, on an early morning run in Concord's woods and meadows, she had felt God's grace imminent in her life. Now she felt God's presence even when no one else cared about her. "If this is experiencing religion, I have done it."[59] She defended Parker's radical theology and his agreement with George Ripley that Christianity must change society as well as individuals. If some thought Parker no Christian, Louisa countered, "He is my sort; for though he may lack reverence for other people's God, he works bravely for his own and turns his back on no one who needs help as some other pious do."[60]

What Louisa called "practical Christianity" bridged the gap between her adventurous "tomboy" self and her role as cranky, overburdened "Aunt Lu." Parker provided safe transport from childhood to young womanhood by recognizing Louisa May Alcott's membership in a large class of young working women. He not only publicly accepted the need of many young women to work, he honored their labor. Inspiring Louisa to call him "Reverend Power" in her novel, *Work*,[61] he strengthened the young author at a crucial moment in her life, helping her learn the difference between eccentricity and Romantic heroism. Indeed, Louisa was not ready for a permanent decision to remain single. Marriage was still the most important event of a woman's life in America.

Louisa assumed that temperament was inherited, as did most of her contemporaries. Nevertheless, she comforted herself with Emerson's promise that balance and serenity could be won through experience, careful introspection, and self-discipline. The effort was worthwhile, not only as a means to personal growth, but also because social progress was still thought to be the aggregate of individual perfections. The difficulty for American women like Louisa was that only young men enjoyed the worldly experience that encouraged much personal and social growth. In the eyes of conventional society, women remained fixed in the private domestic world, the lifelong dependents of men. Parker thundered that it was not so, validating Louisa's feminist experience—experience which increasingly found its way into her short stories and novels.

Young Women and Young Ladies

The same culture that prescribed childlike innocence and isolation from the real world as ideals of young womanhood expected a miraculous transformation on a girl's wedding day. As soon as a woman became a matron, she was expected to keep household accounts, discipline her children, counsel her husband, and in short, mother the Republic. Louisa seized upon this contradiction in women's lives for *Moods*. She laid out the critical shortcomings of a young girl's conventional upbringing claiming her right to an adolescent period of experience and self-reliance. Only this transitional period in the female life cycle could give women the mature individuality that both Emerson and the feminist movement both claimed for all Americans.

Louisa had already rehearsed this new dimension of the woman problem in her stories for the *Gazette*. At first she created Patient Griseldas, only a trifle more realistic than "Violet," the self-sacrificing little fairy in "The Frost King." Little Genevieve, for instance, the heroine of one *Gazette* story, flees into the snow, a motherless victim of her heartless father who had deserted Genevieve's mother and taken their baby with him.[62] Years later, little Genevieve seeks and finds her mother, now a fallen woman. Patiently waiting for her mother outside her apartment in the bitter cold night, Genevieve freezes to death and the heartbroken mother enters a convent.

Louisa's storytelling abilities gradually matured beyond such sentimentality. Slowly she integrated her own experience into her fiction. In "The Sisters' Trial" four young women fulfill a promise to their dead mother by finding happiness in doing their duty.[63] They bravely attempt a year of independent work to earn their living, and in so doing find their true vocations for both useful labor and marriage. In another story Louisa examined differences between independent and dependent women. Written in the fall of 1856, "The Lady and the Woman" defends the virtues of the kind of wife sought by true men.[64]

Louisa was happily attending Theodore Parker's Sunday evening discussions at this time, reporting that they "did her good."[65] Emboldened about presenting young women closer to herself, she wrote about two female friends in their early twenties who take a rural holiday accompanied by a young bachelor both admire. A sudden fierce storm sends the young "lady" into fainting fits. While the young man stays behind to tend the unconscious girl, her friend Kate sets out to bring help in the face of an impending flood.[66] Strong and self-reliant, Kate is a "true woman," seasoned by years of supporting her orphaned brothers. The doctor she brings back observes that she must be a spinster because no husband would allow her out in such a storm. The young bachelor is not at first attracted by Kate's courage. The author tells us that he dislikes "strong minded women," and idolizes "beautiful, tender creatures, submissive to the will." Kate informs him, however, that "an affectionate or accomplished idiot is not my ideal of a woman." She sets forth her own ideal, really a portrait of herself:

> I would have her strong enough to stand alone and give, not ask, support, brave enought to think and act, as well as feel. Keen-eyed enough to see her own and other's faults and wise enough to find a cure for them. I would have her humble, self-reliant; gentle though strong; man's companion, not his plaything; able and willing to face storm as well as sunshine and share life's burdens as they come.

Remarkably, she wins the affection and respect of the doubtful bachelor.

These short stories form the basis of a narrative formula Louisa progressively refined throughout her writing career. Her heroines demand a period of independence or even modest adventure, not as an alternative to domesticity, but as a necessary precondition to its success. If special talents, family responsibilities, or "moods" bar a companionate, equal marriage, the alternative is honorable spinsterhood. According to Alcott, society must grant women a measure of the same experiences that test men in order that women too may be prepared for important roles in the family and in society.

From February 2–25, 1861, Louisa wrote and revised *Moods*, a book that explores the Romantic path to female individuality. She paused only for a run at dusk. Otherwise, she remained sitting, cuddled in a green and red "glory cloak" with a matching silk cap that Abba sewed for her.[67] Surrounded by groves of manuscripts, living for immortality," as May observed, she was also the center of her family's devoted attention.[68] Abba wandered in and out with cups of tea, and Bronson brought cider and apples to "Pegasus." Louisa found it "very pleasant and queer while it lasted."[69] She read it all aloud to the family. Abba and Anna, both bursting with pride, thought it was wonderful, while Bronson thought "Emerson must see this." Louisa admitted, "I planned it some time ago, and have had it in my mind for ever so long; but now it begins to take shape."[70]

In April President Lincoln declared war against the South. Louisa longed to be a man and fight, but had to content herself with "working for those who can." Her war experiences resulted in her writing *Hospital Sketches*.[71] A notable popular success, its publication in 1862 led A. K. Loring to accept *Moods*. After badgering Louisa for months to change the lesson of the book, so that readers might find themselves purified and ennobled by it, he finally published the first edition of *Moods* in 1865. Loring knew the public would be shocked that Louisa allowed her heroine to decide that youth and inexperience had led her to marry the wrong man. Even worse, the heroine seriously considers leaving her husband for her romantic lover. Loring urged Alcott to preach a different moral:

> when the sad awakening comes to either party each should straitway confess to the living and before God resolve that with his aid the vows shall be kept, the marriage sanctified and together, forever they will live out the noble life a sanctified marriage renders possible to all.[72]

Louisa agreed to have her heroine die at the end, unable to remain married to the wrong man. *Moods* was not revised to the author's satisfaction, allowing the heroine to survive her mental adultery, until 1881, when she bought the copyright back from her publisher for one dollar.[73] By that time her international reputation as the author of *Little Women* assured a devoted audience convinced that Miss Alcott would not suggest an immoral course of action. The two versions of *Moods* measure what had changed in Alcott's life and in the world during seventeen crucial years of American history—and also what had remained the same. By 1882 Louisa had long passed out of her "Romantic period," and Transcendentalism had all but faded from American culture. The feminist movement she formally joined had altered some social conventions and a great many state laws, especially those governing divorce and married women's property rights.

Louisa's experiences as a single young woman, however, remained embedded in both editions of *Moods*, testimony to the fact that some obstacles facing young women had not changed much, she thought, by the end of the nineteenth century. Having begun her outward journey, she did not retreat, except to retrace the paths and adventures she had taken for her readers.

CHAPTER VII

Moods

Life is a train of moods like a string of beads, and as we pass through them they prove to be so many coloured lenses, which paint the world their own hue and each shows us only what lies in its own focus.

R. W. Emerson, "Experience," 1844–45

In 1865 Henry James Jr. dismissed *Moods* as an unconvincing version of "the old story of the husband, the wife and the lover."[1] Since a thirty-year-old spinster author could scarcely possess much insight into the eternal triangle, James assumed that the attempt to deal with any deeper problem was laughable. "Has Miss Alcott proposed to give her story a philosophical bearing? We can hardly suppose it," James wrote acidly.[2] His review was only one of many discouraging notices that Louisa Alcott tried to answer in her preface to a revised edition of the novel in 1882. She maintained that the first work was so altered for the publisher that "marriage appeared to be the theme instead of an attempt to show the mistakes of a moody nature, guided by impulse, not principle."[3]

For seventeen years, Alcott remained firmly convinced that the novel's themes offered "philosophic bearing" on relations between the sexes. The "woman problem," after all, was being argued everywhere when she wrote *Moods*. Forwarded by Woman's Rights conventions, the cause was debated in every newspaper and popular magazine. Alcott dealt with the issue in her first edition through the Romantic perspective she knew best.

Henry James Jr. notwithstanding, *Moods* in fact deals deeply with moral and social questions. Alcott attempted to analyze the effect of Transcendentalism on the lives of women. Years of living out the principles of American Romanticism with her family had made her an expert on the problems it posed for women. *Moods* pointedly includes a defense of experience for young, unmarried women; an attack on passion and romantic love; and an insistence on friendship and equality as the best basis for lasting relationships between the sexes.

Alcott hoped that women might win the struggle against older patriarchal arrangements in her own life-time, in lieu of imminent victory, she proposed a transitional solution. Like other feminists, she argued that women should band together as a balancing force against unchecked male dominance. She recognized two kinds of sororal relationships: "the sad sisterhood," whose disappointed members were victims of a power they could not resist, and "happy women," whose fortunate members had found their individual identities and maintained their domestic lives.[4] "Happy women" and "the sad sisterhood" could protect women's interests together until the final battle for equality was won.

Bronson Alcott described Louisa as "Duty's Faithful Child," but she was also a daughter of the Transcendentalist movement he helped found. As such, she and many of her female contemporaries struggled for a sense of individual identity within the context of traditional domesticity. Trying to combine both domesticity and individuality into a workable feminist perspective, they directly challenged established sex roles integral to nineteenth century social order.

Learning to Be a Woman

That girls as well as boys be granted a period of adolescence was Louisa's special, though not original contribution to Woman's Rights. She began fighting for it with the *Gazette* stories, offerred philosophic justification for it in *Moods*, and finally made it an accepted part of normal growth in *Little Women*.[5] The heroine in *Moods*, Sylvia Yule, shut away at home because she has reached the dangerous age of seventeen, prefigures "Jo March" in *Little Women*.[6]

Sylvia is poised between childhood and young womanhood. She lives with her widowed father and an older brother and sister in material luxury but without spiritual guidance. Knowing nothing of the world, her character is unformed. A motherless childhood has left her undisciplined and starved for love. However, she has honesty, intelligence close to genius, and a face that just misses beauty for its "want of harmony." Intensely "moody," yearning for companionship and experience, she joins her brother, Max, and his friends, Geoffrey Moor and Adam Warwick, on a week-long holiday excursion which proves pivotal in Alcott's narrative.

Both Warwick and Moor fall in love with Sylvia. Cherishing Moor as a valued friend, she feels romantic stirrings toward Warwick. Earlier in the first edition of the novel, however, Warwick had a passionate encounter with Ottila, a dark and dangerous Creole woman. Seducing Warwick into believing that she might become principled in time, Ottila had extracted his promise to consider her for marriage. Warwick consented, but secretly had no intention of marrying her.

Before Sylvia fully identifies her feeling for Warwick as adult, sexual attraction, he leaves to visit Ottila; unfortunately, he does not explain the reasons for his departure to Sylvia. Soon after the outing, Sylvia accidentally meets Ottila at a party and learns that Warwick is engaged to her. Angry, feeling rejected, she accepts Moor's offer of marriage. But on their honeymoon in the mountains she meets Adam Warwick, returning to marry her. Realizing her mistake too late, she tells Moor, at Warwick's urging, that her love for Adam Warwick stands between them.

Moor's distant cousin, Faith Dane, a maternal spinster about thirty-years old, counsels Sylvia to accept a separation from her husband, but not to marry Warwick. She knows Warwick well; he is "an eagle," and little Sylvia a "wood dove."[7] Unequal partnerships inevitably lead to the domination of the weaker spirit by the more powerful. On the other hand, separation and time to grow on her own will may make Sylvia a fit, contented companion to Moor. If not, living alone will keep her integrity and at least grant Moor his self-respect.

Moor and Warwick depart as comrades-in-arms to fight for Italy's independence, leaving Sylvia with Faith as her sole friend and guide. Sylvia cares for her aging father, finds comfort in her brother's young family, and maintains a cordial but patronizing relationship with her older sister. After a year of separation, Warwick is drowned while saving Moor's life. Moor returns to America, and husband and wife are reunited. The first edition of *Moods* does not end happily, however. Exhausted by her trials, Sylvia has developed consumption and dies, surrounded by her grieving her husband, father, brother and sister-in-law.

Alcott uses Sylvia Yule's life to illustrate what can happen to a young girl with little or no experience in the world. Alcott's own youth had prepared her to understand Sylvia's limitations, and novelists such as Hawthorne and Bronte supplied fictional models for her own narrative. In both *The Scarlet Letter* and *Jane Eyre*, women suffer from love partly because they know little of life.[8] Hester Prynne leaves her parental home without any preparation for worldly experiences, and Jane Eyre has only a charity school education and a cold outcast life to prepare her for romantic ventures.

Despite her deprivations, or perhaps because of them, Jane speaks in defense of women's human feelings and aspirations:

> Nobody knows how many rebellions besides political rebellions ferment in the masses of life which people the earth. Women are supposed to be very calm generally: but women feel just as men feel; they need exercise for their faculties, and a field for their efforts as

much as their brothers do; they suffer from too rigid a constraint, too absolute a stagnation, precisely as men would suffer; and it is narrow-minded in their more privileged fellow-creatures to say that they ought to confine themselves to making puddings and knitting stockings, to playing on the piano and embroidering bags. It is thoughtless to condemn them, or laugh at them, if they seek to do more or learn more than custom has pronounced necessary for their sex.[9]

Alcott tried to show that Sylvia, like Jane, needed "exercise," and that at seventeen she was ignorant of the choices available to her. Untried in the world outside her garden, a prisoner of childhood, Sylvia could only boyishly rebel and demand experiences reserved to young men. Throughout the novel Alcott contrasts Sylvia's struggle with the easy, unobstructed male acquisition of experience. Thus her brother Max explores the world without restraint while Sylvia sits at home, trying to sew placidly, but thinking about forbidden pleasures: "I don't see why I must sit here and hem nightcap strings when the world is full of pleasant places and delightful people," she sighs. "If I could only be allowed to go and find them . . . . I wish I were a boy, or could be contented with what other girls like."[10]

The disparities in male and female experiences become even more apparent in the holiday journey Sylvia takes with Max, Warwick, and Moor. For source material Alcott drew on expeditions in her own youth and on Thoreau's famous trip down the Concord and Merrimack rivers. Although the friends' voyage lasts only seven days (like Thoreau's), it is crucial both to the transcendental union with nature and the concomitant realization of unique individuality; these rites of passage are familiar in all classical literature.[11] Both rites, however, are forbidden to women, as Henry James made clear in his review. Caring not a whit for the female pilgrim's progress, he described the incident purely in terms of the heroine's indiscretion. Sylvia

> goes off on a camping out expedition of a week's duration, in company with three gentlemen, no superfluous luggage, as far as we can ascertain, 'cockle shell stuck pilgrim wise in her hat.' It is hard to say whether the impropriety of this proceeding is greater or less from the fact of her extreme youth, the fact is at any rate kindly overlooked by two of her companions who become desperately enamored of her before the week is out.[12]

James overlooked the fact that Sylvia was undertaking a form of pilgrimage when he acidly noted the young men's improprieties. His insensitivity to the heroine's aims was of course not unusual for the time.

The domestic novels of the nineteenth century make little note of what Harriet Martineau calls the "substantial, heartfelt interests for women of all ages and under ordinary circumstances, quite apart from love."[13] The quest to satisfy these interests were reserved to men, with the exception of certain discreet travel books designed for ladies' vicarious education. For Alcott such limitations prevented more than picnics. For instance, they prevented any true religious experience; without it, women were fundamentally cut off from the divine order and left to languish in disquieting "moods."

Through Flood and Field and Fire

Warwick and Moor indulge Sylvia's wish for romance, but remain ignorant of what the journey really means to her. In humble gratitude for their companionship, Sylvia performs a series of dramatic sketches with a rug, shawl, and cloak from her wardrobe. (Contrary to James' allegation, she appears to have brought more than a cockle-shell with her). She creates a full evening of illusion for her admirers on their first evening of camping. Moor considers her performance only the result of a lady's education in parlor arts. Warwick, however, understands that a woman may have natural genius and declares she "has it all in her and needs no master."[14] He approves of her playacting, because for women "pent up emotions can find a safer vent in this way than in melancholy dreams of daring action," although he denies Sylvia's need for the journey as anything but "romance." He advises the others to "let her alone, give her plenty of liberty, and I think time and experience will make a noble woman of her." Here Warwick ironically strikes at the moral center of the novel.[15] Through him Alcott argues that self-expression, although perilous in an undisciplined child-woman, can be a treasured possession in a mature woman, the very soul of her capacity for creativity. Yet Warwick, who momentarily supports Sylvia's independence, is more intent on creating a fit playmate for his own romantic needs.

A berry hunt with Warwick reveals an important disparity in their attitudes. Sylvia bets Warwick that she can gather more berries, and when the two compare their harvest, Warwick is touched by her efforts: "You are a true woman, Miss Sylvia, for though your palm is purple there's not a stain upon your lips, and you have neither worked nor suffered for yourself it seems."[16] Sylvia responds, "I don't deserve that compliment, because I was only intent on outdoing you if possible, so you are mistaken again, you see."[17] Her companion remains positive that her fair face is an index to her womanly heart; she is "pleased, yet somehow abashed." Warwick sees her as exemplifying womanly self-sacrifice; he fails to perceive she wants to be his equal.

A Golden Wedding

True womanhood, Alcott admits, cannot develop through competitive berry picking. Instead, Sylvia hungrily seeks her identity in the past world of domestic self-sufficiency. A summer storm drenchs the campers and they seek shelter in a "red farm-house standing under venerable elms, with a patriarchal air which promised hospitable treatment and good cheer." Three generations of farm folk are celebrating Grandma and Grandpa's golden wedding anniversary and the travellers are welcomed into the family circle. They enter fully into the festivities, exchanging their wet camping costumes for old-fashioned, homely farm clothes. The golden wedding couple are a priest and priestess of an older faith, in which "this human father turned to the Divine, as these sons and daughters turned" to him, "as free to ask, as confident of reply."[18] The authority of the old farm couple is tangible and unqestioned; their values and skills are happily reproduced in the loving progeny gathered to celebrate family ties. Grandma "a culinary general," no less commanding than her patriarchal spouse, gives orders to her forty-year-old son and daughters, organizing their domestic arrangements with calm good humor.[19]

Sylvia feels the difference between this home and her own troubled family. Not only motherless, but in a sense, fatherless too, she suffers the emotional conflicts created by a weak father who provides material comforts but little else. Even his wealth is suspect, because he married Sylvia's mother for her money and social position, not for love. Briefly however, borrowing the "second best gingham gown" of the farmer's daughter, Sylvia becomes a farm daughter herself, cuddling babies and singing "John Anderson, my Jo" as an anniversary gift to her fictive kin.[20]

Sylvia's brief contact with this lost world of corporate domesticity is filled with nostalgia and regret, a nostalgia only heightened by her own fragmentary, vulnerable existence. It is the only scene in *Moods* that evokes the homely details of kitchen abundance Alcott ultimately made famous. During the family banquet, she summons up lessons "not learned from books": the fragrance of coffee and "babies borne away to simmer between blankets until called for."[21] "The women unpacked baskets, brooded over teapots and kept up a harmonious clack as the table was spread with pyramids of cake, regiments of pies, quagmires of jelly, snowbanks of bread, and gold mines of butter; every possible article of food, from baked beans to wedding cake, finding a place on that sacrificial altar."[22]

This scene is partly based on Alcott's reading of the biography of the German novelist, Jean Paul Richter. A writer popular with the Concord circle, Richter delighted in all "these humble, simple religous ceremonies."[23] In one of his novels, *Jubelsnoir*, he depicted "the beautiful and simple celebration of an aged minister and his equally aged wife, celebrating the anniversary of their marriage festival."[24] Alcott uses the "Golden Wedding" as a foil to establish the tragic character of Sylvia's journey. She plainly views Sylvia as a member of a newer generation of women no longer supported by a patriarchal tradition. According to Alcott, that tradition, although limiting and provincial, did allow women clear domestic authority. It did guarantee them an honorable old age, surrounded by progeny who would respect them. Above all, woman's abundance is honored and the patriarch, surrounded by his children and grandchildren, stands in stark contrast to Adam Warwick and Geoffrey Moor. Adam, like Bronson Alcott, sees persons as "but animated facts or ideas."[25] As Faith Dane says, "he seizes, searches, uses them and when they have no more for him, drops them like the husk, whose kernel he has secured."[26] Geoffrey Moor possesses Bronson's delicate sensibilities, his veneration of holy family life. Like Bronson, he also fears the earthly family and the consequences of passionate involvement with a grown woman. Sylvia is distracted by the incompleteness of each suitor, momentarily turning back, with longing, to a rural self-sufficiency where Grandpa and Grandma acknowledge their interdependency.

In the next chapter "Sermons," Alcott moved the voyagers to a church in the woods. Here New World nature offers another alternative for a girl in search of original relationships and experience. Moor preaches a Thoreau-like sermon promising nature's sweet solace to the weary pilgrims, while Warwick, as Theodore Parker, expounds the new social gospel to his friends. "Golden Wedding" rituals are forgotten as new choices appear for Sylvia's consideration. Warwick is particularly compelling because Alcott has named him after Warwick Castle in England. In an *Atlantic Monthly* essay, Hawthorne told readers that Warwick was "founded by King Cybeline in the twilight ages." The English, he points out, have based their "new things" on sturdy old foundations.[27]

Adam Warwick in *Moods* is a confusing, if attractive New World product constructed out of Old World materials. He appears conversant with European philosophies and politics, but needs the freedom of the American wilderness to maintain his unique distance from ordinary domesticity. In several ways Warwick resembles Reverend Dimmesdale in the *Scarlet Letter*. He journeys from England to New England, and thunders against the sins of his companions while concealing his own. He points out that Max is indolent, while Geoffrey Moor is too self-sacrificing, and Sylvia's character is flawed by uninformed self-interest. Warwick advises Moor to be more manly. "For years you have lived for others," Warwick says, "Now learn to live a little for yourself, heartily and happily else the feminine in you get the uppermost."[28] But while Moor must remember himself, Sylvia is counseled to efface herself and work for others, which will bring her a "happy soul in a healthy body" and make her "what God intended . . . a brave and noble woman."[29]

But sermons do not a saved soul make in the New Zion. Sylvia lay awake half that night, the experience of the voyage offerring her a glimpse of the promised land:

> like the fairy Lady of Shallott, she had
> left the web and left the loom,
> Had seen the water-lilies bloom
> Had seen the helmet and the plume,
> And had looked down to Camelot.[30]

The Child-Bride

That Warwick and Moor become desperately enamored of Sylvia is a two-fold tragedy. First, Sylvia is seeking a friend, not a lover; raised as a motherless child she is "heir to ceaseless craving for affection" and therefore vulnerable to any proposal that promises security, warmth, and love.[31] As Alcott knew, Sylvia's attempt to gain both friendship and love in marriage was made improbable by her failure to gain experience and independence in life. Sylvia's plight was hardly unique in the transatlantic fiction of the time. Like Sylvia, Bronte's Jane Eyre cannot resist the offer of love, and marries before her heart is mature enough to join principle to love. Such women, Alcott argues, will yield to impulsive moods and romantic dreams.

Alcott read Mrs. Gaskell's *Life of Charlotte Bronte* a few years before she began *Moods*. Harriet Martineau's review of *Jane Eyre* is paraphrased by Mrs. Gaskell.[32] "All female characters," wrote Martineau,

> in all their thoughts and lives, are full of one thing, or are regarded by the reader in the light of that one thought—love. It begins with the child of six years old, at the opening—a charming picture—and it closes with it at the last page; and so dominant is this idea—so incessant is the writer's tendency to describe the need of being loved—that the heroine, who tells her own story, leaves the reader at last under the uncomfortable impression of having entertained either a double love, or allowed one to supercede another without notification of the transition. It is not thus in real life. There are substantial, heartfelt interests for women of all ages, and under ordinary circumstances, quite apart from love; there is an absence of introspection, an unconsciousness, a repose in women's lives— unless under peculiarly unfortunate circumstances of which we find no admission in this book.[33]

As Alcott must have surely noted, Martineau understood the central theme of *Jane Eyre*, which is also that of *Moods*. Most women were largely unrecognized as principled individuals guided by principle precisely because men loved them best as little girls. The "peculiarly unfortunate circumstances" were more the rule than the exception, as indicated by Alcott's census of the "sad sisterhood, a larger class than many of us deem it to be."[34]

The heroine of Alcott's next adult novel, *Work*, discusses *Jane Eyre* at length and condemns Jane's marriage to Rochester as "an unequal bargain." In *Jane Eyre*, as in *Moods*, the union between the main characters is rendered dangerous by disparities in age, education, and experience. In both novels, moreover, the heroes have dangerous, passionate affairs with Creole women who are consumed by ungovernable appetites. Unlike Warwick, who is only briefly drawn to the fiery Ottila, Rochester marries his Bertha. Forcibly restrained, Bertha behaves like a mad animal, endangering Jane's safety and ultimately causing the destruction of the house of Rochester by fire. Jane flees the house, endures lonely poverty and near starvation, and is finally rescued by the kind sisters of a cold, dogmatic minister. These women, really her long lost cousins, act as her surrogate sisters, providing the orphaned Jane with family protection. Successfully evading a loveless marriage to the minister, Jane returns to find Rochester blind, crippled, and helpless. In spite of the inequalities between Jane and Rochester, Jane at last has gained experience and self-reliance. She has become strong enough, and Rochester is weak enough, for them to be happily married. The marriage between Sylvia and Moor, however, is a seriously flawed domestic idyll.

Moor, confident that he can teach Sylvia to love him, has married a child who plays at being a dutiful housewife. She vainly tries to put her husband's happiness above her own. In a few months however, he finds her a lonely girl in a matron's gown, her fingers grown so thin that the wedding ring slips off without a guard. Her condition worsens when Warwick appears in the company of Moor's cousin, Faith Dane, and crushes Sylvia's hand in his passionate grip, breaking the guard and leaving the wedding band rather loosely encircling her finger.

Hoping to avoid choosing again between Geoffrey Moor and Adam Warwick, Sylvia tries to believe that Faith is Adam's new lover. But Faith's ideal is too high for more than friendship. She tells Sylvia that she "never met the man who would satisfy me." "Not even Adam," says Sylvia, "surely he is heroic enough for any woman's ideal." "No, not even Adam," is the reply.[35]

Adam confides to Faith that he would not marry Sylvia if she were free, suggesting that he is afraid of both domestic responsibilities and commitment to a mature, passionate woman. Faith, on the other hand, has given up looking for a man who will accept her as an equal and share the comfortable domesticity she has already created for herself. As

Moor's cousin, Faith knows his limitations as well; he is really trying to replace his mother and sister. In her study of *Moods*, literary historian Hannah Bewick has pointed out that "the enraging quality of Moor's love is heightened by its persistence and possessiveness."[36] Faith offers her home to Sylvia as a sanctuary from Moor, who almost deliberately ignores his wife's unhappiness. He hopes she will magically move from the "gay innocence of childhood to the mature devotion of adult womanhood," skipping over a passionate adolescent stage He exhibits no awareness of her need for self-hood, and even relieves her of any household responsibilities on the presumption that she is still a child. When she pines away, he puts his dead sister's signet ring on her finger to keep the wedding band from slipping off. Sylvia draws back "because his touch was more firm than tender, and his face wore a masterful expression seldom seen there."[37]

Before she married Moor, Sylvia used to enjoy playing with a little servant's child, Tilly. Through marriage Moor himself has lost Sylvia as a boyish companion. Hoping to entice her into motherhood, Moor brings Tilly home for the evening and presents her to Sylvia "so you can dress your dolly to suit yourself or leave her as she is."[38] Sylvia sadly concludes, "No, I find I cannot be a child again."[39]

The Sisterhoods

In an interesting discussion of nineteenth-century sororal relationships in New England, historians Christopher Lasch and William Taylor observe a connection between female friendships and the limitations of genteel womanhood. Simply put, they claim that women affirmed their purity and established important relationships with one another as a defense against the insensitive, materialist world of their men.[40] Louisa May Alcott offered a different explanation for what she called the "sad sisterhood." She argued that the basis for such friendships was not a denial of male sensitivity, nor even an affirmation of female purity, as Lasch and Taylor suggest, but a positive commonality of status as women. Commonality meant at least two things to Alcott— first, that most women were denied direct experience with the world, which would fit them for independence; second, that they were dependent upon men whose status in the world was materially based on a competitive, unstable foundation. These women were "sad" because they were denied freedom and independence, and they recognized one another because their experiences enabled them to see through the stereotyped masks that women were expected to wear. They did not band together as a sisterhood of crippled, helpless victims, however.

Instead, they reached out to nurture and protect one another, and to struggle for reform. Disappointed, abandoned by those who should have protected them, they learned self-reliance through sad experience.

Female friendships were also forged in response to patriarchal relations, which preserved the sexual division of labor but destroyed the recognition and compensation of women's work. Faith and Sylvia developed such a sororal relationship, and so did many women in real life. As Alcott shows in her novels, they did so often at the risk of incurring shame upon themselves and abuse from society.

The theme of sisterhood between ordinary women who have departed either in thought or action from conventional social roles begins in *Moods* and continues throughout all of Alcott's novels. Hester Prynne is the grande dame of this sisterhood (The *Scarlet Letter* is mentioned in at least three Alcott novels). Her scarlet letter illuminates the sins in other bosoms. In *Moods* Sylvia dreams that the scarlet letter burns in the sky, a holy benediction upon the death of Warwick, who is fulfilled in battle if not in love. Alcott likens Sylvia to Hester Prynne, "living in the shadow of a household grief," she

> had joined that sad sisterhood called disappointed women, a larger class than many deem it to be, though there are few of us who have not seen members of it. Unhappy wives, mistaken or forsaken lovers; meek souls, who make life a long penance for the sins of others; gifted creatures kindled into fitful brilliance by some inward fire that consumes but cannot warm. These are women who fly to convents, write bitter books, sing songs full of heartbreak, act splendidly the passion they have lost or never won; who smile, and try to lead brave uncomplaining lives, but whose tragic eyes betray them, whose voices, however sweet or grand, contain an undertone of hopelessness, whose faces sometimes startle one with an expression which haunts the observer long after it is gone.[41]

In a feminist version of Emerson's command, "Trust thyself, every heart vibrates to that iron string," Faith Dane says to Sylvia, "You shall be a law unto yourself, my brave Sylvia."[42] In fact, Sylvia's conversion by "Faith" is the moral heart of *Moods*. Yet Sylvia's decision to take her friend's advice does not make her an outcast the like of Hester Prynne or Jane Eyre. Unlike Jane, Sylvia need not flee her comfortable home; nor does she suffer poverty, isolation, and ill-paying teaching jobs. And unlike Hester, Sylvia suffers no banishment to a cottage at the end of the village, she is not forced to wear a badge of shame.

Alcott has broken her main character into two personalities: gently reared, child-like Sylvia, and adversity-hardened, maternal Faith. Sylvia, unlike Jane or Hester, has a "sister." Faith is described as "shapely and tall, with much native dignity of carriage, and a face singularly attractive from its mild and earnest beauty. Looking at her one felt assured that here was a right womanly woman, gentle, just and true; possessed of a well-balanced mind, a self-reliant soul . . . her presence was comfortable, her voice had a motherly tone in it, her eyes a helpful look."[43] Nothing could be more unlike Sylvia, with her want of harmony and tendency to willful moodiness. Sylvia and Faith represent two paths for women. Sylvia, like Alcott, has passionate impulses that may only be romantic fancies; she also has a tendency to hero-worship. Faith is another part of Louisa; fervent abolitionist and self-reliant daughter of a contentious home, she chooses direct experience with life. She also knows that romantic heroes do not make very good husbands.

The reader half suspects that Faith will become the ultimate heroine of *Moods*, but she never fully emerges from the shadows of her mountain cottage. Faith Dane is the heroine of another Alcott story, however. Faith's enormous capacity for nurturance, expressed in her care of Sylvia, emerges in "The Brothers," a story Alcott published in *Atlantic Monthly* two years before the publication of *Moods*.[44] In "The Brothers," Faith leaves home to nurse at a Union hospital; her assistant is a convalescent freedman named Robert. It turns out that Robert and a rebel officer she tends are half-brothers. Robert tries to kill his brother because the white man has forcibly raped Robert's wife after selling Robert off the plantation. Although Faith saves the rebel by persuading Robert to go north, she admits, "God forgive me! Just then I hated him as only a woman thinking of a sister woman's wrong could hate."[45]

In the end, Robert joins a black regiment and changes his name to Robert Dane. He kills his brother on the battlefield and receives a mortal wound himself. Faith, having gone to nurse at Port Royal, is with him at the last moment, murmuring that in the next life "my contraband" will find "wife and home, eternal liberty and God."[46] Faith's treatment of Sylvia also displays her experienced nursing of a convalescent bondslave. She has learned her craft well in the abolitionist struggle and expanded her sympathies to those white women she recognizes as her equals through "sad sisterhood."

Faith Dane represents Alcott's fullest answer to the challenge (in *Moods*) of combining domesticity and feminism. Dane's cottage, a refuge for Sylvia, offers a wholesome female domesticity. Also, Faith has painfully forged an individual identity. She never rejects marriage; she simply admits she has never found a man who lives up to her "ideal." She does not expect Sylvia to have an equally iron will, but only to find her own honest solutions. "Trust thyself," she says. Although not ready to present a nonconformist heroine as the main character in *Moods*, Alcott rehearses the alternatives available to women in this period: Faith, Sylvia, her older sister Prue, and Max's pretty, conventional wife.

Louisa felt herself part of a transitional generation of women who sacrificed, organized, and placed great faith in the future generation. In fact, the postwar period brought enormous changes for womanhood. Louisa explored the possibilities in her later novels, and incorporated some in the later version of *Moods*.

Moods Revised with Experience

The most interesting change in the 1882 edition of *Moods* concerns Sylvia's ultimate fate. In the first edition, Sylvia dies while still loving Warwick, and makes everyone else feel guilty (as James points out). In the revised edition, Sylvia not only survives, but realizes that her love for Warwick was a passing fancy.

Alcott reinforces Sylvia's centrality in the second version of *Moods* by removing the opening chapters about Adam and Ottila. Moreover, the youthful Sylvia appears in the opening of the second version dressed in sensible girls' clothing rather than being disguised in a boy's smock as in the first version. The author thus corrects two of Henry James' objections to *Moods*. Adam Warwick, who James dismissed simply as a cad, is now a worthy model of romantic individualism. Sylvia demands a freedom of the will not unlike Adam's; neither of them can be accused of seeking license for adventurous impulses in the second rendering of *Moods*.

While Geoffrey Moor remains attracted to Sylvia as a "dear child," even after marriage, Sylvia is unmistakably a woman. Her coming of age is not accomplished by marriage but rather by her discovery that both she and her husband possess secret, inner lives, "private experiences." Her discovery, even though it is prompted by her own adulterous impulse, is nevertheless maintained in the second version of the story as an important challenge to the conventional perspective of a wife as simply part of her husband. The narrator announces, "Sylvia the girl was dead, but Sylvia the woman had begun to live."[47]

Alcott's friends were somewhat perturbed by the changes. Ednah Cheney, for one, complained mildly that Sylvia's simple year of quiet living and mild charity was an inadequate penance for being allowed to live *and* keep her husband.[48] Cheney felt that Louisa at thirty was simply young, inexperienced, and too little interested in love to really present Sylvia's case properly. No matter that Alcott had told Cheney of a real life "double relation" in Concord, similar to the one portrayed in *Moods*. Faith Dane, like Louisa, shrewdly observed the "old story."[49]

Faith Dane does not change at all in the second version of *Moods*. Always threatening to upstage Sylvia, she remains a secondary character. An invincible spinster, she cannot instill in her young friend the courage to remain unmarried, either in 1865 or 1882. Alcott in fact never wrote a full-length novel with an unmarried heroine. In *Jo's Boys*, written in the late 1880s, the surrogate daughter of a heroine chooses spinsterhood, lives happily and usefully, but we only learn this fact at the end of the book.[50] It is likely that the small but significant rise in spinsterhood during the last decades of the nineteenth century came too late for Alcott to portray such women in fiction. She herself prefigured those single, creative, "useful" women who founded settlement houses, wrote books, and helped organize successful suffrage campaigns.

Faith Dane's life is presented as an honorable alternative to unhappy marriage. Nevertheless, it is not true, as Cheney intimates, that Louisa Alcott knew nothing at all about marriage and disdained fictional analyses of wedded life. After all, Louisa observed her parents for years and used them as models for her fictional characters. Alcott is seriously concerned with two aspects of marriage in *Moods*: the personality each marital partner brings to the relationship, and the dynamic interaction between married people. Sylvia Yule brings some of Abba's social and personal problems to her marriage. Sylvia is also the pampered youngest daughter of comfortable gentry, and like Abba remains motherless during her "romantic period." Abba, of course, did mature through great hardships; Louisa greatly valued her mother's comforting "maternal" air. Faith Dane consequently bears a resemblance to Abba Alcott in her generally nurturant, competent demeanor. Faith's experience in the Civil War is, of course, reflective of Louisa May Alcott's own service.

Louisa's perceptions of her father and her struggles with him also found subtle expression in *Moods*. Warwick, Moor, and Mr. Yule, in both editions of the novel, have something of Bronson Alcott in them. Sylvia learns to love her father after Moor and Warwick go off to Europe. In the first *Moods*, Sylvia dies, and a grieving Mr. Yule survives her. In the second version, Mr. Yule dies, after which she is reunited with Moor and lives happily ever after. In 1861 perhaps even a father's belated love was insufficient to save a sinful daughter from death. In 1882, however, Sylvia in a sense outgrows the need for her father's loving approval. Having matured, she need not fear Moor's persistent patriarchy either. Now her father's equal, she can establish a "household democracy" of her own. In both editions Alcott wrote,

> How many roofs cover families or friends who live years together, yet never truly know each other, who love and long, and try to meet, yet fail to do so till some unexpected emotion or event per-

forms the work? In the year that followed the departure of the friends, Sylvia discovered this and learned to know her father. No one was so much to her as he; no one so fully entered into her thoughts and feelings; for sympathy drew them tenderly together and sorrow made them equals. As man and woman they talked, as father and daughter they loved; and the beautiful relation became their truest solace and support.[51]

Between the two versions of *Moods* lay thirty years of Louisa May Alcott's life. The older woman of the 1880s, evidently witnessed a reformed domestic scene, graced by more experienced and politically sophisticated women. In 1881, when she sent the revised *Moods* to her publisher, she also recommended that he publish Mrs. Robinson's *History of the Suffrage Movement*:

Do you scorn the whole thing? Better not, for we are going to win in time, and the friend of literary ladies ought to be also the friend of women generally.[52]

And the next month she added,

I can remember when antislavery was in just the same state that suffrage is now, and take more pride in the very small help we Alcotts could give it than in all the books I ever wrote or ever shall write.[53]

She was secure enough to state that "the observation and experience of the woman have confirmed much that the instinct and imagination of the girl felt and tried to describe."[54] She was certain, for instance, that inequality destroys marriages but also that marriages in her lifetime invited inequality. So long as women's lives outside the family were subject to political and social constraints, the choice of a husband loomed as an escape or refuge from exploitation and misery. At the same time, men also looked to domestic life as a refuge, and expect wives to play a subordinate, self-sacrificing role in the home. *Moods* begins Alcott's exploration of this theme; *Modern Mephistopheles* deals with it as Faustian melodrama; and *Little Women* treats it as domestic comi-tragedy.[55]

It is easy to perceive that the pattern of Louisa's own life underlies this theme of domination and subordination in marriage, but that is only a partial explanation either for the theme's persistence, or for her own lifelong spinsterhood. Much of the answer lies in Transcendentalism, which had elevated the search for individual identity to a holy cause. Louisa's fear of domination was a personal, psychological one, of course, but it also reflected a national concern with human freedom and individualism. The limits of Romanticism were as much a problem in life as they were in her fiction.

Adam Warwick, like Bronson Alcott, believed that proper education and spiritual development create stable marriages and happy families. He expresses this view in a remarkable drawing-room conversation about adultery and divorce initiated by Sylvia's older sister, Prue. In both versions of the novel, Prue tells the assembled guests that a woman in the neighborhood, Helen Chesterfield, "has run away from her husband in the most disgraceful manner." All the guests present have a say about the matter. Warwick argues in favor of preventive education. If he had his way he would

> begin at the beginning and teach young people that marriage is not the only aim and end of life yet would fit them for it, as for a sacrament too high and holy to be profaned by a light word or thought. Show them how to be worthy of it and how to wait for it.[56]

The practical Prue responds, "That is all excellent and charming, but what are poor souls to do who haven't been educated in this fine way?"[57]

Faith Dane then offers the pragmatic woman's rights answer. Modestly declining to speak at first, because she is a spinster with no right to talk about marriage, Faith counsels the hypothetical wife to "leave no effort unmade" to save her marriage. Failing that, she has "the right to dissolve the tie that has become a sin, because where no love lives inevitable suffering and sorrow enter in, falling not only upon guilty parents, but upon the innocent children who may be given them."[58]

Through Faith Dane Louisa makes a familiar feminist demand for the reform of marriage and divorce.[59] By the 1880s, certainly, divorce laws had become more liberal and Faith's arguments seem standard for progressive circles.[60] They were less so in 1861. Alcott herself was familiar with the demands of Woman's Rights congresses from the 1850s on, but she may not have fully realized how unacceptable these domestic reforms seemed to people like A. K. Loring, the first publisher of *Moods*.[61] In context of the novel, it is significant that Faith, knowing of the secret romance between Warwick and Sylvia, gave her approval to divorce in parlor conversation. She sympathizes with Sylvia, whispering in her ear, "Dear child, if you ever need any help that Geoffrey cannot give, remember Cousin Faith."[62] Faith offers both an assertion of woman's rights and a personal promise of continued support for Sylvia, her distressed sister.

The reform of nineteenth-century society, many felt, demanded the efforts of mature women who had taken the journey begun by Sylvia Yule, and who resisted "that ceaseless craving for affection" in order to develop their principles and live by them. That Alcott chose to reissue

Moods when she was a fully established author and an active figure in the Woman's Rights movement is of some importance. Her later novel, *Little Women*, deals more successfully with the reality of domestic life and reforms of it. *Work* relates the experience of single women in the world, but *Moods* dealt with the prelude to those experiences.

Alcott's first important heroine struggles to resist an untimely marriage and loses. Her fate in the first edition of *Moods* is death, by which, as Henry James insisted, "she puts her husband and everyone else in the wrong by dying the death of the righteous." But thirty years later the heroine comes to life, and strengthened by her experience. "For now she had learned to live by principle, not impulse, and this made it both sweet and possible for love and duty to go hand in hand."[63]

Louisa May Alcott never fully rejected her Romantic inheritance, although she moved far beyond the limits it imposed on her life and craft. The Transcendental impetus to find one's unique self-hood through a union with nature sanctified the Woman's Rights cause for her, as it did for many reformers of her generation. Rational, balanced community was Alcott's next demand for American women. Both the national union and the domestic union required reform and reconstruction when *Moods* was first published in 1865. The process was still incomplete in 1882.

CHAPTER VIII

Saving the Union

I set forth in the December twilight, with May and Julian
Hawthorne as escort, feeling as if I was the son of the house
going to War.

Louisa May Alcott, Journals, Dec. 1862

Louisa May Alcott enlisted in a Civil War being fought, as one
observer put it, "in the housewife's front yard."[1] Going to war was
usually reserved to "the son of the house," as she knew, but in this war
the traditional boundaries of sex, race and class were blown apart.[2] For a
moment, the careful distinction between public and private spheres of
activity lay strewn about the countryside like miles of splintered rail
fences. Louisa's deepest desires for independence and domestic order
were unleashed in the disorder of the 1860s.

She seized the opportunity for direct action, and out of her experiences fashioned an unusual, diverse body of fiction that included "hospital sketches," "camp and fireside stories," a novel, and several lurid
tales about men and women falling prey to the full range of human
passions. Her preparations for wartime service, the brief period spent
nursing, and the long recovery she endured, all combined to discipline
her talents and focus her energies. A connection emerged in Louisa's
mind, never to be severed, between the needs of men dying in drafty,
makeshift hospitals and the rights of women and slaves.

After the war, a generation of romantic reformers committed their
energies to reconstructing a rational order. For many of them, like Louisa,
personal and national needs merged together. They were sure that the
breakdown of family life, like the war between the states, was due to
inequalities between men and women, black and white, rich and poor.
Universal laws of balance and harmony must replace selfish, unrestrained individualism. Before the war, fashionable Boston took up the
cause of antislavery and considered the merits of "free religion" and

"universal laws" of progress and democracy—much as it had relished
"Conversations" on the "newness" a generation earlier.[3] The Alcotts and
their well-known causes were almost fashionable in certain parlors as the
war clouds gathered and then burst.

The Anti-Slavery Set

Family links to what she called the "regular anti-slavery set" were
especially crucial to Louisa's own feelings of self-respect and authenticity
in her year of "good luck."[4] Although the Boston gentry Louisa reluctantly depended upon for literary contacts had some "insolent" hostesses
(who she felt humiliated her), the true reformers, newly augmented by
young Hegelians and disciples of August Comte, valued the Alcotts for
more than their ability to "amuse" guests.[5] Among the reformers was
Franklin Sanborn, first introduced to the Alcotts by Ednah Littlehale in
1853; he became the family's loyal and intimate friend.[6]

In 1859 Captain John Brown spoke in Concord at a meeting organized by Frank Sanborn, among others. They had formed the New
England Emigrant Aid Society to help fugitive slaves and stop the spread
of slavery into the territories.[7] The Alcotts, Sanborn, and most of the
"regular anti-slavery set" raised funds for Captain Brown, and they
rejoiced when his small force moved against the Federal Arsenal at
Harper's Ferry, Virginia in hope of sparking a slaves' rebellion. Louisa
wished to do her part in the effort, but Brown was caught and imprisoned. Sanborn and Bronson discussed the possibility of Bronson's slipping into Virginia and leading a small party to assault the jail and free
Brown. Finally, they agreed to ask Thomas Wentworth Higginson, abolitionist leader and soon commander of the first free black troops, to lead a
rescue.[8] Every member of the reform circle tried to stay the execution, free
Brown, or at least bring comfort and medical supplies to the jail. Elizabeth
Peabody travelled to Virginia to beg the governor for clemency. It was no
use; John Brown was hanged on December 2, 1859. Concord went into
mourning for the liberator whose name became a legend in the battle
hymns of the Union army.

Thoreau, Bronson and Emerson participated in a public memorial
service for Brown. Louisa wrote a poem, "With a Rose that Bloomed on
the Day of John Brown's Martyrdom," humbly observing that "No
monument of quarried stone, no eloquence of speech, Can grave the
lessons on the land his martyrdom will teach."[9] Frank Sanborn helped
Louisa publish the poem in *The Liberator* one month later.[10]

The following spring Sanborn received a federal subpoena to testify
about his part in the conspiracy to free the slaves. In the middle of the

night a party of proslavery men dragged him out of bed in Concord and tried to take him away without a warrant. He fought them off, still in his bare feet, while his sister tried to stampede the carriage and horses to prevent his kidnapping. Both Sanborns yelled loudly for help and succeeded in rousing a crowd of angry Concord residents, including Emerson. They chased the would-be captors out of town and then formed a committee of vigilantes to protect Sanborn, with Louisa a proud member of the defense force.[11]

A schoolmaster as well as an abolitionist, Franklin Benjamin Sanborn was just Louisa's age when he offerred May Alcott a job teaching drawing in his Concord school. He was by all accounts a handsome, six-foot-four reformer, committed to abolitionism and woman's rights.[12] Moreover, he not only gave May a job and promoted Bronson's lectures, he also solicited Louisa's work for antislavery publications while reading and praising all her serious fiction. He was a member of the younger generation of reformers which included Moncure Conway, Sam May's daughter, Abigail, Ednah Cheney, William Torrey Harris, and Sally Holley, all of whom turned towards "positive" rationalism without losing their faith in "idealism."[13] Eventually, after the war, Sanborn became president of the American Social Science Association.[14]

In July Mrs. John Brown stayed in Concord with the Alcotts, who invited a group of supporters to meet her. It was an unforgettable experience for Louisa, who greatly admired the widow even though she drank her tea out of her saucer, and used the plainest speech."[15] Louisa dashed about offering tea and gingerbread to the other guests and tried to take special care of the antislavery "regulars."[16] The reality of slavery and the perils of the antislavery rescue missions were brought home even more graphically when she later heard Harriet Tubman describe her many trips leading fugitives out of the South.

That winter Louisa wrote a story about a mulatto hero who is loved by a white female abolitionist. *Atlantic Monthly* rejected the piece and prompted Louisa's acid comment that "Mr. L— won't have M. L. as it is anti-slavery and the dear South must not be offended."[17] James Russell, the editor, had earlier published Louisa's sentimental "Love and Self-Love," thinking at first it was a translation of a German romance.[18] The fifty dollar payment she received was as important as the prestige of being Emerson's literary associate in the pages of the *Atlantic Monthly*.

She kept writing in every spare moment while also doing the housework and sewing for the Concord household. In March of 1860 she stitched a ball dress for May, two riding habits for herself and her sister, and still managed to complete "A Modern Cinderella," with Anna and John Pratt as hero and heroine of the tale.[19] The story also included Anna's

sisters as "Laura", a cool blonde artist, and "Di", as inkstained intellectual who reads esoteric German literature, adores Carlyle, and scribbles
away at her own great works. Anna's fictional counterpart, "Nan", does
all the housework while her sisters selfishly develop their artistic talents.
But "Nan" is rewarded with a proposal from John, a household of her
own to manage, and domestic bliss while her sisters rejoice for her and go
off to Europe. *Atlantic Monthly* accepted "Cinderella" and paid Louisa
another fifty dollars.[20]

As the "irrepressible conflict" drew nearer, Louisa watched her
older married sister become ensconced in domesticity. At the same time
Louisa lost her most admired exemplar of Romantic rebellion. Thoreau
was only forty-four when he died on May 6, 1861.[21] In an advanced state
of tuberculosis, he had taken a brief trip west for his health with Horace
Mann Jr., Hawthorne's nephew. His disease was not arrested. He came
home to die, and had his bed moved downstairs so that friends, including
Louisa, Bronson, and Frank Sanborn, could visit him. Emerson gave the
funeral oration, and afterward Bronson read from Henry's books at a
service all Concord attended. Thoreau had arranged the exercises for
John Brown's memorial; now friends arranged them for his. He was
buried in Sleepy Hollow Cemetery, near the Alcotts' plot.

Thoreau had said that "the mass of men lead lives of quiet despera-
tion." Like Adam Warwick in Louisa's *Moods*, he wanted men to submit
solely to the control of higher principles, to obey no commandment above
nature's dictum that each living being be true to itself. John Brown alone
fulfilled the ideals Thoreau outlined in his "Essay on Civil Disobedience".[22] Louisa May Alcott never forgot Thoreau's message, although
she was ambivalent about its effects upon women left to tend the home
alone. She nevertheless felt her own heart marching to the beat of
Thoreau's drum.

She could not volunteer for war work immediately. Abba's increasing infirmity and Anna's preoccupations with her own family left Louisa
with enormous household responsibilities. As Bronson's earnings barely
supplemented her own, she furiously wrote short tales both for instant
cash and to lay away a supply of publishable fiction. May gratefully but
unquestioningly accepted her sister's self-sacrifice. Louisa sewed the
young artist's summer wardrobe and also took care of John Brown's
daughters, who had come to board with the Alcotts for the summer. She
put aside her literary work for a time and "fell to work at housekeeping."[23]
In the spring she was one of three hundred women sewing union uniforms in the Town Hall. Louisa, who had been wearing Anna's and May's
cast-off clothing as she stitched for the boys in blue, received a parcel of
new clothes from her sisters.

Women joined the war work in both the North and South. In the North, a network of female benevolent societies and women's rights groups became part of a vast civilian auxiliary to the War Department's medical bureau. The official title was the United States Sanitary Commission. In some ways a forerunner of the Red Cross, it had wide responsibilities during the Civil War for hospitals, relief work, and the transport of wounded from the battlefields. Its staffing and funding were all voluntary, and both its branches and more than 10,000 local relief societies were run largely by women.[24] In such cities as Boston, Chicago, New York, and Philadelphia, women held Sanitary fairs which raised millions of dollars for medical aid and relief. In December of 1863 New York City alone contributed $1,000,000.[25] Louisa contributed poems, stories, hand-sewn flags, and clothing for the Boston fair. In many of the larger cities, workers set aside regular portions of their wages for relief work. Theaters gave benefit performances. The Alcotts worked for every war effort, from fairs and benefits to the collection of household silver and jewelry that were sold for the Union cause. Louisa, without money to contribute, acted in benefit amateur performances.

Thousands of women, including the Mays, Sewalls, and Alcotts, presided over public meetings, drafted the constitutions and by-laws of various medical branches and relief societies, kept the accounts of the Sanitary Commission, and also wrestled with the endless red tape produced by the Quartermaster Corps and the Medical Bureau. Mary Vaughan, a friend of Louisa's and a collector of *A Record of Women's Work in the Civil War*, observed that men, who were "usually jealous of woman's extending the sphere of her life and labors, welcomed in this case her assistance in a public work."[26]

Both Dorothy Dix and Clara Barton supervised the processing of applications for hospital nurses. They rejected women they thought too young or romantic, who might "give way under the labors which required a mature strength, a firm will and a skill in all household duties." Housewives, mothers, sisters, and daughters were gradually recruited to serve the union. Louisa had spent a year impatiently writing, sewing, and teaching. She sent in her name as a candidate for Union nurse. If accepted, she would receive meals and twelve dollars a month from the government.

She was thirty years old when she received an acceptance letter a few weeks before Christmas; it instructed her to report to the Union Hotel Hospital in Washington. Louisa suddenly realized that she "had taken my life in my hand and might never see them all [her family and friends] again."[27] She reassured herself with the familiar mixture of self-denial and determined autonomy. It was necessary to "let out my pent up energy in a new way." Besides, there was the Union cause, and if that were not enough, her service would relieve the family of one more Alcott to "feed, warm and worry over."[28]

Hospital Nurse

Louisa's small trunk was packed by her mother and sisters with the aid of Sophia Hawthorne. The Sewalls gave her a small cash fund for her own expenses and for the relief of her patients. She set forth in December, arriving at the Union Hotel in Georgetown, Washington, where several Massachusetts women were already at work.[29] It was an overcrowded, run-down, and poorly ventilated building, hastily converted into a hospital. Washington was still thought threatened by Confederate capture, and Union troops were garrisoned everywhere. The windows of the hotel, already shattered, were half-boarded up against artillery fire, so fresh air was either nonexistent or a permanent cold draft on patients and nurses. Wards were improvised in old ballrooms, reception areas, and vacated suites; every room was heated separately by a small stove, and hot water was carried to each bed for washing wounds and bodies. The hospital used convalescent soldiers as orderlies, and contrabands (escaped slaves) ran errands, acted as waiters for the staff, and did enormous loads of wash each day. Bandages were often made from old clothes and had to be washed for reuse daily.

Louisa and two other nurses shared a small bedroom furnished with one wardrobe closet, their trunks, one chair, and a tin saucepan as a mirror. A small fire was fed with woodchips; oversized logs from the hotel woodpile had to be pushed into the small grate inch by inch. When no one was there to tend it, the fire went out and plunged the room into damp chilliness. The Sewall fund enabled Louisa to buy apples, crackers, and cheese to supplement the barely edible salted beef and pork rations that were accompanied by mouldy, hard bread and watered-down, boiled coffee. Louisa, "a vegetable product," as she called herself, lost most of her private food supply to an army of mice who lived in the wardrobe.

On her first morning she witnessed a death in her ward, nursed pneumonia cases, and viewed a man shot fatally through the lungs. She tried very hard to be "motherly" to her patients, succeeding even when her favorite charge was a handsome Virginia blacksmith named John Sulie, who was just her own age. The most gratifying aspect of patient care to Louisa was her observation of "manly" men who could be as sensitive "as any woman to their stricken comrades." There was a large measure of androgynous conviction in Louisa's feminism. Like many advocates of equal rights, she thought the problems between men and women could best be solved by the cultivation of "masculine" virtues in women and "feminine" virtues in men.[30] The war-wounded had clearly demonstrated their bravery and strength in battle; that they exhibited tender feelings for one another and wrote loving letters to mothers and sweethearts was fine proof to Louisa that her convictions were correct.

She felt "ignorant, awkward and bashful", but she found comfort in her ability to tend her charges.[31] She wrote long letters home about the hospital routine and described each patient and his progress or decline. The men responded to her care with small, hand-made gifts. Many wrote to her for years after the war and followed her records of the Union Hotel Hospital as they were published in *Commonwealth* (and later reprinted as *Hospital Sketches*).[32]

On a typical day she would be "up at six, dress by gaslight, run through my ward, and throw up the windows, though the men grumble and shiver; but the air is bad enough to breed a pestilence."[33] She would tend the fires and provide blankets and emergency aid for men whose wounds ached after a long, cold night. After a quick breakfast with the other nurses, she dished out rations for her wards, brought food for the "helpless boys," washed all the patients and supervised bedmaking and floor sweeping. Then she assisted the physician to dress the more serious wounds and changed minor bandages herself.[34] Louisa found the many amputations hardest to bear, but she assisted in the painful process of picking out bone fragments from shattered limbs. She always wished that the doctors would be "more gentle with my big babies."[35] In those days, prior to the modern division of labor in nursing care, Louisa and the other nurses found themselves in charge of the medication trays for their wards; they also scrounged up bandages and linen, which were always in short supply.

The afternoon began by serving the standard Union hospital lunch; "fried beef, salt butter, husky bread and washy coffee."[36] There was never enough to satisfy the men, so Louisa as well as the many other nurses wrote letters both to the soldiers' families and their own, asking for fruit, jams, pickles, and other niceties. Visitors might bring homemade wine or even bunches of grapes, which were especially cherished. The patients napped in the afternoon, but the nurses had no rest. They read to the sleepless, ran errands, and wrote letters for their patients. Supper at 5:00 P.M. was followed by the doctor's last round and by the nurses' administering medicines and sleeping draughts. Then, Louisa wrote, "night nurses go on duty, and sleep and death have the house to themselves."[37]

Within a few weeks she took night duty herself, thereby gaining a chance to tour Washington during the day. Once she visited the Senate chamber, but found herself too late for the session; she boldly sat in Senator Sumner's chair and imagined herself cudgelling his assailant, Brooks, within an inch of his life. It was an exciting city. Long trains of army wagons rumbled through the capital's streets with supplies for the front lines while pigs rooted en masse in gutters, all contributing to an air of distracted bustle that entranced Louisa. She watched the passing throngs with interest, and wrote letters for the folks back home in which she described officers in their tight, colorful finery, and tired "Billy Yanks" with knapsacks and muskets.

Her "colored brothers and sisters," she said, were more interesting than any of the officers and ladies who promenaded the streets. Southern "colored folk" were different from the few blacks she knew in New England. Warned "not to be too rampant on the subject of slavery," she repressed her most radical thoughts, but still felt affronted by men who "would put two g's into negro" and by nurses who "were willing to be served by the colored people, but seldom thanked them, never praised and scarcely recognized them on the streets."[38] Like the New England abolitionist, Miss Ophelia (in *Uncle Tom's Cabin*), one nurse sniffed at Louisa playing with a contraband baby in the kitchen. "Gracious, how can you?" She said. "I've been here six months and never so much as touched the little toad with a poker." Louisa kissed "the toad" in response.[39]

Louisa did not entirely dismiss the common view that blacks were obseqious, lazy, ignorant, and childish "Samboes". Yet she saw these characteristics as the product of slavery, and noted that they quickly disappeared in the face of respectful treatment by whites. Even more, she observed that "Sambo" was a shrewd disguise for slaves who knew how to use it for their own survival. She was nursing at the hospital on New Year's Day in 1863 when Lincoln's Emancipation Proclamation took effect, declaring that slaves in the rebellious states should be "then, thenceforth and forever free." The government would no longer "repress such persons in any efforts they may make for their actual freedom." Outside the Union Hotel the bells rang out at midnight and Louisa "threw up her window and cheered in answer to the shout of colored men in the street below. All night they tooted and tramped, fired crackers, and sang Glory Hallelujah."[40]

A few days before, the Union Hotel received many of the Fredericksburg casualties. Some 9,600 men had been wounded in General Burnside's unsuccessful frontal attack against Stonewall Jackson's and Robert E. Lee's entrenched forces.[41] The nadir of Northern hopes, it precipitated Lincoln's most serious cabinet crisis, one the Concord Alcotts followed anxiously in the newspapers. That winter the conflict had reached proportions never dreamed of in 1861.

Night and the Dark Spaniard

The war dragged on for two more years, but not for Louisa. By January she was a victim of one of the common diseases that claimed as many deaths in the Civil War as did the rifle fire and cannonades.[42] Scarlet fever, typhus, pneumonia, even measles and chicken pox raged in the wards. Doctors prescribed heroic doses of calomel for patients like Louisa, fearing that bodies weakened by fever would yield to pneumonia, consumption, and ultimately death. At first disoriented by the early stages of fever, Louisa refused to take her illness seriously, but the matron, without telling her, telegraphed news of her condition to Concord. Bronson came to Washington, and on January 21, following the death of the matron herself from typhoid pneumonia, took Louisa home. Dorothy Dix brought a basket of wines, tea, and a Bible to comfort Louisa on her feverish, semiconscious trip home to Concord.[43]

For three weeks a severe case of typhoid raged throughout Louisa Alcott's tired body. After glimpsing May's shocked face at the railroad depot and her mother's frightened demeanor at home, Louisa sank into delerium, haunted by nightmares powerful enough to linger in her mind after she woke. The fever had broken, but she found herself "queer, thin-faced, big-eyed."[44] The terrifying dreams suggest the conflicts that troubled her and influenced her writing for the next ten years. "Strange fancies" assumed the shapes of familiar people and danced about her.[45]

Like Abba, Louisa had an olive complexion, dark eyes and hair, perhaps a reflections of the Portugese ancestry on her mother's side of the family. Was it a fear of her own passionate self that haunted her? Certainly Latin figures were stock characters in the lurid romances of her day, but why should they appear to haunt her dreams just after her work as a Union nurse? It may have been that Louisa's experience of close, physical contact with male patients, many of them her own age and younger, reminded her of passions she chose to avoid. Perhaps she only partly denied the awakening of desire by emphasizing the maternal nature of her role in the wards. Then, too, she had met Dr. Winslow, a friendly Quaker physician who lent her books and took her to dinner.[46] Did these experiences, innocent as they were, evoke specters of herself as a witch, a woman whose carnal lust, once aroused, might be "insatiable?"[47] Unquestionably, Louisa felt that her spinster status at thirty was deviant. If not safely "on the shelf" in married domesticity, was she then inherently licentious?

Nancy Cott's observation that "a single conception of women's sexuality never prevails" in any one historical period is a useful reminder when considering the complexity of Louisa Alcott's feelings. By mid-nineteenth century, the evangelical Protestant views of womanhood had elevated woman's moral influence to a plane of passionlessness. Since sincerity was the cornerstone of female moral power, it followed that women's sexually passive behavior was not simply an affectation, but a true reflection of natural purity.[48] Louisa Alcott, however, was not an evangelical Christian. She was both a Transcendental product and a birthright Unitarian; as such she never denied the existence or the legitimacy of female sexual drives. Her opinions were close to those of Elizabeth Cady Stanton and Rebecca Harding Davis, both of whom acknowledged a healthy sexual instinct in women. "In these rough and tumble days," said Davis, "we'd better give women their places in flesh and blood, with exactly the same wants and passions as men."[49] Alcott agreed with Davis's demand for a single sexual standard in order to eliminate the sexual exploitation of women by men. In *Moods*, Alcott had Faith Dane insist that Sylvia should not yield to her passionate feelings for Adam Warwick because yielding would invite his domination over her untried and consequently weak sense of self. As we have seen, that same intrepid spinster (in "My Contraband") argues that male passion (both sexual and emotional) must also be controlled if a freed slave is to achieve citizenship.[50]

Sexual propriety, Alcott maintained, did not give chaste women any overriding moral power in society. Unlike her parents, Louisa did not believe that the good influence of one woman over one man eventually added up to social perfection. The rational feminism which emerged in Alcott—influenced by her experience in the Union Hotel—rejected romantic love because it inherently promoted a dominant-subordinate relationship between the sexes. Alcott's liberal Unitarianism moved rather easily into secular social science, affirming not only that both men and women possessed sexual appetites, but that all such desires could be domesticated. So tamed, the two sexes could pull evenly towards a balanced, peaceful society.

As Bronson had taught her, life-long domestication of animal passions began in the innocence of childhood; children loved to be good because it was "natural" for them to be so.[51] Sexual development proceeded through coeducation with plenty of healthy physical exercise (as opposed to promiscuous kissing), and from there through a long adolescent stage of travel and education for middle-class youths of both sexes. For poorer youths, public education and healthy exercise was followed by the mastering of work skills spiced with experience through "knocking about" a bit—but never far from the watchful eyes of middle-class reformers and benevolent guardians.

Ideally the pattern was not sexually differentiated, a point Louisa emphatically developed in the March family trilogy. If her "domestic dramas" hardly seem so radical, it may be because she wove liberal feminist programs into sentimental, literary forms. In her hands equal relationships between the sexes often seems like bygone rural simplicity.[52] In other stories she sensationalized the wreck of domesticity upon the rocks of inequality, separation of spheres, and surrender to unchecked passions. Her critique of Romantic individualism permeated all her literary forms—sentimental novels, gothic romances, even fairy tales.

The reconstruction of order in Louisa's personal life was as usual paralleled by the literary order she created through her writing. Her first effort, "with weak wits too tired to read much," was "Thoreau's Flute," a poem composed one night on hospital duty. Sophia Hawthorne admired it and recommended it to James Fields, the new editor of *Atlantic Monthly*.[53] He printed it, pleasing Louisa, but she was more pleased on learning that she had become an aunt. Anna Pratt, Louisa's sister, had given birth to a boy on March 28.[54] Hoping (like Aunt Betsey in *David Copperfield*) for a girl who would be her namesake, she nevertheless rejoiced and busily sewed shirts and gowns for Frederick Pratt as she convalesced.

Domestic jubilation over Anna's son did not subdue Louisa's dreams, for "the old fancies still lingered." She kept repeating the incidents in her nightmare to family and friends, all of whom prodded her to pick up her old life again. Frank Sanborn and Moncure Conway suggested that Louisa arrange her "war letters" into printable form and publish them in *Commonwealth*.[55] Like Sanborn, Conway was a friend her own age, committed to stripping away the irrational layers of Romantic illusion, revealing the "real, rational and unambiguous core of human life."[56] A former Methodist preacher and the son of southern slaveholders, Conway was now a Unitarian, a graduate of Harvard Divinity School. He was deeply interested in all cultural manifestations of the irrational and in finding means of exorcising demons through the exercise of the rational will. Conway was precisely the man to encourage Louisa to describe her experiences with war and death.

Unsure of any popular welcome for the letters which Sanborn and Conway found "witty and pathetic," Louisa set about revising them into *Sketches*. At the same time, keeping her eye on the surest source of income, she wrote another tale for Frank Leslie's *Illustrated Weekly*.[57] As A. M. Barnard, Louisa had just won a hundred dollar prize from Leslie for "Pauline's Passion and Punishment." Using Cuba as a setting, as she did for the opening scene of *Moods*, Louisa created a new Spanish heroine, Pauline, who unlike Ottila gains her revenge upon a heartless lover. Through her handsome young Spanish husband, Manuel, Pauline wreaks vengeance upon Gilbert Redmond, once Pauline's suitor, because he deserted her for an American heiress. Later, as this gothic melodrama becomes even more nightmarish, Manuel, whom Pauline has learned to love, falls in love with Gilbert's young American wife, Barbara. Gilbert kills Manuel, Barbara dies, and "Pauline's long punishment begins"—a life-long penance for surrendering to a fatal passion. Pauline glimpsed true love too late and lost it.

Louisa spared no gory detail in satisfying both the requirements of Leslie's readers and her own need to expose the perils of passion. The most telling element in "Pauline" is that both couples are married, but domesticity offers no peaceful haven. Beginning with secrecy and sexual deception, all four marital partners descend into bottomless passion from which light and reason are hopelessly barred.

In this story Louisa sought to exorcise the Spaniard, a dream figure who enters through windows and closets, and threatens her unprotected household. He appears again and again in her gothic tales over the next ten years, a literary manifestation of Louisa's struggle to protect herself and her household from the unlicensed chaos brought about by willful selfishness.[58] Murder, divorce, child abandonment, nervous disorders degenerating into madness—all these figure in Louisa's novels, and even creep into the *Little Women* trilogy, as we shall see. Without a rational, sexually egalitarian society, Alcott felt these abuses would invade daylight reality as well as midnight fantasies. They were the potential outcome of her own desires, and they were visible in the excesses around her.

Hospital Sketches

Reworking her letters into *Hospital Sketches* was a literary departure for Louisa, and it created several novel problems. Her solutions marked a turning point in her career. She had written fairy tales and thrillers before, but for the first time she was sending a well-bred, single young woman into a life-threatening, intensely masculine environment. The heroine was herself.[59]

The prospect of publishing this book troubled her in two ways. First, she feared revealing herself as the narrator of the sketches, having previously hidden behind pseudonyms (or behind the guise of an eccentric old lady, a Dickensian "character" for charity plays). She felt that her "strong mindedness", abolitionism, and critical condemnation of leisured excess were unfashionable. She had already constructed literary devices for presenting her opinions; these preserved her privacy and guaranteed her freedom to write for a variety of audiences. Second, Alcott was concerned about defying literary and social conventions by placing a young unmarried woman in an army hospital. As Dorothy Dix knew, only respectable married women could safely extend their maternal responsibilities to such places.[60]

As a result of these problems, her narrative voice in *Sketches* is at first uncertain. In the opening pages, in fact, she tries different narrative tones to disarm the reader and win a sympathetic audience. Nurse Tribulation Periwinkle, Louisa's fictional stand-in, is variously described as embarking on a bridal trip, a jolly boyish voyage, and an errand of mercy. The spinsterish depiction of the trip to Washington, on the other hand, is from the viewpoint of an eccentric railway traveller, encumbered by a "cavernous black bonnet, fuzzy brown coat, a hairbrush, a pair of rubbers, two books, and a bag of ginger-bread distorting the pockets of same."[61]

Eventually Louisa abandoned the eccentric costume and self-deprecating humor; Trib Periwinkle firmly declares herself a "woman's rights woman" and apparently takes courage as from Theodore Parker's defense of useful, happy spinsters.[62] Parker argued that a woman who had done everything for house and home was entitled to enter the world. Arguing that technology and free enterprise would one day render most domestic tasks superflous, he envisioned a day when all women would finish their domestic duties before noon and spend the rest of their day in good works. Although he lamented the rise in spinsterhood, which he saw as a national phenomenon, he believed it merely an historical accident brought on by the unrest of the time and by the prevalence of unequal, unhappy marriages. It was natural, even virtuous, he claimed, for some women to choose honorable spinsterhood over unhappy marriage; ultimately, the reform of domesticity and the expansion of women's social and political rights would restore marriage and the family again.

Louisa treated Nurse Periwinkle's unmarried state as if she were a fictional example of Reverend Parker's sermons. Yet Trib never declares herself a voluntary permanent spinster; instead, it appears as if the circumstances for her (inevitable) marriage were somehow not right. This impression is reinforced by the touching relationship between Trib and John Sulie, a fatally wounded Virginia blacksmith. Sulie is tall, handsome, and possesses all the attributes of true manhood. He never asks for the nurse's attentions, but when told he is dying, she volunteers "the gentle tendancy of a woman's hands, the sympathetic magnetism of a woman's presence."[63] Seeing his silent tears of pain and loneliness, "Straightaway my fear vanished, my heart opened wide and took him in, as gathering the bent head in my arms, as freely as if he had been a little child, I said, 'Let me help you bear it John.' " After that, he can touch her dress and grasp her hand without a suspicion of impropriety. He must die, of course, and does, uttering only one last cry of pain. Nurse sends a lock of his hair and his mother's wedding ring to his family. "Bashful and brave," he comes close to the childlike, yet fatherly portrait Louisa drew of Frederick Bhaer in *Little Women*. A true man will be tender-hearted as a woman, brave but not quite able to manage life alone. He needs a motherly sort of woman to be his partner and, as Jo says to Frederick Bhaer, help share his burdens.

Franklin Sanborn submitted *Hospital Sketches* to *Commonwealth*, and the editions carrying Louisa's letters sold out immediately, prompting both Redpath and Roberts Brothers to offer a publishing contract.[64] Louisa chose Redpath. Scarcely pausing as the proofs and notices of her book travelled back and forth from Boston to Concord, she also sent "My Contraband" to *Atlantic Monthly*. It was accepted, but publication in *Atlantic Monthly* paid better in prestige than in cash; its checks were slow to arrive, and Louisa depended more on Frank Leslie.

The publisher of "Pauline's Passion and Punishment" catered to a public that enjoyed sensational gossip, reports of murder trials, and lurid thrillers. He liked "A. M. Barnard's" work and offered the author a regular sum of fifty dollars for a guaranteed monthly story.[65] And so Louisa began a dual writing career. As Louisa May Alcott she published conventional domestic tales like "Cinderella," patriotic sketches and stories of the Civil War, poems, and occasional children's fiction. As A. M. Barnard she supplied not only Frank Leslie but the new Boston paper, *Flag of Our Union* with thrillers.[66] Designed for family reading, *Flag* nevertheless featured blood and thunder tales of criminals, dope addicts, and fallen women. Its editor, James R. Elliott, eventually tried to persuade A. M. Barnard to yield to Louisa May Alcott's byline. But she was adamant and continued to produce pieces only under her assumed name. One of A. M. Barnard's stories, "V. V., or Plots and Counterplots," was eventually republished by Elliott in his dime novel series, but neither the three dollars per column she received from the newspaper nor the sixty-five dollars she eventually received for the exciting "Behind a Mask" persuaded her to emerge from behind her own mask.

The first edition of *Hospital Sketches* ran to one thousand copies, bringing Louisa five cents a copy. She was hardly going to become rich on patriotic works, but she sensed that a "respectable" literary career depended upon keeping her more lurid creations under the name of an unknown male author.[67] A. M. Barnard's regular income was welcome, but his work revealed fantasies unacceptable in a Concord spinster.

Louisa wanted to travel to Port Royal on the Sea Islands of South Carolina, where a substantial experiment was taking place in the contraband community.[68] The former slaves were producing valuable cotton for the Union and organizing themselves with the help of relief societies.

Louisa had hopes of teaching contrabands like her friend, Sally Holley, and sending letters home for another book. Sanborn warmly encouraged her: "Any publisher, this side of Baltimore, would be glad to get the book."[69] She privately exulted that

> there is a sudden hoist for a meek and lowly scribbler, who was told to stick to her teaching and never had a literary friend to lend a helping hand. Fifteen years of hard grubbing may be coming to something after all; and I may yet pay all the debts, fix the house, send May to Italy, and keep the old folks cosey, as I've said I would so long, yet so hopelessly.[70]

But it was difficult for the "scribbler" to reconcile her feelings of generous self-sacrifice with the resentment she also felt at May's easier life. Her fictional characters began to display their author's ambivalence about good and bad fortune. She still tried to accept hard times as character-building for herself, and easier times as May's natural reward for a sunny disposition and an amiable talent. On the other hand, she enjoyed her self-sufficiency and the dependency of her family; she could find no other way to justify her writing. While constantly asserting that she was no good for anything but "peddling her poor stories," Louisa continued to read the works of the great authors she admired, and snatched hours, sometimes days, to rework *Moods* and plot out a new book, *Work*.[71]

Like many other women, she was discovering a new freedom through her work and was unsure of her right to say so. And also like others, she avoided the dangers of her own passion in a sexually unequal society by channeling her feelings into work. In her own lifetime, women emerged as writers, painters, and sculptors in unprecedented numbers. Louisa wrote about them. Still other women found outlets in the women's rights movement, in teaching, and in relief work of all kinds; these too she described in fiction. All of Louisa's respectable heroines achieved a precarious balance between reason and desire through some form of self-sacrifice. Either they gave up their talents for home and family, or they remained single and developed their gifts for art, music, or suffering.[72]

Only a spinster, Louisa felt, could take advantage of the opportunities newly won by women. Alcott was not a Margaret Fuller; she had a well-known family to judge her actions even as she provided for them. If her career as a respectable author depended upon her celibacy, however, it did not preclude gorgeously passionate heroines who dared the most outrageous acts in compensation for their betrayal or exploitation as women.

Whether her stories depicted lurid fallen women or saintly sacrificing heroines, Louisa advised her female readers to beware of marriage unless by upbringing and temperament they felt suited to domesticity. Marriage, she felt, depended upon women who found fulfillment of others' needs to be the satisfaction of their own. Unfortunately, female self-sacrifice was rarely reciprocated; the unchecked drive of willful men to possess and dominate might still be the ruination of an unsuspecting bride. Louisa now believed, like many feminists, that the great age of Romanticism unwittingly promoted excessive individualism, especially in men. A superman was as dangerous to a woman's precarious sense of self as an overt, rapacious scoundrel in Louisa's melodramas. The harm to society at large was as great as the harm done to individual women. The Civil War was proof of that.

Bronson Alcott's new circle of admirers, which included Cheney, Sanborn, Conway, and William Torrey Harris, agreed with him that human beings went through an animal-like stage in childhood and then through a barbarous stage of adolescence to reach the highest stage of civilization in mature adulthood. This analysis has led to assume Bronson that Louisa's and Anna's childish temper resulted from animal passions overwhelming their immature moral senses. By the late 1850s and 1860s this view of personal development was being tempered by the ideas of Hegel and Comte. "Scientific" observations refined the somewhat crude older theory, resulting in a "progressive" understanding of social development that united prison reformers, educators, and feminists. Every individual needed a properly developed moral censor within himself or herself. A loving, firm, homelike atmosphere with regular routine and gentle discipline might restore even the most hopelessly insane person to sanity. Remorse in the most hideous criminal, fallen woman or delinquent child was happy evidence that the germ of moral sense still survived, yearning to be strengthened by loving surrogate parents. By the 1870s Louisa May Alcott would expand her concept of a surrogate family to include public regulatory institutions.[73]

By midcentury, Louisa's writings contained countless humorous remarks about "disciples of Hegel" and "secesh" ministers who thought themselves cultivated if they "quoted Emerson and Carlyle."[74] Nevertheless, she was influenced by these new reform circles quite as much as by the old Concord band. Bronson's public lectures, including those delivered at Harvard in 1853 and Yale in 1856, not only won admirers like Cheney, Sanborn, Conway and Harris, but also helped shape the late nineteenth-century reform movement. Louisa May Alcott incorporated their ideas because she shared them.[75] The new faith in regulatory institutions emerged from the same observations of individual and social malaise that Louisa portrayed in the 1850s and 1860s. However startling the combination of Hegel and Comte may appear, William Leach is right that "both these philosophical systems, as they took shape in the minds of many feminists, tended ultimately to lead to the same intellectual consequences."[76] Virtually all American reformers came to believe that unchecked individualism must yield to community interests.

The reformers were a remarkably close-knit group. William Torrey Harris, the St. Louis Hegelian and a friend and host of Bronson on his western tours, was also the teacher of Anna Brackett.[77] In turn, Louisa recommend Brackett's famous book, *Education for American Girls*, in the *Little Women* trilogy.[78] W. T. Harris, who later with Franklin Sanborn wrote Bronson's biography, partly based his program for "progressive" education on the "model children," as Margaret Fuller once called the Alcott girls.[79] Cooperative, egalitarian marriage was perhaps the most important tenet of Brackett's book. Designed to promote more feminine traits in boys and more masculine traits in girls, thereby balancing sexual relationships, the book promulgated reform of the very evils described in Louisa's Civil War fiction.[80] *Moods*, the Civil War stories, the pseudonymous thrillers—all exposed the dangers of a "house divided." No wonder that the most frequent contemporary image for the Civil War was that of fractured domesticity, "Columbia mourning her lost children."

Hegelian notions of duty and self-sacrifice as the highest form of patriotism fit feminist concepts of domesticity perfectly. By cultivating familial interdependence and mutual self-sacrifice as social goals, one could argue that domesticity expanded into social housekeeping. It was a logical step from the earlier notion that an aggregate of individual virtues would result in a perfect society. Indeed, the destruction of American patriarchy could be viewed as a patriotic act, a necessary step leading to a truly democractic family. This view certainly appealed to Louisa May Alcott.

Louisa portrayed white women as slaves in bondage, as did feminists throughout the 1850s and 1860s. After the Emancipation Proclamation, Stanton and Anthony joined the League of Loyal Women; Louisa, Anna, and Abba were members already. These women hoped that their own emancipation would follow that of the slaves. Thousands of women worked unselfishly throughout the Civil War, demanding nothing, but many hoped that their devotion and skilled service would not be lost on white male voters.

Several underlying motifs create striking links between Louisa's Civil War pieces and the thrillers she produced for Frank Leslie and *The Flag of Our Union*. Paternalism masks incest and exploitation in her stories about slavery, while patriarchy conceals incestuous passion and sexual exploitation in her gothic tales of infidelity and marriage. In "An Hour," a Civil War piece, a beautiful slave girl named Milly masterminds a bloody revolt on one of the Sea Islands.[81] Her master, a young northerner who inherited his plantation, averts the massacre of his cruel stepmother and stepsisters by appealing to Milly for mercy and by guaranteeing immediate emancipation for all his slaves. Mistrustful of Milly's promise to stay the revolt, he provokes her proud retort, "Who taught us to be treacherous, and left us nothing but out own cunning to help ourselves with?" The theme of oppressed victims who seek revenge in treacherous schemes (learned from the duplicity of their oppressors), recurs constantly both in the Civil War tales and the lurid romances. When these victims of injustice do feel remorse, it is heightened by the compassion and love they themselves have been denied.

In "V. V., or Plots and Counterplots," by A. M. Barnard, a gorgeous dancer named Virginie falls in love and weds a wealthy young Scottish nobleman on his holiday in Paris.[82] Victor, her companion and self-appointed guardian, also loves her passionately and refuses to let her seek a more respectable life. He murders her young husband and threatens to implicate Virginie in the deed. They flee together, and years later Virginie appears with Victor's help at her dead husband's castle, disguised as the wealthy Widow Vane. She seeks to seduce and marry Douglas, her dead husband's cousin, and thereby win her former husband's fortune for her own little son, the issue of her brief marriage. Her scheme involves her in the deaths of Douglas' fiancée, Victor, and her own son. Her history is uncovered by Douglas, who threatens to imprison Virginie for life in an ancient tower. She drops a deadly poison from her opal ring into a glass of wine, and murmers as she dies, "I have escaped."

Brilliant, selfish, and guilty of multiple deaths, Virginie is still portrayed as a victim. A poor, vulnerable girl, the illegitimate child of a peasant and an aristocrat, she had only one chance for repectability. With that chance shattered by her husband's death, her fragile morality collapses completely and she becomes obsessed with revenge and greed. Her disguises are sumptuous, and her alternating feelings of deprivation and passionate love make her a fascinating heroine. Her deep love for her son makes the reader waver between condemning her machinations or excusing them because she only wants to provide security for the boy. Louisa cannot allow Virginie's proud spirit to suffer a lifetime of lonely imprisonment. Her suicide is not so much a punishment as an escape from further domination.

In "Behind a Mask," by A. M. Barnard, written at the end of the Civil War, a demure governess named Jean Muir turns out to be a dangerous seductress.[83] Much older than she appears, she uses her arts as an actress to appear as a fresh, innocent young orphan to her employers. Alone in her room, she "unbound and removed the long abundant braids from her head, wiped the pink from her face, took out several pearly teeth, and slipping off her dress appeared herself indeed, a haggard, worn and moody woman of thirty at least."[84] Louisa's own hair, the one proud vanity of her womanhood, had been cut from a yard-and-a-half in length to a boyish crop during her typhoid fever. Like her creator, Jean Muir is haggard from her years of struggle for independence in a hard world.

When Jean's plot to marry the young heir of the house is foiled, she quickly seeks the protection of an elderly, widowed nobleman next door. He is entirely deceived by her touching, feminine performance. She becomes Lady Coventry in a matter of hours, and in so doing finally wins the respectable security she needs. She then allows herself a moment of genuine remorse, and consequently promises to devote her life to the fatherly husband who adores her. For Sir John's sake, the affronted neighbors keep silent about Jean's real identity, and she is assured that "the game was won."

From "Little Genevieve" in 1856 to "Behind a Mask" ten years later, A. M. Barnard had moved from exiling her fallen heroine to a convent to allowing Jean Muir victory and even respectability. Robert, Faith Dane's contraband, assumed her name and declared, "I'll fight fer her till I'm killed." But by 1866 fallen women (who, like contrabands, are outside conventional society) are able to fight for themselves in Louisa's pseudonymous works. Although they still need nurturance, they not only redeem themselves, but triumph in the end.

The more respectable heroines who appear under Louisa's real name tend to put abolitionism ahead of feminism. Yet Louisa agreed with the Christian and idealist assertion that slaves are at least spiritually more free than their masters. In accepting a temporal and hence limited en-slavement on earth, they can still affirm eternal freedom in heaven. Women encountered a somewhat different problem. They were in bond-age not only to external authority, but also to their own feelings of love for their masters. Love usually entailed powerful enslavement in Louisa's thrillers, unless domesticated by a model family. In "The Marble Woman, or the Mysterious Model," the longest and most complex of her pseudo-nonymous stories, a dying mother leaves her orphan daughter to the protection of a reclusive bachelor sculptor.[85] Again, the absence of a nurturing family gives the heroine more scope to act, but also threatens her with arrested moral development unless a surrogate parent steps in. This heroine is called Cecilia, after her mother, but her guardian insists on calling her "Cecil," in effect treating her like a little boy and thus masking his incestuous feelings for her. Bazil Yorke, the sculptor, is far from the selfless Faith Dane. He demands that Cecil call him Yorke, and she obeys him while also addressing him as "Master." Cecil grows into beautiful young womanhood in virtual isolation from school, friends, or suitors.

Bazil treats her coldly but firmly as his apprentice, and they spend long hours together in his studio as he models a marble statue of Psyche, using Cecil as his unwitting model. The girl produces her own small masterpiece in a marble Cupid, after the young man next door (the only companion Bazil grudgingly tolerates for her) tells her the story of Psyche and Cupid.

Cecil loves her "master" and rejects a boyish proposal from her only friend. To stay with Yorke, she must agree to a permanent, affectionless apprenticeship to him, which she does. But fearing gossip about their cohabitation, Bazil finally proposes marriage to Cecil. He makes it clear that the wedding is a mere formality that will not alter their relationship. But once a bride, Cecil cannot control her real need for affection, or her developing awareness of more passionate needs. She is driven to take opium to render herself the passive "marble woman" acceptable to her husband. Yorke has contributed to her addiction by his rejection of her sexuality, and more specifically by giving her laudanum when she is unable to sleep. One night, having devoured all the pellets, she drinks most of the laudanum in her guardian's cabinet and falls into a stupor for two days. A doctor is summoned and informs Bazil that Cecil will survive the normally lethal dose because she is an addict and can tolerate heroic quantities of narcotics. Her generally passive demeanor actually masks her retreat into a dream world where she can satisfy her repressed passion.

The "marble woman" is allowed no easy solution to her problems. She promises to give up the drug and to work toward control of her emotional needs. Yorke's hidden feelings for Cecil emerge after he takes her to a ball and is humiliated by his friends' comparison of her cold beauty to the warmth of a pretty newlywed at the party. To prove the superiority of his possession, Yorke bids Cecil to act the role of a happy affectionate bride, which she does, while he pretends to be a loving groom; he finds the role strangely agreeable. But it is his turn to suffer. If passive self-sacrifice reaches its outermost limit in Cecil, her revenge lies in stating that she finally has no heart to be broken by Bazil's coldness.

Gradually the truth is revealed: Cecil's mother was once engaged to marry Bazil, who might have been her father. Her real father, Germain, a dissolute rake, eloped with Cecil's innocent mother. Unable to support a wife, he committed a murder. Later imprisoned, Germain escaped only to find his wife dead. Germain finally tracks his daughter down. Repentent, he tells her the truth before he dies. Yet for a brief moment Cecil had assumed that Germain was a potential, desirable lover. (Germain is only forty-two years old, Bazil thirty-eight, and Cecil seventeen.) It is only after Germain's death that Bazil and Cecil are able to live together as a genuinely married pair. Her real father's love has empowered her to transform her "master" into a loving husband.

Louisa aimed a powerful blow at the patriarchal notion that a husband can assume a father's power over a young wife. When Bazil finally seeks Cecil's mature love, he can gain it only by treating her as an adult equal. Nevertheless, the story presents a tempting, forbidden union, suggesting once again that domesticity can be dangerously close to incest.

Intentionally or not, the story also reveals Louisa's feeling that a father's validation of his daughter's sexuality is necessary for her to become a happy wife. Germain's brief wooing of his daughter awakens Cecil's sense of her own powers and enables her to trust them in winning over her husband. In real life, however, Louisa's diaries from the 1860s (and thereafter) describe Bronson as "the old gentleman." Bronson in fact did not seem particularly aware of Louisa's sensuality, although he praised her older sister's womanliness. Both of her parents increasingly accepted her as "the son" of the household, committed to providing both comfort and prestige for the family.[86]

By the end of the war Louisa's fiction provided her family with subsistence and small comforts, if not affluence. Richmond fell in April of 1865, but Lincoln's assassination that same month dampened the enthusiasm of victory in Concord and Boston. At home, Anna was expecting her second child, and on June 24, 1865 John Pratt Jr. was born. Married on her parents' anniversary, Anna had her second baby on the anniversary of her sister Beth's birth. Her father found Anna's happy domesticity a confirmation of her parent's efforts. He said of her, "I am sure she is one of the best women I have known, will all the wealth of heart her mother gave her. . . . she had every social exce-lence I may covet and is a treasure for every heart."[87] May too was a "fortunate girl;" she easily found patrons and admirers, and never resented temporary dependency because she was fully confident of rewarding her benefactors with her talents.

Louisa, however, turned her story of "Success" into "Work" before she could complete it. In July she prepared for a working holiday. Mr. William Weld had asked her to accompany his ailing daughter, Anna, on a year's trip to Europe as a nurse and companion. Bronson sent Louisa, but admitted in his journal that he would miss her "activity and her money, she having contributed largely of her means derived from writing to the payment of family debts and gladly will more as her ability shall allow. A serving visit will be of great profit to her and brings spoils for future literary labor."[88]

The war had drastically changed Louisa's status inside her family, confirming her decision to remain single. It also changed her place in society.

Louisa was not the romantic heroine of a poem, but she had seen the larger world and chose to live in it, leaving Concord to Bronson and Abba.

She would return to Orchard House for the next twenty years to serve the household when they needed her, but she wanted something more. To the Alcotts, Louisa's career was proof that she lacked an instinct for marriage and motherhood; without these, any overt sexuality was unthinkable. In the 1860s even most feminists thought that genteel women could not pursue both careers and families. Many working women were forced to combine both, but their lives were scarcely to be envied.

A career certainly allowed little escape from domestic self-sacrifice. Bronson, who had accepted the largesse of friends in providing a European trip when he needed relief, sanctimoniously approved Louisa's earning her own way with a "serving trip." He was so generous as to forego her regular contribution to his living expenses and debts.

She certainly experienced a full year of self-sacrifice in Europe as the paid companion of Anna Weld. Sailing down the Rhine and living in Swiss pensiones for Anna's health cures eliminated much of the sightseeing available to wealthier young women. But she found a romantic young companion, Ladislas Wisneiwski, an eighteen-year-old Polish refugee, during their stay at Vevay. She and Anna Weld listened to his exciting tales of fighting for Polish liberation and then fleeing for his life. His experiences contrasted dramatically with months of fetching shawls and pushing Anna about in a wheelchair, a genteel servitude Louisa could scarcely bear. Yet she considered "Laurie," as she called him, a mere boy despite his heroism; she had a family to support. She wrote home that his real name was unpronounceable, a cross between "two hiccoughs and a sneeze," but she remembered his dark eyes, curly hair, and his piano playing well enough to use him as one of the models for "Laurie" in *Little Women*.[89] When Louisa finally decided to leave Anna Weld after nearly a year abroad, she found a friendly guide around Paris in her Polish "boy." As Jo's rejected suitor and Amy's eventual husband, "Laurie" captivated *Little Women* readers. He confided in "sister Jo" just as Louisa claimed the real Laurie and another friend, Alfred Whitman, had confided in her.

In somewhat less than luxurious accommodations on the *Africa*, Louisa sailed back to America. In New York John Pratt met her at the dock and escorted her to Concord. During her absence the Alcott family had hired a housekeeper, but they dismissed her on learning of Louisa's return. So in addition to her family's open arms, magazine offers, and the debts for her English holiday, Louisa was greeted by household chores. Moreover, Abba was feeling old, sick and tired; she needed costly medical attention and careful home nursing all that fall. Louisa fell into her old routine; she nursed Abba, wrote "Behind a Mask," and even found time to act in Concord plays.[90] When Abba felt strong enough to move about the house, Louisa noted in her diary that "all her fine hair was gone and face full of wrinkles, bowed back and every sign of age. Life had been so hard for her and she so brave, so glad to spend herself for others. Now we must live for her."[91] Despite bouts of nursing at home, Louisa was fiercely determined to live alone and write in Boston. Only writing could take care of the accumulated bills and provide the housekeeping services that Louisa frankly dreaded. Again and again she confided to her journal that she was ill, stifled, and depressed in Concord.

Children's fiction was a reliable source of income for women writers by mid-century, and Louisa received an attractive offer from *Merry's Museum*, a popular juvenile magazine. She would receive five-hundred dollars a year for her editing skills and her contributions of stories, poems, and advice column.[92] Children's fiction had changed. In the earlier nineteenth century it had been generally pious, dull, and curiously unspecific about the details of everyday life. But by the 1860s Bronson's Romantic faith in the innocence of infants had become part of a popular sentimentalization of childhood. It helped improve the quality of juvenile fiction, at least in terms of rich detail and mildly adventurous plots. Even the Sunday School Societies, which published their own tracts and stories for children, agreed that lively fiction was a positive moral aid to parents. Secular publishers developed a large market for juvenile literature, and they encouraged their authors to write in detail about children's dress, food, and games.[93] Most important, the children themselves were now the central figures in their stories; adults were only accessory characters. Louisa May Alcott became editor of *Merry's Museum* and "A. M. Barnard" disappeared under her new aliases, "Aunt Wee" and "Cousin Tribulation". Those two worthies contributed stories, advice, and poems to the magazine.

By the time of the Civil War, childhood was accepted with equanimity as a stage in life, but youth or adolescence was increasingly regarded as a troubling period both for parents and their offspring. Most of all, adults feared precosity, the tendency of young people to grow up too fast and make impetuous decisions that would affect their whole lives. Also, some social goals were contradictory. The family was expected to teach young people about the land of opportunity outside the cottage door, but it was also supposed to preserve innocence by protecting youth from reality. Reading material for older youth developed quickly as an aid for parents in coping with this unsettling period.[94]

Thomas Niles, Robert Brothers' literary representative, suggested that Louisa write a girls' book.[95] It was not an idle suggestion, because Niles wanted to tap the market for girls created by popular writers of boy's fiction like "Oliver Optic". The author's real name was William

Taylor Adams, and like Louisa he was a member of a respectable Massachusetts family. In addition to boys' "Great Western Series," "Lake Shore Series," and "Yacht Club Series," he had also produced a promising girls' story about "Katy Redmond." His heroine was a self-reliant twelve-year-old whose exploits signalled a change in girls' fiction that struck a responsive note in Louisa.[96]

She considered the possibility of writing a two-hundred-page girls' story for Roberts Brothers. She was thirty-five years old and a little bored with writing the idealized versions of her own and her sisters' childhood adventures. Still, she wrote them easily and the Alcotts needed the money she sent home from thrillers, children's stories, and poems. After her European trip she had turned out a two-hundred-page adult novel, *A Modern Mephistopheles*, only to have it rejected for serialization in *The Flag of Our Nation*.[97] To keep up her apartment in Boston and the Alcott's home in Concord, as well as help May teach art in Boston and Concord, Louisa decided to try her talents at what paid best, a girls' book. She had earned the $1,000 she set as her goal in 1867, but now she needed spectacles to work and called herself "Minerva Moody."[98] She wrote to Abba, "Keep all the money I send; pay up every bill; get comforts and enjoy yourselves." She also sent regards to Bronson as "Plato" and asked if her father didn't want any new socks or other clothes.[99]

Bronson urged Louisa to accept Niles' offer for a story, and he assumed that she would move back to Concord to write it. He was anxious to please Niles, who had agreed to publish parts of Bronson's diaries under the title, *Tablets*.[100] In May of 1868 Louisa did move back to Concord, and in her old room at Orchard House, seated at the tiny desk her father had built years ago in front of her window, she began to write her girls' book.

She sent the first twelve chapters to Niles in June, and admitted to herself that "he thought it dull, so do I."[101] On July 15 her diary notes, "Have finished Little Women and sent it off—412 pages.[102] May is designing some pictures for it. Hope it will go . . . very tired, full of pain from overwork, and heart heavy about Marmee who is growing feeble." Robert Brothers gave her the choice of a few hundred dollars as a flat fee, or a percentage of the sales and her own copyright. She took a chance on the copyright, and years later wrote gratefully, "an honest publisher and a lucky author, for the copyright made her fortune and the dull book was the first golden egg of the ugly duckling."[103]

Little Women made the case for an enlightened family life as the best means for raising a new woman and saving the Union. By setting her story in the Civil War years she easily linked the cause of domestic reform to patriotism and abolition. Within a few years after its publication, the problem of uniting female rights and Negro rights split the feminist movement. Louisa herself insisted that the two were inseparable even if woman's suffrage withdrew for a moment in support of "the hour of the Negro".[104] She continued writing a series of domestic dramas. These gradually expanded the egalitarian nuclear family of *Little Women* into personalized, public institutions to educate, support and house Americans.

CHAPTER IX

Writing *Little Women*

I don't understand it. What can there be in a simple little story like that, to make people praise it so?

"Jo March," Little Women

Little Women portrays fifteen years in the life of the March family. As all her readers know, it is essentially the story of her own family and its domestic adventures, and contemporary readers could also recognize the author's friends and acquaintances. Perhaps the novel's greatest strength lay in Louisa Alcott's comfortable assertion that domesticity and feminism were not only compatible, but essential to one another.[1]

Beneath this conventional story, in which girls learn to sacrifice and conquer faults on their way to becoming true women, flows a subterranean river. Partly buried within the girls' everyday experiences runs a troubling current of sexual definition, an intrinsic part of the woman problem in Alcott's time. Does achieving one's individual identity, for instance, mean nothing more than growing up to be male or female? In the second chapter of *Little Women* the "Laurence Boy" enters the story as the March sisters' invisible benefactor. Laurie, who lives next door in his wealthy grandfather's mansion, in effect becomes a fifth sister. Jo is his sponsor, and together Jo and Laurie become the best loved and most memorable characters in all of Alcott's fiction. Introducing an adolescent boy into a mid-nineteenth-century all-female household was no small feat. Moreover at any given moment (in the first part of *Little Women*) it is difficult to tell whether Jo is a boy, Laurie is a girl, or vice versa; that is exactly the author's intent.[2]

Romantics and Rationalists

By mid-November of 1868, Louisa had been working on the second half of *Little Women* for more than two weeks, completing a chapter a day.[3]

She was pressed by devoted fans who wanted to know "who the little women marry." Louisa was determined not to marry Jo to Laurie to please anyone—"as if marriage were the only end and aim of a woman's life."[4] She was also tired of writing. For diversion she accompanied her father to a meeting of the Boston Radical Club to hear the Unitarian minister, John Weiss, read a "fine paper on Woman Suffrage," as she later recorded it. The "good talk afterward" pleased her as much as the paper did.[5] In fact she incorporated what some called the "rose colored view of the future" into *Little Women*.

The essential point of Weiss's paper was that women and men should combine in political as well as domestic arrangements. Emerson, who was in attendance, did not agree. Given to understand that most women did not like public life, he declared, that "women of refinement and culture" would shrink from engaging in political reform. Ednah Cheney countered that refined men were as indifferent to political activism as refined women. Nothing would be accomplished towards the "purification of politics" until "refined intellectual men and women" worked for political reform together. Neither Emerson, who had once spoken in behalf of mechanics and farmers, nor Cheney, who represented the new, educated and "refined" women reformers, had much faith in conventional political parties. There were others present, however, who wanted to create a reform coalition of laboring people, farmers and reformist intellectuals.[6]

The contested terrain was nothing less than the reconstruction of all American society. Behind the parlor exchange lay a major debate in Alcott's circle about the means and ends of such reform. Two perspectives represented overlapping generations of reformers. Louisa's generation, including Cheney, Sanborn, Harris, as well as Abigail May, Abigail May Alcott's younger cousin, had been inspired by the Romantic individualism of the older generation, who believed with Carlyle that great men make history.[7] The new historical perspective, which Louisa learned partly at the Radical Club lectures on the English historian Henry Buckle, was being disseminated widely through such books as John Lothrop Motley's *The Rise of the Dutch Republic*.[8] Cheney recommended Motley's book to the Alcotts and urged them even more strongly to read his *Historic Progress and American Democracy*. Opposing the view that individuals make history, Motley placed individuals *within* history and under the contraint of a historical law that governs "all bodies political as inexorably as Kepler's law controls the motions of planets. The law is Progress: the result is Democracy."[9]

Buckle and Motley argued that the history of humankind displays the unfolding of "order, symmetry, and law."[10] Persons are only instruments of history, having little or no power to influence the course of events. The progress of events is the progress of impersonal ideas and tendencies working through human society. Only the steady application of existing laws, not the intervention of individual "will," would create a new rational order in the world.

The proponents of each perspective claimed that democracy was incarnated in their viewpoint. The Romantic or Transcendental view of the "will" elevated the inner voice of each individual to a commanding position above the restricting laws and institutions of conventional society. Bronson Alcott, Emerson, Margaret Fuller, and Thoreau had all found the courage to be individuals and reformers in opposition to existing social mores. At the Radical Club Bronson still argued that "great men were always the prophets of an age to come; the world has to be educated up to them. Through the great minds, the revelations are made to the multitude."[11] Even in 1868 Bronson saw who conflict between this patriarchal conception of leadership and genuine democratic aspiration. He added Queen Elizabeth to his list of great figures, but insisted that she carried the sceptre of female culture and beauty, without which there would have been no Raleigh or Shakespeare. Perhaps for the first time in a public discussion Elizabeth I was credited with exercising "spiritual influence, rather than naked power over her subjects."[12]

From the point of view of Louisa Alcott, Ednah Cheney, and others, Buckle and Motley promised a different and grander democratic notion of history. The new rationalist progressives held that God "does not and cannot incarnate himself wholly in any one person, but must have all humanity for his organs. He works through the whole."[13] The question was how to reconcile personal will and responsibility, which none of the Idealists wanted to discard, despite their enthusiasm for new theory of social law.

Thomas Wentworth Higginson, very much a feminist in this discussion as he was an abolitionist, invoked the great Transcendentalist himself, Emerson, to reconcile individualism with the new theory. Emerson "had shown how the leader was fed from all sources and all other times were constantly pressing upon him."[14] As for himself, Higginson (who would later embrace an American variant of socialism) maintained that "the longer he lived, the more weight he attached to the general voice."[15] William T. Potter, a liberal Unitarian and a member of the Radical Club, also extolled the virtues of the new historical perspective. The Civil War, he said, was most emphatically "a people's war." Lincoln and Stanton, however great as individuals, were effective leaders because they represented the "courage, patriotism, and love of justice, in the heart of the nation."[16]

As for woman, she was the heart of the nation in this new view.[17] The universal laws of symmetry and balance held as true for social as for personal relationships. Theodore Parker had said something similar years before, so it was appropriate that a meeting of the Radical Club should end with a reading from one of Parker's speeches. Parker's words seemed to unite everyone in the room. "Everywhere," he had declared,

> in the family, the community, the Church and the State, we want the masculine and feminine element co-operating and conjoined. Woman is to correct man's taste, mend his morals, excite his affections, inspire his religious faculties. Man is to quicken her intellect, to help her will, translate her sentiments to ideas, and enact them into righteous laws. Man's moral action, at best, is only a sort of general human providence, aiming at the welfare of a part, and satisfied with achieving the 'greatest good of the greatest number.' Woman's moral action is more like a special human providence, acting without general rules, but caring for each particular case. We need both of these, the general and the special, to make a total human providence.

Granting men and women social equivalence, Parker had said, would redress the evils of history. Without it, "property must be theft, law the strength of selfish will, and Christianity what we see it is, the apology for every powerful wrong."[18]

After this inspirational conclusion, Louisa lunched with women friends and relaxed at the Women's Club. The next day, however, she was back at work, so inspired that she could scarcely stop to eat or sleep, going out only for her usual, solitary run.[19] Her thirty-sixth birthday came and went, her single gift a copy of her father's new book, *Tablets*.[20] She had already satirized the Radical Club debates in her "Jo's Journal" chapter in *Little Women*.[21] In that chapter Jo and Friedrich Bhaer attend a fashionable "select symposium" in New York, in which debates about "speculative philosophy" and "universal laws of progress" are presented the fictional philosophers, each riding his favorite "hobby."[22]

Despite the satire, the John Weiss lecture and discussion helped clarify Louisa's plan of action for Jo. Her heroine could not remain a child forever, even for so good a cause as liberty. The rationalist argument that society needed the harmonious blend of both male and female principles suited the author, who would not marry Jo to Laurie. Instead, Alcott created a situation in which Jo could share in supporting a home with a husband who could share in nurturing. The Radical Club discussions were only the culmination, after all, of domestic reforms which Alcott supported ever since the Syracuse Woman's Congress of 1852. They included coeducation, household democracy, woman's right to individual development of her talents, work, and of course, suffrage.[23]

Significantly, Louisa's first biographer was Ednah Littlehale Dow Cheney, who had sat with Bronson and his daughter at the Radical Club debate. Cheney found it necessary to remind Alcott readers, only twenty-one years after *Little Women*'s publication, that there had once been another "newness:" "the great question of the transcendental period was truth to the inward life instead of the outward law."[24] She compared Jo March in *Little Women* to Sylvia Yule in *Moods*, and observed that *Moods* fails because "the marriage question is not stated strongly, it does not reach down to this central principle."[25] A "double relation" such as Sylvia's marriage to Moor when she really loved Warwick could only be endured if the situation is "completed by fate, fate of character and overpowering circumstances."[26] In other words, Sylvia does not obey the laws of circumstance; she is in a "double relation" because she obeys only her romantic fancy. On the other hand, "stormy Jo," the creation most like Louisa herself, "is a real presence to us . . . whom we take to our hearts, in spite of her faults."[27] Louisa, like "Jo," was saved from Sylvia's fate "by the discipline of family work and love." Jo did not marry the wrong man and she did demand respect for her individuality and hard work.

Cheney had difficulty once again with the fact that Alcott, whom Cheney claimed was not much interested in "love and marriage," presented an important treatment of marriage from the liberal feminist perspective. She was well aware that Alcott had written a tribute to spinsterhood shortly before writing *Little Women*. Louisa wrote an advice column for the *New York Ledger* on "Happy Women,"[28] and Cheney discreetly observes that the professionals and artists Louisa portrayed were all "easily recognizable" as the sort of unmarried women Theodore Parker called a "glorious phalanx of old maids."[29] It seems likely that Alcott intended Jo's words to be taken seriously: that she preferred to remain unmarried. Readers, however, did not prefer it that way. Alcott was saved herself from making a phony romantic compromise by presenting a new kind of egalitarian marriage.

Cheney, like Frank Sanborn, was a family friend who knew both the models for Louisa's characters and the issues they dramatized. In fact, Louisa's journal entries for the year she wrote *Little Women* describe an expanding social life, full of new issues and friends.[30] In the New Year of 1868 she enjoyed more than Radical Club lectures with her friends. With her cousin Abigail May, she watched Fanny Kemble perform in "The Merchant of Venice." Afterward they went to the home of Mrs. Mary Parkman and dined with Fanny Kemble herself.[31] Mary Parkman and Abigail May, both Republicans and members of the American Social Science Association, invited Louisa to attend the New England Woman's Suffrage Association meetings. May and Parkman were (respectively) recording secretary of the Social Science Association, and executive board member. In its early years the association had a strong feminist orientation; this was the work in part of Caroline Dall, a found and close friend of Abba, who had read Dall's book on women and work. Sanborn and

William Torrey Harris were also leading Social Science members. They published numerous articles in its journals, and disseminated the rationalist views of Buckle along with their own more Romantic versions of Hegelian idealism. As she finished the last pages of *Little Women*, Louisa helped her father pack for his westward trip to visit William Torrey Harris.[32]

In November 1868 she also joined the New England Woman's Suffrage Association. Formed by feminists, including her own family and friends, the association favored the Republican Party as a vehicle for women's enfranchisement. As the widely recognized author of *Hospital Sketches* and *Little Women*, Louisa was an asset to the feminist cause. She attended the first organizational meeting of the Suffrage Association and listened to reformers debate the relative political importance of suffrage for blacks and women. Frederick Douglas, the famous black abolitionist and supporter of women's rights, told the group: "Woman has a thousand ways by which she can attach herself to the ruling power of the land that we have not." He urged his audience to put the cause of black suffrage ahead of women's rights for the moment.[33]

Lucy Stone replied that the women's cause was no less pressing than that of the Negro. But the political struggles of the previous year had convinced many that the coalition between women's and negro's rights was unproductive. In 1867 the national Equal Rights Association had been badly defeated trying to gain black and women's rights to vote on the Kansas referenda. Republican lack of enthusiasm for the women's cause had led to a shameful alliance between feminists and racist Democrats. Late in the campaign, a number of Republican men including Gerrit Smith and Henry Ward Beecher finally issued an "Appeal to the Voters of Kansas" that urged a vote for women's rights. It was too late. When both referenda failed, the united front of abolitionism and feminism collapsed.[34]

The New England Association attempted to repair the coalition by making votes for women its ultimate goal while giving priority to black suffrage. Julia Ward Howe was elected the first president of the Association; she made it clear that her right to vote could wait upon black male enfranchisement. In Februrary 1869, when Louisa had just finished the second part of *Little Women*, Congress passed the Fifteenth Amendment to the Constitution of the United States. It ensured the right of citizens to vote regardless of "race, color, or previous condition of servitude." It ignored the rights of black and white women.[35]

Like many other radical abolitionists in the woman's movement, Louisa tried to believe that universal male suffrage would inevitably lead American men to accept women's political rights. The women worked state by state, hoping to secure the right to vote from state legislatures. Louisa signed the "Appeal to Republican Women in Massachusetts."[36]

Lucy Stone wrote Sam May that the temperance reformers in the Massachusetts legislature would favor women's rights, but they did not, voting twenty-two to nine against female suffrage.[37]

Although Louisa devoted much of her energies to the cause of woman's rights over the next twenty years, her domestic fiction constituted her most important feminist contribution. She made woman's rights integral to her stories, and above all to *Little Women*. And she remained convinced that woman's rights were linked to universal human reform efforts despite the betrayals of party politics.

Louisa was never actively involved in party politics again, although she campaigned locally in Concord for temperance. Having sent Bronson to visit the St. Louis Hegelians, and settled Abba at Anna's house, the two "working sisters" left for to the Bellevue Hotel in Boston, where Louisa made the final corrections on *Little Women*. Owned and operated by Dio Lewis, principal of Boston's Normal Institute for Physical Education, the Bellevue Hotel was a haven where reformist women could exercise freely and learn the principles of preventive medicine. Living on the seventh floor, which Louisa called their "sky parlor," the Alcott sisters had the advantages of steam baths, elevator service, and lobster salad lunchons.[38] An active life and healthy food accompanied coeducation, household democracy, and woman's suffrage in the liberal circle of fashion. In her notes for "Happy Women" Louisa wrote, "Liberty is a better husband than love to many of us."[39] With May for company and plenty of writing to do, Louisa found herself both exhausted and happy.

How did the woman who hated to "pack for home" and leave a "quiet room" of her own manage to write the most exquisite tribute to American home life?[40] She was often lonely, in ill health from the effects of over-medication and over-work, and chose to remain unmarried. The answer lies in being close to the realization of her "dream of supporting the family and being perfectly independent."[41]

Louisa never questioned the value of domesticity; instead, she challenged the price ordinarily extracted from women like herself. On the other hand, Anna and John Pratt seemed ideally suited to marriage and home life; she portrayed them as Meg and John Brooke in *Little Women*. As a sort of private family joke, she memorialized the fact that John Pratt's family had been at Brook Farm by giving Anna's fictional husband the family name "Brooke." The "old people," as she called Bronson and Abba, lived in the same Orchard House cottage as their fictional counterparts, Mr. and Mrs. March—all provided for by Louisa.[42] For her part, Louisa wanted to believe that a democratic household could evolve into a feminist society. In *Little Women*, she imagined that just such an evolution might begin with Plumfield, a nineteenth-century feminist Utopia.

CHAPTER X

Reading *Little Women*

I may be strong minded, but no one can say I'm out of my sphere now, for woman's special mission is supposed to be drying tears and bearing burdens. I'm to carry my share, Friedrich, and help to earn the home. Make up your mind to that, or I'll never go.

"Jo March," Little Women, *Chapter 46*

The title of Louisa May Alcott's most famous book is taken from a commonplace nineteenth-century term. In the opening chapter, Marmee reads a Christmas letter from her absent husband to his daughters, which tenderly admonishes them to "conquer themselves so beautifully that when I come back to them I may be fonder and prouder of my little women."[1] This sentimental diminutive is puzzling in a feminist who was concerned with augmenting, rather than diminishing, woman's status. Such belittlement was part of the woman problem, as Alcott knew. The title appears even more puzzling when we consider that *Little Women* deals with the problems common to girls growing into womanhood.

Alcott had no intention of sentimentalizing the struggles of young women, so we must look elsewhere for an explanation of the title. We find one in the works of Charles Dickens, which Alcott read and took with her to the Union Hotel during the Civil War. For several decades Dickens had moved English and American readers to tears with his tender depictions, imitated but never equalled, of childhood woe. Dickens cared most deeply for the misery of exploited children, abused strangers in a venal adult world, but often remarkably capable of fending for themselves. Dickensian girls are particularly self-reliant, able to care for their siblings by the time they are "over thirteen, sir," as the girl "Charley" says to Mr. Jarndyce in *Bleak House*.[2] In *Bleak House*, in fact, the term "little women" makes a prominent appearance. Esther, ward of the generous, sweet-hearted Mr. Jarndyce, has the distinction of becoming the first well-known "little woman" in literature. Her guardian says to her, "You have wrought changes in me, little woman," indicating that she has widened and deepened his sensibilities and hence his philanthropy.[3]

Esther saves many people during the course of the novel, including the girl "Charley" whom she takes in and nurses through a bout of smallpox. Charley herself had contracted the disease from Jo, another pathetic Dickensian orphan. Inevitably, Esther comes down with smallpox, which leaves her face scarred and sets her musing about the meaning of "little woman."

Although only twenty-one years old, Esther has been close to death and realizes how short time is for "little women." No longer a child, yet not an adult, she finds life fleeting and precious. Dreadfully confused, she talks about the stages of her life, feeling herself at once "a child, an elder girl, and the little woman I had been so happy as." The problem, she thinks, is that the stages are not so distinct as she had once innocently supposed. Rather, they seem joined together and weighted down by similar "cares and difficulties," which are hard to reconcile or understand.[4]

When Louisa May Alcott employed the term "little women," she infused it with this Dickensian meaning. *Little Women* portrays just such a complex overlapping of stages from childhood to elder child, little woman to young woman, that appears in *Bleak House*. Like Esther in that novel, each of Alcott's heroines has a scarring experience that jars her into painful awareness of vanished childhood innocence and the woman problem.

Esther's job as part-time narrator in *Bleak House* is given to Jo in *Little Women*, but there the resemblance between the two characters ends. Jo comes close to bounding off the pages of her book; an American heroine, she has fits of exuberance alternating with sighs of half-chastened humility. Unlike Esther, and very much like her creator, Jo writes a story that succeeds miraculously even though she "never knew how it happened." "Something," Jo declares, "got into that story that went straight to the hearts of those who read it."[5] She put "humor and pathos into it," says saintly Mr. March, sure that his daughter had "no thought of fame or money in writing" her story.[6]

In fact, of course, Louisa May Alcott, unlike Jo, produced the story of *Little Women* in record time for money. As she reviewed the first page proofs, she found that "it reads better than I expected; we really lived most of it and if it succeeds that will be the reason of it.'"[7] Five succeeding generations have laughed and cried over *Little Women*. It may well be that each generation has its own favorite incidents and lessons. What remains indisputable is that every generation's critics and fans love Jo. What appeals to readers across time may therefore be Alcott's depiction of the woman problem, the conflict between domesticity and individuality that first presents itself at just the moment when little women move from girlhood to womanhood.

Themes in *Little Women*: Domesticity

The novel develops three major themes: domesticity, the achievement of individual identity through work, and true love. The same motifs appear in *Little Men, Jo's Boys, Eight Cousins, Rose in Bloom* and *An Old Fashioned Girl*. None has been out of print since first written. Together they comprise a fictional record of liberal feminist ideology, process, and programs from 1867 through 1886 in America.

From the outset Alcott established the centrality of household democracy, underscoring the importance of "natural" cooperation and mutual self-sacrifice within family life. The March cottage shelters the four sisters and their parents, all of whom love and depend upon one another. Even the family poverty, so reminiscent of Louisa's own, serves to reinforce democratic practice in the family. With the help of Hannah, who worked as a maid for Mrs. March in better days and now considers herself a "member of the family," all the women work together to accomplish household chores, making the most of meager means by sharing everything.

The virtues of mutual self-sacrifice and domestic cooperation, however, must be proven to the March girls before they can recognize how important such virtues are to their self-realization. Independent-minded and childishly selfish, the girls must learn how to shape their individualities in harmony with the interests of the family. In an important episode Alcott describes the tactics used by Mrs. March to win her daughters to a higher social standard.

After listening to Jo, Meg, Beth, and Amy pine for the "vacations" enjoyed by wealthier friends, Marmee agrees to release them from domestic duties for one week. She allows them to structure their time in any way they please. On the first morning, the neat inviting cottage is suddenly a different place. Meg, coming down to a solitary breakfast, finds the parlor "lonely and untidy," because "Jo had not filled the vases, Beth had not dusted, and Amy's books lay about scattered."[8] Before long, selfishness produces more domestic disasters, which increase alarmingly as the week progresses. Jo gets sunburnt boating too long with Laurie, and headachy from spending hours devouring her cherished novels. "Giving out" her ordinary sewing chores, Meg falls to "snipping and spoiling" her clothes in an attempt to be fashionable. Amy sketches lazily under a hedge and getting drenched by a summer rain, ruins her best white frock. Beth makes a mess out of her doll's closet, leaves the mess, and goes off to practice some new music. By the end of the day, she is left with "the confusion of her closet" and, "the difficulty of learning three of four songs at once."[9] All these small troubles make the girls grumpy and ill-tempered.

The experiment, however, is far from over. Excessive attention to self-pleasure produces a scarcity of necessities, including food. Emulating the little red hen, Mrs. March decides that those who do not work shall not eat. She gives Hannah a holiday, and the maid leaves with these parting words: "Housekeeping ain't no joke."[10] Unable to rely on the experience and counsel of Hannah and their mother, the girls produce a breakfast featuring "boiled tea, very bitter, scorched omelette, and biscuits speckled with saleratus."[11] Jo caters a luncheon for friends, only to discover that she can't make anything "fit to eat" except "gingerbread and molasses candy." So she sails off to purchase "a very young lobster, some very old asparagus, and two boxes of acid strawberries." She boils the asparagus for an hour until the heads are "cooked off" and the stalks "harder than ever."[12] She undercooks the lobster and the potatoes, and sprinkles salt instead of sugar on the strawberries.

In the midst of this culinary chaos, Beth discovers that her canary, Pip, is dead from lack of water and food. Her sisters, and the assembled guests, including Laurie, try to help, but to no avail. Amy proposes that they warm the bird in an oven to revive him. "Overcome with emotion and lobster," sickened by the death of her bird, Beth rebels. "He's been starved," she says of her bird, "and he shant be baked, now he's dead . . . and I'll never have another bird . . . for I am too bad to own one."[13]

Returning home to find her daughters miserable over the death of Pip and their failures as homekeepers, Mrs. March easily persuades them to admit that "it is better to have a few duties, and live for others."[14] This experiment, she says, was designed to show you "what happens when everyone thinks only for herself. Now you know that in order to make a home comfortable and happy," everyone in it must contribute to the family welfare.[15] Marmee has also proven to the girls that domestic work is real work, giving women a "sense of power and independence better than money or fashion."[16] She has shown them that home life becomes a "beautiful success" only if work alternates with leisure, independence with cooperation and mutual concern.

Although this episode deals almost exclusively with girls, Alcott integrated men into her vision of cooperative family life. Men too should benefit from and participate in this family experience, but only on the grounds that they respect the independence and equal authority of women within the home.

Accepting, even glorifying the importance of women's domestic work, Alcott emphasizes that men are homeless without women. Since the ability to create a home and sustain a family supercedes fame and money as evidence of success and civilization, it follows that women have already proved themselves in the world; thus their ability to extend their sphere is unquestioned in *Little Women*. Homeless men, despite wealth, wages and worldly experience, are motherless children. Meg's suitor, John Brooke, is attracted to the March cottage in large part because he is a lonely young man who has recently lost his mother. Laurie is motherless, which excuses most of his faults, and Mr. Laurence, his grandfather, has neither wife, daughter, or granddaughter. Mr. March alone has a proper home and knows his place in it, returning from the war to augment, but not supercede, Marmee's authority. He wholly accepts the female abundance around him, tending the flock of his tiny parish and leaving domestic arrangements to his womenfolk.

The question of whether men can be integrated into domesic life on feminist terms first appears in the relationship between young Laurie and the March sisters. Laurie starts out right. The gift of food is an excellent way to gain acceptance into an alien tribe. Meg, Jo, Beth and Amy, having given up their Christmas breakfast for a starving German immigrant family, are happily surprised by a compensatory feast sent over by the Laurences. Mrs. March has encouraged her daughters to pack up their hot muffins, buckwheat cakes, bread and cream early Christmas morning and deliver the meal to the hungry Hummels. After a full day spent giving gifts to Marmee and then performing a homemade opera for their friends, a fashionable supper of "ice cream actually two dishes of it, pink and white, cake and fruit and distracting French bon-bons" is exactly what the unfashionable March girls crave.[17] Three huge bouquets of hothouse flowers complete the Laurence boy's offerings. Under the guise of rewarding their self-sacrifice, he is courting them.

Laurie and Jo reverse the gift-giving and also their sexual personnas when Jo visits her new friend on his home ground, the "Palace Beautiful," as the girls call the mansion next door. Having spied "a curly black head leaning on a thin hand at the upper window," Jo throws up a snowball and promises to visit Laurie.[18] She suggests a visit from girls, because her sex ordinarily is "quiet and likes to play nurse." Laurie does not want boys to visit, he tells Jo, because "they make such a row and my head is weak." "I am not quiet and nice," she says, "but I'll come."[19]

In a moment, appearing "rosy and quite at her ease" in Laurie's parlor, Jo unpacks a maternal abundance of gifts, including Meg's blancmange, decorated with Amy's "pet" geranium leaves, and a basket of Beth's kittens to amuse the sick "sister." Jo's gift is her own womanly touch; she brushes the hearth, straightens books and bottles, and plumps Laurie's pillows. He has been observing the March sisters through their parlor window, "where the flowers are," and when the lamps are lit he can see them around the table with Marmee. It is this shy confession, coupled with the "hungry, solitary look in his eyes," that turns Jo from boy to little woman to foster mother in a twinkling. Skeptical readers are warned away from any other interpretation of the unchaperoned visit by Alcott's firm assertion that Jo "had been so simply taught that there was no nonsense in her head, and at fifteen, she was as innocent and frank as any child."[20]

A boy's acceptance of motherly abundance entices an innocent young girl to treat him as her sister and also make him, as Jo says, her "boy" or foster-son. An adult romance, emerging out of this familiar relationship, is fraught with incestuous complications. The worst one, from Jo's viewpoint, is that such frozen domestic roles preclude female independence within marital union; democratic households cannot be incestuous.

Alcott advances ideas about the place of men in the family that emerged out of her domestic experiences with her parents, despite her belief in universal laws of progress and democracy. On the whole, she does not paint a compelling picture of marital equality in *Little Women*. Instead she presents the possibility of educating and parenting a new generation of little men and little women. In the second part of *Little Women* Alcott describes the married life of John and Meg Brooke. Theirs is no deal egalitarian marriage, but then John Brooke was not raised by Marmee. The single wage-earner for his family, John provides a domestic servant but does not share domestic chores himself, except for disciplining his son in the evening. Meg is totally dependent upon his income both for household and personal expenses. Careful of her household accounting, she nevertheless often behaves like an impulsive child. On one occasion, she is tempted by a length of lovely violet silk while shopping with an old friend, Sallie Moffet. The silk costs fifty dollars, an enormous sum to the young couple. When Meg tells John that she has bought the silk, he responds only that "twenty-five yards of silk seems a good deal to cover one small woman, but I've no doubt my wife will look as fine as Ned Moffet's when she gets it on." Meg is overwhelmed with remorse at her own selfishness. Sallie generously buys the silk, whereupon Meg uses the fifty dollars to buy a new overcoat for her husband.

In a chapter called "On the Shelf," Meg's docility appears as her greatest virtue and her most serious domestic flaw. Docility is a fine quality in a daughter, even a sister, Alcott admits, but dangerous in a wife. Meg becomes dowdy and dependent, isolated in her little cottage with two small children. John spends more time away from home, provoking Marmee to confront Meg, but not her son-in-law, reminding her that "it's mother who blames as well as mother who sympathizes."[21]

Mother shares her domestic secret: a good marriage is based on mutuality of interests and responsibilities. Marmee herself learned this as a young wife, when after a hard time caring for her children, she welcomed father's help. Now, she says, he does not let business distract him from domestic details, and she remembers to interest herself in his pursuits. "We each do our part alone in many things, but at home we work together, always."[22] Marmee's advice is heeded; Meg pays more attention to the niceties of her dress, tries to talk about current affairs, and cedes to her husband some measure of child management.

According to Alcott, the reform of domestic life required restoration of a mutuality that had vanished with the separation of home and work. Yet of all the domestic advice presented in *Little Women*, this lesson carries the least conviction. Mr. March is the minister of a small parish and presumably home a great deal. John Brooke, on the other hand, is a clerk, far removed from his home and children. As we shall see, Alcott can only offer model domesticity in utopian settings where cooperative communities reappear in feminist forms.

Flying Up: Little Women Grow Up to be Themselves

When Louisa finished writing part two of *Little Women*, she suggested "Wedding marches" as a possible title. She changed it, however to "Birds Leaving the Nest," or "Little Women Grow Up," because she did not wish to suggest that marriage should be the focal event for growing girls. Instead she argues that girls who take trial flights from secure homes will find their own paths to domestic happiness. They might choose independent spinsterhood or some form of marital bonds that range from partial to complete "household democracy." For Alcott, sisterhood and marriage, though often contradictory, are equally valuable possibilities for women. Fully realized sisterhood becomes a model for marriage, not simply an alternative to it. Together, marriage and sisterhood guarantee that individual identity and domesticity will be harmonious.

Meg, the eldest and most "docile daughter," does not attain Alcott's ideal womanhood. Democratic domesticity requires maturity, strength, and above all a secure identity that Meg lacks. Her identity consists of being Marmee's daughter and then John's wife. Yet she and John are well matched. Neither really wants sexual equality in the dovecote. When Meg leaves home to work as a governess she accepts a three-year engagement period, dreaming that she will have much to learn while she waits. But John says, "You have only to wait; I am to do the work."[23] Alcott accepts the limitations of temperament and circumstance in Meg, as she does in all her characters. In *Little Men*, however, Meg's widowhood grants her the circumstances to develop a stronger side of her character.

Fashion provides a counterpoint to feminism in *Little Women*. Jo's strong sense of self is established in part by her rejection of fashion, which she perceives as a sign of dependency and sexual stereotyping. Amy, on the other hand, struggles against her burden of vanity, which has its positive side in her "nice manners and refined way of speaking." Amy must learn that appearances can be deceiving, whereas Jo must learn that appearances do count in the larger world. Meg's vanity may be one reason she is linked to Amy in the game of "playing mother," wherein Meg and Jo watch over their sisters "in the places of discarded dolls." Jo obviously rejects Amy early in their lives. Amy's flat nose, her chief "trial," as she says, is supposedly the result of careless Jo's dropping her baby sister onto a coal-hod.

Jo's lack of vanity about clothes at first conceals her pride both in her writing talent and in her exclusive relationship to Laurie. Laurie enjoys Jo's vivid imagination; it gives color and vivacity to his own lonely childhood. Keeping Amy out of pleasurable excursions with Laurie is one of Jo's main "faults." Left at home once too often, Amy burns a collection of Jo's painstakingly written fairy tales as revenge. Furious, Jo leaves her behind again when she and Laurie go skating. Amy follows behind and is almost killed by falling through the thin ice. Penitent, Jo vows to curb her temper and cherish Amy. Accepting the fact that she is not the only independent and talented member of the family is part of Jo's growing up.

Her notion that she is "the man of the family" is a more serious problem in the story. In a strange way this too plays itself out around fashion. Jo has her first serious encounter with Laurie at a neighborhood dance, where she is uncomfortably dressed up to accompany Meg on their first "grown up" social expedition. Meg's woes arise from her desire for fashionable frippery; she dances in overly tight high-heeled slippers that cripple her before the dance is over. Jo wears sensible shoes, but cannot dance because "in maroon, with a stiff gentlemanly linen collar and a white chrysanthemeum or two for her only ornament,"[24] she is pledged to hide the scorched back of her "poplin" gown. Therefore she must stand quietly or hide in a corner in penance for her habit of standing too near the fire. The Laurence boy is shy, a stranger to the neighborhood who has spent much of his childhood in a Swiss boarding school. He wears two "nice pearl colored gloves" and dances well, volunteering to polka with Jo in the privacy of a hall. Jo is suddenly aware that the gentility she rejects as too "lady-like" can be quite acceptable when it is "gentlemanly," or in other words, gender-free. Her regret at having only one good glove (the other is stained with lemonade) signals her growth from tomboyhood to womanhood in the feminist sense of the term. Jo is somewhat confused, having made a cause celebré out of being a sloppy, rough boy who clumps about in unlaced boots. Now she finds herself attracted by Laurie's "curly black hair, brown skin, big black eyes, handsome nose, fine teeth, small hands and feet." She observes her new model closely: "Taller than I am," says Jo, and "very polite for a boy, altogether jolly."[25] Finding her sartorial model in the opposite sex, Jo decides she can grow up to be a splendid woman with neatly laced boots and clean linen. She does not want Laurie as a sweetheart; she wants to adopt both him and his air of freedom and elegant comfort.

Meg can easily sympathize with Amy. Both love pretty things and are well regarded by wealthy relatives who appreciate their social graces and attention to niceties of dress. Mr. Laurence buys Meg her first silvery silk dress, a seemingly harmless and generous act. But because she is always dependent upon someone else's generosity, poor Meg must forego her next silk gown five years later. Meg elicits the reader's sympathy, however, while Amy's tastes seem symptoms of a selfish, superficial character.

First of all, Amy is too young to care about jewelry or fashionable frocks in the first half of *Little Women*. Nevertheless, she cares a great deal for them; she covets a schoolmate's carnelian ring, and preens and postures in front of her friends while exaggerating her family's lost wealth and status. Amy's pretensions lead her into trouble in the famous incident of the "pickled limes." Fashionable little school-girls have allowances, but Amy has none. As a result she has gone in debt to chums who treat her to the current delicacy—pickled limes. Meg then gives Amy a quarter, and the delighted girl purchases a bag of limes.

Mr. Davis, the school master, has forbidden treats in his classroom. Discovering that Amy has hidden limes in her desk, he calls her to the front of the room and humiliates her with "several tingling blows on her little palm." The author suggests that this incident might mark the beginning of Amy's maturation. Instead, Marmee and Jo rescue Amy by giving her a vacation from school. A small lecture by Marmee on the "power of modesty" does not alter the fact that Amy has had her burden lightened.

Later, at a charity fair, Amy is unfairly treated by rich and envious girls. This time she tries to "love her neighbor" and modestly allows her trinkets to be sold by a rival. Once again, this time augmented by Laurie and his friends (who have been commandeered by Jo) the family sails to Amy's rescue. They buy back Amy's trinkets and all the bouquets (provided by the Laurences' gardener) on sale at Amy's unfashionable booth. If this were not enough, Amy's Aunt Carrol, hearing of her niece's delicate manners, talented fancy work, and Christian forbearance at the charity fair, rewards her with a trip to Europe as her companion. Poor Jo, who engineered the rescue, is left behind, too unfashionable and forthright to be patronized. On one occasion Jo tells Amy, "Its easier for me to risk my life for a person than to be pleasant to him when I don't feel like it." Amy replies that "women should learn to be agreeable, particularly poor ones; for they have no other way of repaying kindnesses they receive. If you'd remember that, and practice it, you'd be better liked than I am because there is more of you." It is precisely because Jo is indeed more substantial that the author grants Amy a free holiday in Europe and eventually a wealthy indulgent husband.[26]

Amy and Laurie grow up together in Europe. Both are fashionable, inclined to indolence and coquetry. Both have talent, Amy for painting and Laurie for music, but only enough to please friends in polite salons. Neither is put to the test of earning a living. Both are also inclined toward "illusion" in dressing themselves and appreciating each other's refined taste. Their growing up, however, does require a degree of honesty: they admit that "talent isn't genius and you can't make it so."[27]

Despite the sniping and competition for parental love, social approval, and material rewards, Amy and Jo share one great loss that matures them both. The central tragedy of *Little Women*, one that generations of readers remember, is Beth's death in the final part of the book. Loving home the best, gentle Beth never wants to leave it; perhaps she would never have done so. She grows more fragile each year, and in her last months confides to Jo feeling that she was never intended to live long. Her short speech is also her longest in the novel:

> 'I'm not like the rest of you; I never made any plans about what I'd do when I grew up; I never thought of being married, as you all did. I couldn't seem to imagine myself anything but stupid little Beth, trotting about at home, of no use anywhere but there. I never wanted to go away and the hard part now is the leaving you all. I'm not afraid, but it seems as if I should be homesick for you even in heaven.'[28]

Jo's maturation is sealed by her grief over Beth's decline. The chapter entitled "Valley of the Shadow" sketches a household that revolves around Beth's room for one year. Everyone, including Beth, knows she is dying. Jo writes a long poem to her sister in which she acknowledges that true sisterhood is born in shared domestic experiences, and that such loving ties cannot be severed:

> Henceforth, safe across the river,
> I shall see forevermore
> Waiting for me on the shore.
> Hope and faith, born of my sorrow,
> Guardian angels shall become,
> And the sister gone before me
> By their hands shall lead me home.[29]

Wasted away, suffering with "pathetic patience," Beth's death releases her parents and sisters to "thank God that Beth was well at last." Beth's self-sacrifice is ultimately the greatest in the novel. She gives up her life knowing that it has had only private, domestic meaning. Only the March family knows and loves her sweet "household spirit."

Nobody mourns Beth more than Jo, her opposite in temperament as well as her partner in the bonds of sisterhood. Beth is shy and Jo is as frank and fearless as her fictional heroes. Beth never has any plans, and Jo is full of plots and dreams. Their commonality lies in the simple fact that both of them value their sororal relationship above any other unions.

When Meg becomes engaged and Jo feels she is about to lose her "best friend," Laurie declares that he will stand by Jo forever. Jo gratefully shakes his hand, saying "I know you will, and I'm ever so much obliged; you are always a great comfort to me, Teddy."[30] But Laurie turns out to be a boy, not Jo's sister after all. Jo's rejection of Laurie's suit is her first grown-up act, and her trip to New York to become a writer is her first flight into the world. Beth's death, through which she escapes the awful problem of growing up, triggers Jo's maturation. She does leave home to go "across the river." Jo's journey is the only fully complete one in *Little Women* and it involves her learning to tell true love from romantic fancy. She must do so in order to reproduce her lost sisterhood in a new, feminist domestic union.

True Love Found

The ability to distinguish true love from romantic fancy is a prerequisite for a woman's growing up in *Little Women*. True love involves mutual self-sacrifice and self-control, and requires the kind of man who can make the household the center of his life and work. Romance, on the other hand, is inherently selfish, passionate, and unequal.

Ultimately all the surviving heroines are paired off in true love. Jo, however, proves closest to Alcott's ideal because she rejects Laurie Laurence. At one point Jo tells Laurie that they are unsuited to one another because both have strong wills and quick tempers. Unpersuaded and unreasonable, the spoiled young man presses his suit, forcing her to tell him a harder truth: she does not love him as a woman loves a man, and never did, but simply feels motherly toward him.

Jo does not want to be an adoring adornment to a fashionable man's home. Nor will she give up her "scribbling" to satisfy Laurie. She knows he would hate her writing, and that she "couldn't get on without it." Laurie shared the secret of Jo's pseudononymous stories in the past, but he really views her writing as just another glorious lark. Laurie's proposal reveals just how much "scribbling" really means to Jo. If merely saving her "pathetic family" from poverty were her only motivation, she might marry Laurie and enrich them all. She might even produce leisured, graceful literature under his patronage. But she won't be patronized and she won't concede. "I don't believe I shall every marry," she declares. "I am happy as I am, and love my liberty too well to be in any hurry to give it up for any mortal man."[31]

Laurie stubbornly refuses to believe her, even though she has made perfectly clear that, like Louisa Alcott, she prefers "paddling her own canoe." Laurie insists that Jo has some unknown romantic rival in mind who will induce her to give up her foolish notions of independence and "live and die for him." Exasperated, her limited patience turns to defiance. "Yes, I will live and die for him," she declared, "if he ever comes and makes me love him in spite of myself, and you must do the best you can."[32] We do not know if Jo really means that she would yield to a "great romance," or is merely angry enough to tell Laurie that his worst "envious" fantasy is what he deserves. Possibly, Jo also recognizes passions in herself, however hard she struggles to keep them under control. She certainly experiences more than "moods;" she has genuine emotional depth and active fantasies, which she usually transforms into tragi-comic family operas or melodramatic stories.

In the nineteenth-century world of *Little Women*, there are only two alternatives following the sexual equality of childhood: romantic love or rational affection. With considerable regret Jo chooses the latter, because she must forego forever the equality she once knew with Laurie, her exuberant companion in childhood. Jo's decision, as Alcott knew, presents the reader with a bitter pill, for nearly everyone wants Laurie to win Jo. Yet the author has her heroine firmly reject any "silliness" from the start. She enjoys being Laurie's chum, plays at being his mother, but is never tempted to be his domestic companion.

It is precisely because Alcott makes Laurie such an irresistible boy-man that the reader must take Jo's refusal seriously. The youthful sweet surrogate sister develops into a handsome, passionate suitor. Moreover, Jo is physically attracted to Laurie, and frequently observes his handsome face, curly hair, and fine eyes. She hates it when he briefly ruins his romantic looks with a collegiate pose. The reader as well as Jo feels the power of Laurie's sexuality and the power he tries to exert over her. Yet if he calls her "my girl," meaning his sweetheart, she calls him "my boy," meaning her son.

Jo's refusal is not prompted by love for a rival suitor. In New York she works as a governess to children in her boardinghouse and scribbles away for the penny-dreadful newspapers. Soon she encounters Friedrick Bhaer helping a serving maid. Bhaer's life, unlike Laurie's, is not the stuff of romance. Forty-years old, "learned and good," he is domestic by nature and darns his own socks. He loves flowers and children and reads good literature. Moreover, he insists that Jo give up writing blood-and-thunder tales and learn to write good fiction. He gives her his own copy of Shakespeare as a Christmas present. "A regular German," Jo says,

> rather stout with brown hair tumbled all over his head, a bushy beard, good nose, the kindest eyes I ever saw, and a splendid big voice that does one's ears good, after our rusty, or slipshod American gabble. His clothes were rusty, his hands were large, and he hadn't a really handsome feature in his face, except his beautiful teeth; yet I liked him, for he had a fine head, his linen was very nice, and he looked like a gentleman, though two buttons were off his coat, and there was a patch on one shoe.[33]

Bhaer is a man Jo can love and marry.

A mature adult capable of raising his two orphaned nephews, he does not need Jo to mother him, although she is drawn to do so. Bhaer is more attracted to her youth and independent spirit. Nevertheless, he bestows his affection upon her by appreciating both her Old World "gemutlichkeit" and her American self-reliance. In a way he is Santa Claus, giving gifts despite his poverty to friends and servants alike. In one scene Bhaer buys oranges and figs for small children while holding a dilapidated blue umbrella aloft for Jo in the rain. Unlike Father March, who is a fragile invalid, Father Bhaer is a strapping, generous man.

There is no end to his domesticity or his capacity for cooperative self-sacrifice. Matching his paternal benevolence to Jo's maternal abundance, Bhaer does the shopping for both himself and Jo. As Alcott describes him, he "finished the marketing by buying several pounds of grapes, a pot of rosy daisies, and a pretty jar of honey, to be regarded in the light of a demijohn. Then, distorting his pockets with the knobby bundles, and giving her the flowers to hold, he put up the old umbrella and they travelled on again."[34] Contrast this fulgent account of a man who understands the "household spirit" with Laurie, who cannot even direct the maids to plump his pillows properly, or with John Brooke, who magisterially sends the meat and vegetables home to Meg (no knobby bundles in his pockets!).

Meanwhile, Laurie has returned from Europe with Amy, and they tell the story of their Swiss romance. Laurie has found a perfect mate in Amy, who will be very good at giving orders to their servants, having practised in her imagination for years. Theirs will also be an equal marital partnership, though somewhat different from that of Jo and Fritz, and very different from the frugal conventions of Meg and John.

Jo, the last sister to leave home, might never have accepted Professor Bhaer's proposal were it not for Beth's death. Fritz has found a poem of Jo's expressing the deep love and devotion she feels for Meg, Amy, and

Beth. We are "parted only for an hour, none lost," she writes, "one only gone before." Tenderly Bhaer declares: "I read that, and I think to myself, she has a sorrow, she is lonely, she would find comfort in true love. I haf a heart full for her."[35]

Bhaer has all the qualities Bronson Alcott lacked: warmth, intimacy, and a tender capacity for expressing his affection—the feminine attributes Louisa admired and hoped men could acquire in a rational, feminist world. As Marmee says, he is "a dear man." He touches everyone, hugs and carries children about on his back. Bronson, despite all his genuine idealism and devotion to humanity, was emotionally reserved and distant. Fritz Bhaer loves material reality, is eminently approachable, and values all the things that Bronson Alcott rejects, such as good food, warm rooms, and appealing domestic disorder, even though he is a "bacheldore" when Jo meets him.

Bhaer's love for Jo gives him courage to conquer the barriers between them, including his poverty and age, his foreignness and his babbling, unromantic self. They decide to share life's burdens just as they shared the load of bundles on their shopping expedition. Jo hopes to fulfill "woman's special mission" of which is "drying tears and bearing burdens," so that nobody will ever again call her unwomanly. She resolutely adds the feminist postscript: "I'm to carry my share Friedrich and help to earn the home. Make up your mind to that, or I'll never go."[36] She has her family duty and her work to keep her busy, while Fritz goes west to support his nephews before he can marry. The marriage contract they arrange is very different from that of Meg and John at the end of *Little Women*, part one.

The Model Society: A Harvest of Rationalism

Jo March and Friedrich Bhaer embark on more than a model marriage in part two of *Little Women*. Together they also set out to construct a model society which institutionalizes many of Jo's (and Louisa Alcott's) feminist ideals. Both Jo and Bhaer are keenly interested in new ideas and reforms. At one point they attend a symposium in New York City which Alcott based on her experience with the Boston Radical Club in the late 1860s.[37]

At this symposium Jo and Bhaer participate in a wide-ranging discussion in which "the world was being picked to pieces and put together on new and according to the talkers, on infinitely better principles than before." At first disturbed by the flirtations and by the disillusioning talk around her, Jo soon becomes enthralled by the debate. Speculative philosophy fascinates her, "though Kant and Hegel were unknown gods, the subjective and objective unintelligible terms."[38] Less delighted by the discussion, Bhaer defends older beliefs, standing "his colors like a man." Not the intellectual equal of the philosophers in the room, he nevertheless insists upon speaking up because "his conscience will not let him be silent." It is that conscience that Jo so admires. "Character," she believes, "is a better possession than money, rank, intellect and beauty and to see that if greatness is what a wise man has defined it to be, 'truth, reverence, and good will,' then her friend Friedrich Bhaer was not only good but great."[39]

Bhaer again reminds the reader of Bronson Alcott, albeit a transformed, lovable Bronson. Indeed, Louisa May Alcott had finally come to accept what she could of her father. She was delighted, for instance, with a discussion of "The Historical Views of Jesus" held by the Radical Club a few months before she began writing *Little Women*. Bronson had been villified in the Temple School days for taking similar views of Jesus, and Louisa was pleased that members of polite society "listen and applaud *now* what was hooted at twenty years ago."[40]

If Bronson moves through part two of *Little Women* idealized as Mr. Bhaer, he takes on a more "muffled" guise as Mr. March. Madeleine Stern observes that Bronson "would be atypical in a book on the American home . . . with his vegetarianism, his fads, and his reforms."[41] Hence Louisa divides him into two characters. The older Bronson surely resembles Mr. March, and in Friedrich we see the man he might have been with the aid of a rational, feminist reform movement. Bhaer's devotion to humanity, embodied in his acceptance of a "merry little Quadroon" at Plumfield and also by his brave speech at the "Symposium," are direct homages to Bronson.

Long ago she had wanted to praise him warmly for all those things she herself was now achieving—published writing, an earned income sufficient to support his family, and attention paid to the small, domestic comforts dear to Abba and her daughters. Now Louisa felt that "as I grow myself I begin to see much of the beauty of my father's life." His power, she said, was in "silent influence of character. Even so, we, his family, often misjudge and reproach him, unjustly perhaps, for he seems to live by a higher law than any we can see."[42]

Louisa's modified view of her father paralleled the emergence of her conception of a model society. In part two of *Little Women*, she remakes her father's experiment at Fruitlands into her own fictional experiment at Plumfield. A fortunate inheritance from Jo's former employer, Aunt March, enables Jo to turn the suburban estate of Plumfield into a "good happy, homelike school" with herself as headmistress and Fritz as headmaster. Laurie and Amy provide scholarships and Meg sends her son and daughter as model pupils, which ensures that the school will be coeducational from the start. Mr. and Mrs. March beam like benevolent household gods at the assembled, extended family as the book closes on Mrs. March's sixtieth birthday celebration.

As Jo watches John and Laurie playing cricket with the boys at Plumfield, she speaks to Amy in a "maternal way of all mankind." Jo, the tomboy, has attained the final stage of true womanhood; she has accepted maternal responsibility for the whole world. The conflict between feminist selfhood and domestic self-sacrifice has been resolved by expanding the home to include the world, making everyone equally responsible for human nurturance. If woman's rights are enlarged with her responsibilities, men's rights are also granted to them—but "nothing more," as Elizabeth Cady Stanton demanded in *The Revolution*.

Sororal bonds, Alcott argues, are forged between equals. A female family, therefore, is naturally democratic; while accepting conflict, like "birds in a nest," sisters must share household tasks, pool their incomes, and lend one another their personal treasures. The Marchs' household democracy is perfectly represented by Hannah's daily provision of hot turnovers, which warm Jo and Meg's hands on the way to work. Hannah is loved by the March girls, who understand that their domestic worker must get up early to provide hot turnovers for women who go out to work. Meg and Jo, even while they labor outside the home, have no special exemption from domestic chores in *Little Women*.[43]

Louisa made little attempt to conceal the parallels between her life and her fiction. The family name of March is a simple substitute for May. Unlike Fruitlands, however, with its disappointing poverty Plumfield is a feminist Utopia that promises an abundance of puddings, free fields to roam in, and festivals in apple-picking season. Having admitted the "female element" to full equality with the male, Plumfield's harvest will have "more wheat and fewer tares every year."[44] Lest the reader forget the bittersweet fall of Fruitlands, Louisa tucks in a last reference to Mr. March strolling about with Mr. Laurence enjoying "the gentle apple's winey juice."[45] Since Alcott admitted that Mr. Laurence was modelled on Grandfather May, we may assume that the Mays would smile approvingly on Plumfield. And unlike Sam May, who withdrew family monies from Fruitlands, the Laurence family provides scholarships to Plumfield.

True love is not denied at the end of *Little Women*; it is linked, as Fritz Bhaer put it, "to the wish to share and enlarge that so happy home."[46]

CHAPTER XI

The Natural Bridge

"Never mind: I'm tired of dolls, and I guess I shall put them all away and attend to my farm; I like it rather better than playing house," said Mrs. G. unconsciously expressing the desire of many older ladies, who cannot dispose of their families so easily however.

Louisa May Alcott, Little Men

Louisa May Alcott published eight popular novels and countless short stories in the next twenty years of her life. Nevertheless, her biographers are almost apologetic about her career following *Little Women*; some feel that success permanently imprisoned Alcott in sentimental conventions.[1] As we have seen, however, the first history of the March family did not depend on a sentimental formula; neither did its sequels, which nevertheless contributed to what Ann Douglas terms "the feminization of American culture."[2]

Alcott's later heroines, unlike their Adamic contemporaries, Tom Sawyer and Huckleberry Finn, cannot run away from civilization to nature; this fact underpins the sexual division of labor.[3] Domesticated by their mothers, little women in their turn cleanse and order the natural world. They must do so in order to gain half a day for themselves, as Theodore Parker predicted.[4] A New England regionalist, mistress of its vernacular, Louisa Alcott makes this perspective a national, even universal truth in her later works.[5]

If men return to the natural world to gain liberty, women create civilization to gain theirs. Alcott gradually accepted "progress" as the only solution to the woman problem. A progressive society would free women because it needs their labor and influence. She uneasily set aside the Romantic notion that only great men and women are the principal actors in history. Ordinary men and women also make history, she asserts, because impersonal historical forces work through common people. The heroines of *An Old Fashioned Girl*, *Little Men*, *Jo's Boys*, and *Shawl Straps* are talented women, Alcott's version of Emerson's exemplary social types.[6] But they are not Romantic rebels like Jo in *Little Women* or Sylvia in *Moods*.

A Natural Bridge

An Old Fashioned Girl, Shawl Straps, and *Little Men* form a natural bridge from the Romantic reform movement to a new progressive coalition for institutional change. *Little Women's* success gave its author access to a popular audience, one receptive to proposals for social change presented within the familiar construct of domesticity. Throwing off the "pink and white tyranny" of Alcott spent the next twenty years in an uneven battle against the exploitation of conventional female identity.[7] The idle rich and fashionable of both sexes, she claimed, were responsible for hollowness of heart, and consequently for a mistrust between men and women. She criticized sentimentalism and attempted to restore genuine trust by depicting true love, health and dress reform, and woman's right either to work and live independently, or to create egalitarian marriages. Moreover, she presents these reforms as "old-fashioned" virtues.

Alcott argues for woman's rights as nothing less than the restoration of democracy. Making women useful and dignified citizens will restore domestic tranquility in the largest sense. Grandmother's tales in *An Old Fashioned Girl* ignore patriarchal history and install in the minds of children a grand legacy of women's heroism in revolutionary America. The novel's subsequent action frees women to organize around a single national standard of values. Polly Shaw, the novel's active do-gooder, moves from girlhood to womanhood by leaving her family home and serving as missionary to the rich. Of course the March sisters had essentially accomplished that old-fashioned task in *Little Women* but Polly also joins a boarding house sisterhood—a foreshadowing of the settlement houses that spread throughout the United States between the 1880s and early twentieth century. Polly's supportive establishment is part of a genuine neighborhood; it gains the confidence of its poor inhabitants by sharing their troubles, and informs the rich neighbors of the horrors outside townhouse doors.

Abba May Alcott had begun with giving advice to the poor on chastity, sobriety, and thrift before shifting her concern to the social causes of poverty. Her daughter now moved farther, and asserted that causality lay beyond the individual greed of employers even as social remedies lay beyond the capacity of the poor to achieve prosperity through self-restraint and diligent work. Although causes as well as remedies lay beyond the individual, Alcott thought self-sufficiency could be restored by giving the less privileged an institutional helping hand—

above all, some experience in cooperation and self-government. Voluntarism might be restored if a sense of community, similar to that of village life, could be instilled in a modern nation of strangers.

Reformers like Alcott were aware that an integrated identity is forged within a political process; such a process could not be shaped, they thought, by an ignorant backward populace. In *Little Men, Jo's Boys* and *Work*, Alcott spelled out the gentry's role in reconstructing urban society. As her focus shifted, the personal battle between an individual's sinful nature and God's redeeming grace gradually disappeared from her fiction even as it disappeared from the American reform perspective at large. The essence of modernity (however reluctantly and unevenly digested) lay in a symmetrical fit between individuality and social role. If men or women felt alienated from themselves in the performance of a given social role, they needed the warm approval of caring authorities and peers. At the same time, Alcott's own experience had taught her that inner struggle shaped courageous, creative people. Romantic characters are therefore present throughout her later fiction; however, they are all "gentled" or "tamed," much as (she herself noted) a wild colt is domesticated through love and dependence upon its captors.

Ultimately the private space available to a Hester Prynne in her outcast's cottage or to Sylvia Yule on the river, or even to Jo March in the attic, disappeared. Alcott tried to assure her readers that Jo's long struggle with herself had ended; her many roles as author, housemother, sister, and teacher left her no time for personal rebellion or angst.

An Old Fashioned Girl

Little Women, Part Second went on sale on April 14, 1869. In one month thirteen thousand copies were sold at one dollar and fifty cents for each illustrated volume.[8] That summer, as a reward for their labors, Louisa and her sister May vacationed in the Canadian summer home of their cousin, Octavius Brooks Frothingham. A New York City leader of the Free Religion movement and a close friend of the late Theodore Parker, he had also contributed to the *Cincinnati Dial*, as had Conway, Sanborn, and Bronson Alcott.[9] Through the *Dial* Louisa was familiar with rational reform proposals and philosophies, and even had read a spirited review of Darwin's *Origin of the Species*.[10]

Frothingham was a perfect host. Louisa relaxed in the company of sympathetic liberal reformers, drinking tea, playing croquet, and going for long drives about the countryside. The Alcott sisters then travelled to Maine for another month, where Louisa learned that twenty-three thousand copies of *Little Women* had been sold.[11] Her royalties amounted to ten cents on each volume; she was almost rich and certainly famous. By

New Years Day the thirty-seven year old author had a check from Roberts Brothers for $8,500.[12]

That late summer and fall in 1869 are a chapter in Louisa May Alcott's life that sympathetic biographers never tire of retelling. It seemed that her worries were finally over. Having paid off every penny of the Alcotts' old debts, Louisa seized her chance to please *Little Women* fans clamoring for more stories. The result was *An Old Fashioned Girl*. If it sold nearly as well as its predecessor, she would earn the "competence" that brought independence.[13] Yet she was slightly mystified by her popularity, unsure to what extent her own character in the guise of Jo had created her success. Nor could she help recalling her readers' disappointment at Jo's refusal of Laurie. Quickly she revised the *Hospital Sketches* and even *Camp and Fireside Stories* to be reissued together by Roberts in one handsome volume. The tales of soldiers longing for home and kin would appeal, she reasoned, to readers of *Little Women*.[14]

Louisa settled Abba and Bronson in Anna's home for the winter, and rented rooms on Beacon Hill for herself and May. The circumstances for writing *An Old Fashioned Girl* were certainly better than the cold, lonely fourteen-hour days spent on *Little Women* and *Merry's Museum*. Louisa also enjoyed May's circle of convivial artistic friends. Encouraged by the presence of sister and friends, she wrote her new novel as a feminist critique of fashionable life. In its place she offered a program for domestic reform with an enlarged, more equal position for woman in society.

The freedom of May's circle contrasted sharply with Abba's state of mind, a constant reminder to Louisa of the contradiction between traditional domesticity and female independence. Abba was in fact ill, at times deeply depressed. A year earlier she penned a notation that might pass for humor in one of Louisa's domestic dramas, but followed by a series of similar protests and longings, it seems only pathetic. She wrote, "All alone! Alone! Alone! . . . I love all family employments but cooking—I think I should live on rice and apples if I lived alone—ha! I should have a cordial cup of tea once a day."[15] Louisa perceived that for her mother's generation of women, domestic duties were eternal. Moreover, the strained relationship between the Alcott sisters and their parents could only be eased if Louisa earned enough money for housekeeper services as well as full maintenance for herself and parents.

Abba wanted to live with Anna, to be cared for by her eldest daughter as if she were Anna's child. She spoke of being proud of her daughters, happy that they enjoyed "a larger better woman-hood" than she had known. But she added that it would be hard to find "a freer life than my husband leads."[16] This left Abba the only enslaved family member in her own eyes. Wistfully she hoped that "some arrangement be made for me by which May and Mr. Alcott can be cared for and leave me free."[17] In fact, she was no longer able to keep up with the housekeeping or the valet services attendant on preparing Bronson for his Western trips.

Louisa's own independence would only follow that of her family. It all depended on her earnings.[18] The task was now complicated by constant illness. Louisa's formerly strong constitution was now a memory; she was hoarse from a chronically sore throat probably worsened by heroic applications of caustic remedies. Constant neuralgia affected her facial muscles, and her joints were inflamed; one leg was lame. She did not yield to the pain, but scribbled away with her "left hand in a sling, one foot up, head aching and no voice." She added sarcastically, "Yet as the book is funny, people will say, 'didn't you enjoy doing it?' "[19]

A Missionary to the Rich

An Old Fashioned Girl is funny because the Shaw family's fashionable world is seen through Polly Milton's critical gaze. A "fresh faced little girl" of fourteen, graced with pretty brown curls and a "half-shy, half-merry look in her blue eyes," she is a country mouse come to the city to visit Fanny Shaw.[20] Fanny is two years older than her friend, a spoiled, affected lady fond of her own reflection in the mirror. Polly, dressed in blue merino, "stout boots, and short hair," stares at Fan's elaborately frizzed bangs, topped by a false chignon, and her suit with its big sash and panniers. Innocently she asks, "Don't you ever forget to lift your sash and fix those puffy things before you sit down?"[21]

Alcott quickly introduces the rest of the Shaws. Brother Tom, just Polly's age, is an unhappy, red-haired scapegrace who constantly cracks peanuts and stirs up trouble to get attention. Maud, aged seven, alternately roars and wails because she is a "fwactious" unlovely burden to Mrs. Shaw. That pale and nervous matron serves no other purpose than to consume faster and more fashionably than her social-climbing competitors. On one occasion she rejects her small daughter's (rare) hug because grimy little hands may soil an exquisite ensemble. Even kind, hardworking Mr. Shaw receives little attention from his wife, but he is usually oblivious to the emotional poverty around him, imprisoned as he is in the mysterious world of business. That leaves only Madam Shaw, who likes Polly but spends most of her time closeted upstairs—grandmotherly advice being unwelcome in the fashionable world.

A bewildered Polly notes that all the Shaws need love, but not one knows how to give or receive it. Lacking a sensible Marmee, the Shaw children must nevertheless grow up through all the complex stages of adolescence and young adulthood identified in *Little Women*. Grandma

Shaw can only offer the memory of a time when girls and boys were children until eighteen; then, having learned their chores at home, they left to create new homes for themselves. The narrative tension in *An Old Fashioned Girl*, unlike that in *Little Women*, does not stem from the relationship between external hardship and internal self-discipline, at least at first. Polly observes that the Shaws have no material problems, but gradually she and the reader learn that rich, fashionable society has hard times of its own.

If the Shaw household has invisible hands to do its domestic chores, the source of their money is likewise invisible, making it easy to fritter away a fortune. To Polly's amazement and discomfort, the purchase of one pair of bronze dancing slippers, a "necessity" for attending Fan's ball, eats up her spending money. She had intended to buy presents for her brothers, sister and parents. She consequently spends stolen hours making gifts for her family.

Without Polly, a motherly missionary for woman's rights in her "simple gray cloak and blue knitted mittens," the Shaws would continue without a chance of redemption. It takes eight years to complete Polly's mission. She visits the Shaws annually, setting a good example by growing up to be an independent woman capable of cooking, cleaning, dressmaking, and earning her own living by teaching music. She never gains much in the way of property, but she does rent a room of her own furnishes it with a shining teakettle and a kitten and canary who dwell harmoniously together by the hearth.[22] Polly domesticates both animals and people. Her cheery fire attracts the shivering, unloved, and unloving Shaws, who thaw out and become quite human, if not entirely lovable, by the end of the book.

The novel does not end with a happy, old-fashioned girl making her way in the world. Polly is lonely, conscious of the fact that her wages enable the Miltons to educate their second son for the ministry. She loves her brother, Will, but he is studying at college and she is alone in her room most of the week. "Yes, by the time the little teakettle had lost its brightness, Polly had decided that getting one's living was no joke, and many of her brilliant hopes had shared the fate of the little kettle."[23] As she listens to the carriages going by and glimpses the excited faces of wealthier girls going to the theater, Polly discovers in "the thicket that always bars a woman's progress" that "working for a living shuts a good many doors in one's face even in democratic America."[24]

At this turning point of the novel, Alcott introduces two remarkable, wholly different sewing circles. They illustrate the distance between women who work for a living and those who do not. Polly's landlady, Miss Mills, who is "old and homely, and good and happy," sits quietly sewing away.[25] Finishing a nightdress, she tells the story of little Jane, a seamstress unable to find work at a decent wage, homeless and hopeless, who leaves a suicide note and swallows half a bottle of laudanum. She writes her landlady (Miss Mills) that she has sold her few things for the rent, and finally defends taking her own life, "I hope it isn't very wicked, but there don't seem any room for me in the world, and I'm not afraid to die, though I should be if I stayed and got bad because I hadn't the strength to keep right."[26]

The woman who is truly independent has a home to share with others. Miss Mills takes Jane in, vowing that she shall have a home so long as Miss Mills has one to share. The unconditional sharing of home is again one of the most powerful links between individual identity and household democracy. Without loving cooperation, the individual can literally disappear without a tear shed by anyone.

Before Polly leaves her boarding house to join Fan's sewing circle, Miss Mills reminds the young woman of her vow to "bear a little ridicule for the sake of a good cause."[27] The cause Polly is pledged to uphold is "to help your sex as far and as fast as you could."[28] Her first task is to ask the fashionable young women to give out sewing for Jane to do as she recovers. Miss Mills insists that the rich may not really be hard of heart, but they are ignorant and careless of the poor. They pay low wages and do not trouble themselves to find out how much it costs working women to live. Rather than attempting to convert the rich, Miss Mills merely insists that Polly get from them what they will give: work for capable hands to perform.

Through her landlady Polly comes to know "a little sisterhood of busy, happy, independent girls, who each had a purpose to execute, a talent to develop, an ambition to achieve, and brought to the work patience, and perseverance, hope, and courage." Teachers, artists, writers, and sculptors, they don't care about "money, fashion or position," but instead help one another and rejoice in mutual successes.[29]

In the midst of a wonderful impromptu female picnic, the reader spies Louisa herself in the person of Kate King, a "shabby young woman" who has written "a successful book by accident, and happened to be the fashion, just then." Kate's contribution to the feast is "a bag or oranges and several big, plummy buns."[30] Polly runs out to get a pot of jam and cake, because Fan likes sweets; then coffee, milk, sardines and nuts appear, the contribution of the other women. Kate sets the example, eating with "such a relish" that the others fall to, and following her directions "take the sardines by their little tails,"[31] wipe their fingers on brown paper napkins, and enjoy a meal which nobody cooked and nobody served.

The specifically female friendship in the "little sisterhood" stands as one alternative to marriage for women who have special vocations. A sculptor, Rebecaa Jeffrey, and an engraver, Lizzie Small, live together and take care of one another in what Alcott refers to as "true Damon and Pythias style:" "They are all alone in the world, but as happy and independent as birds; real friends, whom nothing will part."[32] Polly shows them off to Fanny as examples of the emancipated life to come. Fanny remarks that sooner or later a male lover will part the two artists, but Polly vehemently disagrees and sees the two as dedicated to art and to each other.

By way of proof she introduces Becky's latest piece of sculpture, "a beautiful woman, bigger, lovelier, and more imposing than any woman I ever saw . . . strong minded, strong hearted, strong souled and strong boned."[33] Kate, the author, wants to give her a ballot box as a symbol, to which the sculptor agrees, and adds "needle, pen, palette and broom." But Polly's idea of a man's hand to "help her along" is rejected by the sculptor, for the new woman must "stand alone and help herself." The figure also stands without a child, for Rebecca Jeffries insists that the new woman is "more than a nurse." The statue rejects both marriage and motherhood as determinants of womanhood, insisting that "men must respect girls such as these and yes love them too, for inspite of their independence they are womanly."[34]

The model Alcott offers to a transitional generation is spinsterhood and the friendship of other dedicated women. They new woman may have a palette and a ballot box while also keeping the needle and the broom as symbols of her sex. Domesticity and working for a living, Alcott implies, are possible, even pleasurable, to free single women. Husband and child, rejected as accessories for the statue, might unbalance the new woman still struggling for individual identity in a world that makes wives and mothers wholly responsible for a family's domestic life.

In all of Alcott's novels, a woman who accepts the love of a man thereupon owes her first allegiance to childrearing. It is this fact which makes spinsterhood the preferred status for a first generation of woman's rights "graduates." Just when the reader considers the new possibility of Polly's happiness as a useful spinster, however, her personal charity case, the Shaws, diverts her attention to themselves. Mr. Shaw loses all his money; his family's only compensation is the knowledge that his failure was an "honorable" one. He has "gone under" as a result of relentless, impersonal forces of competition, Alcott intimates. The Shaws are thus thrust down into a world they scarcely knew except through Polly's stories.

She rescues them in just the same way that Miss Mills taught her to rescue little Jane, by helping them to help themselves. In the following months she teaches Fan and Maude to cook, clean, and make over their old clothes. Madam Shaw is dead by this time; Mrs. Shaw takes to her bed, wailing that she will soon be carried off to the poor house, so Polly must be mother and friend to the family. True love and Christian charity go hand-in-hand, and Polly's reward is Tom. Young Shaw braces up with the help of Mr. Sidney and the offer of a job out west from Polly's ambitious older brother, Ned. A hard year's work in the West turns Tom's carroty curls to a genteel brown, he grows a big brown beard to match his hair, and shows that he has disciplined his energies towards earning a living for his family.

Mr. Shaw and Tom are now a proper father and son; they talk about trade and commerce in the West and Tom admits that he used to be ashamed of his father for being a self-made man. Now the reader understands the source of Mrs. Shaw's frantic attempts to achieve social status and Madam Shaw's bewilderment at her children's life style. Mr. Shaw and his son must both start out afresh to climb their way into the market-place.

Alcott is poised on the edge of a social situation close to that depicted a few years later in William Dean Howells' *The Rise of Silas Lapham*. A self-made man one generation away from farm life, Mr. Shaw could return to that simple life, as does Silas Lapham after his failure. But Alcott does not fully share Howells' suspicion of the entrepeneurial class. She is more a Cory than a Lapham herself, comfortable in the genteel world Howell admires, describes, but only visits. Alcott, like her heroine Polly Milton, comes from a long line of illustrious ancestors; her branch lost its money, but not its pride. Fanny Shaw, like Miss Lapham, achieves a distinguished marriage, but here the resemblance between the two stories ends, with Alcott's novel the poorer for it.

As a fourteen year old "child", Polly Milton has the tomboy spirit of Jo March. She gets along "capitally" with Tom Shaw as a coasting partner. In this "child-world" Polly allows herself a "delicious go" down the snowy slope on a borrowed sled "with her hair blowing in the wind, and an expression of genuine enjoyment which a very red nose didn't damage in the least."[35] Her innocent enjoyment of coeducational sport, however, results in gossip about a flirtation with Tom. Reluctantly she gives up her outdoor freedom, and six years later takes only sedate walks with gentleman admirers.

Offered the example of a band of independent women, Polly draws back, suggesting that a man's hand is necessary to help the new woman along. Unlike Sylvia Yule, who takes a "masculine" voyage down river in *Moods*, or Jo who longs to soldier in the Civil War, Polly yearns only to dress up and go to the opera. She has neither nature nor war to provide a rite of passage into maturity. Almost impatiently (it seems), Alcott tries to make marriage Polly's great adventure by depicting Tom as poor and unremarkable. He wholly lacks the dark-eyed pathos of young Laurie in

Little Women, and he is scarsely more appealing later as a young western businessman. Nevertheless, he is part of Louisa's propaganda for rational feminist reform.

The Woman Who Did Not Dare

Alcott offers a new reform strategy, one familiar to readers of *The Woman's Advocat* and its successor, *The Woman's Journal.* Women must make the cause of their sex paramount in their lives because women's participation in all areas of life is essential to universal reform. Those who accept dependency in marriage because they are infatuated or because they seek higher social status or economic survival, are dangerous to themselves and to the rest of society; they perpetuate sexual injustice. Finally, it is every woman's duty, married or single, to form associations with other like-minded reformers.

An Old Fashioned Girl offers convinced feminists a strategic argument. Alcott uses a colonial and revolutionary dame, Madam Shaw, as a model for the stalwart independent woman, disdainful of vapors and lack of domestic skills. To the fashionable reader the author points out that business cycles may turn this year's belle into next year's sewing woman. She goes farther, noting that fashionable young women commonly become engaged several times and calculate the "respective values" of their fiancés; they should know, she says, that men do the same. Every bride must face the tawdry fact that her husband has probably discussed the fortune of girls he preferred, but "could not afford to marry." Such a system is not calculated to make either partner very secure, and marriages based on such a material base will certainly break apart in economic crisis. Romance and sentimentality are just disguises for the "business" of courtship and marriage in the Shaw's set.

Polly offers her friends the alternative of her love for Tom. The most important quality in a man, to Polly, is a warm generous heart. Having known Tom since they were both fourteen, and watched his moral progress, she knows that he is "one of the men who can be led by their affections, and the woman he marries can make or mar him." She would not save him if he were "weak or bad." Like Jo and Fritz in *Little Women,* Polly and Tom are friends and partners in adversity.

As a semi-private joke to reformist readers, Alcott entitles the chapter in which Polly and Fan wait for marriage proposals, "The Woman Who Did Not Dare." In 1869 Epes Sargent wrote a novel, *The Women Who Dared,* in which a woman artist proposed to her chosen mate and married him. The heroine manages to combine marriage, career, and later motherhood as well; she states (in the novel's free verse form', "Passion may lead to Love, it may lead away from Love, but Passion is not Love."[36]

Polly is much too bashful to propose to Tom, so she waits, fearful that he has fallen in love with a Western girl. Tom is fearful that Polly loves Arthur Sydney, but it is Fan who loves Sydney. Sydney is a "domestic man," and Fan must perfect her housekeeping and her temper in order to win a proposal. The friendship between Fan and Polly grows deeper and more genuine as they exchange confidences about their hearts' desire. Polly is able to make Fan see that loving a man despite his poverty is not enough to prove true love. Polly's feelings are genuinely unselfish; she is willing to let Maria Bailey, the Western girl, have Tom is she is "all he thinks her." Fan cries out that such an event would surely break her friend's heart, and Polly replies that she would "bear it; people always do bear things somehow."

Finally, Alcott proves that perfect equality and true love may admit sentiment as a touching embellishment. Tom proposes to Polly, and they agree to start "rather low down" rather than wait for Tom to make more money. Working together is the best way, as Polly knows from the example of her parents' marriage. Readers of *Little Women* trust Polly's family without a single scene sketched by the Milton fire; they are obviously kin to the Marches. The tiny piece of sentiment introduced at the end is a "small brown object which gave out a faint fragrance." Tom has been carrying a rose from the birthday cake Polly baked him the previous year. Keeping it carefully in his pocketbook, he explains that this "bit of nonsense kept me economical, honest and hard at it, for I never opened my pocket book that I didn't think of you."[37] Tom's dried momento contrasts favorably with a clandestine bouquet of hothouse flowers sent by a rake to sixteen-year-old Fan at the beginning of the novel. Her angry father sends back that token to the young man, who (with Fan's help) was making a mockery of true love and serious courtship.

The author ends her book with "a matrimonial epidemic," which she offers as a compensation for ending a "certain story as I like." This time she intends to pair off "everybody I can lay my hands on."[38]

Spinsterhood Forever: Les Dames Americaines

Having married off almost everyone in *An Old Fashioned Girl*, Louisa, her sister May, and a friend named Alice Bartlett—a triumphant trio of spinsters—escaped to Europe. They sailed March 31, 1870 on a French steamer, the *Lafayette*, bound for Brest and the start of their Grand Tour. Louisa's happiness abroad can best be understood through the letters and notes she turned into sketches and stories. It was partly her new-found financial security that prompted these remarkably open, feminist pieces. Gathered together they eventually became *Shawl Straps*, one of the volumes in Louisa's series, *Aunt Jo's Scrap Bag*. Already a sure success, twelve thousand copies of *An Old Fashioned Girl* were sold in advance, and the Boston *Transcript* printed a sketch of Miss Alcott paying glowing tribute to her "genius for naturalness," the day she sailed away.

Louisa detailed the itinerary of their tour in narrative sequence. They first visited Brittany, then France, Italy, Switzerland, and finally England. Alice Bartlett spoke French fluently, and Italian and German well enough to interpret for her friends. There was no shortage of money, and Louisa, who described herself variously as Lavinia, Livy, the Raven, Granny, and the Old Lady, enjoyed spoiling her sister and pleasing herself with odd bargains. In her stories, May was Matilda and Alice was Amanda, and each represented a type of American female independence. Together they proved that their countrywomen need "wait for no man;" instead, as Lavinia advised,

> Take your little store and invest it in something far better than Paris finery, Geneva jewelry, or Roman relics. Bring home empty trunks, if you will, but heads full of new and larger ideas, hearts richer in the sympathy that makes the whole world kin, hands readier to help in the great work God gives humanity, and souls elevated by the wonders of art and the diviner miracles of Nature.[39]

Louisa and her companions did not bring home empty trunks. In fact, what they purchase, pack, and unpack tells us much about them as individuals. We also enjoy what they see and what we see of them. Lavinia is immediately "edified" by the spectacle of a brisk, cheery widow of some sixty years "with the color of a winter-apple in her face."[40] Dressed in Breton costume, she hoists their big boxes up on her cart and trundles away with herself as carthorse. Then she shoulders their trunks one by one and climbs two steep flights of hotel stairs and smiles cheerfully at the Americans; their gratuities feed the widow and her many children. Everywhere, in fact, the travellers see peasant women keeping house, rearing children, knitting garments, tending shops, markets, gardens, and farm animals with ease and skill. Their labor, however, brought no more equal reward in Brittany than in America. Watching two men split logs and "one brisk woman" carry them in and pile them up, they find that her steady day's work is worth half a franc, while the men, who have paused to smoke, drink cider and rest every hour, receive two francs a day.

The Americans were perhaps most amazed at the contrast between the power and strength of older married women and the cloistered, child-like dependency of young unmarried girls. The European custom of arranged marriages, the elaborate property settlements between families, and the fact that Pelagie, the French bride in their pensione, was more interested in her trousseau than her fiancee both amused and horrified the American women. Pelagie looks forward after her marriage to wearing the camel's-hair shawl of a proper bourgeois wife. Lavinia senses, however, that Pelagie will be more independent as a wife than as an unmarried girl. Even so, Europe seems to offer nothing better than a poor choice between unmarried seclusion and married woman's exploitation. The Americans vow "spinsterhood forever."[41]

As they travel Louisa paints a comical but not demeaning picture of herself as an old maid who loves plain English beef and ale, angora cats, and cuddling by the fire to warm her aching bones. She describes Amanda, a young lady of considerable taste and sophistication, who enjoys eating snails, carries a heavy volume of Shakespeare about in her shawl-strap, and appears to possess no clothes though she is always well-dressed. This feat is much admired, especially since Livy is concerned with comfort and respectability, two mutually exclusive goals in women's dress, and Matilda is interested in finding the longest, most outrageously colored, six-buttoned gloves available on the Continent. Matilda's predilection for fashionable constumes, moreover, runs afoul on her appetite for art and art supplies. She must pack ribbons, hats, gowns, and gloves along with paint pots, brushes, and sketch pads into one huge trunk.

Wonderfully various activities attest to the fact that independent women can be frivolously feminine and boyishly active at the same time. They clamber up and down rocks, "do" the churches and castles, and spend one whole evening in France drinking mulled wine and manicuring their fingernails, "pruning and polishing" so that each achieved "ten pointed pink nails." Avoiding the Franco-Prussian war was a more serious matter, however, and they leave France to enjoy Switzerland and Italy, with Lavinia cheering the Prussians because they had supported the Union.

Reaching London, the companions part company. Matilda remains to study art, as did May Alcott; Amanda returns home to Alice Bartlett's family; and Lavinia, like Louisa, goes back to Concord. Livy's sorrow at their parting seems the most touching, because Amanda is "the friend to her mind" she has searched long years to find. But comforted by the example of a model Englishwoman, Mrs. Taylor, and recalling her previous visit with the Taylors and the Moncure Conways five years before, the now famous author enjoys a last trip to Aubrey House under different circumstances.

The English suffragists seem more sensible than the Americans to Lavinia, and with their "cheeful, well balanced minds, in strong, healthy bodies"[42] they seem likely to win the vote sooner than American feminists. Quiet orderly ways suited Louisa, and so did Mrs. Taylor's school for poor girls and Moncure Conway's Free Religion. She begged forgiveness for her unpatriotic support of English reformers on account of the "fact that reforms of all sorts had been poured into her ears till her head was like a hive of bees." The sight of London's poor, familiar to her from Dicken's novels, roused Lavinia to attend a Free Church where the congregation is of "all nations, all colors, all ages, and nearly all bearing the sad marks of poverty or sin." The preacher announced evening meetings at which mothers could meet and talk over the "best ways of teaching and training children."

This church was better by far, Louisa wrote, than the High Church "mummery" abroad or the "drowsy Unitarianism at home."[43] Moncure Conway described his South Place Chapel in London, the model for one of Louisa's fictional chapels, as one of "advanced rational free thought;" it welcomed Elizabeth Cady Stanton, Ernestine Rose, and Mary Livermore as guest preachers in the following years.

Only two factors kept Louisa May Alcott from semipermanent residence abroad. The first was her discovery that increasing lameness and constant attacks of neuralgia were not just the effects of overwork and constant worry. Her Grand Tour was a completely delightful holiday, except for the fact that her health did not really improve. As Lavinia says, in packing she "confined herself to a choice collection of bottles, and pillboxes, fur boots and several French novels—the solace of waking nights."[44] She travelled carrying a scarlet army blanket "with U.S. in big black letters on it" to hold her travelling medical chest. On a summer's day, travelling from St. Malo to Le Mans, she had one brief respite from pain. So exilharated was the Raven that "she smashed her bromide bottle out of the window, declaring herself cured, and tried to sing Hail Columbia, in a voice like an asthmatic bagpipe."[45] The description is funny and chilling at the same time, because Louisa discovered from a friendly English surgeon in Brittany that her pains were due to mercury poisoning from the old calomel dosing. He recommended iodine of potash to try and purge her system of the mercury, and Louisa, relieved at what seemed a simple and sensible prescription, followed his advice. Still, she needed opium to sleep.

Her ill health linked her to Anna's husband, John, who also suffered from neuralgia and had been dosed with calomel. In Rome, in a comfortable apartment on the Piazzi Barberini just a day before Louisa's birthday, Louisa and May received news from Boston that John Pratt had died. Louisa wrote her sister a long and heartfelt letter, telling her that John Pratt "did more to make me trust and respect men than anyone I know and with him I lost the one young man whom I sincerely honored in my heart."[46] He was only thirty-seven years old, and Louisa worried that her sister and her nephews would be without that secure competence she so desperately wanted for her whole family. She set to work immediately on a sequel to *Little Women*.

Little Men, a thoroughly American Utopia, was written at Number 2 Piazza Barberini in Rome, interrupted only by the great flood when the River Tiber overflowed its banks three days after Christmas in 1870.[47] Louisa's incentive to write *Little Women* had been the Oliver Optic series, which before the Civil War sold three million copies of the adventures of such heroes as Bobby Bright and Harry West. The moral in the Optic stories was a simple one: with integrity and hard work the individual triumphs over himself and social adversity. Without integrity and hard work the individual triumphs over himself and social adversity.

William Taylor Adams (the real name of Oliver Optic) spared no pains to paint a gruesome picture of the institutions designed to house, nourish and employ poor orphans, widows and elderly folk. In *Try Again*, young Harry West, "most twelve," is a resident of the poorhouse "situated thirty-one miles southwest of Boston."[48] According to its overseer, it is a place where boys should learn to know their place and how to treat their superiors. Young Harry is a modest but unflinching young democrat; daring to look his superior in the eye brings the wrath of the Squire down on his head. Harry is kicked out, and the rest of the novel consists of Harry's climb upwards once free of institutional constraints. All the Oliver Optic books are variations on Harry West's adventures. In every one the major adventures take place outside a conventional home, and the hero travels far and wide before finding domestic security. Home is the reward which at last brings his adventures to an end.

Even though William Taylor Adams himself saw the need for better houses and education for the poor, he never recommended cooperative institutional solutions. In 1867 his adult novel *The Way of the World*, suggested that one or two model tenements at cheap rents would serve as an incentive to "prudent men's investment" because such houses were sound, paying property.[49] The old-fashioned personal charity baskets delivered by the protagonists, Eugene and Mary Hungerford, enabled men and women to seek work with "well filled stomachs and well covered bodies, leading them to feel a self respect and a self reliance which refused charity."[50] Mary Hungerford herself had once known poverty, before her marriage, and she had endured the loss of a factory job because she was falsely accused of being a fallen woman. Never mind, said Adams, it is "the way of the world," and ultimately virtue shines forth and is rewarded. Mary had asked her future husband, in the face of her poverty and trials and the social conditions they both wished to change, "What kind of an institution do you propose?" He had answered, "No institution whatsoever."[51]

Louisa May Alcott, however, presents an institution so invitingly sugared and toasted that it warms the hearts of readers and coaxes them to accept democratic institutional responses to the problem of social inequality. Alcott maintained her belief that men and women could live together equitably and therefore harmoniously if they were trained to do so in their earliest years. Moreover, citizens accustomed in their youth to a prosperous equality, would help generate change in the larger society. A school for boys proved a socially acceptable device to promote the spirit of cooperation and democracy, but coeducation especially in a boarding school, was another matter. Alcott solved this difficulty by gradually introducing three very different little girls to the fifteen assorted boys at Plumfield.

As in *Little Women*, Louisa's special gift lay in her ability to create fireside, family adventures. *Little Men*, however, is set at Plumfield. Having established the estate's origins in the March family, the author smoothly woos her readers to accept a public institution in lieu of the private family. Polly Milton's missionary work began and ended with one family in *An Old Fashioned Girl*, but she identified larger problems than even the best, feminist family could solve. Chief among them was the increasing geographical and social distance between rich and porr. Rich citizens, never having worked, did not know the value of labor and stinted wages to the poor. The lower classes despaired, and in their distress became the "dangerous classes."

A ragged, homeless little chap, Nat Blake arrives in the first scene of *Little Men* at Plumfield's suppertime. He is immediately greeted by Meg Brooke's twins, Daisy and Demi, on the first floor of an old-fashioned hospitable house aswarm with boys. A delicious aroma tantalizes his "hungry little nose and stomach." To his left, just inside the hallway, a long supper table is laid with "great pitchers of new milk, piles of brown and white bread, and perfect stacks of the shiny gingerbread so dear to boyish souls. A flavor of toast was in the air, also suggestions of baked apples."[52] As Nat, an orphaned street musician, is welcomed and gradually won over by Plumfield's routine, the reader discovers along with him, that this model farm school raises most of the food that appears in scene after scene of nutritious abundance.

Unlike Fruitlands, this experiment has a resident experienced farmer, Silas, who is in charge of the students' outside work and all the tasks necessary to a profitable farm operation. It is never clear how much of Plumfield's income comes from tuition and how much from the farm and charitable contributions. We do learn that there are all sorts of pupils in residence. Some from very wealthy homes have afflictions related to their affluent backgrounds, such as greed, sloth, and in the case of poor Billy, feeble-mindedness resulting from his ambitious parents' stuffing their promising son with useless "knowledge." Others, like Nat and

Dan, bear the marks of brutal neglect. They are sensitive and inclined toward the petty dishonesties that have enabled them to survive in the world.

The domesticity that nourishes them all is created by Jo Bhaer (in her roles as wife, mother, and aunt); Jo is ably assisted by at least three other women. The kitchen is presided over by Asia, a black cook whose dominion in her sphere is unchallenged. She is aided by Mary Ann, the maid, and by "Nursey," the pathetic Frau Hummel in *Little Women*. Mrs. Jo is famously uninterested in domestic chores, though she insists that the three female students learn simple cooking. laundry, and sewing. The coeducational experiment begins when Daisy is joined by Naughty Nan, or little Annie Harding, as her father knows her. Nan, where mother is dead, is a tomboy and a perfect foil for the naturally domestic Daisy. Mrs. Jo says forthrightly to Fritz, "You know we believe in bringing up little men and women together, and it is high time we acted up to our belief."[53] The third little girl is really just a frequent visitor, loved by all for her baby lisp and golden curls. Men's hearts, we are told, can be won to respect for women through the memory of some lovely girl-child. Alcott therefore gives us Bess, the only child of Amy and Laurie, whose sole function at Plumfield is to love and be loved by everyone.

Bess, as faithful readers of *Little Women* will recall, is named after Beth March, and like Beth she is a fragile creature who almost perished from an unnamed ailment in her infancy. In *Little Men* she has become a gentle but all powerful queen. "Loud voices displeased her and quarreling frightened her; so gentler tones came into the boyish voices as they addressed her, and squabbles were promptly suppressed in her presence by lookerson if the principals could not restrain themselves." Her beauty is armed by her firm ability to withdraw favor from those who indulge in rude screams and romps; she helps tame Nan. Bess occasionally evokes the sentimental dominion of little Eva in *Uncle Tom's Cabin*, but she does not die out of sheer goodness. Also, she can and does control those who need her love, especially with a disdainful lisping ("Do away, dirty boy!").

By the 1890s Bess has a successor in the famous "Little Colonel," a creation of Annie Fellows Johnston.[54] That lovely girl-child virtually reunites the new South and the new North by joyously wiggling her toes in the dust, "just like a little nigger." She then proposes to educate May Lilly, daughter of her family's black cook. The "Little Colonel" has inexhaustible energy and self-will; Johnston even allows her a temper tantrum in the name of national redemption. It is of note that this incarnation of ideal beauty uses her femininity and infant innocence to re-socialize conflicting races and classes. Everyone wants her love and everyone knuckles under to the new standard she represents. Bess is a transitional heroine, more active than little Eva, but less powerful than Lloyd Sherman, "the little colonel."

All the Plumfield children (except the visiting Bess) have garden plots and projects of their own to earn money, acquire useful skills, and incidentally to learn that cooperation is both necessary and efficient in a model political economy. Two of the boys raise potatoes which they sell to Fritz Bhaer "at a fair price" for the household's dinners. His nephews grow corn, husk it and have it milled into enough meal for puddings and johnnycake for everyone. They accept no payment because their uncle has supported them for years. Some of the crops turn out less well. Tommy's beans dry up, his peas grow unharvested, and at last he leaves his patch to nettles which are eaten up by Toby, the family donkey. Daisy grows flowers, of course, and Nan cultivates and dries herbs. Most importantly, they learn the advantages of helping one another, and gain wisdom from learning that different skills as well as temperaments are useful at certain times.

Alcott allows one slip in the perfect combination of morality and political science at Plumfield; she introduces Nat and the reader to a new form of cooperative capitalism on a Sunday. Tommy Bangs has a flock of speckled hens whose eggs he sells to Plumfield's kitchen. Nat has no capital to start such a fine venture, and sighs sadly, possessing no more than an "old empty pocketbook and the skill that lay in his ten finger tips." Tommy understands the sign and offers to give Nat one egg out of every twelve that he gathers. It is a good deal for Tommy, who hates to hunt eggs, and a source of investment capital for Nat, who agrees to be the egg hunter for both of them. Mother Bhaer pays twenty-five cents a dozen, so as soon as Nat finds his first egg, Tom chalks up "T. Bangs and Co. on the side of the winnowing machine in the barn, with Nat as proud investor in the "company." Later, suspected of thievery, Nat's name is temporarily erased. Petty capitalism, in Alcott's story, is a moral system.

Future lives are of great concern to Jo and Fritz Bhaer. Alcott makes it clear that differences in temperament and class, as well as sex, will greatly shape children's futures. But there is some hope, through the Plumfield regime, of greater equality of opportunity for the poor. Wealthier pupils learn to admire the good qualities of their poorer schoolmates, and by working themselves rich boys and girls may learn the labor theory of value. Dan and Nan represent the two most appealing leftovers of Romantic rebellion. Both are passionate, self-willed, proud, and imaginative; they possess qualities of leadership that Mrs. Jo hopes to preserve and tame. If Nan and Dan can develop the necessary self-restraint, they can become exemplary reformers, leading their fellow citizens as they lead their schoolmates at Plumfield.

Nan gets lost with one of Jo's sons, little Rob, on a huckleberry hunt. Responsible for the younger child's welfare, she must be punished for her carelessness, and Aunt Jo ties her to the sofa with an apron string to teach Nan that selfish hedonism results in loss of liberty. Nan "loves her liberty above all things," and so the cure works. In the meantime, loving little Rob ties himself to the sofa to keep Nan company; after all, as he says to her, "we got lost together."

Alcott, like Mark Twain, presents a longed-for world of childhood in her most popular fiction. Unlike Twain's boys, however, Alcott's male characters are "little men," the functional partners of "little women." Neither boyhood nor girlhood in Alcott's novel inherit the sacred liberty found in Twain's Mississippi odyssey. Plumfield has a small, tame stream with a playhouse refuge in the willow tree overhanging its banks; grown-ups and children climb up and share confidences with one another. In Twain's scheme of things neither girls nor white adults can really be trusted. Only boys and "niggers," social outcasts because they are primitives, are existentially free.

Huck Finn is historically anachronistic even as Twain evokes his countrymen's deep faith in nature as the repository of liberty—and their equally deep suspicion that civilization inevitably betrays freedom. Yet Alcott's longing for a Romantic reunion with nature is still present in *Little Men*; like Sylvia Yule in *Moods*, poor Nan find herself done in by competitive berry picking. Like Sylvia, Nan also throws off the domestic half of the division of labor, only to find herself branded an irresponsible citizen. By the time Nan grows up (one year after Twain's publication of Huckleberry Finn in 1885), the individualist escape to freedom disappears for girls entirely. The civilization of both sexes is made inevitable by the sentimentalization of childhood, a fact Twain understood well.

Children's good feelings, Alcott maintains, should be evoked to socialize them. Nan is temperamentally no less wild and freedom-loving than Dan in *Little Men*. The motherless daughter of a genteel family, she is nevertheless as easily tamed by loving discipline as Dan; she too is hungry for home. Nan is also bound to her friend Daisy because they are two girls in a boy's world. When separated, each falls victim to the domination of little men. Daisy's domesticity leaves her prey to exploitation by hungry, selfish little boys who devour her cooking and leave her with the messy remains of their feasts. Nan's determination to be one of the boys is thwarted by their primitive male bonding, and her life and limbs are endangered by mean-spirited dares to prove herself in reckless physical competition. The girls find safety, support, and maturation in sisterhood. Learning to value one another despite their differences, Alcott intimates that Daisy and Nan are models for the woman's movement. Girls, like boys, must learn that females are not all the same.

Plumfield has often been interpreted as Louisa Alcott's tribute to her father's Temple School. Certainly the Alcotts continued to hope that Bronson was a genius before his time (especially after Louisa's success with *Little Women*), and they were delighted with public pedagogical reforms that seemed to vindicate Temple School. Plumfield, however, goes far beyond Temple School in advocating peer-group pressure and Socratic dialogues to evoke children's natural purity. *Little Men* does not retreat from the world any more than *Little Women* did. Consequently, the holy bonds of children's friendship are not forged against adults as they are in Twain's more radical novel, *Huckleberry Finn*. If Alcott's second March family history is not a female *Huckleberry Finn*, it is not Fruitlands either.

Self-control seemed to Louisa less and less the product of the independent human will; indeed, she joined many of her contemporaries in presenting human personality as largely the product of social interaction. The problem, she argues, is that the stable and organic social code which shaped individual character has vanished. The answer to that problem lies in Plumfield, where the old virtues (cooperation, hard work, patience, and thrift) are presented as means to loving acceptance by one's peers and betters.

In effect, the author of *Little Men* steals America's children. She removes them from their parents unreliable care and makes their school the center of learning in the fullest sense. Intellectual and practical skills, peer group approval, adult love, and authority are all included in one institution. Public schools were to take another forty years to achieve what Plumfield represents: an integrated social institution.

There is no conflict between the values espoused by Jo and Fritz and the true nature of their pupils. Resistance to the house parents' code of behavior is treated much like evidence of a physical disease; the adults offer love, warm soothing cough syrup, clean linen, and a reassuringly firm schedule of engaging daily activities. Social approval is Plumfield's household god, and it works because there are no alternative deities to venerate or propitiate.

It is sufficient, Alcott argues, to prepare children to be useful, self-supporting citizens who understand the need for corporate welfare. And so Daisy, Demi, and even Dan and Nat join forces to soften Nan's bondage, but the children do not form a band of brigands and run away to the river. Instead, Daisy picnics her dolls on the lawn so Nan can watch the show, Demi reads a story aloud for her amusement, Nat plays her a tune, and Dan brings her a little tree toad as sign of his sympathy. Grownups always maintain their authority in Alcott's fiction, in large measure by posing as children's best friends and companions. They accomplish this by recalling that they too were once children, a fact Miz

Wilson and the Widow Douglas seem to have forgotten in *The Adventures of Tom Sawyer*. Sarah Josepha Hale understood the source of Alcott's power over her juvenile fans quite well: "Miss Alcott has a faculty of entering into the lives and feelings of children that is conspicuously wanting in most writers who address them; and to this cause, to the consciousness among her readers that they are hearing about people like themselves instead of abstract qualities with names, the popularity of her books is due."[55] Plumfield, in short, is a kind of settlement house. It employs neighborhood people and offers shelter while allowing its clients to move in and out at various stages.

The heroism of boys finds an acceptable outlet at Plumfield in the Damon and Pythias friendship of Dan and Nat. The delicate young fiddler is accused of stealing his partner's money. It is a serious crime because Tom has trusted Nat in their joint business enterprise, and a good name is really all Nat has in the way of capital. He is doubly suspect because as Fritz Bhaer remarks, beggar boys have a proclivity for lying and stealing to make their way in the world. Since Nat does not own up to the crime, Fritz charitably suspends judgment, leaving him to the "coventry" of his mates' rejection. Dan, feeling sorry for his best friend and fellow street urchin, replaces the money and takes the blame on himself. Just as everyone—including Aunt Jo, who dearly loves him—believes him guilty, a letter arrives informing Fritz that a wealthy "sharp" boy, Ned, is the culprit. Dan is a hero, his small lie forgiven for the true friendship and compassion it shows. But his troubles are far from over, because wild Dan, like Nan, loves his freedom. He runs away, comes back and is finally tamed by Jo's love and a part-time job as a delivery boy.

The extended March family is present but muted, usually off stage in this domestic drama, and even Fritz and Jo play minor roles. The children themselves take center stage. There is no real plot in *Little Men*, but the book holds reader interest because Plumfield seems, as Daisy says, "the nicest place in the world,"[56] and in such a place it seems there are no really bad people or serious misfortunes. It is a safe haven, subject only to two natural tragedies. The first is the death of John Brooke, Daisy, and Demi's father and Meg's husband. So many of the children are orphaned at Plumfield that Jo, at least, finds comfort in "their blundering affection." In fact, the children hold their own memorial service for Uncle John, and eventually Demi grows up a good deal, no longer so pampered and bookish a child. He takes on chores to earn dollars for his mother and sister, and insists on being called John instead of Demi.

Alcott presents the second problem as the inevitable consequence of democracy unrestrained by a mature, educated citizenry. Guardians of the uneducated masses are a necessity in order to prevent dictatorship and the worship of false gods. The smaller children, closer to tribal life, enjoy scaring up an imaginary creature, called Kitty-Mouse, who threatens terrible punishments for disobedience to its commandments. Demi, who is the inventor and prophet of Kitty-Mouse, announces the event of "sacerryfice." The children build a big fire, and according to Demi, who has heard a garbled version of Uncle Fritz's lecture on Greek sacrifice, they must all burn their most cherished possessions. Rob throws on his wood toy village on the fire, Daisy gives up a new set of paper dolls, and Teddy, not knowing what is happening, comes along with his stuffed lamb and his favorite doll, Annabella. The entranced children watch the destruction of their toys, and when the wooden people of the toy village are burned, Teddy throws his lamb and then poor Annabella on the "funeral pyre." What ensues is a horrible lesson about giving up what one loves most to dictators. Annabella,

> being covered with kid, did not blaze, but did what was worse, she squirmed. First one leg curled up, then the other, in a very awful and lifelike manner; next she flung her arms over her head as if in great agony; her head itself turned on her shoulders, her glass eyes fell out and with one final writh of her whole body, she sank down a blackened mass on the ruins of the town.[57]

Teddy ran screaming for "Marmar" as loud as he could. Lions, lambs, and the sacrifice of dear possessions resonate back to Fruitlands; they also testify to a fear of demagoguery among the "dangerous classes," who, like children, are prey to their primitive instincts.

Such foolish plays are unusual in Alcott's story, however. Most of the children's mistakes are harmless, real enough to provoke sympathy and calculated to teach the moral of the story. That moral, in direct contrast to the Oliver Optic books, is that cooperative, democratic institutions prove, as Aunt Jo says, "If men and women would only trust, understand and help one another, as my children do, what a capital place the world would be."[58]

Jo's father urges her to keep on with Plumfield because the world will see a utopian possibility "by the success of your small experiment."[59] In the last scene of the book, Jo replies that she is not so ambitious as that. She simply wants to give the children a home and teach them things that will make their life less hard in the outside world. Father and Mother Bhaer are a successful, miraculously unconflicted example of reform domesticity. They address each other as Jo and Fritz, but have no roles outside of "Mother and Father" in the novel. If they have a more private life, the reader never learns of it, and perhaps does not care, because the Bhaers seem so united and fulfilled as overseers of Plumfield. There is a gentle refuge in social roles, Alcott intimates to her readers.

Little Men was published in England while Louisa was still there in 1871. When her ship docked in Boston harbor, she found that the American publication date coincided with her homecoming that same year. Fifty thousand books sold out in advance. That June was pleasant, despite the fact that Louisa saw Abba so enfeebled that her second daughter vowed never to go far away from Marmee again. That summer Samuel J. May died. Louisa determined at thirty-nine to put off any more holidays, taking her turn at family responsibilities until May came home. Her earnings bought a steam furnace for the Concord house. By December, May was in charge at home and Louisa could enjoy Boston and the Radical Club again.

Louisa turned her letters and notes into a series of European travel sketches, but she never ventured on the lecture curcuit as Mark Twain did after publishing *Innocents Abroad* in 1869.[60] Both authors loved acting, but Louisa was never comfortable appearing as herself on stage. And unlike Twain, Alcott accepted both old world "romance" and the value of aristocratic ancestors—especially if one views Quincys, Sewalls, and Mays as America's only aristocracy. Yet she also perceived the impressive housewives of Brittany and France as relations of Madam Shaw in *An Old Fashioned Girl*—as kin, in short, to our lusty, hardworking foremothers. American women could recover their former industry and get paid for it this time, she argued.

By 1872, aware that neither literary success nor secure earnings brought a dimunition of her domestic responsibilities, Louisa wrote in her journal,

> Work is my salvation. . . Got out the old manuscript of Success and called it Work! Fired up the engine and plunged into a vortex with many doubts about getting out. Can't work slowly; the thing possesses me, and I must obey till its done.[61]

Her most autobiographical novel, *Work*, written for adult readers, was Alcott's attempt to mediate between classes and so to provide a domestic and civil union, with justice for all. Independence and a home remained her cry on behalf of American women. *Diana and Persis*, together with *Jo's Boys*, completed her analysis of the proper means to that end.

CHAPTER XII

To Earn a Home

It is not always want, insanity or sin that drives women to desperate deaths; often it is a dreadful loneliness of heart, a hunger for home and friends, worse than starvation, a bitter sense of wrong in being denied the tender ties; the pleasant duties, the sweet regards that can make the humblest life happy; a rebellious protest against God, who, when they cry for bread seems to offer them a stone.

Louisa May Alcott, Work

Despite literary and financial success, Louisa Alcott never created a permanent domestic environment of her own. As a single woman, the "tender ties" of home and friends remained elusive. It was not until 1880, when her niece came to live with Louisa, that the fifty-two year old author wrote, "I do mean to set up my own establishment in Boston," adding "Now I have an excuse for a home of my own, and as the other artistic and literary spinsters have a house, I am going to try the plan, for a winter at least."[1]

Alcott's hunger for home and her fierce desire for independence were part of a larger social issue she examined in her adult fiction. In *Work* she argues that expanded education, training, and jobs for women would give the next generation of women what had been denied hers; such changes, however, would come about through the hard work of reformist associations and sustained mutual sacrifice. Louisa portrayed the experiences of working women as powerfully as she lived them, faltering only in her earnest depiction of social mediators between "the helpers and the helped." In a valiant effort to bridge the growing chasm between races, classes, and generations, she wrote of her proposed alliance as if it were an imminent reality.

Then, in a brief romance about herself and May, she sketched the lives of two artists who choose different paths to fulfill their need for creative work and domestic ties. One chooses spinsterhood and friendship; the other tries egalitarian marriage, motherhood, and an expanded family circle. An individual might be lucky enough to find personal solutions to a social problem, she argued. At the same time, she knew that the woman problem could be solved only through institutional changes in society.

Success and Work

The Christian Union asked Louisa for a serial story in November of 1872. Having just spent a good deal of money on clothes and a trunk for Bronson, who left on another western trip "all neat and comfortable," she was delighted to oblige the editors in return for a payment of three thousand dollars. The serial was Work: A Story of Experiences.[2]

Short tales for useful sums, the great Boston fire, and visits from Anna and the boys interrupted the manuscript's completion. In letters to Marmee from her "writing room" in Boston, Louisa also admitted, that she had "transcendental days" in which the Radical Club claimed her attendance with its "funny mixture of rabbis, and weedy old ladies, the 'oversoul' and oysters." She was keeping a separate account for the "family income" and living off the money earned by her "little tales."[3]

By January she managed to get back to Work in marathon writing sessions. A month later her diary recorded family obligations that could not be bought, it seemed, for money:

> Anna very ill with pneumonia; home to nurse, Father telegraphed to come home, as we thought her dying. She gave me her boys, but the dear saint got well and kept the lads for herself. Thank God! Back to my work with what wits nursing left me. Had Johnny for a week to keep all quiet at home. . . . Finished Work—twenty chapters. Not what it should be—too many interruptions. Should like to do one book in peace and see if it wouldn't be good.[4]

Louisa quoted Thomas Carlyle on the title page of her new novel: "An endless significance lies in work; in idleness alone is there perpetual despair." She dedicated the book "To My Mother, Whose Life has been a long labor of love;" appropriately enough, Work argues powerfully for female independence and cooperative domesticity.[5] Alcott's earlier books reasoned that young women were incapable of sensible child care if they were excluded from education and employment in the larger society. However, the principles of loving service, compassion, and sisterhood were increasingly threatened by the same marketplace that provided women's sole source of independent income. Alcott struggled to resolve this contradiction. Her first task was to find a satisfactory definition of the status and role of women. Once again she looked to Theodore Parker for confirmation of "The Public Function of Women."[6]

Moncure Conway remembered that during Parker's last illness the Alumni Association of the Harvard Divinity School refused to pray for his restoration to health and work. Parker's denial of divine miracles and his radical political stand in behalf of working people, women, and slaves cost him the support of conservative Unitarians.[7] While in Italy Louisa had visited Parker's grave with memorial flowers, but her best tribute to him was the character Reverend Power in *Work*.[8] As she told Ednah Cheney, "Christie's adventures are many of them my own; Mr. Power is Mr. Parker."[9]

Christie Devon, the heroine of *Work*, is an orphan and thus freed from the obligations that customarily befall the daughter of a farm household. She uses the language of the Seneca Falls Convention to claim her rights ("There's going to be a new Declaration of Independence") and emphasizes "her speech by energetic demonstration in the bread trough, kneading dough as if it were her destiny, and she was shaping it to suit herself."[10] This conversation is carried out in the large farm kitchen, her Aunt Betsey replying in the form of a recipe. Though humorously done, the scene bids farewell to rural life with its timeless pattern and prescribed stages of women's life and work.

Christie's experience so far has been entirely rural and domestic; all her skills have been learned either at a village school or at home. She leaves knowing that "work was always to be found in the city," and perceives the wage system as the means to independence.[11] She finds a room in a boarding house and begins hunting for a job, free for the first time from the endless round of tasks that define domesticity and dependency. At an "intelligence office," aptly described as the "purgatory of the poor," Christie learns that the skills of general housewifery are not wanted by employers.[12] She must define herself by one particular skill. Unable to call herself a professional cook or nursemaid, she goes into service as the lowliest maid-of-all-work, just as Louisa Alcott did.

When her first employer refuses to call Christie by her own name, she learns the anonymity of wage earners first hand. Her employer is pleased that, unlike the Irish servant girls previously employed (all called "Jane"), Christie does not object to working with a black cook. It is the cook, Hepsey, who gives Christie a lesson in humility, kindness and patience. Directed to pull off her master's boots and clean them, Christie is horrified, regarding the order as a direct humiliation. This incident mirrors Louisa's actual experience, and in fact led her to quit the job. Hepsey, however, offers to perform the bootblacking for Christie:

> "Dere's more 'grading works dan dat chile, and dem dat's bin bliged to do 'em find dis sort bery easy. You's paid for it, honey . . . I's shore I'd never ask it of any woman if I was a man, less I was sick or ole. But folks don't seem to 'member dat we've got feelins."[13]

Domesticity produces a consciousness of work not only as "craft," but also as a process quite apart from wages and hours. Consequently, many servant "girls" preferred factory work to the long hours and endless tasks set by household employers. Lucy Maynard Salmon, in discussing the "social disadvantages of domestic service," found the lack of "home privileges" to be a serious source of distress to female servants.[14] "Board and lodging do not constitute a home, and the domestic can never be a part of the family whose external life she shares."[15] As one girl reported, "One must remember that there is a difference between a house, a place of shelter, and a home, a place where all our affections are centered."[16]

Domesticity was quite different from domestic service, and it was the substitution of a wage for affection and interdependency that made the one a house to clean and the other a home to live in. This consciousness of work as distinct from job was to cause some confusion in Alcott's heroine. In her first twenty-four hours of service Christie learns that she is expected to do tasks with the devotion of a family member but without the rewards of a family relationship.

Christie's first job does not last long. Her employers, a family of upwardly mobile social climbers worse than the Shaws in *An Old Fashioned Girl*, exploit and then fire her in the first chapters of *Work*. The elegant mistress, forgetting any pretense to gentility, screams at Christie like a fishwife, and thereupon is too embarrassed to retain her. "Jane," of course, saw through the "lady" all along.

Christie is on her own once again, though she remains linked to Hepsey Johnson by friendship and a new commitment to abolition and racial integration. Hepsey's loyalty to her enslaved family, whom she hopes to free with her wages, had its real counterpart in many black families. Louisa's knowledge of this was more than secondhand. Winnie Beale, a freed slave, gratefully acknowledged the receipt of a barrel of clothing and household linens from Abba Alcott. She sent a message through Sally Holly to Louisa, "I wish I had something to send the lady. Why! She is a mammy to me. I shall be warm now."[17] Winnie Beale sent something more valuable—the long sad tale of her struggles to reunite her family. Later, during the war, Louisa had hoped to teach in Port Royal before typhoid invalided her to Concord. Instead, she combined what she knew of Harriet Tubman and Winnie Beale in the character of Hepsey.

Hepsey is the first link in a chain of sisterhood forged by Christie Devon, who discovers (as did her creator) that jobs are better than chattel slavery, but do not bring full independence. Female friendship in her boarding house subsequently gives Christie the opportunity to try a stage career. Alas, Christie finds that actresses can remain true women only with the greatest difficulty. Sexual familiarities were commonplace, rivalries between actresses prevented real companionship, and so Christie leaves acting. Warned that stage experience is an impediment to "genteel'' employment, she refrains from mentioning it and secures an appointment as governess to a wealthy family. She soon leaves for the seashore with the mother, two children and the bachelor brother of her employer.

The bachelor, Philip Fletcher, is a wealthy snobbish invalid; nevertheless, as a rich single man he is considered a "catch." He proposes to Christie, despite having learned that she was formerly an actress. Lonely and tired, she is tempted to "marry for a living."[18] Fortunately, realizing that marriage to Fletcher can only mean subordination and dependency, she rejects his proposal after a conversation about *Jane Eyre*, which she has been reading. Her suitor suggests that a man's faults can be cured by the love of a good woman, such as herself. Christie replies, "If he has wasted his life he must take the consequences, and be content with pity and indifference, instead of respect and love. Many good women do 'lend a hand,' as you say, and it is quite Christian and amiable I've no doubt; but I cannot think it is a fair bargain."[19] Later in the novel Fletcher goes to war and becomes a more worthwhile suitor as a result of his adversity training. Christie still refuses him because she does not love him.

All the jobs Christie finds in the first half of *Work* are ill-paying and humiliating. Her female employers are not true women; as the husbands and fathers participate in the competitive marketplace, their wives and daughters maneuver in the social world of fashion to augment their husbands' chances for success. They never extend hands in friendship to those who serve them. Theodore Parker had remarked that it was not work which crushed the spirit of the laboring people, but rather

> the tacit confession on the part of the employer, that he has wronged and subjugated the person who serves him; for when these same actions are performed by the mother for her child, or the son for his father, they are done for love and not money, they are counted not as low but rather ennobling.[20]

The turning point in the novel is Christie's employment as a seamstress in a factory-like workroom. She holds herself aloof from the other factory "hands," but is attracted to Rachel, a quiet romantic-looking girl. Clearly fallen gentry hired for her "superior taste," Rachel is Christie's first friend of her own age and sensibilities, a true heart's companion. The respectable workshop manager, however, has neglected to check Rachel's background, doubtless over-impressed by her genteel dress and demeanor. When she discovers that Rachel is a fallen woman, she fires her. The legitimacy of the factory system depends on its reputation for hiring only girls of good character. Charity to one's fallen sister must yield to secure profits.

The importance of Rachel and Christie's friendship cannot be overemphasized. The power of female friendship in *Work* redeems a fallen woman, as it does in Harriet Beecher Stowe's novel, *We and Our Neighbors*, published in 1875. Rachel's plight, like that of Stowe's heroine, points to the inadequacy of conventional charity institutions. Her dismissal from work is the beginning of Christie's search for a religious faith more liberal than conventional Christianity, a faith that can link her to others and change a society that promises opportunity and delivers oppression.

Christie leaves her job as a sign of protest and solidarity with Rachel, but soon finds herself alone, ill, and reduced to piecework. Just as she seriously contemplates suicide, Rachel appears and sends Christie to stay with Cynthie Wilkins, a humble laundress with a shiftless husband and a brood of small children. Cynthie's greatness of heart resembles Peggotty's in *David Copperfield*.[21] A new alliance and a new agenda for reform emerge from the domestic haven of Cynthie's humble cottage. Mrs. Wilkins is a laundress who advertises her services with a sign: "Cynthie Wilkins, Clear Starcher," and her vision of the world is as clear as her starching: social change will come about through a new Christian union in which Christ washes whitest of all. Her chaplain and the head of this new union is the Reverend Power, who as Cynthie says, "starts the dirt and gits the stains out, and leaves 'em ready for other folks to finish off."[22]

Reverend Power sends Christie to David Sterling for a job. Sterling, the owner of a greenhouse, is Alcott's idealized portrait of Henry David Thoreau. It is through friendship and growing recognition of their common interests in equality and reform that Christie and David fall in love. They marry during the Civil War, and both wear uniforms at the ceremony. David leaves to fight and Christie becomes a nurse. After only a few months together, most of them spent visiting on the battlefield, David is killed. Christie survives the loss only because she finds hope in bearing his child.[23]

Her daughter, Pansy, becomes the focus of her energetic plans for a new generation of women. Instead of retiring on her widow's pension, Christie runs a cooperative greenhouse with her mother-in-law, Pansy, and Rachel. Rachel turns out to be David's long-lost sister, and together the old and young women work and share their profits equally. Christie's old Uncle Enos, now a widower contemplating his own death, looks for a good cause to support in his will. Christie quickly names the multitude of causes she herself supports—"Help the freed people . . . Wounded soldiers, destitute children, ill-paid women, young people struggling for independence, homes, hospitals, schools, churches, and God's charity all over the world."[24] She has formed a "loving league" with Hepsey, Reverend Power, Cynthie Wilkins, and the rest of her family and friends; they are a band of dedicated reformers.

A new field of labor opens for the heroine of *Work*, when at the age of forty she joins an association of working women. She notices the widening gap between middle-class reformers and working people. "How difficult it was for the two classes to meet and help one another in spite of the utmost need on the one side and the sincerest good will on the other."[25] As the wife of a war hero and friend of Reverend Power, Christie is trusted as mediator by both groups. This will be her chosen work. As a symbol of her role, she speaks to an audience from the bottom of the speaker's platform: "I am better here, thank you; for I have been and mean to be a working woman all my life."[26]

A woman's rights polemic, *Work* is also Alcott's strongest portrayal of women's lives. Christie moves through a period of adolescent struggle in which she demands her individual rights as a daughter of the American Revolution, and then learns she is only one of "that large class of women, who moderately endowed with talents, earnest and true-hearted, are driven by necessity, temperament, or principle out into the world to find support, happiness and homes for themselves."[27] By herself she cannot find work, happiness, or home. Her progress throughout the novel depends upon mutuality, cooperation, and loving league with others.

Christie finds true womanhood in association with all the social classes Alcott wants to unite in a search for democratic harmony. Middle-class women can aid their working sisters by using their social status and influence to open education, jobs, and homes for the less privileged. The problem, Alcott insists, is a lack of communication between those who have much to give and those who desperately need help to get started. The creation of institutions to provide that help is proper work for the veterans of the first fight for emancipation. Christie's greenhouse and cooperative household are further examples of Alcott's settlement-house proposals.

Alcott distributed the money earned from the sales of *Work* according to her sense of family and social responsibility. One thousand dollars went to May to help her study art in Europe. Part of the royalties went into the "Alcott sinking fund," as she called the family investments, and some money went as a "thank offering" to "the silent poor to which we belonged for so many years—needy, but repectable and forgotten because too proud to beg."[28]

The publication of *Work* had two additional results. The first was a new housekeeper. Alcott was curious "how she came to us," and discovered that "she had taught and sewed, was tired, and wanted something else; decided to try for a housekeeper's place, but happened to read *Work*, and thought she'd do as Christie did—take anything that came."[29] Her new housekeeper found that Miss Alcott practiced what she preached, and the author remarked that employer and employee "had a good time together." The second outcome of *Work* was a small but disquieting stream of criticism. *The Lakeside Monthly* condemned the book "as an immoderate apotheosis of Madam Work pointing out to the author that slavery had been abolished and with it the necessity of cant on the subject of Negro rights."[30]

Harper's reviewer argued that Alcott's name and reputation would carry the book, and not the book itself. Ignoring *Moods*, the review called *Work* "Miss Alcott's first real novel." As a "serious didactic essay on the subject of woman's work," the novel came dangerously close to "preaching in the guise of story telling." The reviewer was quite right in recognizing the defects of *Work* as fiction; it was a factual report on laboring women.[31]

In 1869, at a meeting between working and middle-class women of Massachusetts, one Miss Phelps stood up and spoke about working women in much the same language later used by Christie Devon in *Work*:

> "We do not think the men of Massachusetts know how the women live. We do not think if they did they would allow such a state of things to exist. Some of us who signed the petition have had to work for less than twenty-five cents a day, and we know that many others have had to do the same. . . . Do you not think that they feel the difference between their condition and that of rich, well dressed ladies who pass them? If they did not they would be less than human. . . . Only help us to earn a home that we can attach ourselves to, that will make us feel that we have a country. It has been said that we can go anywhere and be at home. Women cannot. It is because they have no homes. They have a husband's or a father's home, but none of their own. . . . I am often met with the objection that these women can go to California or Nevada. But our mothers live here. We know not these distant places. . . . Girls love independence, girls love society, just as much as men do. A woman must have some intellectual society or she goes down. I am no speechmaker—only a worker."[32]

Bread and Roses

Alcott knew enough about adversity to write powerfully about woman's wrongs as a social question. But her most puzzling problem remained the contradictions between private domestic life and woman's individuality. For herself there was no longer a personal question. Forty years experience with the difficulties of supporting a family while gaining a modicum of independence led her to cry out, "Spinsterhood forever." But she also knew the familiar loneliness for "tender ties" and "pleasant duties" performed by and for loved ones. She came close to proposing a social answer to this problem when she created a happy community of dedicated spinsters in *An Old Fashioned Girl*, the model school run by family members and open to homeless waifs in *Little Men*, and a cooperative household and business in *Work*.

For the most part, however, she presented the problem as a simple alternative: a woman must choose either a single life dedicated to truth, art, and humanity at the cost of those "pleasant duties" and "sweet regards," or marriage to a man who supports woman's rights and accepts her work, maternity, and wifehood as compatible vocations. In 1879 she wrote a romance in four chapters about Diana and Persis, two artist friends who try different paths to domesticity and feminism.[33]

Louisa is the Diana of her unfinished story, and May, her youngest sister, is Persis. May's daring try for independence, love, and maternity leads us to ask what extent the order of the children's birth and the fluctuating family circumstances of the Alcotts affected the lives they chose to lead. Abba Alcott dreamt that women would be bankers, teachers, judges, writers, artists and doctors by the year 1900, and Louisa depicted them in training at Laurence University. But these hopes were clearly incompatible with the subordination of self to husband and children. Could girls brought up to value self-sacrifice learn to cherish individual identity and demand freedom from household drudgery with no regrets? May was able to do so, while Abba and Louisa watched her with pleasure perhaps tinged with envy.

After finishing *Work* Louisa gave up her "writing room" in Boston and moved back to Concord to take up family chores. She sent May to Europe, expecting her to return eventually, or if fortune favored them both, to visit her there. Although thirty-three, May's letters home seem written by a young girl. She describes her housekeeping arrangements as if she were playing house. She was also aware of fashion, art galleries, and good food: "My artistic sister will appreciate as I do, shops abounding with cheap clothing of all sorts, ready made. Work's also so cheap that a young woman of moderate means can get up a neat and handsome wardrobe for half the sum it costs at home."[34]

May's copies of Turner won John Ruskin's praise in London. She was learning to turn out "pot boilers," as her sister called her own quick novels and May's art copies.[35] In 1874, when May returned once more to help at home, Louisa's health seemed much worse. Rheumatism and blinding neuralgic headaches made writing and caring for the family too heavy a burden. But in the spring of 1876 she agreed to send May back to Europe. Louisa wrote, "She cannot find the help she needs here and is happy and busy in her own world over there. God be with her, she has done her distasteful duty faithfully and deserves a reward."[36]

May never returned to Concord. She established herself in Paris, living close to several other woman artists. She described working in an all-woman studio with nude models and criticism of students' work by leading painters. She wrote a guide book for American artists abroad, and carefully listed those male artists who took female students. Her vivid letters describe a comfortable, supportive group of young female artists who shared breakfasts, Thanksgiving dinners far from home, and encourage one another's ambition. "Kate, Rose and May" were "three jolly spinsters," and knowing her mother and sister's intense interest in the minute details of a female artist abroad, May added sketches and a verbal portrait, of Mary Cassatt, whose teas were a mecca for the young artists.[37]

Abba's health was failing as she faithfully copied her "good child's" letters into her journal. Meanwhile, her youngest daughter was "making plans to stay in Europe having proved to my satisfaction that there is enough talent to pay for educating it and giving my life to it."[38] She reassured the family that she would make occasional summer visits home "if you want me very much." Better yet, "Why not shut up Apple Slump for a year and let Nan have all the pretty things and a general pick and let Lu come for a year's vacation, if Mother continues well and can spare her."[39]

This tug of war with silken cord between Concord and Paris continued for a year. Abba wrote, "I think she has realized what a sacrifice to me it has been to have her gone so far, and has conscientiously tried to gratify me and her sisters by these frequent and interesting accounts of her progress in Art."[40] May's still life won a red ribbon at the Paris Salon, and Bronson sent her a congratulatory note in red ink. At the same time he mentioned Louisa's book (*Modern Mephistopheles*) in the forthcoming "No Name Series," and testily remarked, "If you know the title you are better informed than I am."[41] But Abba had already read it and Louisa had directed Thomas Niles to send May a copy.

Abba's insistence upon the primacy of obligations within the family did not deter her from taking strong public positions on woman's rights in her last years. Concord's centennial celebration led her to pen a fiery declaration demanding "no taxation without representation;" she addressed it specifically to women in their status as "wives, mothers, daughters, and sisters."[42] The signatories include not only Abba herself, Louisa, and Anna, but also Lydian Emerson, Sophia Thoreau, and eighty-seven other "Female Taxpayers of Concord."[43] Pasted beneath this declaration in Abba's journal is a handbill for the Woman's Suffrage Association with the names of William Lloyd Garrison, Julia Ward Howe, Elizabeth Blackwell, Lucy Stone and Amos Bronson Alcott. At the Concord Centennial, the speakers' platform collapsed. Abba commented that its structural weakness was due to the omission of a woman's rights plank.[44]

On her seventy-seventh birthday Abba Alcott penned her last words, a notation of "the coming of May's letter full of pleasant news."[45] Abba died a few days later.

May wrote repeatedly of her remorse at being so far away when her mother died, but she did not return. Instead she praised Louisa and encouraged her to

> be grateful enough that *you* have been the one who could make dear Marmee, and Papa too, so comfortable and happy these last years by your generosity and devotion, for money has done what affection alone could never do, unromantic as it sounds to say so, and you have delighted in making us all happy in our own way tho' much of your own life and health has been sacrificed in doing it, and this I feel more perhaps than anybody.[46]

May went on with her work. "If mine can't be a happy domestic life . . . perhaps the Good God meant me for great things in other ways."[47] Also, "Perhaps this sacrifice I have freely chosen to make in losing one year of Marmee's life may make me work better."[48] In this fashion May manages to argue that the duties of work force her to sacrifice her responsibilities at home. One month later May had a new admirer in Ernest Nieriker, a handsome young Swiss businessman, fourteen years younger than herself. Four months after Abba's death she married him.

Undoubtedly May was emotionally vulnerable in the months following her mother's death. Indeed, Louisa had portrayed both Amy and Jo March as vulnerable to matrimony after the death of Beth in *Little Women*. But if one accepts the conviction in May's letters, she married Nieriker because she loved him. He fully encouraged her to keep working as a serious artist, and his family joined him in urging her to continue her career.

May wrote repeated invitations for Louisa to stay with them in Paris:

> Not a wish seems ungratified except that Louisa is not well enough to come and see and enjoy my good fortune with me . . . She must not think my own happiness has made me unmindful of her, for it only draws us nearer. But I have laid out my future life and hope not to swerve from purpose. I do not mean to be hindered by envious people, or anything to divert me from accomplishing my dream. . . . For myself this simple artistic life is so charming, that America seems death to all aspiration or hope of work. . . . It is the perfection of living; the wife so free from household cares, so busy and so happy. I never mean to have a house or many belongings, but lead the delightfully free life I do now with no society to bother me, and nothing to prevent my carrying out my aims.[49]

Louisa would have loved to come, but "at the last moment gave it up, fearing to undo all the good this year of ease had done for me and be a burden on her."[50] May was pregnant in 1879, and Louisa feared that the household would have two women to care for if she went to visit the Nierikers. By some strange irony Louisa recovered, while May herself died a few weeks after giving birth to Louisa May Nieriker. May had noted in her diary that Louisa is "at the Bellevue writing her Art story in which some of my adventures will appear."[51]

The uncompleted romance of Diana and Persis is only four chapters long.[52] In the first chapter we meet two female artists, Diana, a sculptor, and Persis, a painter. Both are orphans; they are also dear friends who encourage each other's work and share small pleasures. Persis longs for some "sort of motive in her life," and Diana warns her sternly, "Don't look for it in marriage, that is too costly an experiment for us." Resolved to study in Paris, Persis leaves Diana for a year, hoping to rendesvous there to continue their life and work together. Fearing that the younger Persis, already a collector of male hearts, will find a lover abroad, Diana exacts a promise of fidelity. Persis says, "I will keep myself like a vestal virgin and keep the vow I make to my chosen goddess Diana."[53] Diana kisses "Percy" and reluctantly lets her go.

The second chapter provides descriptions of the artistic life led by young American women studying in Paris which are almost direct copies of May's letters to her family. Mary Cassatt appears as Miss Cassal, "rich, motherly and strong." Persis's letters urge Diana to join her quickly. Diana is, however, hard at work, "no nun in her cell ever led a more austere and secluded life than this fine creature intent upon her self-appointed task."[54]

Then the course of the story changes. Persis quickly marries and has a baby in Paris. Diana, meanwhile, has gone to Rome, and while wandering the streets thinking of Percy she is observed by an expatriate American sculptor, Anthony Stafford. His motherless son, Nino, eventually introduces Diana to Stafford. The sculptor is described as having "lost his power" after his wife died. He admires Diana's work, particularly her statue of a mother and child: "I am glad a woman did that . . . because it is so strong. There is a virile force in this, accuracy as well as passion—in short—genius."[55] Diana notes that "few men would say that to a woman," and the author adds, "The masculine fibre in her nature demanded recognition as it does in all strong natures and, having won it, she could permit the softer side of her character to assert itself without forming the accusation of weakness which she hated like a man."[56] The chapter ends with the insinuation that Stafford and Persis may be "comrades;" no hint of sexual desire, however, escapes Diana's lips. Instead she decides to visit Persis.

The last chapter, "At Home," finds Percy married and caring for her baby. Like May Alcott Nieriker, she insists that she means to be a happy wife and mother and also go on with her art. The fictional husband is August Muller (the name of one of May's Parisian teachers). Persis, like May, is quite happy, and Muller says, "I believe a woman can and ought to have both if she has the power and courage to win them."[57]

Louisa's narrative voice, here separate from Diana's inner thoughts, records some disturbing signs: the studio is full of dust and Persis' eyes, "as beautiful as ever," nevertheless wear the "tender anxiety of a mother's eyes." The scene moves swiftly to the healthy baby napping naked on a sunny balcony and the three adults dining, drinking wine, and conversing. While August and Diana become friends, debating Persis' future as an artist and mother, "Percy was thinking what they should have for breakfast since morning would inevitably bring that dreadful question."[58] Here the romance breaks off.

The White Marmorean Flock

A larger history, remains hidden behind this obviously personal story of the Alcott sisters. May had written a grateful description of the brave women artists who lived and studied abroad before her generation. Louisa in turn entitled one chapter of her story "Puck," a tribute to May's work and to Harriet Hosmer's sculpture. Years before, in one of her "stage struck" periods, she admired the great actress Charlotte Cushman. A visitor to the Alcott's home, Cushman was also a member of the Radical Club, and sent letters to the club when world-wide engagements kept her from regular attendance.[59] Cushman befriended Harriet Hosmer, the New England sculptress, and urged her to come to Rome. There Hosmer created a famous marble figure, "Puck." Copied many times, it also served as the motif for Hawthorne's famous novel, *The Marble Faun*. For several reasons Hosmer and Cushman did not remain close friends. First of all, William Wetmore Story, the American expatriate sculptor, became Hosmer's patron. Under his protection, Harriet developed a child-like behavior to escape the social disapproval usually attending a woman artist's independence. Cushman, along with Emma Stebbins, her life-long companion, and Edmonia Lewis, disdained such disguises. Living together in Rome, entertaining widely and famously, Cushman's group was described by Henry James as "the white marmorean flock that settled on the seven hills of Rome."[60]

How many levels of meaning attend Alcott's brief romance we shall never know. She knew about the Roman circle, and she debated the choice between companionship within the egalitarian marriage and spinsterhood with the tender ties of friendship. Given the circumstances of her own life and the relative ease of May's new opportunities, financial security, and status as the "baby of the family," it is not hard to imagine that Louisa depended upon sisterhood and mistrusted marriage a great deal more than May.

The years between 1846 and 1880 recorded a small but significant rise in the percentage of American women who never married. Louisa's birth cohort included about 6.5 percent of women who remained spinsters throughout their lives. By the immediate postwar period, girls born between 1866 and 1870 might have a 9.6 percent chance of remaining spinsters. The small rise remained a demographic fact until the late 1890s, when the upward curve reversed itself and dropped to a new low of 4.8 percent for the group born between 1921 and 1930.[61]

Historians have been hard pressed to explain this rise of spinsterhood in the late nineteenth century, but they have generally agreed with Dan Scott Smith that "the numerically tiny majority who remained single had far larger historical significance than their numbers would suggest." Smith does not find the rise surprising in view of the "tides of the woman's movement."[62] Alcott's works and her own life experience enlarge the dimensions of such an observation. Certainly there were new educational and vocational opportunities for women, and as Louisa repeatedly noted and publicized, the opportunities were best seized by spinsters. Perhaps more important was the problem of reconciling domestic responsibilities, conventionally borne by women, with the desire for individual identity and achievement. A sense of self was highly prized by Romantic reformers; it was not abandoned in the shift to a more rationalist perspective.

May Alcott tried to solve the problem of marriage and female individuality by marrying later than most women, and by marrying an enlightened Swiss gentleman of means. She was outspoken in blaming her mother's lifelong problems on Bronson's stubborn, if comfortable ignorance of the economic facts of everyday life. He took domestic comforts for granted when he had them, and praised his own simplicity of taste when times were hard. Louisa, however, agreed with May and Abba that financial independence made the woman problem easier to bear; she devoted most of her life to securing a "competence," thereby maximizing the choices available to her sisters, nephews, and niece. But this personal solution did not satisfy Louisa as a prescription for society. She went on to write *Jo's Boys*, developing Plumfield into Laurence University, a feminist Utopia graced with cooperative housekeeping and coeducation. Dress and health reforms shared center stage with Greek, chemistry, and philosophy in Louisa's educational curriculum.

Moreover, Alcott argued that for many "the social influence was the better part of the training they received." Middle-class, genteel taste in dress, manners, social and political values assured a single standard without violating the principle of individuality, at least in Alcott's view. She assumed that the greatest inequalities, were the lack of opportunity to acquire the May refinement and taste, and the lack of independent means to dignify the humblest home with "a good picture or two hung on the walls," books, and blooming Christmas roses.

She presented a two-fold plan for reform. First, hungry young women could find the means to earn a decent living once they acquired a college education equal to that of young men. Women's success at academic studies would prove their fitness to hold jobs and occupy professions hitherto reserved to males. Second, "especial care was taken to fit them to play their parts worthily in the great republic which offered them wider opportunities and more serious duties." They would become practical missionaries of the "social influence" acquired at college. If they could earn a decent living and having acquire refined tastes and congenial friends, these young women would possess the essential requirements for freely choosing between egalitarian marriage or spinsterhood.

CHAPTER XIII

The Social Influence

"The female population exceeds the male, you know, especially in New England, which accounts for the high state of
culture we are in, perhaps," answered John.

"It is a merciful provision, my dears, for it takes three or four
women to get each man into, through, and out of the world.
You are costly creatures, boys, and it is well that mothers,
sisters, wives, and daughters love their duty and do it so well,
or you would perish off the face of the earth," said Mrs. Jo
solemnly.

Louisa May Alcott, Jo's Boys

The 1870s and 1880s witnessed a challenge to woman's rights in the
name of science. The notion of woman's limited mental ability, supposedly the product of her specialized reproductive capacity, was never
"more fervently held or more highly elaborated than it was in America
after the Civil War."[1] Alcott impatiently took up this challenge in the
pages of *Eight Cousins*, *Rose in Bloom*, and *Jo's Boys*. Woman's minds, she
insisted, were every bit as curious as men's; female anatomy, however
biologically suited for procreation, presented no impediment to serious
mental work.

Motives for the renewed differentiation between the sexes were
complex, but clear enough to Alcott and her liberal contemporaries.
Women were working outside their homes in even greater numbers, and
they were often played out against men in the labor market. Middle-class
women, both conservative and liberal, were uniting in serious campaigns
to reform public life and public policy in the name of family welfare. Each
new role played by women seemed to spur their sex on to greater
demands for education, suffrage, and even equal pay for equal work.

As a consequence, "Many Americans believed the need to draw a
clear line between appropriately male and female activities had become
acute."[2] Dr. Edward Clarke drew that line on Louisa's homeground,
speaking at the New England Woman's Club of Boston in 1872.[3] He cited

Darwin and Spencer, arguing that it was not so much that one sex was superior, but that the sexes were widely different. His arguments were embellished in his book, *Sex in Education: or A Fair Chance for the Girls.*[4] Men, he claimed, had evolved with a higher metabolic rate than women and a greater tendency to vary; hence they grew progressively stronger and more intelligent than women over the long *Descent of Man.*[5] Because of their biological specificity (and consequently diminished capacity for variance) women were dependent upon men for protection. Motherhood therefore granted women a gentle immunity from the struggle of natural selection, but that same immunity also rendered woman biologically unfit for the mental exertions that stimulated and developed man.

Yours For Reform of All Kinds

Feminists replied to Clarke in *The Woman's Journal*, and Julia Ward Howe eventually assembled a brilliant array of essays under the title *Sex and Education: A Reply to Dr. Clarke's "Sex in Education."*[6] Louisa May Alcott began her own refutation of Clarke's theses with the novel *Eight Cousins*. She wrote the first chapters on a farm in Conway, Massachusetts during a summer holiday in 1874. Anna and her sons had accompanied her, and Louisa drew heavily on the boy's adventures and also upon her own childhood recollections. At first she seems intent on creating another version of *Little Men* for *St. Nicholas*, the most successful and prestigious magazine for children in late nineteenth-century America.[7] But unlike *Little Men* the new serial focussed on one particular heroine. Attacking the presumption of woman's innate fragility, it demonstrates that mental and physical strength are products of environment and education.

Rose Campbell, the sheltered rich orphan in Alcott's tale, joins an array of strong-minded girls depicted in *St. Nicholas* from the 1870s through the early twentieth century. Its editor, Mary Mapes Dodge, set a remarkable standard for young people's literature. She published the fiction of Rebecca Harding Davis, Sarah Orne Jewett, Helen Hunt Jackson, and Helen Stuart Campbell, among others, as well as impressive nonfiction works. *Eight Cousins* appeared for twelve months in 1874 and 1875 alongside reports of a gassiz Club's naturalist projects and reports of children's temperance union meetings.[8] All of these offerings were aimed directly at a middle-class audience, but though the tone was uniformly patriotic and genteel, the pervading message was that character is environmentally rather than biologically formed. This conviction enabled Alcott to claim woman's rights as a benefit both for girls' health and America's social welfare.

Rose arrives at the refined home of her Aunt Peace and Aunt Plenty, who cosset and spoil her. The seven male Campbell cousins assume that

Rose is a "delicate little creter," which indeed she is at the start of the book.[9] To the proud and prosperous Campbells, Rose's delicacy seems no more than the price of a good breeding. Her first friend is Phoebe, the household's maid and an orphan, like Rose. Phoebe, however, has survived because she is sturdy and self-sufficient. Like Dickens' Charley, she announces, "I'm fifteen now, and old enough to earn my own living."[10] Part of Rose's education involves learning (through Phoebe) how the other half lives. Her schooling also includes learning to make "bread and button holes," because her remarkable Uncle Alec, physician and guardian, believes that all men and women should be self-reliant. The good Doctor, once a sailor, has his own work bag "out of which he produced a thimble without a top, and, having threaded his needle, he proceeded to sew on the buttons so handily that Rose was much impressed and amused."[11]

Doctor Alec Campbell must battle his fashionable sisters-in-law and his own spinster sisters to provide a sensible wardrobe of warm, loose clothing, and a healthy diet of milk and gingerbread instead of hot bread, coffee, and patent medicines for his niece. He wins out, and with the aid of shiny ice-skates and plenty of outdoor exercise, Rose's character, intelligence, and physical strength bloom harmoniously during the year-long educational experiment.[12]

Phoebe does not need lessons in domestic science, nor is her life lacking in physical exertion. Rose finds her "maid, friend, teacher" in silent tears, however, frustrated in an attempt to teach herself to read and write. A "broken slate that had blown off the roof, and inch or two of pencil, an old almanac for a reader, several bits of brown or yellow paper ironed smoothly and sewed together for a copy-book, and the copies of sundry receipts . . . these, with a small bottle of ink and a rusty pen" make up Phoebe's school supplies.[13] In contrast, Rose possesses one of the most delightful chambers imaginable. Her bath, toilet table, curio cabinet, and desk are all arragned to facilitate a young lady's love of both reading and primping. At this point Rose realizes that her own well-stocked library and her leisure for reading are unusual privileges, and she sets out to share her knowledge and supplies with Phoebe. Greek and Latin, courtesy of the Campbell cousins, follow literacy, and finally Uncle Alec takes a hand, agreeing to send Phoebe to school. Fortunately, a new cook and maid are being hired, so Phoebe's work may be taken over by others.

Phoebe, however, is not the only person who needs help. Rose is subsequently sent on monthly sojourns to her cousins' homes as a missionary. The indulgent, well-meaning efforts of the boys' mothers are unable to offset problem fathers and powerful male peer groups. The adolescent male Campbells reenforce one another in smoking, drinking, fighting, betting, and a general lack of old-fashioned deference to elders.

Rose's missionary efforts not only benefit her cousins, they improve her own character and physical health. Alcott's message is clear: true womanhood involves setting a civilized example to rude male savages; in turn, such cares strengthen and improve little women. Rose announces that she has learned what little girls are made for—"to take care of boys."[14]

Rose in Bloom

Even in Concord Alcott found that "young American gentlemen, as well as farmers and mill hands" did a great deal of drinking. She expected it, she said, "among the Irish," but such dissolution among native-born Yankee men testified to the need for a wider social influence on the part of reformers. At Franklin and Louisa Sanborn's home she met regularly with Mrs. Julia Ward Howe and William Torrey Harris, and at least once partook of tea with Walt Whitman.[15] Her network of intergenerational reformers stretched from Whitman, with his professed love of cold water baths and plain carpenter's dress, to the Woman's Congress at Syracuse, New York, where Julia Ward Howe led the "Battle Hymn of the Republic," and even to elegant New York City drawing rooms, where an international coterie of free religionists, actresses, writers, and charity organizers met regularly.

Between the publication of *Eight Cousins* and *Rose in Bloom*, Lousia Alcott travelled the full range of this reformers' network. At Vassar College she listed her duties: "talk with four hundred girls, write in stacks of albums and schoolbooks, and kiss every one who asks me." Vassar students even formed a Little Women Club.[16] Their famous teacher, the astronomer Maria Mitchell, refused to give grades; she acknowledged her ties to Emerson and the Transcendental Circle: "You cannot mark a human mind because there is no intellectual unit."[17] Vice-president of the American Social Science Association, mature both intellectually and emotionally, Mitchell embodied Alcott's ideal of true womanhood.

In 1875, Mitchell offered an opening prayer from the platform of the Woman's Congress at Syracuse, New York.[18] Louisa, who hated making speeches, attended this conference and signed numerous autographs while listening carefully to the full range of woman's issues. Temperance, coeducation, domestic science, suffrage, and the wrongs of poorly-paid working women were all represented and eloquently described. *Rose in Bloom* and *Jo's Boys* put these issues before a sympathetic middle-class audience.

Later she visited New York City, where she found the contrasts between rich and poor described at the woman's congress all too visible. Dressed in silks, she attended the opera, the theater, and found herself the honored guest of Sorosis, the most advanced and liberal women's club in the city. At Mrs. Croly's reception she found herself sharing guest-of-honor status with the young poet, Oscar Wilde. Twenty-seven years old, he had just won the Newdigate Prize for English verse.[19] Louisa met socially prominent people at the Frothinghams' and the Botta's, and also sampled the water cure and spartan diet of the Bath Hotel in lower New York. Thanksgiving Day found her sharing a carriage ride with her friend Sallie Holley, teacher and missionary to freedmen and women.[20]

On Christmas Day during the same trip to New York, Louisa visited the Tombs, a well-known home for newsboys, and Randalls Island Hospital. She helped give out toys and sweets to poor babies "born of want and sin" who suffered "every sort of deformity, disease, and pain." In letters to Concord she described "one mite so eaten up with sores that his whole face was painted with some white salve—its head covered with an oilskin cap; one eye gone, and the other half filmed over." This babe, she said, could only "moan and move its feet till I put a gay red dolly in one hand and a pink candy in the other; then the dim eye brightened, the hoarse voice said feebly, 'tanky lady' and I left it contentedly sucking the sweetie and trying to see its dear new toy."[21]

The vivid contrast between fashionable drawing rooms and Randalls Island became the focus for *Rose in Bloom*[22]. Alcott has her heroine, Rose Campbell, take up the causes of poor children, ill-paid working women, and temperance, Alcott also portrays (through Rose and Phoebe) the growing gap between reform-minded middle-class women and their working-class sisters. Rose and Phoebe, can no longer overlook the material and social distances between mistress and maid. After several years abroad with Uncle Alec, the two young women return sharing a belief that "it is as much a right and a duty for women to do something with their lives as for men."[23] Phoebe's imperative is clear: she must support herself. However, Prince Charlie, the most dashing of Rose's Campbell cousins, reminds Rose that a well-to-do girl's proper career is marriage and motherhood. Rose angrily asks him, "Would you be contented to be told to enjoy yourself for a little while then marry and do nothing more til you die?"[24] The fact that women possess minds, souls, hearts, ambition, and talent does not preclude marriage and motherhood, but Rose vows to prove that she is something beside "a housekeeper and a baby tender" before yielding to love.[25]

Phoebe's natural gift for music is cultivated by professional training, and she launches a career as a choir singer and music teacher. A brilliant concert appearance on behalf of an orphan home eventually leads Archie Campbell, Rose's eldest cousin, to propose marriage to Phoebe. Although love is unquestionably his only motive, and although Phoebe returns his affection, Alcott plays out their courtship for the entire length of the novel because Phoebe must overcome the objections of snobbish

Campbell mothers and aunts. Not surprisingly, it is Phoebe who feels obliged to prove her worth, and Rose who cannot understand why the young couple should not marry at once. Rose naively tries to minimize the differences between Phoebe and herself by wearing simple gowns and fresh flowers when the two young women attend the same dances. Phoebe, however, continues to call her patroness, "little mistress." Working in the city is Phoebe's only escape from social inferiority.

Left to her own devices, with only lazy cousin Charlie to "play with Rose," the young heiress falls prey to his charming attentions. She mistakes romance for love, and in the fashionable social season she also finds that gift-giving is a sentimental mask for ordinary greed. Charlie himself is gradually revealed as an alcoholic, lured by fast male chums to overindulgences he cannot control. The temperance message is strong in *Rose in Bloom*; liquor is the downfall not only of working men who abuse their families, but of gentlemen who cannot observe the old-fashioned moderation exemplified in domestic holiday toasts. Alcott draws a clear line between domestic abundance and a secretive popping of corks behind the closed doors of all-male smoking-rooms. In fact, it hardly matters if the drinking environment is private library or public saloon; the effect is disastrously the same. Similarly, contra dancing represents an old-fashioned intergenerational amusement, while "round" dancing at fashionable balls leads to a romantic intensity that is perilously separate from the safe circle of kin and friends. With the exception of Uncle Alec, all the adult men in the Campbell clan desert domesticity, bent on making money or escaping an imperfect homelife. Fashionable women, Alcott argues here as in earlier novels, are somewhat to blame, failing to create happy homes for husbands and children. Happy homes, in turn, are part of a dense social network which protects and sustains the individual.

Louisa Alcott's own background included her father's enjoyment of New England hard cider, and the author herself admitted she liked a glass of champagne at fashionable New York suppers. Her temperance advocacy is nonetheless genuine; it was immoderate indulgence in members of their own class that led many liberal, sophisticated reformers to support temperance. A founder of the Concord Women's Temperance Society, Louisa linked that cause to woman's suffrage. She wrote her publisher, "We are going to meet the Governor, council and legislature at Mrs. Tudor's next Wednesday and have a grand-set-to. I hope he will come out of the struggle alive."[26]

Conservative church women, previously aloof to woman's rights activities, often became public activists in the Women's Crusade, the temperance organization which soon became the Women's Christian Temperance Union. Frances Willard, subsequently president of the W.C.T.U., regarded the issue of alcohol as the single most important vehicle in persuading women of the helplessness of their sex to defend self and family. If women were dependent upon men as a natural consequence of biology, they were also helpless before the ruin visited upon them by intemperate men. Historian Barbara Epstein concludes further that "in the context of discussing mens' drinking, it was possible for women to talk about their own isolation and loneliness." Moreover, "Women could hardly object to their husbands' involvement in their work, since women's livelihood depended on it, but they could object to their husbands' socializing with other men in their free time. The saloon thus became a symbol for the larger issues of the exclusion of women and children from men's lives."[27]

Charlie Campbell takes the pledge in *Rose in Bloom* on the eve of sailing to India with his mother. He does so, however, in order to prove he is dependable enough to join the family mercantile business. Predictably, he is lured by friends for a farewell round of drinks in a saloon. Later that cold, snowy night, he is thrown from his horse in a drunken stupor. Eventually discovered and taken home, Charlie develops pneumonia and dies repentent. Rose is thereby saved from marriage to the wrong man, and soon finds herself happily involved in philanthropic work with her bookish cousin, Mac, now a physician and poet.

Rose's true partner for life, Mac, is interesting to Alcott's readers because he so closely resembles Jo March. Like the heroine of *Little Women*, Mac Campbell is shy, honest, and bookish, but occasionally sarcastic when provoked by too many conventional restrictions. He accompanies Rose to a ball, properly garbed in borrowed broadcloth and white gloves, but before the last German can be danced, "His tie was under one ear, his posy hung upside down, his gloves were rolled into a ball, which he absently squeezed and pounded as he talked, and his hair looked as if a whirlwind had passed over it."[28] Mac becomes a physician because he enjoys science as an alternative to fashionable banter and because he wishes to serve the poor. That is not enough to win Rose, however. In the end he achieves her love by proving himself tenderhearted and poetic, an admirer of Emerson's *Essays* and Thoreau's "Week on the Concord and Merrimac Rivers."[29] Mac, we are told, admired, "Heroism" and "Self-Reliance," while Rose preferred "Love" and "Friendship," as they discuss Emerson's *Essays*. Friendly arguments over Concord's distinguished ante-bellum literature proves a proper basis for true love, especially if the reader recalls that Charlie Campbell had admired Jane Eyre's Rochester as a hero.

Drawing upon her Christmas visit to Randalls Island and the Newsboys Home, Alcott uses Mac's work in a charity hospital to impress a middle-class audience with the enormity of the social problems around them. After Charlie's death, Rose takes up the cause of poor children who have no chance of fresh air or decent food; she establishes the Campbells' summer farmhouse as a vacation asylum for slum children. This asylum, in addition to the refurbishing of two old tenements as cooperative, low-cost homes for working women, constitutes the philanthropic careeer Rose chooses as an alternative to fashionable life. Mac, however, is in daily contact with the worst social inequities. One day while on his hospital rounds he comes across a destitute, dying woman who begs him to take care of her baby. He locates the infant in "a miserable place, left in the care of an old hag, who had shut her up alone to keep her out of the way, and there this mite was, huddled in a corner, crying, 'Marmar,' 'marmar' fit to touch a heart of stone."[30] The baby has been beaten and starved. Mac's own mother refuses to have an unlovely, dirty orphan baby in her house, and none of the "overcrowded institutions" can give the child the care and love she needs. Rose adopts the child, naming her Dulcinea, and a few months of kindness, food, and fresh air restore the little girl. Her new mother admits, however, that she will never really be a "gay, attractive child," having been born "in sorrow and brought up in misery."[31]

The point Alcott makes with this incident is that woman's rights and motherhood go hand in hand; Clarke's books, in fact, help feminists to unite the two. Frances Willard, for example, used the slogan of the Canadian temperance women, "Home Protection ballot," in the 1870s.[32] Women, she argued, needed suffrage in order to protect their homes from demon liquor. Certainly there was opposition within the woman's temperance movement itself to Willard's firm linkage of woman's suffrage and temperance, but she and her allies persevered in making the connection. In 1879 Willard was elected president of the WCTU and remained in that office until her death. Alcott, who was committed somewhat contradictorily both to woman's special virtue and woman's natural rights, corresponded with President Willard. She notes a letter written to her (in 1880) by a reformed convict; the man had heard Louisa read a story at Concord Prison, and wished to explain that drink had led him to steal in the first place. Alcott kept track of him, after checking his story with the prison warden, and she kept up correspondence until he left for work in South America. Alcott's letter of reference and the interest of Frances Willard in the case helped his cause, and Louisa wrote proudly, "Glad to have said a word to help the poor boy."[33]

Rose must marry because a spinster heroine might prove Clarke's charge that education and full-time public service made women unfit for motherhood. Alcott's fictional couples, however, reflect the demographic transformation in her own lifetime; she limits the March women's progeny to three children for Meg, two for Jo, and only one for Amy. *Jo's Boys* also offers the full range of demographic changes: each of the March women lives out a genuinely representative mid-nineteenth-century woman's life cycle.[34] Although Alcott marries her heroine, Rose, to young Doctor Alec Campbell in a final chapter appropriately entitled "Short and Sweet," Alcott acknowledges spinsterhood as a real choice in *Jo's Boys*. In any case, Rose and Mac are a reformist couple, pledged to "work together and try to make the world better by the music and the love we leave behind us when we go." Rose admittedly has no special talents; she does possess inherited money, which Alcott darkly intimates could only leave her prey to unscrupulous fortune hunters in the absence of a watchful, temperate mate and philanthropic endowments.

A Social Whole

Louisa May Alcott took seven years to finish the last of the March family chronicles, working on *Jo's Boys* only fitfully. She described herself as a "tired historian" in the last chapter. From 1875 through 1885 her success brought a flood of invitations to appear at reform meetings, women's colleges, prisons, and refuges. Family responsibilities scarcely diminished either, although her stream of fiction assured the Alcotts of a comfortable living. Louisa and her sister Anna shared the care of Bronson, Anna's two sons, and Louisa May Nieriker, May's daughter. It seemed for a few years that Miss Alcott could be everywhere at once. Despite recurring lameness, severe headaches, and digestive problems, she was enjoying her hard-won success.

Bronson Alcott, Frank Sanborn, and William Torrey Harris, with the aid of Julia Ward Howe and Elizabeth Peabody, among others, organized and taught the Concord School of Philosophy for several successive summers.[35] When they proposed that Louisa write a biography of her father, she gently told Sanborn that Sanborn himself was better equipped to write the biography. Sanborn's lectures on the new social science, along with Julia Ward Howe's courses on the ancient and modern views of women, touched on Louisa's new concerns.[36] Bronson was now popularly known as the grandfather of the little women because his past eccentricities had been forgiven in the new national enthusiasm for institutional reforms. Unquestionably Bronson enjoyed Louisa's success and, even more, he and Louisa both took pleasure in his later career as an educational ambassador to the West where he included Alcott family anecdotes in his lectures.

William Torrey Harris thoroughly reconstructed Bronson Alcott and his philosophy for the new order. Once, Harris claimed, Bronson had "broken himself against the old order of things."[37] Like John Brown, Garrison, and Theodore Parker, Bronson Alcott had been a heroic moral censor, braving the disapproval of the mobs. Torrey argued, on the basis of long conversations with his mentor, that the founder of Fruitlands had been converted by his family after the failure of that experiment. Alcott's later career was marked by "a growing compromise with things as they are."[38] Now Bronson was sympathetic with the "spirit of progress, which is more or less outspoken belief in evolution."[39] Clinging to his idealism, Bronson Alcott saw evolution as the spiritual development of all mankind, accompanied by great material advancement.

Newly converted to the industrial age, Alcott now saw socialism, in all its forms, as a reversion to more primitive types of human development. History, he claimed, witnessed a steady upward march from the family (the most natural social unit) to village, feudal manor, and finally to the highest stage of civilization, "free industrial competition, free suffrage and representative government."[40] Mechanical inventions were helping man to recover his lapsed omnipotence in nature; relieved of earning his bread by the sweat of his brow, humanity could at last achieve spiritual perfection. Moreover this glorious promise was now close to democratic realization. Wealth, Bronson assumed, was now more diffused, "capitalists holding kings and presidents in check while playing the better game of civilization." Criminals were being cured as well as punished and "all things are undergoing reform and reconstruction . . . laying broad and deep the foundations of new institutions."[41] Such institutions, which Louisa described in *Work* and *Jo's Boys*, included prisons, shelters, churches, schools and hospitals. She signed herself "Yours for reform of all kinds" in letters to *The Woman's Journal* and wondered, "why discuss the unknowable till our poor are fed and the wicked saved."[42]

Louisa could not have repeated the simple landscape of *Little Women* in her last March story, and did not try. The "tired historian on the March family" knew that the "walking city" of Jo's girlhood was gone, taken over by the streetcar.[43] The direct personal charity she depicted earlier was also impossible. Large numbers of Irish and German Catholic immigrants had changed the image and cultural life of northeastern cities. Many genteel residents were frightened by the possibilities of engulfment in the immigrant tide; after all, there was a decline in the native-born birth rate, a proportionately higher immigrant fertility rate, and a doubling of American divorce rates between 1870 and 1890.

The leaders of American reconstruction still believed, along with the Alcotts, that a "social whole" in which "each helps all and all help each" was possible.[44]

They conceived of society as one physical organism, not unlike the human body, with each class and sex interdependent in its functions. Individuality would be respected; as William Torrey Harris interpreted Bronson Alcott, "Respect for the self activity of others is necessary, or else the individual ego will collide with all other egos, and they will make common cause against him, and thus return on him his own negative deeds.[45] The individual "will" was now socially related; indeed, only social activity could preserve one's reason. Institutions were necessary not only to educate children and immigrants and to reform criminals, but also to readjust those individuals gone mad through social isolation or denial of organic symmetry and interdependence.

Education was now women's work.[46] The old faith in an individual's ability to earn a living and rise to a better class had to be restored, Alcott felt, and taught to poor people, immigrants, and freedmen, and women. All these classes were suspicious of gentry. Mutual mistrust, in turn, prevented orderly progress through economic and geographic expansion. "True relations with each other" were needed, and Louisa insisted that working people were eager for light, "ready to be led if some one would only show a possible way."[47] The Civil War experience demonstrated that it was possible to organize vast numbers of citizens; Louisa's old "set," in fact, had mobilized a million and a half men and vast supplies in behalf of the Union. After the war, her set prospered along with the new middle class. The new educators, including many of the old "radicals" like Bronson Alcott and Louisa herself, believed in economic expansion and social influence as progressive partners.

The expansion of territory and industry on a national scale was linked to the expansion of reform institutions both in Alcott's life and in her fiction, particularly in her later novels. Samuel Sewall, Abba's cousin, chose to invest Louisa's earnings in railroad stocks and other "sure" securities after the war.[48] In view of the vast expansion of track from 35,000 miles at the start of the war to 70,000 by 1875 and 166,700 miles fifteen years later, Sewall was not risking Alcott's savings by his choice of investments.[49] In retrospect, however, these investments embody contradictions that seem to have escaped the reformers. Alcott, for instance, was genuinely and deeply sympathetic with the plight of American Indians forced off their lands; she enthusiastically endorsed Helen Hunt's novel, *Ramona*, a romantic indictment of both settlers and governments for stealing Indian homelands.[50] *Jo's Boys* takes up the plight of the Montana tribes, yet manages to present western lands as the just spoils of manifest destiny, a white man's paradise of cheap land and social mobility.

The railroads brought white settlements west, and helped by the Homestead Act of 1862, railroads and settlers drove the Indian tribes out. Western farmers subsequently depended upon railroads as carriers of grain and beef to market. By the end of Louisa's life, railroads were locked in bitter conflict with small farmers and shippers who could not compete in markets dominated by monopolistic and unequal freight charges.

During the years Alcott wrote about the freedom available on the prairies for enterprising young businessmen and farmers (in *An Old Fashioned Girl* and *Jo's Boys*), many of them began to demand regulation of railroad charges and an end to corporate control of markets.[51]

Louisa's ideal in the last twenty years of her life was to make bourgeois entrepeneurship a genuine possibility for all Americans. At the same time she was critical of money-making and cities full of "temptations with nothing to do but waste time, money and health."[52] Her notion of the safeguards against individual corruption were still "good principles, refined tastes, and a wise mother."[53] Some people were lucky enough to be born with all three; for the others she was willing to provide both public and private institutions to act in loco parentis.

The Brave and the Strong: *Jo's Boys*

The tamers of the west, healers of the sick, and missionaries to the poor are being trained and sent forth from Laurence University. There the March women with their husbands and children live and work together again, ten years after the last chapter of *Little Women*. Three houses— Plumfield (still inhabited by Fritz, Jo and their children), Parnassus (a new mansion inhabited by Amy, Laurie, and Bess), and the Dovecote (a replica of Meg and John's Dovecote)—stand on the grounds of Aunt March's old estate. Endowed by Mr. Laurence's will, it has become a university in *Jo's Boys*. As Alcott describes it, the little women had no choice but to move together:

> For when the rapid growth of the city shut in the old house, spoilt Meg's nest and dared to put a soap factory under Mr. Laurence's indignant nose, our friends emigrated to Plumfield and the great changes began.[54]

In *Little Men* Mr. March suggested that a small family experiment could serve as a model for society. By 1886, after firmly rejecting both the family and the utopian colony as practical agents for solving social problems, Alcott created a college community with Fritz Bhaer as President, Mr. March as chaplain, and Jo as unofficial educator of social missionaries.

The young institution

> had not yet made its rules as fixed as the laws of the Medes and Persians, and believed so heartily in the right of all sex, colors, creeds and ranks to education, that there was room for everyone who knocked, and a welcome to the shabby youths from up country, the eager girls from the West, the awkward freedman or woman

from the South, or the well born student whose poverty made this college a possibility when other doors were barred. There was still prejudice, ridicule, neglect in high places, and the prophecies of failure to contend with, but the Faculty was composed of cheerful, hopeful men and women who had seen greater reforms spring from smaller roots and after stormy seasons blossom beautifully, to add prosperity and honor to the nation.[55]

Feminist demands for a coeducational environment proceeded in harmony with their demands for household democracy. Coeducation, not surprisingly, was decried by Alcott's reviewers. One critic came directly to the point: "The book is apparently intended to champion co-education, the uninterrupted acquaintance of boys and girls in their everyday life and a good comrade sort of marriage." He reminded the American public that marriage was not supposed to be based on either equality or romantic love, but on a "dignified and holy relation which brings sweetness and self-sacrifice to a woman's life."[56]

The dangers of Alcott's scheme were evident to another reviewer, who foresaw that young women might demand more than a passive role in family decision-making, not to mention in society at large. Girls should be taught to respect and obey their future husbands, not to argue or challenge their supremacy:

> We would add that while co-education needs no advocate at this day, it might be possible to look for a co-educational institution where the ordinary rules of good breeding are as little observed as among these students of "Laurence College." In our opinion, no respectable boy would stand some of the abuse which several of these boys receive from their high spirited girl friends.[57]

What the reviewer saw as "abuse" the author saw as healthy signs of the new woman.

Long-Haired Men and Short-Haired Women

Nan Harding is just the sort of "spirited girl friend" Alcott presents as the model for a new woman. Nan had already dumped her dolls overboard in *Little Men*. Then, in response to Daisy's dream of keeping house, she replied, "I shall have an office with lots of bottles and drawers and pestle things in it, and I shall drive around in a horse and chaise and cure sick people. That will be such fun."[58] Her notion of fun did not change in *Jo's Boys*; dosing Tommy Bangs, her faithful suitor, with sugar pills, she finally gets him to leave her alone and then dedicates her life "to her suffering sisters and their children." Nan represents one of a group

Alcott now called "a third class of ambitious girls." They were a mixed group. Some "hardly knew what they wanted, but were hungry for whatever could fit them to face the world and earn a living, being driven by necessity, the urgency of some half conscious talent, or the restlessness of strong young natures to break away from the narrow life which no longer satisfied."[59]

The primary coeducational experiment in *Little Men* sowed the seeds for the adult women's challenge to male dominance. Nan could run "splendidly," like Louisa herself, and she could endure scrapes as well as any boy. Still, in 1871 Alcott had been unsure how much freedom girls might aspire to. Jo had importuned the indulgent Fritz, "Don't let us snub her restless little nature, but do our best to give her work she likes, and by and by persuade her father to let her study medicine." In *Jo's Boys*, Nan is a physician and "the pride of the community."[60]

The coeds who flock to Meg, Jo, and Amy's weekly sewing circle are given a feminist education in just such possibilities. In a chapter called "Among the Maids," a happy sisterhood passes on domestic skills and reform literature along with genteel hints on dress and deportment. On Saturdays, Amy's sewing room becomes a meeting place for the "sweet privacy that domestic women have and can make so helpful by a wise mixture of cooks and chemistry, table linen and theology, prosaic duties and good poetry." They read aloud to each other, taking turns, and "Mrs. Jo gives little lectures on health, religion and politics and the various questions in which all should be interested, with copious extracts from Miss Cobbe's Duties of Women, Miss Brackett's Education of American Girls, Mrs. Duffy's No Sex in Education, Mrs. Woolson's Dress Reform, and many of the other excellent books wise women write for their sisters now that they are waking up and asking what shall we do?"[61]

Alcott had at last harmonized her personal and political perspective. Her new generation of girls notes that "old maids aren't sneered at half as much as they used to be, since some of them have grown famous and proved that woman isn't half but a whole being and can stand alone."[62] Nevertheless, traditional family life still offered the only "tender ties" allowable in conventional society. Work, social life, and ultimately security were shaped by the sexual division of labor. Coeducation challenged that division, and by implication it then challenged the right of one social unit, the conjugal family, to stand as the only basis for social harmony and progress.

It is not only that Laurence College makes spinsterhood a viable choice, or that it provokes women to demand egalitarian marriage, that makes *Jo's Boys* so interesting for its time. Despite its acceptance of a single standard of middle-class morality and taste, the book presents women who are willing to criticize free enterprise as the means of life; no longer hostages to fortune, women want men to free themselves too.

Meg Brooke, the most dependent and "housewifely" little woman (she moved to Laurence University after being widowed), objects to her son choosing bookkeeping as his profession. In *Little Men* John Brooke died revered by all who knew him for being "conscientious almost to a fault as a businessman and above reproach in all things,"[63] His widow wants something better for her son. "No," she says, "you'll get round shouldered writing at a tall desk; and they say, once a bookkeeper always a bookkeeper."[64] She grows even bolder in demanding social mobility and some restoration of entrepeneurial opportunities:

> I don't want my son to spend his best years grubbing for a little money in a dark office, or be knocked about in a rough and tumble scramble to get on. I want to see you in some business where your tastes and talents can be developed and made useful; where you can go on rising, and in time put in your little fortune, and be a partner; so that your years of apprenticeship will not be wasted but fit you to take your place among the honorable men who make their lives and work useful and respected.[65]

Young John obeys his mother and finds work with Aunt Jo's publishers, where he can sell books even though he agrees that writing them is more satisfactory work. Above all he will deal with a refined class of people, and his name may yet be listed among the partners. He marries Alice Healey, also a graduate of Laurence University, and the reader knows that Alice will work because she has already considered spinsterhood, having ailing parents to support. A respectable girl, though impoverished, Alice's taste is never questioned and she is praised by Meg March Brooke, guardian of the March family line.[66]

Virtuous Ancestors

Louisa May Alcott never resolves contradictions between Romantic individuality and the standardized shaping and control of "all sex, colors, creeds and ranks" inherent in rational feminist reform efforts.[67] If society was truly one social organism, she imagined that it resembled her friends in the "regular anti-slavery set." After all, a "long line of virtuous ancestors," as she called them, were everyone's "founding fathers" by right of acculturation. The opportunity to acquire that culture and its values was a right she championed for all Americans.

Great fortunes in the hands of old families are a mainstay of Laurence University. Theodore Laurence, having outgrown his vulgar college-boy pranks, now dedicates himself to helping worthy, impoverished students. They all want to dress like the Laurences and appreciate art and music just as their patrons do. Amy and Meg, in particular, provide advice on making over coeds' cheap and vulgar green or pink silk gowns with muslin over-layers, trimming them with suitable fresh flowers. The coeds cannot afford to copy Mrs. Laurence's "India mull and Valenciennes lace," but they learn that her taste is the proper standard of excellence.[68] When Laurie says to Jo, "Come and have a dish of tea, old dear, and see what the young folks are about," the contemporary reader of *Jo's Boys* is reassured that progress and reform are in capable hands.[69]

Nevertheless, Jo does not relinquish her old belief in the sanctity and privacy of each individual soul. Her system of "conscience books" is put aside once the little men and women have grown up, but she still chooses private moments to have missionary chats with each errant young student. In a conversation with one coed, she admits to preferring Charlotte Bronte over George Eliot because "the brain is there" in Eliot, but the "heart is left out."[70] The key to her preference is more fully expressed in a novel Alcott wrote in 1877, *A Modern Mephistopheles*, wherein a self-sacrificing heroine reasserts the romantic message of *The Scarlet Letter*.[71] The unpardonable sin is still a "want of love and reverence for the human soul, which makes a man pry into its mysterious depths, not with a hope or purpose of making it better, but from a cold philosophical curiousity."[72]

The possibility of separating intellect from feeling is Alcott's only problem with the new social sciences, one she solves by placing Jo Bhaer, like Penelope, among the maids at Laurence. Jo's notion of household democracy expands with utter self-confidence into social housekeeping. Theodore Parker's vision is fully realized at Plumfield, but it is not technology which frees the little women. Jo is finally revealed as a successful author in this novel. Her earnings buy security for the whole family, and together with the Laurence endowment, help create a cooperative domesticity involving all three houses. The sisters spell one another at entertaining, cooking, and supervising children. Jo, Meg, and Amy are thus free to reform and control their society, each with her own area of expertise. The question of who really benifits from women's unpaid housework is never really answered.

Their own children do not present much of a challenge to the power of benificent social influence. Jo's sons, Rob and Ted, do display a few unsavory tendencies. Like his father and grandfather, Rob is a bit too passive and bookish. Teddy has inherited Jo's taste for larking and scrapes, and he has been so indulged that he teases animals when he cannot get his way.[73] Nevertheless, these faults can be gently corrected. Meg's daughter, Josie, a wild, harum-scarum girl, becomes a famous actress and a competitive athlete by virtue of inherited talent, Laurence

University connections to a famous actress, and the settling influence of a good college education.[74]

Nat and Dan, the two boys whose origins are largely unknown, present the real dilemma of the novel. They have quite opposite but equally troubling flaws, presumably inherited, and both fall in love with genteel daughters of their benefactors. Dan's father was a handsome wastrel. His mother, who ran away from her husband to save the boy from a bad example, dies young, leaving her son on his own. By the time he arrives at Plumfield Dan is a wild colt, only half tamed by the end of *Little Men*. As *Jo's Boys* progresses, it is obvious that the Bhaers still love him, but do not consider him college material. Instead, he tries his hand at ranching in Australia, hunting and riding with Indians in Montana, and on a visit to Laurence proposes to invest his money in large-scale farming in Kansas. On his way west he saves a young boy from the clutches of card sharks. One of them draws a gun and Jo's quick-tempered hero strikes the cheat a killing blow.[75]

The central chapter of the novel, a moral turning point, occurs as Dan spends a bleak Christmas in prison, doing hard labor for his crime. Ashamed and hopeless, he does not contact his friends at Plumfield. But he is touched by a sermon from a visiting, middle-aged woman missionary, and he accepts responsibility for his crime and prays that he can make the rest of his life decent and self-sacrificing.[76] After his prison term Dan finds work in a rough mining town where violence and anarchy are common. The mining of that wealth, Alcott intimates, is fit employment for the rougher sort of romantic American hero.

The Marches and Laurences learn of Dan's whereabouts by chance—through a newspaper account of a mine accident in which he rescued several men.[77] He was seriously injured in the rescue, and Laurie and Jo's son Ted travel west to bring him back to Plumfield and Jo's care. Slowly recovering, he falls in love with one of his nurses, Laurie and Amy's beautiful golden-haired daughter, Bess. Jo, however, barely needs remind him that killing in self-defense, which he had paid for, is much less important than his unreliable temperament and unknown origins in making him an unacceptable husband for wealthy, delicately bred Bess.

Dan goes off with a lock of Bess's golden hair, determined to devote his life to the Indians. He makes a commitment to plead their cause himself, but Fritz Bhaer insists that "one honest agent among many would not do much, and noble as the effort would be, it would be wiser to think over the matter carefully, get influence and authority from the right quarters."[78] Laurie then goes to Washington to ensure that Dan will have that influence, prudently taking Bess and Amy with him so that the impressionable "little princess" will not be tempted by a last romantic farewell with Dan.

Government, Alcott knows, is slow to right wrongs, and so Dan's mission is more designed to supply him a noble end than to reform society. He dies defending his "chosen people" in the western mountains. His selfless heroism wins no earthly reward, and Alcott makes it clear that Dan, despite any visible flaws save his passion for justice, is best exiled beyond the frontiers of ordered, passionless society.[79]

Nat, Dan's best friend, is weak and suffers from a lack of initiative, presumably inherited. He has grown up with Daisy, Meg's older daughter, and fallen in love with her; Daisy reciprocates the feeling. Jo is forced to tell Nat that Meg "objects". Poor Nat must go off to Europe to perfect his musical talent with a scholarship from Laurie. Jo advises the brokenhearted suitor to prove his faithfulness and love by "being not only a good musician but an excellent man, and so command respect and confidence." Angered, Nat declares: "Other fellows poorer and stupider than I have done great things and come to honor. Why may not I, though I am nothing now? I know Mrs. Brooke remembers what I came from, but my father was honest though everything went wrong and I have nothing to be ashamed of though I was a *charity* boy."[80]

Aunt Jo is equally defensive and somewhat confused in her reply to Nat: "Daisy's mother is not really a snob, she does not despise your poverty or your past, but mothers are very tender over their daughters and we Marches, though we have been poor, *are* I confess, a little proud of our good family. We don't care for money, but a long line of virtuous ancestors *is* something to desire and be proud of."[81]

The story ends happily enough, for Nat eventually becomes a modest success after running through his scholarship funds and taking two part-time jobs to avoid debt and disgrace in Germany. He thereby wins Daisy, the most exemplary homebody in all of American fiction, and it seems obvious that he will never stray far from Meg Brooke's careful monitoring. Unhappy union, in Alcott's fiction, usually result from an attempt to unite a woman with a suitor of lesser social standing. A young woman might marry upward, as did Phoebe, the kitchen maid in *Eight Cousins* and *Rose in Bloom*, but only after one's character was proven by hard work.[82] Moreover, Alcott's socially mobile young women are miraculously adopted by the families they marry into *before* romance blooms—characters of lesser origins must become fictive kin before wedlock. Old-fashioned girls with genteel backgrounds may marry monied men with little problem. It is precisely their lack of wealth and fashionable lifestyle that fits these gentlewomen for the task of domestic reform.

Profits and Pleasures

Charity, even when proferred by the most genteel, tender-hearted philanthropists, was not enough for the "deserving" poor in Alcott's later fiction. She tentatively explored the social conditions for self-reliance in a diverse, industrial society. "Mountain Laurel and Maidenhair," a story included in *Garland for Girls* (1888), typically blends Transcendental themes into a social science analysis of society.[83] The plot centers around a developing friendship between two girls. Emily, the dainty daughter of wealthy city-folk, is "tuckered out doing nothing", while Becky Moore, a sturdy "red-haired freckle-faced" country girl, has boundless energy despite a full work-load of farm and family chores.[84] Emily is taken in by Becky's mother to continue her life-long recuperation from leisure. The delicate invalid is served breakfast in bed by Becky, who brings her "a glass of rosy laurel and delicate maiden-fern" with toast, eggs, strawberries and cream.[85] The two girls discover a mutual interest in literature as Emily develops a hunger for farm food in the fresh country air.

Emily's trunk yields up fashionably bound books by Whittier, Tennyson, and Emerson, all of which Becky "hungrily" notices. At first her new friend is disdainful at the idea of a farmer's daughter with a taste for poetry. Emily prefers Tennyson, and "shows that even Emerson's simplest poems were far above her comprehension as yet, because she loved sentiment more than nature."[86] But Becky stoutly defends Whittier as "true and natural", and Emerson's pages are enough to waken in her face "something like beauty."[87]

Alcott invokes the natural environment itself as a teacher for Emily, and she soon ventures out with the "instinct of all young creatures for air and motion," replete with protective hat, wrap, book, and parasol.[88] The Moore family is busy at chores, including a market garden, chickens, butter-making, strawberry picking and the cooking of meals for five paying guests. Mr. Moore is spoken of only in the past tense. Like Bronson Alcott, he was the son of a farmer, and worked hard to clear the stony land and build the spring and bower that is Mrs. Moore's favorite resting place. Becky is the eldest and said to take after her father. Gradually Emily discovers that her friend not only reads and recites poetry, but writes it too, inbetween cooking, weaving carpets, and teaching in the local school—where, at eighteen, she reports that "some of my boys are big fellows older than I am."

Discovering one of Becky's poems, "Mountain Laurel," Emily fancies a brilliant and well-paid career for her friend and herself, the glory of discovering "a feminine Burns among the New Hampshire hills." Becky is at first angry at the intrusion, and then "a few happy tears drop on the hands so worn with hard work, when they ached to be holding a pen and trying to record the fancies that sung in her brain."[89] Only Becky's mother had known that Becky wrote poetry. Then Emily's mother, Mrs. Spencer, is taken into the girls' confidence, but after reading the poems she sensibly concludes that they "would bring neither fame nor money." Mrs. Spencer is a friend of Whittier and the patron of many aspiring "unfledged scribblers." She advises them all to "work and wait," then to "first live, then write," and finally to "do the duty that is nearest." Becky's life is not to be spoiled by "rash projects."[90]

Instead, another summer visitor, a wealthy and practical widow who was once a country girl herself, presents a way for the Moores to keep their farm. Unlike "Eli's Education," this story argues that a widow and her daughters can be self-supporting.[91] The worldly widow believes in Mrs. Moore's capabilities, and goes about the neighborhood talking to farmers about a means of getting their collective produce to market more efficiently. She encourages them to push for a "branch railroad down to Peeksville" which "would increase the value of the land, and enable them to get their strawberries and asparagus to market."[92] Becky delightedly tells her friend that "some of the rich men took up the plan and we hope it will be done this fall. It will be the making of us, for our land is first rate for crops, and the children can help at that, and with a depot close by it would be such easy work. That's what I call helping folks to help themselves."[93]

There are some interesting turns to Emersonian theories of nature and democracy in this late-nineteenth-century story. The mountain laurel is a sturdy flower, like Becky herself, but the delicate maidenhair fern will not grow as luxuriantly in the wild as it does in Emily's greenhouse. Becky has transplanted the ferns, from "nooks on the mountain hidden under the taller ferns and in sly corners." The laurel, however, will not thrive in a greenhouse, and Becky warns Emily to "leave the dear bushes alone, and come up here and enjoy 'em in their own place."[94]

Mrs. Spencer's mottoes, superficially so like Emerson's and Alcott's in affirming natural capacities, are very different in their denial of the individual's ability to step out of historical circumstances. Her counsel, which is buttressed by Becky's botanical lessons, argues that the laws of progress derive from empirical relationships in the real world. These female reformers, moreover, are not planting a new Eden based on self-culture and denial of material abundance. On the contrary, one young woman strengthens another with mouth-watering meals, and a female-headed family stays together by shipping strawberries and asparagus to market on the railroad. This band of reformers includes three social science-minded guests of the Moore's—affable lady schoolteachers who also forsake the more fashionable resort hotels to summer on the farm. *Garland for Girls* does not overlook men, but they always appear as fathers, brothers, and sweethearts saved from the excesses of social drinking by temperance-minded young women.

All the heroines are like the "May flowers," Alcott writes, who "being Boston girls, of course got up a club for mental improvement and, as they were all descendents of the Pilgrim Fathers, they called it the May

Flower Club."[95] The less well-to-do young women work for a living at teaching, sewing, even fishmongering. Becky Moore, however, is the most advanced of these new little women, because in the end she remains a happy spinster, helping out at home until the younger children are able to manage the farm. Then she turns to teaching "in which she found both profit and pleasure."[96]

In *Little Men* Alcott suggested that proper training for female abundance begins in the nursery. Banned from boys' games, Daisy is compensated by Mrs. Jo with a play kitchen. It had "a real iron stove, big enough to cook for a large family of very hungry dolls. But the best of it was that a real fire burned in it, real steam came out of the nose of the little teakettle, and the lid of the little boiler actually danced a jig, the water inside bubbled so hard."[97] Daisy, however, did not cook just for dolls. She ordered groceries from Asia, the cook and with much sighing over her "sweet rolling pin, darling dish tub and cunning pepper pot" she produced meals as rewards for good boys. Alcott insisted that "if little men are like big ones, good cooking will touch their hearts and soothe their tempers delightfully."[98] None of the little men, however, ever learn to cook.

Domesticity and Feminism

Only one young man in Alcott's later fiction actually cooks. He is a foundry watchman, "a young and pleasant-looking fellow, with a merry eye, an honest brown face and a hearty voice."[99] A poor orphaned sewing girl finds a friend in him, and "Letty's Tramp" (who is not a tramp at all) offers her shelter from a snowstorm, a pallet by his fire, a sandwich and hot coffee. The author knows that a working girl needs the stimulant that only overexcites a lady of leisure. Letty and her friend Joe fall in love because he "tried to express his sympathy in deeds as well as words."[100] Not only does he cook her supper and share his breakfast next morning, he also finds work for her after learning that the putting-out system pays Letty only six cents, "sometimes only four," for each shirt she sews. Joe decides to reject the products of this sweat labor: "Hanged if I buy another."[101] Instead, he orders a bale of red flannel and stakes Letty to a small shirtmaking business, the finished products to be sold to his fellow foundrymen. Joe and Letty marry eventually, but we never learn if he continues to make the coffee and sandwiches.

Moods presented a large class of women identified as a "sad sisterhood," forced by unfortunate circumstances into the world. *Work* expanded on their trials and sufferings in a hostile world. *Little Women*, in turn, gave domestic reformers an opportunity to demonstrate the possibilities for women in democratic households. Alcott later reached towards enlarged institutions to reproduce the March family's mutual sacrifice. *Little Men* began a coeducational experiment in cooperative democracy. Then, in the uncompleted *Diana and Persis*, Alcott expresses her suspicion that a private domestic solution to the woman problem is not possible. Even at Lawrence University, in *Jo's Boys*, the true union of domesticity and feminism is incomplete. Jo herself is free to write and supervise community morality, but her domestic freedom depends upon the excellent money she earns; moreover; Fritz never challenges her household authority. Even earning a living and having an agreeable, almost invisible spouse is not enough; Jo's liberty also depends upon Daisy's migratory cooking, Meg's baby-sitting, and her own paid household staff.

The March sisters and their progeny at Laurence University never really yield control of their lives to anyone. It is not even clear that children of the March family attend classes there. The college really exists for those who lack family, wealth, or social influence to place them comfortably in the world. The March sons and daughters find their way in that world through a network of family and friends, with only vague references to college educations. Laurence, then, is a vehicle for presenting the feminist demand for coeducation in a pleasing, comfortable way. It is also Alcott's means of reassuring her public about new reformist institutions. Like *Little Women*, *Little Men* and *An Old Fashioned Girl*, the final March novel tries to make social change seem like old, familiar history.

Little Women has a timeless resonance which reflects Alcott's grasp of her historical framework in the 1860s. The novel's ideas do not intrude themselves upon the reader because the author wholly controls the implications of her imaginative structure. Sexual equality is the salvation of marriage and the family; democratic relationships make happy endings. This is the unifying imaginative frame of *Little Women* which then expands into *Little Men* and bravely attempts to work itself out as historical law in *Jo's Boys*.

The last effort fails, but Alcott is in good company. The progressive social imagination embodied in the utopian works of Twain, Howells, and Gilman (only a few years after *Jo's Boys*) accepted human nature as constant, but posited history as advancing toward ideal freedom. The inherent contradictions of this position troubled all utopian writers, perhaps Alcott the most of all. She made her choice after the Civil War in favor of the progressive framework, but its concepts never fully live in the fictional worlds she created. Also, despite her debt to the Romantic belief in conflict as the source of creativity, she feared the radical implications of conflict after the war.

It was not enthusiasm which frightened her. Alcott was on the side of Anne Hutchinson and Hester Prynne; it was time to realize the brave new relationship between the sexes prophesized in *The Scarlet Letter*. By the 1880s, that new relationship was as contradictory in her own work as it was in the woman's rights movement itself. She insisted on the full human status of her heroines while also claiming that women must play a major role in society because of their capacity for nurturance. Daisy exercised that gift traditionally by caring for her extended family, while Nan demonstrated her womanly nature by becoming a woman's physician and healing the members of her own sex. Both heroines, of course, deserve suffrage, and therefore the right-minded heroes in *Jo's Boys* support their claim. The best of Jo's boys, in fact, learn to expand their nurturing capacities, and in becoming more like women they become more fully human as well.

Sexual segregation permitted Harvard's President Eliot to claim that "the world knows next to nothing about the natural mental capacities of the female sex."[102] Alcott therefore insisted that coeducation was the best method of teaching one sex about the capacities of the other. To that end, Josie competes almost rudely with visiting Harvard students in tennis matches and debates about woman's suffrage. Such competitions, incidentally, separate the real men from the boys; weaker members of the male sex give up quickly in the face of feminist challenge. Defeated men, Alcott says, seek feminine balm for their wounded vanity; they marry girls who are willing to mother them. Having made a strong case for women's natural rights, Alcott then admits a fear that girls, overly protected in youth, might lack the aggressiveness necessary in traditionally masculine territory. She recognized that intellectual and physical skills alone were not enough, and notes in *Rose in Bloom* that "we do our duty better by the boys . . . the poor little women are seldom provided with any armor worth having; and, sooner or later, they are sure to need it, for every one must fight her own battle, and only the brave and strong can win."[103] Young women needed the experience of a male-dominated society, she thought, in order to prepare themselves for the "ups and downs of life."

At the same time, the author of *Little Women* suspected that democratic domesticity was itself a product of women's segregation from the power struggles of the larger world. In order to reform society, women must have some means of maintaining their own sense of idealism and mutual sacrifice in a coeducational world. The March sisters therefore re-create the old sewing circle, passing on the little women's spirit of egalitarian domesticity to a new generation of coeds who might otherwise succumb totally to male values—and consequently reject the domestic habits that link them to ordinary women outside the university community. Women, Alcott argues, will not remake the world by becoming just like men. Both sexes are united in the old familiar way at the close of *Jo's Boys* when Nat plays "the street melody he gave them the first night he came to Plumfield." All of the others remember it and join in singing.

> Oh, my heart is sad and weary
> Everywhere I roam, still
> Longing for the old plantation
> And for the old folks at home.[104]

Ancestors and Immigrants

Next to civil war, the conflict Alcott and her friends feared most was brewing in the struggles of immigrants, freedmen, women, industrial workers, and angry small farmers. These groups constituted a growing numerical majority in the United States. True, progressivism at its most rigorous argued that "The Law is Progress: The Result Democracy."[105] But for Alcott a popular victory was cause for celebration only when the victors were familiar native stock whose leaders were of unquestioned good breeding and reputation (such as her friends).

When late nineteenth-century American society expanded beyond the communal myth of the March cottage, Louisa Alcott shifted her perspective uneasily. The primacy of biology over culture, an idea which had never really been defeated by ante-bellum reformers, made a strong come-back in reaction to the woman's rights movement. Combatting this resurgence strengthened Alcott's conviction that no inherent differences existed between races and ethnic groups either. If environment actually shaped human behavior, then Alcott and her set were more determined than ever to provide a single national culture fashioned in their own image. They generally assumed that their own dominance was the result of social laws beyond individual control, thereby absolving themselves from responsibility for institutionalizing poverty, racial and sexual discrimination, and the virtual annihilation of American Indian tribal life. Much of the injustice seemed a regrettable by-product of progress; ultimately there would be abundance for all. They counted upon social influence to blend Americans within a balanced society. In *Jo's Boys*, for instance, Alcott tries to accept the social structure around her as given.

She never questioned its historical origins. Believing that her beloved band of reformers had fought for progress, she found it hard to question their achievement. Indeed, there had been great changes: the emancipation of slaves was the greatest of all victories. Louisa deliberately used the old antislavery language as proof of her women's rights allegiance; in 1885 she told Lucy Stone, "After a fifty year acquaintance with the noble men and women of the anti-slavery cause, the sight of the glorious end to their faithful work, I should be a traitor to all I most love, honor and desire to imitate, if I did not covet a place among those who are giving their lives to the emancipation of the white slaves of America."[106]

Although they defend social stability, Alcott's last works also attempt to persuade readers to accept and advance social change. That there were contradictions between democratic ideals and social reality, Alcott never denied. She had lived through a period of extraordinary social ferment. Like many of her circle, including Harris, Sanborn, Cheney, Croly, Abba May and Julia Ward Howe, she was less fearful of destroying the individual than she was of civil war. In any case, molding society into line with the values already held by her set seemed more or less the natural working out of Providence—with a little help from the "best people." It must be said as an explanation, if not an excuse, that Alcott never forgot the examples of David Thoreau, Frank Sanborn, and John Brown. Once she had fiercely supported the effort to arm slaves against their masters, knowing that ownership of human beings is the worst example of property rights. Similarly, she thought that good people would refuse to accept the degradation and exploitation of their fellow human beings after emancipation.

Social roles now seemed to have some intrinsic merit. In Alcott's earlier fiction, stepping out of a role allowed her heroines to see society more truly—as Jo does when she stomps aound in unlaced boots uttering rather mild boyish slang. But Jo's role-swapping did not change society. In *Jo's Boys*, her namesake, Josie, does not need to pretend at being a boy. A modern girl, never outside her role, she plays tennis in comfortable clothes, swims and dives like a porpoise, and insists on acting as a profession, not as a mere vent for pent-up feelings. Woman's social role had indeed changed between 1868 and 1885, and the "great changes" are evident in the hope Alcott holds out to a generation of coeds at Laurence University.

From a nineteenth-century feminist perspective, women needed a social structure to replace the code of laissez faire individualism. They could not desert society and light out to the territories as Dan does in *Jo's Boys*. Alcott, moreover, does not set her utopia backwards, as Twain does in *A Connecticut Yankee in King Arthur's Court* (1889), or forward, as Bellamy does in *Looking Backward* (1888). Although her society at Laurence University somewhat resembles Charlotte Perkins Gilman's *Herland* (1915), Alcott does not remove men from utopia to achieve social harmony and rational planning.

Jo's Boys is set in Alcott's last historical moment. It chronicles the gains made in her lifetime, but gathers them up into one great cornucopia at Plumfield. There her readers may observe the scattered gains already integrated into a social system. Young men and women have a free, open relationship with one another. They eat healthily, exercise, and work hard in anticipation of happy useful lives. Their educated talent is dedicated to social welfare. Only indolent, dull sons of wealth loll at Harvard with no important plans for the future; Alcott intimates that they will be superfluous in the new order.

For all her energy in depicting a brave new world, Alcott cannot make its inhabitants compelling. Josie at fourteen is a "pretty little lass" with "curly dark hair, bright eyes, and a very expressive face." But she does not capture our hearts as Jo did with her wonderful mixture of self-will and self-sacrifice. Josie has talent but little imagination; she is all common sense. Moreover, she has no apparent ties to her sister Daisy, and unlike Jo, who resented her sisters' marraiges, Josie willingly serves as John's go-between in his courtship of Alice Healey. The earlier little women had clung to their childhood and their siblings, but Josie cannot wait to grow up. Young womanhood, Alcott argues, is now glorious independence for those with talent, discipline, and a college education.

There are moments of nostalgia in *Jo's Boys*, but they are all for former days of adversity. Moreover, the poor young people at Laurence acquiesce too easily to advice about patience, hard work, and dressmaking. Alcott has not lost her feeling for youth—Dan's plight is evocative of brave John Sulie in Hospital Sketches—but somehow the new little women seem a tame group. It is as if life lies outside the gates of utopia. The ragged children who wander in and out of stories in *St. Nicholas* and the collected tales of *Aunt Jo's Scrap Bag*, for example, have the warm spark of Alcott's earliest heroes and heroines. Her later feminist men and women have benefitted greatly from the earlier band's efforts and they do care about the ragged children and working men and women. Alcott never quite saw the world she imagined in *Jo's Boys* and she could not portray it as reality. To the end, a "cry for bread and hunger for home" was the woman problem as she knew it.

Epilogue

On September 19, 1980, Louisa Alcott welcomed her niece and namesake, Louisa May Nieriker, to Boston. "Miss Alcott's baby" filled the last years of her life with the everyday pleasures and trials of motherhood. It was a new world for her, one in which she told stories, kissed hurts, and escaped occasionally to the Bellevue, where she maintained her traditional, separate "writing room."[107] Maternal feelings now linked Louisa comfortably to women friends—she wrote to Betsey William, "My poppet is a picture of health, vigor and delightful naughtiness."[108]

Louisa's financial success enabled the Alcott family to rent to a succession of comfortable mansions in Boston and to keep up Anna's "Thoreau House" as their stable Concord home. Louisa adopted John

Pratt so that Anna's elder son could file for royalties from her fiction after she died.[109] She made a will, precise enough to satisfy the most conservative May spirit. Her own ill health and a terrible awareness of the Concord circle's passing led her to these precautions. Emerson died in 1882, and then Wendell Phillips too was gone. Together with Frank Sanborn, Louisa edited a new edition of Theodore Parker's prayers as a memorial to the old antislavery set.[110]

In the fall the Alcotts sold Orchard House to William Torrey Harris; it seemed right to pass on reform headquarters to one of Bronson's disciples. Then Bronson was paralyzed by a stroke. Rushing back to Concord, Louisa joined her sister and a team of nurses and doctors in caring for him. He recovered, and although never fully his old self, he could nevertheless sit through sessions of his Concord School of Philosophy on warm summer afternoons.[111] Louisa migrated back and forth between Concord, a summer cottage at Nonquitt, New York, and Boston.[112]

Louisa did not much care for her status as a public figure, but she loved to hear that "the books go well" because the doctors insisted she limit her writing to two hours a day. Her fears of financial distress alternated with periods in which she accepted her increasing fragility. Finally she retreated to a nursing home owned by Dr. Rhoda Lawrence, Louisa's friend and a homeopathic physician. Dr. Lawrence supervised a diet of milk, rest, and regular massage.[113] Lulu was relinquished to Anna's care, but she made daily visits to Aunt Louisa in the Roxbury home. For a while, even after a twenty-five pound weight loss, it seemed that Louisa might be cured. She went on a final holiday with Dr. Lawrence to New Hampshire, where the mountains looked down over the old experiment at Fruitlands. But her list of symptoms, painfully recorded in a red-leather diary, were irreversible.[114]

Louisa was apparently a lingering casuality of the Civil War. Calomel, mercurous chloride, is not normally expelled from the body. Unless taken with saline laxatives, it accumulates through successive doses. The doctors who used calomel to treat typhoid in Louisa's lifetime often seemed indifferent whether or not the drug was administered with a laxative. Her symptoms, which included weakness, fatigue, loss of appetite, weight loss, sore throats, tremors, and lameness all point to slowly incapacitating mercury poisoning.[115]

On March 1, 1888 she drove in a carriage to see Bronson, who was seriously ill at the family's rented house on Louisburg Square. It was cold, and Louisa was carefully wrapped in a fur cloak. Bronson could only murmur, "I am going up, come with me."[116] Hurrying back to her own sickbed, the daughter he called "duty's faithful child" left off her warm wrap. Chilled, weakened, and grieving, Louisa sank into a fever. On

March 6, two days after her father's death, Louisa May Alcott died in her sleep at the age of fifty-six.[117]

In 1889 Robert Brothers brought out a posthumous volume containing two early Alcott romances, *A Modern Mephistopheles* and *A Whisper in the Dark*.[118] Both are treatments of romantic sexual conflict; each heroine resists possession of her soul by a more dominant masculine will. In the "modern" version of Faust, an innocent girl, Gladys, marries a handsome young poet who owes his fame and fortune to a wealthy diabolic genius, Helwyze. Unknown to Gladys, her husband's poetry is really written by Helwyze, who has arranged her marriage to Felix Canaris, the young poet, only because he wants them both under his roof where he can enjoy Gladys' fresh beauty. She almost succumbs to the evil man after he tricks her into taking hashish one night, but her true love for Felix (the young poet) is strong enough to prevent seduction. In the end her unhappy husband confesses his awful debt to Helwyze, and is freed at the cost of Gladys's life. She dies in childbirth, escaping both men.

In *A Whisper in the Dark* a similar scheme confronts young Sybil. Her marriage to her cousin is designed so that he and his wicked father can gain control of Sybil's fortune. When she learns of their plot, she refuses to marry the young man even though she has fallen in love with him. Drugged and kidnapped, she awakens in a strange mansion to discover that she is imprisoned for life. Going mad with isolation and despair, she hears another woman walking in the room above her, singing a lullaby.

The woman upstairs is already quite mad, her closed door guarded by a huge hound who eyes Sybil and growls savagely when she tries to enter the room. Nevertheless, she persists in seeking some communication with the other prisoner. Finally, on a warm April night, awakening to walk in the moonlight, Sybil sees a ghostly hand waving from the single pane of glass in the woman's door. "Shrill through the keyhole came a whisper that chilled me to the marrow of my bones, so terribly distinct and imploring it was," recalls Sibyl. "Find it! for God's sake find it before it is too late!" implores the hidden lady. Then again, "The dog—a lock of hair—there is yet time."[119]

On the next day the room upstairs is open. An empty cradle stands beside the bed, and a lifeless body rests on it. Sybil sees its face, a pale image of her own. It is not her imagination. "The hair, beautiful and blonde," as hers had been," streamed long over the pulseless breast, and on the hand, still clenched in that last struggle, shone the likeness of a ring" identical to the one Sybil wore, a ring bequeathed her by her father.[120] The other prisoner is Sybil's long-lost mother, driven mad by separation from her husband and child, incarcerated by the same wicked step-uncle who persecutes Sybil.

At long last the daughter realizes that there is a message attached to the dog's collar by a lock of her mother's blond hair. The older woman never knew that Sybil was her daughter, yet she tried to warn her and help her to escape, writing in the note: "Child! Woman! whatever you are, leave this accursed house while you have power to do it."[121] A mad experiment by a doctor in the employ of Sybil's step-uncle sets the house on fire. The girl runs away, fortunately encountering her cousin, Guy, who tells her the whole story of her own and her mother's betrayal by his father. Guy, "through the hard discipline of poverty and honest labor," has become a "manlier man."[122] He helps Sybil to health and control of her own wealth, and the two cousins marry and live happily ever after.

Madeleine Stern has suggested that success prevented Louisa Alcott from writing any more of the passionate, feminist tales exemplified by *A Whisper in the Dark*. Sybil's voice, never acknowledged as Louisa's own in her lifetime, nevertheless reverberates across the years. Under the gold-leaf title of a posthumous edition of the story, the "Author of *Little Women*" admits that "over all these years, serenely prosperous, still hangs over me the shadow of the past, still rises that dead image of my mother, still echoes that spectral whisper in the dark."[123]

Notes

Bibliographical Note

Significant use has been made of the following manuscript collections:

Houghton Library, Harvard University
Abigail May Alcott, Fragments of an Autobiography (Incomplete Diaries of Abigail May Alcott; pages saved by Louisa May Alcott for use in a future biography of her mother, including pages from Abigail May Alcott's diaries copied by Louisa. Louisa burned some pages and left instructions to destroy the remaining entries after her own death. Her instructions were not carried out.)
Alcott Family Papers
Alcott-Pratt Collection
Amos Bronson Alcott, Autobiographical Collections
Amos Bronson Alcott, Autobiographical Index
Amos Bronson Alcott, Manuscript Journal
Emerson Papers
Louisa May Alcott, Letters and Papers
Memoir of Abigail May Alcott, Notes and Materials left by Amos Bronson Alcott, 1878

Olin Library, Cornell University
Samuel J. May Papers

Boston Public Library
Alcott Collection
Samuel May Papers

Concord Free Public Library, Concord, Mass.
Alcott Papers
Franklin Sanborn Papers

Onondaga Historical Society, Syracuse, N.Y.
Samuel J. May Papers

Preface

1. Margaret Fuller, *Memoirs: Memoirs of Margaret Fuller Ossoli*, ed. R. W. Emerson, W. H. Channing, and J. F. Clarke, (Boston, 1884), I, 297.
2. Ibid.
3. Ibid., p. 237. See also Bell Gale Chevigny, *The Woman and the Myth: Margaret Fuller's Life and Writings* (New York, 1976).
4. Ednah Cheney, ed., *Louisa May Alcott: Life, Letters and Journals* (Boston, 1928); p. 39.
5. See Madeleine B. Stern, *Louisa May Alcott* (London, New York, 1957), p. 288.
6. Amos Bronson Alcott, "Observations on the Spiritual Nurture of My Children" and "Researches on Childhood," Alcott-Pratt Collection at Houghton Library, Harvard University.
7. Sarah J. Hale's review is quoted as an advertisement in the endpiece for Louisa May Alcott novels after *Little Women*, in the Robert Bros. series.
8. A complete bibliography of Alcott's works is available in Madeleine B. Stern, ed., *Louisa's Wonder Book* (Michigan, 1975).
9. Cheney, ed., *Louisa May Alcott*, pp. 228–29.
10. Thomas Beer, *The Mauve Decade* (New York, 1926), pp. 17–64.
11. Ibid., p. 25. Beer describes the lawyer, Joseph Choate, turning on a witness with the cry, "Good God, Madame! Did you think that your husband was one of Miss Alcott's boys?"
12. Ibid. See also T. Jackson Lears, *No Place of Grace* (New York, 1982) for an excellent discussion of ambiguous "modernity."
13. Louisa May Alcott, "Transcendental Wild Oats," *The Independent* 25, no. 1307 (Dec. 18, 1873).
14. Louisa May Alcott, *Hospital Sketches and Camp and Fireside Stories* (Boston, 1863). Clover Hooper Adams, among other readers, was inspired to work for the Sanitary Commission by reading *Hospital Sketches*. See Eugenia Kaledin, *The Education of Mrs. Henry Adams* (Philadelphia, 1981).
15. Cheney, ed., *Louisa May Alcott*, pp. 223, 234.
16. Louisa May Alcott, *Work: A Story of Experience* (Boston, 1872).

Chapter I

1. Louisa May Alcott, *Little Women* (Boston, 1868, 1869), Chapter 1, "Playing Pilgrims." References to *Little Women* are cited by chapter numbers and titles which remain consistent in all editions of the novel.
2. The May family's history is documented in several sources, including Madeleine B. Stern, *Louisa May Alcott* (London, New York, 1957); Madelon Bedell, *The Alcotts: Biography of a Family* (New York, 1980); Thomas Joseph May, *A Memorial Study, Samuel Joseph May*, by his son, Joseph May (Boston, 1898); Catherine Covert Stepanek, "Saint before His Time: Samuel J. May and American Educational Reform," unpub. M.A. thesis, Syracuse University, 1964.
3. Direct references to Bronson Alcott's ancestry and early life are largely drawn from Odell Shepard, *Pedlar's Progress: The Life of Bronson Alcott* (Boston, 1937); Odell Shepard, ed., *The Journals of Bronson Alcott* (Boston, 1938); and Richard Herrnstadt, ed., *The Letters of Amos Bronson Alcott*, (Ames, Iowa, 1969).
4. Odell Shepard notes that Bronson found his cousin Riley Alcox's copy of John Bunyan's *Pilgrim's Progress*, the Dublin edition of 1802, and that he read it

many times, "memorizing large parts of it and acting it out in some rude dramatic form of his own division" (Shepard, *Pedlar's Progress*, pp. 34, 36).

5. Shepard, *Pedlar's Progress*, pp. 62–63.

6. Bedell, *The Alcotts*, p. 15.

7. Clara Endicott Sears, *Bronson Alcott's Fruitlands* (Boston, 1915), p. 84.

8. Louisa May Alcott, "Eli's Education," *St. Nicholas*, 11 no. 5 (March 1884); rpt. in idem, *Spinning Wheel Stories* (Boston, 1931).

9. Ibid.

10. Ibid.

11. Herrnstadt, ed., *The Letters of Amos Bronson Alcott*, p. 26. The same story is discussed in Bedell, *The Alcotts*, pp. 8–9, with a somewhat different understanding of Bronson's relationship to his mother.

12. Herrnstadt, ed., *The Letters of Amos Bronson Alcott* p. 26.

13. *Alcott Memoirs of Dr. Frederick L. H. Willis* (Boston, 1915); William Leach, *True Love and Perfect Union* (New York, 1981), p. 216.

14. Stepanek, "Saint before His Time," p. 399.

15. *Boston Recorder*, May 11, 1827, clipping of an article on Amos Bronson Alcott, at Houghton Library, Harvard University.

16. Samuel May, *Common School Journal* (Boston 1839), II, 220.

17. See Samuel J. May, "The Importance of Our Common Schools," *Lectures Delivered Before the American Literature Institute of Instruction at Pittsfield, August 15, 16, 17, 1843* (Boston, 1844), p. 231; Samuel J. May, "Address Delivered by the Rev. S. J. May at the Opening of A New and Highly Improved District Schoolhouse in Hanover, Mass., June 20, 1839," *Common School Journal*, II, 14. Samuel J. May, "Capital Punishment: Six Reasons Why It Should be Abolished," *New York Tribune*, July 25, 1851. William Andrus Alcott, Bronson's cousin, *Juvenile Rambler* (1831, 1832), probably the first magazine for children published in the United States. William was much better known as a public educator than his cousin.

18. See Bedell, *The Alcotts*, pp. 3, 4.

19. Ibid.

20. Ibid.; Abigail May Alcott's Diary, Aug. 5, 1828, Fragments of an Autobiography, Alcott Collection at Houghton Library, Harvard University.

21. Rose Hawthorne Lathrop, *Memories of Hawthorne* (Boston, 1897), p. 16; Bedell, *The Alcotts* p. 15.

22. Amos Bronson Alcott's Manuscript Journal, Sept. 21, 1828, at Houghton Library, Harvard University.

23. Ibid., Apr. 9, 1830.

24. Stepanek, "Saint before His Time," p. 11.

25. Ibid., p. 9.

26. Ibid., p. 31.

27. Ibid., pp. 69–70.

28. Abigail May Alcott, "Autobiographical Sketch," Fragments of an Autobiography, Alcott Collection at Houghton Library, Harvard University.

29. Samuel May to Abigail May, July 21, 1828, Alcott Family Papers at Houghton Library, Harvard University.

30. Abigail May to Amos Bronson Alcott, June 10, 1829, Alcott Family Papers at Houghton Library, Harvard University.

31. Abigail May Alcott's Diary, Fragments of an Autobiography, Alcott Collection at Houghton Library, Harvard University.

32. William A. Alcott, *The Young Wife or Duties of Women in the Marriage Relation* (Boston, 1837; rpt. New York, 1972), p. 37.

33. Amos Bronson Alcott's Manuscript Journal, July 28, 1828, at Houghton Library, Harvard University.
34. Abigail May Alcott's Diary, Aug. 1828, from notes and materials left by Amos Bronson Alcott for the Memoir of Abigail May Alcott, at Houghton Library, Harvard University.
35. Abigail May Alcott to Samuel J. May, Aug. 1828, Alcott Family Papers at Houghton Library, Harvard University.
36. Joseph May to Abigail May, July 6, 1829, Alcott Family Papers at Houghton Library, Harvard University.
37. Amos Bronson Alcott's Manuscript Journal, Oct. 15, 1828, at Houghton Library, Harvard University. The two most recent biographers of the Alcotts disagree on the nature of Abigail and Bronson's courtship. Martha Saxton calls Bronson a narcissist and concludes that this journal entry typifies his inability to feel deeply for any other human being except as a reflection of his own idealized self-image. She finds Abigail May to be the personification of Victorian female hysteria. (Martha Saxton, Louisa May, [New York, 1977]) Madelon Bedell is a good deal more sensitive and sympathetic to the young couple. Setting their courtship in the context of their nineteenth-century lives, and appreciating the differences in their backgrounds and temperaments, she finds Bronson to be a shy, inhibited, but still loving man. Abigail's mercurial moments she sees as partly the expression of a passionate nature and partly a sensitive response to family traumas and life-cycle problems (Bedell, The Alcotts). Indeed, Alcott scholars tend to side with one or another of the family members, a difficult tendency to avoid in view of the intensity of the family's relationships and its self-conscious preservation of "face." Still, Bronson Alcott's view of himself as an "original" seems to have infected too many of his biographers, with the exception of Saxton, who unfortunately ignores the impoverished status and desire to be accepted by gentlefolk like the Mays that helped nurture Bronson's self-image. His need to present himself as one of nature's noblemen was reinforced by the expectations of genteel reformers who hoped to find just such examples of modest virtue among the common people. A very small number of acquaintances, among them Father Hecker and Rose Hawthorne Lathrop, caught the subtle mixture of Bronson Alcott's "insinuating" ways and his genuine passion to "be good."
38. Abigail May Alcott to Amos Bronson Alcott, June 10, 1829, Amos Bronson Alcott, Alcott Collection at Houghton Library, Harvard University.

Chapter II

1. A. J. Graves, Women in America (New York, 1843), p. xv, discussed in Mary P. Ryan, "The Empire of the Mother: American Writings on Women and the Family, 1830–1860," Women and History 1, no. 2–3 (Spring 1983).
2. A number of excellent studies exist on the changing aspects of domestic prescription and practice. Among them are Linda Kerber, "The Republican Mother: Women and The Enlightenment—An American Perspective," American Quarterly 28, no. 2 (Summer 1976): 187–205; Anne Kuhn, The Mother's Role in Childhood Education (New Haven, 1947); Ann Douglas, The Feminization of American Culture (New York, 1972); Katherine Sklar, Catherine Beecher: A Study in Domesticity (New Haven, 1973).

3. Amos Bronson Alcott, *Observations on the Principles and Methods of Infant Instruction* (Boston, 1830); rpt. in Walter Harding, ed., *Essays on Education* (Gainesville, Fla., 1960).

4. Madelon Bedell, *The Alcotts: Biography of a Family* (New York, 1980), p. 54. Bedell thinks the printing may have been paid for either by Alcott himself or Robert Vaux.

5. The best discussion of Alcott's unpublished "Observations on the Spiritual Nurture of My Children," is in Charles Strickland, "A Transcendentalist Father: The Child Rearing Practices of Bronson Alcott," *Perspectives in American History* 3 (1969), pp. 5–71. The quotations I cite are from Strickland's article. Strickland's second, longer version appears in *History of Childhood Quarterly: The Journal of Psychohistory* 1, no. 1 (Summer 1973). The complete manuscript of "Observations on the Spiritual Nurture of My Children" can be consulted at Houghton Library, Harvard University, bound in one volume with Alcott's "Researches on Childhood." The complete study of the Alcott girls has never been published.

6. Samuel J. May's library included these works, and May lent them to Henry Barnard and both men lectured publicly on Pestalozzian theory. (Catherine Covert Stepanek, "Saint before His Time: Samuel J. May and American Educational Reform," unpub. thesis, Syracuse University, 1967, pp. 86–87. Social historians of education who find commonality in the reformers' theories include Lawrence A. Cremin, *The Transformation of the School* (New York, 1961); Freeman Butts and Lawrence A. Cremin, *History of Education in American Culture* (New York, 1953); and E. P. Cubberly, *Public Education in the United States* (Boston, 1919).

7. Amos Bronson Alcott, "Pestalozzi's Principles and Methods of Instruction," *American Journal of Education* 4 (Mar.–Apr. 1829): 97–107.

8. M. H. Abrams, *The Mirror and the Lamp: Romantic Theory and the Critical Tradition* (New York, 1953), p. 69.

9. This struggle is detailed in Butts and Cremin, *History of Education*; and in Cubberly, *Public Education*; and in Cremin, *The Transformation of the School*. Recent revisionist treatments of the struggle include an excellent analysis by Michael Katz, *The Irony of Early School Reform* (New York, 1968); and Michael Katz, ed., *Social Issues in American Education* (New York, 1974).

10. Ibid.

11. Bedell, *The Alcotts* p. 54.

12. Strickland, "A Transcendentalist Father," p. 6.

13. Lydia Maria Child, *The Mother's Book* (Boston, 1831).

14. Amos Bronson Alcott, "Observations on the Spiritual Nurture," p. 27; cited in Strickland, "A Transcendentalist Father," p. 6.

15. Abigail May Alcott to Samuel J. May, Mar. 27, 1831, Alcott Family Papers at Houghton Library, Harvard University.

16. Amos Bronson Alcott, "Observations on the Spiritual Nurture," cited in Strickland, "A Transcendentalist Father," p. 76.

17. Ryan, "The Empire of the Mother." Ryan emphasizes Godey's popularity; it was read by 150,000 people in 1860.

18. Amos Bronson Alcott, "Observations on the Spiritual Nurture," cited in Strickland, "A Transcendentalist Father," p. 10.

19. Ibid., pp. 45–46; see also Child, *The Mother's Book*. I wish to stress the similarities between Child's regimen and Bronson and Abigail Alcott's descriptions because their diaries seem very radical only when compared to more conservative advisors, such as the Rev. John C. Abott in *The Mother at*

Home (see Strickland, "A Transcendentalist Father," p. 18). In fact, the general stream of advice in the 1830s and 1840s was becoming very liberal, or at least more inclined toward the emotional persuasion of children. Like Strickland, I agree with Lewis Mumford that a "major legacy of transcendentalism was the belief that childhood could be happy." (Strickland, "A Transcendentalist Father," p. 12). But the believers in happy childhood included many nontranscendentalists.

20. Ibid., pp. 45–46; cited in Strickland, "A Transcendentalist Father," p. 22.
21. Louisa May Alcott, *Little Women* (Boston, 1868, 1869), chapter 38 "On the Shelf." References to *Little Women* are cited by chapter numbers and titles which remain consistent in all editions of the novel.
22. Ibid.
23. Amos Bronson Alcott to Col. Joseph May, Nov., 1832, at Houghton Library, Harvard University. Bedell notes from (Bronson's "Observations on the Spiritual Nurture") that Louisa's life "began in struggle." Her mother's milk did not come in until five days after she was born (Bedell thinks that she almost starved to death). Moreover, she was not washed until she was a week old; during this time she remained soiled with meconium, a condition Bronson thought life-threatening. On the other hand, Bronson also wrote to his mother that the baby was "a very fine, fat little creature" (Bedell, *The Alcotts*, p. 63).
24. Abigail May Alcott to Samuel J. May, Feb. 20, 1837, Alcott Family Papers at Houghton Library, Harvard University.
25. Ibid. Bronson Alcott did observe "detail" about Louisa's character during her infancy. He remarked on her "boldness and amplitude," her luxuriant nature, and called her "fit for the scuffle of things," besides noting her "will" later on (Amos Bronson Alcott, "Observations on the Spiritual Nurture, pp. 73–74). I agree with Bedell that "all we know of Louisa's later life and career, of the invincible, spirited woman of power, talent and drive, confirms this analysis of her character made by her father in the first year of her life" (Bedell, *The Alcotts* p. 66). Bronson granted to baby Louisa some of Abba's obvious sensuality. Both Alcotts thought that Louisa resembled her mother physically and emotionally. See Abigail May Alcott to Joseph May, March 11, 1833, Alcott Family Papers at Houghton Library, Harvard University.
26. Saxton (Martha Saxton, *Louisa May* [New York, 1977]) and Bedell agree that this was a "separation." Bronson wrote that "subtle ties of friendship . . . are worn away by constant familiarity" (Bedell, *The Alcotts*, p. 69). See my discussion of Louisa May Alcott's treatment of such problems in "Reading Little Women."
27. Bedell, *The Alcotts*, p. 69.
28. Ibid.
29. Actually, the figures for Abigail Alcott's cohort are probably higher. Uhlenberg offers a 35 percent rate of infant mortality in Louisa and Anna's cohort— that is, those born in 1830. See Peter R. Uhlenberg, "A Study of Cohort Life Cycles: Cohorts of Native Born Massachusetts Women, 1830–1920," *Population Studies* 23, pt. 3 (Nov. 1969): 407–20. He also reports that the 1867 Massachusetts Vital Registration Report attributed about 10 percent of female deaths to childbearing.
30. Odell Shepard, *Pedlar's Progress: The Life of Bronson Alcott* (Boston, 1937).
31. Amos Bronson Alcott's Manuscript Journal Oct. 10, 1834, at Houghton Library, Harvard University; see also Strickland, "A Transcendentalist Father," pp. 45–55.

32. Louisa May Alcott, *Little Men*: Life at Plumfield with Jo's Boys (Boston, 1871), chapter 3, "Sunday." References to *Little Men* are cited by chapter numbers and titles which remain consistent in all editions of the novel.
33. Strickland, "A Transcendentalist Father," pp. 45–55.
34. Ibid.
35. Ibid.
36. Amos Bronson Alcott, "Observations on the Spiritual Nurture" and "Researches on Childhood," as cited in Strickland, "A Transcendentalist Father," pp. 59–60.
37. See Elizabeth Peabody, *Record of a School: Exemplifying the General Principles of Spiritual Culture* (Boston, 1836).
38. Amos Bronson Alcott, "Observations on the Spiritual Nurture," as cited in Strickland, "A Transcendentalist Father," pp. 59–60.
39. Ibid.
40. Ednah Cheney, ed., *Louisa May Alcott: Life, Letters and Journals* (Boston, 1928), p. 18.
41. Ibid.
42. Madeleine B. Stern, *Louisa May Alcott* (London, New York, 1957), pp. 11–12.
43. Amos Bronson Alcott, ed., *Conversations with Children on the Gospel* (Boston, 1837). Feminists both in the 1870s and later made a strong case for sex education of children. See William Leach, *True Love and Perfect Union* pt. 1 (New York, 1980).
44. William Alcott, *The Physiology of Marriage* (Boston, 1855). See also Sylvester Graham, *Lectures on Chastity* (Glasgow, 1834). Graham assumed that marital intimacy reduced the dangers of romantic passion, in part because it removed the mystery of the sexual act. Sexual excess, he found, was more the result of overstimulated imagination than instinctual drives. A vegetarian, bland diet also helped to insure that "intercourse is very seldom." Bronson became a life-long vegetarian in this period, but Abigail harbored a dangerous taste for meat and occasionally fed it to the children until severe poverty forced her to discontinue the practice.
45. Saxton, *Louisa May*, p. 102.
46. Stern, *Louisa May Alcott*, p. 13.
47. During the Alcotts' separation in Germantown and Philadelphia, Bronson wrote that "sacrifices must be made to the spirit of the age . . . my family must feel the evil of this to some degree, but this should not deter me from striving to effect what has been attempted in conception of duty and right" Amos Bronson Alcott's Manuscript Journal, Mar. 27, 1834, at Houghton Library, Harvard University. For a more detailed analysis of this phenomenon see Douglas, *The Feminization of American Culture*.

Chapter III

1. Martha Saxton, *Louisa May* (New York, 1977), p. 102.
2. Ralph Waldo Emerson, "Self Reliance" (1840, ed. Stephen E. Whicher, *Selections from Ralph Waldo Emerson* (Boston, 1960), p. 147.
3. Odell Shepard, *Pedlar's Progress: The Life of Bronson Alcott* (Boston, 1937), p. 268. I have relied on a number of general and specific treatments of American reform, including John L. Thomas, "Romantic Reform in America, 1815–1865," *American Quarterly* 17, no. 2 (Winter, 1965), pp. 656–81; Henry Steele Commager, *The Era of Reform* (Princeton, 1960); Clifford A. Griffin, *Their*

Brothers' Keepers: Moral Stewardship in the United States 1800–1865 (New Brunswick, 1960); Frank Thistlethwaite, *The Anglo-American Connection in the Early Nineteenth Century* (Philadelphia, 1959); Alice Felt Tyler, *Freedom's Ferment: Phases of American Social History to 1860* (Minneapolis, 1944); Robert Brenner, *From the Depths: The Discovery of Poverty in the United States* (New York, 1964); David Rothman, *The Discovery of the Asylum; Social Order and Disorder in the New Republic* (Boston, 1971); Elizabeth Cady Stanton et al., *A History of Woman Suffrage* 1–3 (Rochester, 1889); Mark Holloway, *Heavens on Earth: Utopian Communities in America, 1680–1880* (New York, 1951); Louis J. Kern, *An Ordered Love: Sex Roles and Sexuality in Victorian Utopias* (Chapel Hill, 1981); Russell Nye, *Society and Culture in America, 1830–1860* (New York, 1974); and Martin Duberman, ed., *The Antislavery Vanguard, New Essays on the Abolitionists* (New Jersey, 1965).

4. Mary Wollstonecraft, *A Vindication of the Rights of Woman* (New York, 1967), p. 108.

5. Madelon Bedell has provided a moving account of Abba Alcott's pregnancies and childbirth experiences, carefully documented from the May and Alcott family papers (Madelon Bedell, *The Alcotts: Biography of a Family* [New York, 1980], chapter 9.

6. The standard work is by Octavius Brooks Frothingham, *Transcendentalism in New England* (New York, 1876). It has the virtues of its defects, namely that Frothingham was involved in the movement and also related to Abigail May Alcott. A new interpretation of Emerson, Alcott, and Thoreau is found in Taylor Stoehr, *Nay-Saying in Concord: Emerson, Alcott and Thoreau* (Hamden, Conn., 1979). For a view of Transcendentalism as a genuine social movement see Anne C. Rose, *Transcendentalism, as a Social Movement, 1830–1850* (New Haven, 1981).

7. Rose, *Transcendentalism.* Rose does not, however, include Thoreau as an active reformer.

8. See F. O. Matthiessen, *The American Renaissance* (New York, 1941).

9. This popular phrase has endured since John Louis O'Sullivan first coined it in the early nineteenth century as a Democratic party slogan.

10. Shepard, *Pedlar's Progress*, p. 279.

11. Ralph Waldo Emerson, "The American Scholar" [an oration delivered before the Phi Beta Kappa Society, at Cambridge, Aug. 31, 1837], in Alfred Ferguson, ed. *Collected Works of Ralph Waldo Emerson* (Boston, 1971), I, 70.

12. Ibid., p. 52.

13. Ralph Waldo Emerson, "Nature," in *Collected Works*, I, 8.

14. Ibid., p. 10.

15. Ednah Cheney, ed., *Louisa May Alcott: Life, Letters and Journals*, p. 20.

16. Ibid., pp. 13, 14.

17. Shepard, *Pedlar's Progress*, pp. 233–45.

18. Ibid., p. 268.

19. Ibid.

20. Ralph Waldo Emerson, "Man the Reformer," [A lecture read before the Mechanics Apprentices' Library Association at the Masonic Temple, Boston, Jan. 25, 1941], in *Collected Works* I,

21. Amos Bronson Alcott to Louisa May Alcott, June 21, 1840, Orchard House reproduction (Concord, 1974). Original letter in Alcott Family Papers at Houghton Library, Harvard University.

22. Shepard, *Pedlar's Progress*, p. 267.

23. The controversies surrounding Col. May's will are substantial. Saxton sets the amount received as $3,000 to each heir (Saxton, *Louisa May*). Madelon Bedell estimates the total amount of the estate at $15,000 with about $2,000 going to Abigail Alcott (Bedell, *The Alcotts*). I have examined the original will, the executor's inventory and the subsequent accounting in probate court which fully enumerates the assets and debts of Col. May, and also the costs of legal services charged to the estate in court actions surrounding disbursements. The will itself is registered #32792, Suffolk County Court. The executors' final accounts are totalled as of Jan. 15, 1844 when the monies were released from probate. The first inventory is dated Boston, Apr. 5, 1841. The entire matter is of some consequence in fully understanding not only the Alcotts' relationship to the Sewall and May families, but also in understanding the subsequent events surrounding the Alcotts', Mays', and Charles Lane's involvement in the "Fruitlands" experiment at Harvard. See my following analysis of the situation in chapter 4, "Transcendental Wild Oats."
24. Will of Col. Joseph May [executors' inventory].
25. Ibid.
26. Ibid.
27. Joseph May to Abigail May Alcott, Oct. 1, 1834, from notes and materials left by Amos Bronson Alcott for a Memoir of Abigail May Alcott, at Houghton Library, Harvard University; also cited in Bedell, *The Alcotts*, p. 136.
28. Abigail May Alcott to Joseph May, Oct. 6, 1834, from notes and materials left by Amos Bronson Alcott for a memoir of Abigail May Alcott, at Houghton Library, Harvard University; also cited in Bedell, *The Alcotts*, p. 136.
29. Abigail May Alcott's Diary, Feb. 1841, from notes and materials left by Amos Bronson Alcott for a Memoir of Abigail May Alcott, at Houghton Library, Harvard University.
30. Stanton et al., *A History of Woman Suffrage* 1.
31. Bedell, *The Alcotts*, p. 167.
32. Shepard, *Pedlar's Progress*, p. 300.
33. Saxton, *Louisa May*, p. 128.
34. Ibid.
35. Cheney, ed., *Louisa May Alcott*, pp. 15–16.
36. The best account of Bronson's English visit is Bedell, *The Alcotts*, chapter 12. Shephard also writes a detailed description of Bronson's contact with the English reformers (Shepard, *Pedlar's Progress*, pp. 303–42).
37. Shepard, *Pedlar's Progress*, p. 318.
38. Ibid., p. 195.
39. Bedell, *The Alcotts*, p. 195.
40. Ralph Waldo Emerson, "Lectures on the Times: Introductory Lecture," in *Collected Works* I, 175–76.
41. Stoehr, *Nay-Saying in Concord*, p. 34.
42. Abigail May Alcott's Diary, Sept. 1842, Fragments of an Autobiography, Alcott Collection, at Houghton Library, Harvard University.

Chapter IV

1. Odell Shepard, *Pedlar's Progress: The Life of Bronson Alcott* (Boston, 1937), p. 352.
2. Ibid. Lane also informed Junius Alcott that "we are learning to hold our

peace, and to keep our hands from each other's bodies—the ill effects of which we see upon the little baby." Both Saxton and Bedell suspect that this line indicates the extremity of Lane's predilection for celibacy (Martha Saxton, *Louisa May* [New York, 1977]; Madelon Bedell, *The Alcotts: Biography of a Family* [New York, 1980]). He may also have been referring to the prohibition against both chastisement of children and verbal abuse in the cottage.

3. Charles Lane to William Oldham, Nov. 30, 1842, in Clara Endicott Sears, *Bronson Alcott's Fruitlands* (Boston, 1915), pp. 12–13.
4. Abigail May Alcott's Diary, Dec. 24, 1842, Fragments of an Autobiography, Alcott Collection at Houghton Library, Harvard University.
5. Ibid., Jan. 30, 1843.
6. Nina Baym, *Woman's Fiction: A Guide to Novels by and about Women in America, 1820–1870* (Ithaca, 1978), p. 257.
7. Sears, *Bronson Alcott's Fruitlands*, pp. 12–13.
8. Shepard, *Pedlar's Progress*, p. 307.
9. Charles Lane to William Oldham, in Sears, *Bronson Alcott's Fruitlands*, p. 18.
10. Charles Lane to Junius Alcott, Mar. 7, 1843, in ibid., p. 11.
11. Charles Lane to William Oldham, May 31, 1843, in ibid., p. 14.
12. Ibid.
13. Ibid., p. 15.
14. Ibid.
15. Ibid.
16. Samuel J. May to Ralph Waldo Emerson, Concord, Jan. 13, 1844, Concord, Emerson Papers, at Houghton Library, Harvard University. Professor Catherine Covert of Syracuse University shared this note from Samuel J. May at a critical moment.
17. Lester G. Wells, *The Skaneateles Communal Experiment, 1843–1846* (Syracuse, 1953).
18. Charles Lane to William Oldham, June 28, 1843, in Sears, *Bronson Alcott's Fruitlands*, p. 28.
19. Anna Alcott's Diary at Fruitlands, in ibid., p. 86.
20. Ibid., p. 36.
21. Ibid.
22. Ibid., p. 209.
23. Anna Alcott's Diary at Fruitlands, June 6, 1843, in ibid., p. 87.
24. Ibid., June 13, 1843, in ibid., p. 92.
25. Ibid., July 20, 1843, in ibid., p. 101.
26. Ibid., Sept. 6, 1843, in ibid., p. 103.
27. Louisa May Alcott's Diary at Fruitlands, Sept. 14, 1843, in ibid., p. 107. "I ran in the wind and played be a horse, and had a lovely time in the woods with Anna and Lizzie. We were fairies, and made gowns and paper wings. I 'flied' the highest of all . . ."
28. Ibid.
29. Ibid., Sept. 24, 1843, in ibid.
30. Ibid., Oct. 12, 1843, in ibid.
31. Ibid., Sept. 24, 1843, in ibid.
32. Ibid.
33. Ibid., Oct. 12, 1843, in ibid., p. 109.
34. Louisa May Alcott, *Little Women* (Boston, 1868, 1869).
35. Sears, *Bronson Alcott's Fruitlands*, p. 108.

36. Annie M. L. Clark, *The Alcotts in Harvard* (Lancaster, Mass., 1902). There are four stanzas to the poem; the second reads:

Oh why these tears
and these idle fears
For what may come to-morrow?
The birds find food
From God so good,
And the flowers know no sorrow.

37. Sears, *Bronson Alcott's Fruitlands*, p. 108.
38. Ibid., p. 109.
39. Ibid.
40. Isaac Hecker at Brook Farm, July 7, 1843, in Ibid., p. 76. Hecker's complete diary at Fruitlands can be found in the Hecker Papers, at the Paulist Archives, New York City.
41. Ibid., p. 884.
42. Isaac Hecker at Fruitlands, July 17, 1843, in ibid., p. 79.
43. Ibid., July 21, 1843, in ibid., p. 81.
44. Ibid., p. 84.
45. Ibid., p. 125.
46. Ibid., p. 113. Mr. Child went to hear Alcott and Lane in a discussion with W. H. Channing. After listening to Lane and Alcott, her husband reported to Lydia Maria Child, "Why, after I heard them talk a few minutes, I'll be cursed if I knew whether I had any mind at all."
47. Samuel J. May, Lexington, Mass., Jan. 13, 1844, copy forwarded to Ralph Waldo Emerson and included in the Emerson Papers, at Houghton Library, Harvard University.
48. Charles Lane to William Oldham, Nov. 26, 1843, in Sears, *Bronson Alcott's Fruitlands*, p. 123.
49. Amos Bronson Alcott and Charles Lane to A. Brooke of Oakland, Ohio in ibid., pp. 40–52; pub. under the title "The Consociate Family Life," in the *Herald of Freedom*, Sept. 8, 1843; copy at Houghton Library, Harvard University.
50. Ibid.
51. Ibid. For a detailed account of the relationship between fertility patterns and women's interest in the Shakers see D'Ann Campbell, "Women's Life in Utopia: The Shaker Experiment in Sexual Equality Reappraised, 1810–1860," *New England Quarterly*, 2, no. 1 (Mar. 1978): 23–27. Kern is quite right that Shaker theology found woman unclean and the separation of the sexes made her "a highly ambiguous entity; at once foundation stone of the new Order; harlot and saint" (Louis J. Kern, *An Ordered Love: Sex Roles and Sexuality in Victorian Utopias* [Chapel Hill, 1981], p. 86).
52. Charles Lane to William Oldham, 1843, in Sears, *Bronson Alcott's Fruitlands*, p. 8.
53. Ibid., pp. 40–52; rpt. in Louisa May Alcott, "Transcendental Wild Oats," *The Independent* 25, no. 130 (Dec. 18, 1873).
54. Taylor Stoehr, *Nay-Saying in Concord: Emerson, Alcott and Thoreau* (Hamden, Conn., 1979), p. 85.
55. Sears, *Bronson Alcott's Fruitlands*, p. 143.
56. Emerson visited Lane in England at Ham in 1848. Lane had a school of sixteen

children and married the matron, Miss Hannah Bond, "who had lived at Owen's Community at Harmony Hall." Writing to Thoreau, Emerson said that Lane was "full of friendliness and hospitality" Sears, *Bronson Alcott's Fruitlands*, p. 134.

57. Richard Herrnstadt, ed., *The Letters of Amos Bronson Alcott* (Ames, Iowa, 1969), p. 656.
58. Stoehr, *Nay-Saying in Concord*, p. 85.
59. Amos Bronson Alcott's Manuscript Journal, in ibid., p. 84.
60. Abigail May Alcott's Diary, Aug. 26, 1843, Fragments of an Autobiography, Alcott Collection at Houghton Library, Harvard University.
61. Ibid.
62. Louisa May Alcott, "Transcendental Wild Oats," *The Independent* 25, no. 1307 (Dec. 18, 1873); rpt. in *Silver Pitchers* (Boston, 1908), pp. 95–120. All references in this chapter are to the *Silver Pitchers* rpt.
63. Alcott and Lane, "The Consociate Family Life," in Sears, *Bronson Alcott's Fruitlands*, pp. 40–52.
64. Louisa May Alcott, "Transcendental Wild Oats," p. 100.
65. Alcott and Lane, "The Consociate Family Life," in Sears, *Bronson Alcott's Fruitlands*, pp. 40–52.
66. Ibid.
67. Louisa May Alcott, "Transcendental Wild Oats," p. 100.
68. Louisa May Alcott, *Little Men: Life at Plumfield with Jo's Boys* (Boston, 1871), chapter 1, "Nat." (References to *Little Men* are cited by chapter numbers and titles which remain consistent in all editions of the novel.) Nat Blake, an orphaned street musician, thinks he has found heaven when Aunt Jo and Nursey ensconce him in a warm flannel nightgown, tuck him in a clean bed, and then administer draughts of "warm soothy stuff."
69. Louisa May Alcott, "Transcendental Wild Oats," p. 100.

Chapter V

1. Annie M. L. Clark, *The Alcotts in Harvard* (Lancaster, Mass., 1902), p. 31.
2. Ibid., p. 34.
3. Ibid.
4. Ibid., p. 37.
5. Suffolk County Probate Court, Abigail May Alcott, Petition addressed to Hon. Willard Phillips, Judge of Probate, County of Suffolk, Mass., May 20, 1844.
6. Suffolk County, Mass., Probate Court, Samuel E. Sewall for himself and Samuel J. May, Aug. 13, 1844.
7. Samuel J. May to Ralph Waldo Emerson, Dec. 22, 1844, Emerson Papers, at Houghton Library, Harvard University.
8. Ibid., Jan. 13, 1844.
9. Ibid.
10. Ibid.
11. Ibid.
12. Ibid.
13. Clark, *The Alcotts*, p. 42.
14. Ibid.
15. Ibid.

16. Carroll Smith Rosenberg, "Sex as Symbol in Victorian Purity: An Ethnohistorical Analysis of Jacksonian America," *American Journal of Sociology* 84, suppl. (1978): S212–S47.
17. William Alcott, *The Physiology of Marriage* (Boston, 1855), p. 12; cited in Smith-Rosenberg, "Sex as Symbol,"
18. Ibid. See also Carroll Smith-Rosenberg, "Beauty, the Beast and the Militant Woman: A Study in the Sex Roles and Social Stress in Jacksonian America," *American Quarterly* 23 (Winter 1971): 562–84.
19. Madeline B. Stern, ed., *Behind a Mask: The Unknown Thrillers of Louisa May Alcott* (New York, 1975), and idem., *Plots and Counterplots: More Unknown Thrillers of Louisa May Alcott* (New York, 1976). Stern's interesting analysis of the separation of domesticity from sexuality is also stated and expanded in Nancy F. Cott, "Passionlessness: An Interpretation of Victorian Sexual Ideology, 1790–1850," *Signs: Journal of Women in Culture and Society* 4, no. 2 (Winter, 1978): 219–436. She notes, "Both women's participation in the creation of Victorian sexual standards and the place of passionlessness in the vanguard of feminist thought deserve more recognition. The serviceability of passionlessness to women in gaining social and familiar power should be acknowledged as a primary reason that the ideology was quickly and widely accepted" (Cott, "Passionlessness," p. 235). I would argue that by the mid-nineteenth century liberal feminists did not reject passion so much as they wanted to "rationalize" it. Co-education, household democracy, and equal pay for equal work would remove the dangers of sexual passion, preserving healthy sexual relations and "true love."
20. Madelon Bedell, *The Alcotts: Biography of a Family* (New York, 1980), pp. 241–46.
21. Ibid. See William Leach, *True Love and Perfect Union: The Feminist Reform of Sex and Society* (New York, 1980), for the most complete and sympathetic account of the links between domestic reform, feminist social theory, and sexuality in mid-nineteenth century America.
22. Clara Gowing, *The Alcotts as I Knew Them* (Boston, 1909), p. 11.
23. Ibid.
24. Ibid., p. 9.
25. Ednah Cheney, ed., *Louisa May Alcott: Life, Letters and Journals* (Boston, 1928), p. 34.
26. Ibid.
27. Dr. Frederick L. H. Willis, *Alcott Memoirs* (Boston, 1915), p. 35. Gowing presents a similar description: Louisa was "tall and slim . . . the fleetest runner in school, and could walk, run and climb like a boy" (Gowing, *The Alcotts*, p. 6.
28. Willis, *Alcott Memoirs*, p. 44.
29. Ibid.
30. Ibid.
31. Cheney, ed., *Louisa May Alcott*, p. 36.
32. Ibid.
33. Harriot K. Hunt, *Glances and Glimpses of Fifty Years Social, Including Twenty Years Professional Life* (Boston, 1855), p. 52.
34. Ibid. See also Eleanor Wolf Thompson, *Education for Ladies, 1830–1860* (Binghamton, New York, 1947). Thompson presents a detailed account of the popular literature and its treatment of the "woman question," particularly education for young ladies in this period. See also H. W. Bellows' column on female education, a plea for women's rights that clearly links abolitionism and

feminism (H. W. Bellows, *National Anti-Slavery Standard* 2, no. 47 [Apr. 28, 1842]: p. 188. Thomas Wentworth Higginson, another friend of the Alcotts, elaborated on the theme "no sex in mind," in the *Atlantic Monthly* 3, no. 16 [Feb. 1859]. Louisa May Alcott was a contributor to the *Atlantic Monthly* in the 1860s and later read Thomas Wentworth Higginson, *Atlantic Essays* (Boston, 1871). Also of note are Catherine Beecher, *A Treatise on Domestic Economy* (Boston, 1841); Catherine Beecher and Harriet Beecher Stowe, *The American Woman's Home* (Boston, 1869), and Mrs. Sigourney, "The Comparative Intellect of the Sexes," *Ladies Magazine* 3, no. 6, [June 1830]: 241–45. None of these writers are as radical as Hunt in linking coeducation, exercise, and work for women. All, however, argue in favor of "healthy" exercise and education for girls.

35. Hunt learned the practice of homeopathy from an English husband and wife team of physicians who treated her sister in 1833. Harriot Hunt, a schoolteacher at the time, went to live with the two Doctors Mott, conducted their business correspondence, and at the age of twenty-eight brought her mother and sister to live with the Motts. The two sisters began nursing and then physician's training with their hosts.

36. Hunt, *Glances and Glimpses* p. 217.

37. Cheney, ed., *Louisa May Alcott*, p. 36.

38. Ibid., pp. 44–45.

39. I have followed the chronology of Thoreau's life presented in Richard Libeaux, *Young Man Thoreau* (New York, 1975). An excellent comparison of Emerson's, Alcott's, and Thoreau's views on nature, community, labor, property, and family is Taylor Stoehr, *Nay Saying in Concord: Emerson, Alcott, and Thoreau* (Hamden, Conn., 1979). Bedell and Stern agree on the significance of Thoreau's life to Louisa May Alcott (Bedell, *The Alcotts*; Madeleine B. Stern, *Louisa May Alcott* [London, New York, 1957]).

40. Ibid.

41. Margaret Fuller, "On Lidian Emerson, Sept. 2, 1842," quoted in Bell Gale Chevigny, *The Woman and the Myth: Margaret Fuller's Life and Writings* (New York, 1976), p. 128.

42. Ibid.

43. Ibid.

44. Bedell offers a full and engaging description of Louisa May and Anna Alcotts' "home-made theatricals" (Bedell, *The Alcotts*, pp. 252–53). Stern quotes generously from the plays, describes costumes and scenery and weaves together the young Alcotts' roleplaying of Dickens' novels with their own original theatricals (Stern, *Louisa May Alcott*, pp. 53–55). Anna Alcott eventually edited Louisa's dramas and wrote an introduction to them according to Cheney, ed., *Louisa May Alcott*. A full explication of the home productions awaits some future scholar's examination.

45. Cheney, ed., *Louisa May Alcott*, pp. 44–45.

46. Ibid.

47. Gowing, *The Alcotts*, pp. 17–20.

48. Ibid.

49. Bedell, *The Alcotts*, p. 269.

50. Ibid., pp. 270–71.

51. Ibid. Bedell mentions that Abba's "first venture into independence had been a failure, but she did not consider herself defeated." I would mildly disagree. Abba Alcott wished for a genuinely romantic union with her husband, something approaching interdependency. I believe that Waterford was a success in

that it gave her the courage to "administer" in Boston. The separation from her daughters also stimulated her awareness of their need for a supervised "trying out" period. Louisa later divided the *Little Women* volumes into "Birds in the Nest" and "Birds Leave the Nest," attesting to the need for adolescent girls' "trial flights."

52. Ibid., p. 272.
53. Chevigny, *The Woman and the Myth*, p. 369.
54. Daniel Walker Howe, "American Victorianism as a Culture," *American Quarterly* 27 (Dec. 1975): 507–32.
55. Ibid., p. 515.
56. I am grateful to Susan Reverby for alerting me to Eric Schneider's fine Ph.D. dissertation, "In the Web of Class: Youth, Class and Culture in Boston, 1840–1940," Boston University (1980). I have followed his guide to novels about Boston's pauperism and poverty in the 1840s and agree with his analysis of the significance of these works. They were cheap and widely available, but I have no direct evidence that Louisa May Alcott read them. Nevertheless, her descriptions of similar scenes in *Little Men: Life at Plumfield with Jo's Boys* (Boston, 1871) and *Work: A Story of Experience* (Boston, 1872) are striking. Schneider also identifies the term "dangerous classes," which was used frequently by reformers, journalists, and missionaries by the 1840s. Alcott's descriptions are closely modeled on her reading of Charles Dickens' novels.
57. Bedell, *The Alcotts* p. 272.
58. Schneider, "In the Web of Class," p. 20.
59. Ibid.
60. Louisa May Alcott, *Work: A Story of Experience* (Boston: 1873).
61. Bedell, p. 274.
62. Joseph Tuckerman, *On the Elevation of the Poor: A Selection from his Reports as Minister-At-Large in Boston* (Boston, 1874; rpt. New York, 1971).
63. Ibid., pp. 121–22.
64. Catherine Covert Stepanek, "Saint before His Time: Samuel J. May and American Educational Reform," unpub. M.A. Thesis, Syracuse University, 1964, p. 110.
65. Ibid., p. 126.
66. Samuel J. May to Andrew Dickson White, Sept. 20, 1857, Samuel J. May Papers, Olin Library, Cornell University.
67. Schneider, "In the Web of Class," pp. 198–57. See also Barbara Brenzel, "Lancaster Industrial School for Girls: A Social Portrait of a Nineteenth Century Reform School for Girls," *Feminist Studies* 3 (Fall 1975): 40–54.
68. Abigail May Alcott's Diary, 1849, Fragments of an Autobiography, Alcott Collection at Houghton Library, Harvard University.
69. Ibid., Apr. 4, 1850. See also, Abigail May Alcott, "To the Ladies of the South Friendly Society," (Apr. 1830), in Abigail May Alcott, "Fragments of Reports while Visitor to the Poor," 1849, 1850, 1851, 1852, at Houghton Library, Harvard University.
70. Bedell, *The Alcotts*, pp. 272–85.
71. *Proceedings of the Women's Rights Convention, Held at Syracuse, Sept. 8, 9, 10, 1852, Including the Worcester Call for the Syracuse Convention* (Syracuse, 1852).
72. Bedell, *The Alcotts*, p. 285.
73. Margaret Fuller, *Woman in the Nineteenth Century and Other Kindred Papers by Margaret Fuller Ossoli*, ed. Arthur Buckminster Fuller (Boston, 1855); cited in Alice Rossi, ed., *The Feminist Papers* (New York, 1973), p. 158.

Chapter VI

1. Ednah Cheney, ed., *Louisa May Alcott: Life, Letters and Journals* (Boston, 1928), pp. 72–73.
2. Ibid., p. 47.
3. Ibid., p. 48.
4. Ibid.
5. Ibid.
6. Louisa May Alcott, *Work: A Story of Experience* (Boston, 1873), chapter 2.
7. Abigail May Alcott, Aug. 14, 1850, from notes and materials left by Amos Bronson Alcott for the Memoir of Abigail May Alcott, at Houghton Library, Harvard University; cited in Madelon Bedell, *The Alcotts: Biography of a Family* (New York, 1900), p. 282.
8. Anna Alcox's Diary, 1850–1851, at Houghton Library, Harvard University; cited in Bedell, *The Alcotts*, p. 282.
9. Cheney, ed., *Louisa May Alcott*, p. 48.
10. Ibid., p. 49.
11. Ibid. Louisa refers to a poem called "My Little Kingdom," written at the age of fourteen. The poem details self-control as the only power worth having.
12. Ibid.
13. Ibid. See Madeleine B. Stern, "L. Alcott, Trouper," *New England Quarterly* 26, no. 2 (June, 1943): 192–93.
14. Cheney, ed., *Louisa May Alcott*, p. 52.
15. Bedell notes that the Reverend Richardson attended Bronson Alcott's "Conversations" (Bedell, *The Alcotts*, p. 318). Louisa May Alcott's own recollection of her service is "How I Went out into Service: A Story," *The Independent* 26 (June 4, 1874).
16. Louisa May Alcott, "How I Went out into Service."
17. Cheney, ed., *Louisa May Alcott*, p. 52.
18. Ibid.
19. Ibid.
20. Bedell, *The Alcotts*, p. 284.
21. Ibid.
22. Louisa May Alcott, "The Rival Painters: A Face of Rome," *Olive Branch*, 17 (Sept. 1851).
23. Cheney, ed., *Louisa May Alcott*, pp. 53–54.
24. Ibid., p. 56.
25. Ibid., p. 55 (Feb. 1854, Pinckney Street, Boston).
26. Ibid., p. 57.
27. Ibid.
28. Ibid.
29. Ibid., p. 58.
30. Ibid., p. 63 (Apr. 1855).
31. Ibid. (Jan. 1855).
32. Ibid.
33. Ibid. (added notation: "L.M.A. 1886")
34. Ibid.
35. Louisa May Alcott, *Flower Fables* (Boston, 1855).
36. Cheney, ed., *Louisa May Alcott*, p. 65. (June 1855, Walpole, New Hampshire).
37. Ibid., p. 66.
38. Ibid.

39. Louisa noted that her sister Anna was "the star" of the Walpole theatricals in 1855, "her acting being really fine." Cheney, ed., *Louisa May Alcott*, p. 66.
40. Ibid., p. 100 (Aug. 1860).
41. Ibid.
42. Ibid.
43. Ibid.
44. Ibid., p. 68 (Oct. 1856).
45. Ibid.
46. Ibid., p. 78.
47. Odell Shepard, ed., *The Journals of Bronson Alcott* (Boston, 1938), pp. 303–05; Odell Shepard, *Pedlar's Progress: The Life of Bronson Alcott* (Boston, 1937), pp. 467–68.
48. Cheney, ed., *Louisa May Alcott*, p. 78.
49. Ibid.
50. Ibid.
51. Ibid., p. 80. Louisa did say she would "forgive" John Pratt for taking Anna away if "he makes her happy."
52. Ibid.
53. Ibid., p. 81 (Oct. 1858).
54. Ibid.
55. Ibid.
56. Ibid.
57. Ibid., p. 82. ". . . for these things are tests of character as well as courage."
58. Ibid. "I feel as if I could write better now,—more truly of things I have felt and therefore *know*. I hope I shall yet do my great book, for that seems to be my work, and I'm growing up to it" (Nov. 1858).
59. Ibid. She added, "But I think it is only the lesson one must learn as it comes, and I am glad to know it."
60. Ibid., p. 84. In 1859 Parker was in Italy, where he died; Louisa called him "my beloved minister and friend," adding, "To him and R. W. E. [Ralph Waldo Emerson] I owe much of my education. May I be a worthy pupil of such men!"
61. Louisa May Alcott, *Work.*
62. Louisa May Alcott, "Little Genevieve," *Saturday Evening Gazette* (Boston), Quarto Series (Mar. 29, 1856).
63. Louisa May Alcott, "The Sisters' Trial," *Saturday Evening Gazette* (Boston), Quarto Series (Jan. 26, 1856).
64. Louisa May Alcott, "The Lady and the Woman," *Saturday Evening Gazette* (Boston), Quarto Series (Oct. 4, 1856).
65. Cheney, ed., *Louisa May Alcott*, p. 82.
66. Louisa May Alcott, "The Lady and the Woman."
67. Cheney, ed., *Louisa May Alcott*, p. 102.
68. Ibid.
69. Ibid.
70. Ibid.
71. Louisa May Alcott, *Hospital Sketches* and Camp and Fireside Stories (Boston, 1863); see also Cheney, ed., *Louisa May Alcott*, p. 103.
72. A. K. Loring to Louisa May Alcott, Sept. 1, 1864, cited in Madeleine B. Stern, *Louisa May Alcott* (London, New York, 1957), p. 383 (courtesy of the late Mr. Carroll A. Wilson).
73. Hannah Bewick, "Introduction to *Moods*," unpub. manuscript, (courtesy of John A. Bewick). I am grateful to Professors Barbara Solomon and Daniel

Aaron of Harvard University for introducing me to Hannah Bewick's work. Bewick's untimely death cut short her promising contribution to Alcott scholarship.

Chapter VII

1. Henry James, "Miss Alcott's *Moods*," *North American Review* 101 (July, 1865): 276; rpt. in Henry James, *Notes and Reviews* (New York, 1968), pp. 49–58

2. James, "Miss Alcott's *Moods*," p. 276, rpt. in James, *Notes and Reviews*, pp. 49–58.

3. Louisa May Alcott, *Moods* (Boston, 1882), preface.

4. The "sad sisterhood" is described in *Moods*. The "happy women" include spinsters, married women, and widows. Three public letters from Louisa May Alcott detail the feminist life-choices she supported: "When Shall Our Young Women Marry?" *The Brooklyn Magazine* 4 (Apr. 1886); "Happy Women," *The New York Ledger* 24 (Apr. 11, 1868); and "Early Marriages," *The Ladies Home Journal* 4 (Sept. 1887).

5. Louisa May Alcott, *Little Women* (Boston, 1868, 1869).

6. Cheney notes the relationship between Sylvia Yule, Jo March, and Louisa May Alcott in Ednah Cheney, ed., *Louisa May Alcott: Life, Letters and Journals* (Boston, 1928), pp. 95–98.

7. Louisa May Alcott, *Moods*, p. 308. The first published version of *Moods* (Boston, 1865) is available on microfilm, Wright American Fiction, v.2, 1851–1875, no. 32, reel A-5. Subsequent references in this chapter to the 1882 edition are also in the 1865 edition of *Moods* unless otherwise noted.

8. Charlotte Bronte's *Jane Eyre* (London, 1847) and Nathaniel Hawthorne's *The Scarlet Letter* (Boston, 1850). Alcott read both novels several times. She and her mother read Mrs. Gaskell's biography of Bronte (Elizabeth Gaskell, *The Life of Charlotte Bronte* [London, 1857; New York, 1873]). Abba noted, "Mrs. Gaskell has told the history of this interesting family well. Their struggle reminds me of my own dear girls" Abigail May Alcott's Diary, May 1869, Fragments of an Autobiography, Alcott Collection at Houghton Library, Havard University.

9. Charlotte Bronte, *Jane Eyre* (London, 1847), chapter 12.

10. Louisa May Alcott, *Moods*, (Boston, 1882), p. 69.

11. Henry David Thoreau, *A Week on the Concord and Merrimack Rivers* (New York, 1849). See also George Whicher, *Walden Revisited* (Chicago, 1945), and Henry David Thoreau, *Poems of Nature* (Boston, 1895).

12. Henry James, "Miss Alcott's *Moods*," rpt. in James, *Notes and Reviews*, p. 49.

13. Harriet Martineau; cited in Gaskell, *The Life of Charlotte Bronte*, p. 420.

14. Louisa May Alcott, *Moods*, p. 84.

15. Ibid.

16. Ibid., p. 103

17. Ibid.

18. Ibid., p. 137.

19. Ibid., p. 126

20. Ibid., p. 125

21. Ibid., p. 131.

22. Ibid.

23. Eliza Buckminster Lee, *Life of Jean Paul Richter* (Boston, 1864).

24. Ibid., p. 266.
25. Lousia May Alcott, *Moods*, p. 248.
26. Ibid.
27. Nathaniel Hawthorne, "Warwick Castle," *Atlantic Monthly* 10 (July–Dec. 1862). That same year the *Atlantic Monthly* also featured Emerson, Thoreau, and Elizabeth Peabody. Such was Louisa May Alcott's reformist inheritance and her early circle of friends.
28. Louisa May Alcott, *Moods*, p. 146.
29. Ibid., p. 147
30. Ibid., p. 155.
31. Ibid., p. 46.
32. Gaskell, *The Life of Charlotte Bronte*, p. 420.
33. Ibid.
34. Louisa May Alcott, *Moods*, p. 322.
35. Ibid., p. 30.
36. Hannah Bewick, "Introduction to *Moods*," unpub. manuscript (courtesy of John A. Bewick). I am again grateful to Professors Barbara Solomon and Daniel Aaron of Harvard University for introducing me to Hannah Bewick's work.
37. Louisa May Alcott, *Moods*, p. 236
38. Ibid., p. 234.
39. Ibid., p. 245.
40. William R. Taylor and Christopher Lasch, "Two Kindred Spirits: Sorority and Family in New England, 1839–1845," *New England Quarterly* 36 (Mar. 1963), p. 154.
41. Louisa May Alcott, *Moods*, p. 322
42. Ibid., p. 311.
43. Ibid., p. 250.
44. Louisa May Alcott, "My Contraband or The Brothers," *Atlantic Monthly* 12, no. 73 (Nov. 1863): 584–90; rpt. in Louisa May Alcott, *Hospital Sketches and Camp and Fireside Stories* (Boston, 1863).
45. Ibid., p. 584.
46. Ibid.
47. Louisa May Alcott, *Moods*, p. 242.
48. Cheny, ed., *Louisa May Alcott*, pp. 95–98.
49. Ibid., p. 239.
50. Louisa May Alcott, *Jo's Boy's* (Boston, 1886). The spinster heroine is Nan Harding.
51. Louisa May Alcott, *Moods*, p. 323. The author also notes in that chapter, Sylvia's older sister, Prue, "both rejoiced at and rebelled against" the newly tender relationship between Sylvia and Mr. Yule. Prue, in fact, marries a widower with nine children because she is "of no farther use at home."
52. Louisa May Alcott to Thomas Niles, Feb. 12, 1881; cited in Cheney, ed., *Louisa May Alcott*, p. 341.
53. Ibid.
54. Louisa May Alcott, *Moods*, preface.
55. Louisa May Alcott, *A Modern Mephistopheles and A Whisper in the Dark* (Boston, 1889).
56. Louisa May Alcott, *Moods*, pp. 252, 253.
57. Ibid.
58. Ibid.

59. See William Leach, *True Love and Perfect Union: The Feminist Reform of Sex and Society* (New York, 1980), especially chapter 6, and Antoinette Brown Blackwell, *The Island Neighbors: A Novel of American Life* (New York, 1871). Blackwell claims that men and women must go forward together or else risk personal and social disunion. Lillie Devereux Blake, *Fettered for Life: Or Lord and Master* (New York, 1874) posed suicide as the alternative to divorce when married women are denied equality. See also Eliza B. Duffey, *The Relation of the Sexes* (New York, 1874). Alcott recommends Duffey to college girls in *Jo's Boys* so they will start out as equals to men.

60. Alcott's knowledge of the mainstream woman's rights position dates back to the *Proceedings of the Women's Rights Convention, Held at Syracuse, Sept. 8, 9, 10, 1852 including the Worcester Call for the Syracuse Convention* (Syracuse, 1852). There Samuel J. May listened to W. H. Channing, Harriot Hunt, and Ernestine Rose link egalitarian marriage and divorce as women's rights. The Reverend May then preached on "The Enfranchisement of Woman" in Nov. 1845, saying "the family is the most important institution on earth." Where marriages are prompted by "sordid, mercenary, or sensual motives," only "sorrow and sin" can flow (Samuel J. May Papers, Olin Library, Cornell University).

61. A. K. Loring to Louisa May Alcott; quoted in Madeleine B. Stern, *Louisa May Alcott* (London, New York, 1957), p. 383.

62. Louisa May Alcott, *Moods*, p. 301.

63. Ibid., pp. 358, 359.

Chapter VIII

1. Bessie Z. Jones, "Introduction to Louisa May Alcott," in Louisa May Alcott, *Hospital Sketches, Camp and Fireside Stories* (Cambridge, Mass., 1960), p. 17.

2. See Ednah Cheney, ed., *Louisa May Alcott: Life, Letters and Journals* (Boston, 1928), p. 115: Louisa wrote that she felt like "the son of the house going to war."

3. As William Leach notes, the *Index*, a journal run by Free Religion advocates, was next door to the *Woman's Journal* on Tremont Place in Boston. Leach details the relationship among feminists, positivists and adherents of Free Religion. Octavius Frothingham was Louisa Alcott's cousin and frequent host. Louisa mentioned enjoying the company of Julia Ward Howe, Caroline Dall, and Jane Croly. In the 1860s, 1870s and 1880s Alcott's fiction shifted from romanticism towards a rational realism that closely followed the bricolage structure of American positivism. Free Religion and universal laws of progress seemed as familiar as the *Index* and the *Woman's Journal* to Alcott (William Leach, *True Love and Perfect Union: The Feminist Reform of Sex and Society* [New York, 1980]).

     In *Little Women* (Boston, 1868, 1869), Louisa May Alcott spoke of Jo March as belonging to "the church of one" and in *Jo's Boys* (Boston, 1886), Alcott recommended the standard rational feminist polemics of the post-war period in the chapter, "Among the Maids." References to *Little Women* and *Jo's Boys* are cited by chapter numbers and titles which remain consistent in all editions of the novels.

4. Cheney, ed., *Louisa May Alcott*, chapter 6.

5. Ibid., p. 106.

6. In Mar. 1853, Bronson Alcott lectured on "Modern Life" to a group of Harvard students including Sanborn and Moncure Conway. Bedell notes that Sanborn visited the Alcotts at home on Pinckney Street, Boston, that same year. Louisa mentions him constantly as a friend and fellow reformer from then until her death in 1888 (Madelon Bedell, *The Alcotts: Biography of a Family* (New York, 1980).

7. In April 1860, Louisa wrote in her journal that "Sanborn was nearly kidnapped for being a friend of John Brown; but his sister and A. W. rescued him when he was hand-cuffed, and the scamps drove off" (Cheney, ed., *Louisa May Alcott*, p. 98).

8. Thomas Wentworth Higginson, *Cheerful Yesterdays* (Boston, 1898). Higginson also related Bronson Alcott's heroism during the attempt to rescue Anthony Burns, a fugitive slave, in 1854, Strangely, Louisa never fictionalized Bronson's lonely march up the steps of Faneuil Hall to confront the armed federal marshalls charged with returning Burns to slavery.

9. Louisa May Alcott, "With a Rose That Bloomed on the Day of John Brown's Martyrdom," *The Liberator* 30 (Jan. 20, 1860).

10. Ibid.

11. Cheney, ed., *Louisa May Alcott*, p. 106.

12. Bedell, *The Alcotts* p. 320.

13. This circle of friends all acknowledged their debt to Transcendentalism and then joined forces in the Concord School of Philosophy and the American Social Science Association in the 1880s. At some stage of their lives, all were also Unitarians. Their dedication to women's rights raises the importance of liberal religion and rationalism to feminism in nineteenth century America.

14. See Thomas Haskell, *The Emergence of Professional Social Science, The ASSA, and the Crisis of Authority* (Urbana, Ill., 1977), and Franklin Sanborn, "The Work of Social Science in the United States," *Journal of Social Science* 6 (July, 1874).

15. Cheney, ed., *Louisa May Alcott*, p. 108.

16. Ibid.

17. Ibid.

18. Louisa May Alcott, "Love and Self-Love," *Atlantic Monthly*, 5 (Mar. 1860).

19. Louisa May Alcott, "A Modern Cinderella: Or The Little Old Shoe," *Atlantic Monthly*, 6 (Oct. 1860).

20. In June 1860, Louisa described Anna and John Pratt as living like "a pair of turtle doves." Nevertheless she stoutly insisted, "I'd rather be a free spinster and paddle my own canoe." (Cheney, ed., *Louisa May Alcott*, p. 100).

21. See Louisa May Alcott, "Thoreau's Flute," Louisa May Alcott's tribute to the "lonely friend," *Atlantic Monthly* 22, no. 73 (Nov. 1863); rpt. in Cheney, ed., *Louisa May Alcott*, chapter 7.

22. Henry David Thoreau, "On the Duty of Civil Disobedience" (Boston, 1848).

23. Cheney, ed., *Louisa May Alcott*, p. 104. While she worked, "stories simmered in the brain." Like Jo in *Little Women*, her creator confided woes to a ragbag in the attic. John Brown's daughters were boarding with the Alcotts in the spring of 1861, making Louisa's writing time even more precarious.

24. L. P. Brockett and Mary C. Vaughan, *Woman's Work in the Civil War: A Record* (Boston, 1867). See especially the introduction by Henry W. Bellows, president, U.S. Sanitary Commission.

25. Ibid., p. 79.

26. Ibid., p. 56. Henry W. Bellows, in the introduction, claimed that these American women were "the products and representatives of a new social era, and a new political development."

27. Cheney, ed., *Louisa May Alcott*, p. 115 (Dec. 1862).
28. Ibid.
29. Ibid. (Union Hotel Hospital, Georgetown, D.C., Jan. 1863).
30. Louisa's views on this subject follow those of Harriot Hunt, Elizabeth Cady Stanton, Julia Ward Howe, et al. Her description of John Sulie, a fatally wounded Virginia blacksmith, expresses the feminist ideal of true manhood: "Under his plain speech and unpolished manner I seem to see a noble character, a heart as warm and tender as a woman's, a nature fresh and frank as any child's." Cheney, ed., *Louisa May Alcott*, pp. 116, 117. See also Louisa May Alcott, *Hospital Sketches and Camp and Fireside Stories* (Boston, 1895), p. 51.
31. Ibid.
32. Louisa May Alcott, "Hospital Sketches," *The Commonwealth* 1 (May 22, 29; June 12, 26 [1863]). See also idem, *Hospital Sketches and Camp and Fireside Stories* (Boston, 1895).
33. Cheney, ed., *Louisa May Alcott*, p. 117
34. Ibid., p. 118.
35. Ibid.
36. Ibid., p. 117.
37. Ibid., p. 118.
38. Louisa May Alcott, *Hospital Sketches and Camp and Fireside Stories* (Boston, 1869), p. 75
39. Ibid., p. 76
40. Ibid., p. 76, 77.
41. See J. G. Randall and David Donald, *The Civil War and Reconstruction* (Boston, 1961), pp. 224–25, 399, 461.
42. Ibid.
43. Cheney, ed., *Louisa May Alcott*, p. 119 (Jan. 21, 1864).
44. Ibid., p. 120 (Feb. 1864).
45. Ibid.
46. Ibid.
47. The Alcotts' friend, Moncure Conway, did not publish his monumental two volume work on demonology until 1879. However, he had authored a tract for the Ladies Religious Publication Society entitled *The Natural History of the Devil* (Albany, 1859). Conway's interest in science and in Free Religion was sparked by his determination to rid the world of both unchecked passion and the force of superstition. Conway and Bronson Alcott took the reality of the devil seriously in the 1850s. Eventually Conway maintained that "Orthodoxy was now pleading for charity at the hands of rationalism," as his biographer, Mary Elizabeth Burtis, said in *Moncure Conway* (New Jersey, 1952), p. 163.
48. Nancy F. Cott, "Passionlessness: An Interpretation of Victorian Sexual Ideology, 1790–1850," *Signs: Journal of Women in Culture and Society* 4, no. 2, (Winter, 1978): 219–36.
49. Rebecca Harding Davis, "Paul Blecker, "*Atlantic Monthly* (June–July 1863), quoted in Cott, "Passionlessness," p. 236. Louisa met Rebecca Harding (Davis) in May 1862 at a Boston party given by Annie Fields. Alcott's journal records that Harding was "a handsome, fresh, quiet woman, who says she never had any troubles, though she writes about woes. I told her I had lots of troubles; so I write jolly tales; and we wondered why we each did so" (Cheney, ed., *Louisa May Alcott* p. 107).
50. Louisa May Alcott, "My Contraband or The Brothers," *Atlantic Monthly* 12, no. 73 (Nov. 1863): 584–90; rpt. in Louisa May Alcott, *Hospital Sketches and Camp and Fireside Stories* (Boston, 1869).

51. See Louisa May Alcott, *Hospital Sketches*, chapter 2, "Model Children."

52. This theme is especially true in *Little Women*, *An Old Fashioned Girl*, *Rose in Bloom*, and *Eight Cousins; or the Aunt-Hill*.

53. Louisa May Alcott, "Thoreau's Flute."

54. Cheney, ed., *Louisa May Alcott*, p. 122.

55. Ibid., p. 123. "Sanborn asked me to do what Conway suggested before he left for Europe; viz., to arrange my letters in a printable shape, and put them in the "Commonwealth".

56. Leach, *True Love and Perfect Union*, p. 122.

57. See Madeleine Stern, ed., *Behind a Mask: The Unknown Thrillers of Louisa May Alcott* (New York, 1975). Stern traces the publication history of these pseudononymous tales and presents "Behind a Mask, "Pauline's Passion and Punishment," "The Mysterious Key," and "The Abbot's Ghost," in their original forms. The companion volume, *Plots and Counterplots: More Unknown Thrillers of Louisa May Alcott* (New York, 1976), includes "V.V.," "A Marble Woman," "The Skeleton in the Closet," "A Whisper in the Dark," and "Perilous Play." Stern's volumes are invaluable, a brilliant piece of literary detective work.

58. Stern, ed., *Behind a Mask*, "Pauline's Passion and Punishment."

59. Louisa May Alcott, *Hospital Sketches*. See also Cheney, ed., *Louisa May Alcott*, p. 115–19.

60. Brockett and Vaughan, *Woman's Work in the Civil War*, p. 71.

61. Louisa May Alcott, *Hospital Sketches*, p. 7.

62. Theodore Parker, "The Public Function of Woman;" rpt. in Theodore Parker, *Sins and Safeguards of Society* (Boston, 1907), pp. 178–206.

63. Louisa May Alcott, *Hospital Sketches*, p. 62.

64. Cheney, ed., *Louisa May Alcott*, p. 124

65. Ibid., p. 126.

66. See Stern, ed., *Plots and Counterplots* for a detailed description of the publishing intrigue surrounding Louisa's "double life" as author of domestic fictions and passionate thrillers.

67. Stern, ed., *Behind a Mask*.

68. Cheney, ed., *Louisa May Alcott*, p. 126.

69. Ibid.

70. Ibid.

71. Ibid., p. 131.

72. This choice is made abundantly clear in Louisa May Alcott, *An Old Fashioned Girl* (Boston, 1870) and *Little Women*. In both novels the ideal feminist goal is mutual sacrifice in friendship, true love or marriage.

73. Louisa May Alcott, *Little Men: Life at Plumfield with Jo's Boys* (Boston, 1871); idem, *Work: A Story of Experience* (Boston, 1873); idem, *Eight Cousins, or, The Aunt-Hill* (Boston, 1875); and idem, "A Visit to the Tombs," *The Youth's Companion* 19, no. 21 (May 25, 1876).

74. Louisa May Alcott, *Hospital Sketches*, p. 81.

75. See Franklin Sanborn and William Torrey Harris, *A. Bronson Alcott: His Life and Philosophy*, II (New York, 1893). Harris claimed that Bronson Alcott finally rejected his own "career of protest against public opinion." Instead, Harris reports that the mature Alcott concluded, "Nor is any man greatest when standing apart in his individualism; his strength and dignity come by sympathy with the aims of the best men of the community of which he is a member" (p. 641).

76. Leach, *True Love and Perfect Union*, p. 341.

77. Ibid.
78. Anna Brackett spoke at the Syracuse Woman's Congress, 1875; Louisa May Alcott was a Mass. delegate to the congress. The mind and body, according to Brackett, worked together, in obedience to hygenic laws of balance and harmony. Criminality and insanity were the result of degenerate, physical unbalance. Her paper, "Organization as Related to Civilization," must surely have appealed to Louisa Alcott, expressing her own integration of social science and moral duty as twin engines of feminist reform.
79. Cheney, ed., *Louisa May Alcott*, p. 39.
80. Anna Brackett, ed., *Education for American Girls* (New York, 1874).
81. Louisa May Alcott, "An Hour," in *Hospital Sketches and Camp and Fireside Stories*.
82. A. M. Barnard, "V. V. or Plots and Counterplots," *The Flag of Our Union* 20 (Feb. 1865); rpt. in Stern, ed., *Plots and Counterplots*.
83. A. M. Barnard, "Behind a Mask," *The Flag of Our Union* 21, nos. 41, 42, 43, 44 (Oct. 13, 20, 27, Nov. 3, 1866); rpt. in Stern, ed., *Behind a Mask*.
84. Ibid.
85. A. M. Barnard, "The Marble Woman: Or, the Mysterious Model," *The Flag of Our Union* 20, nos. 20, 21, 22, 23 (May 20, 27, June 3, 10, 1865); rpt. in Stern, ed., *Plots and Counterplots*.
86. Cheney, ed., *Louisa May Alcott*, p. 115. I argue that Louisa's Civil War experience is the turning point in her own decision to remain single and in her parents' acceptance of her as their "son."
87. Odell Shepard, *Pedlar's Progress: The Life of Bronson Alcott* (Boston, 1937), p. 503.
88. Amos Bronson Alcott's Manuscript Journal, July 5, 1865, at Houghton Library, Harvard University.
89. Cheney, ed., *Louisa May Alcott*, p. 146.
90. Ibid., p. 151.
91. Ibid.
92. Ibid., p. 152.
93. See Jane Benardette and Phyllis Moe, eds., *Companions of Our Youth: Stories by Women for Young People's Magazines, 1865–1900* (New York, 1980).
94. See the works of William Dean Howells, Mark Twain, Rebecca Harding Davis, Sarah Orne Jewett. Two analyses of juvenile and adolescent literature are in Cornelia Mugs, ed., rev. ed. (Toronto, 1969), and Alice Jordan, *From Rollo to Tom Sawyer* (Boston, 1948).
95. Cheney, ed., *Louisa May Alcott*, p. 152.
96. Unfortunately, Adams' adult heroines were not allowed the freedom granted his twelve-year-old girls.
97. *A Modern Mephistopheles* eventually did rather well in the "no name" series (Boston, 1877); rpt. in Louisa May Alcott, *A Modern Mephistopheles and A Whisper in the Dark* (Boston, 1889).
98. Cheney, ed., *Louisa May Alcott*, p. 154.
99. Ibid., p. 155.
100. Ibid., p. 163.
101. Ibid.
102. Ibid.
103. Ibid., p. 164.
104. See Ellen Carol DuBois, *Feminism and Suffrage* (Ithaca, 1978), chapter 6, for a full description of this problem.

Chapter IX

1. I avoid the term "domestic feminism" here, because as used by Daniel Scott Smith it refers specifically to woman's growing power within the household. Smith links the "radical decline in nineteenth-century marital fertility" to the increasing power of woman *within* the family (his emphasis). See Daniel Scott Smith, "Family Limitation, Sexual Control, and Domestic Feminism in Victorian America," in *Clio's Consciousness Raised*, ed. Mary Hartman and Lois W. Banner (New York, 1974), pp. 119–36. As Smith uses "domestic feminism," the term does not convey the links between a woman's power within the family and her extension of that power into the public sphere.

      I would argue that egalitarian marriage was at the heart of liberal American feminism in the nineteenth century. This chapter explores the centrality of feminists' wish for individuality and democratic domestic life.

2. Alcott's readers wanted Jo to marry Laurie; she was flooded with letters after pt. 1 of *Little Women* appeared. Although Alcott depicted Laurie as a rich, handsome "Heathcliff," (or romantic hero), Alcott tried to domesticate him just as she tried to make Jo's boyishness acceptable. Her main characters are not androgynous, but their individuality does not reside in specifically sexual stereotypes either. Manhood and womanhood are a combination of physical resources and socialization.

3. Ednah Cheney, ed., *Louisa May Alcott: Life, Letters and Journals* (Boston, 1928), pp. 162–67. Alcott began writing pt. 1 in May 1868. By June she sent twelve chapters to Thomas Niles at Roberts Bros. Her journal for Nov. 1, 1868 records, "Began the second part of "Little Women." I can do a chapter a day, and in a month I mean to be done" (p. 165).

4. Ibid., p. 165.

5. Ibid., (Nov. 16, 1868). The next day she recorded finishing the thirteenth chapter of *Little Women*.

6. "Woman," the record of a lecture and discussion at the Radical Club appears in Mrs. John T. Sargent, ed., *Sketches and Reminiscences of the Radical Club of Chestnut Street, Boston* (Boston, 1880). Coalitionists present and speaking included: Ednah Cheney, Thomas Wentworth Higginson, Bronson Alcott, Charles Everett, Ralph Waldo Emerson.

7. Louisa read Carlyle; Bronson's visit with Carlyle is described in chapter 3.

8. "Buckle and Carlyle," paper delivered by W. J. Potter at the Radical Club, summarized in Sargent, ed., *Sketches*, pp. 251–58. Cheney specifically mentions Motley's *The Rise of the Dutch Republic* in the discussion following Potter's lecture. That evening Bronson Alcott was still arguing that the world "has to be educated up" to accept the ideas of great "prophets." Higginson, Cyrus Bartol, and Cheney, together with Potter, carried the evening (p. 256).

9. John Lathrop Motley *Historic Progress and American Democracy* (New York, 1869), p. 6; idem, *The Rise of the Dutch Republic* (New York, 1855). The latter was published after *Little Women*, Motley's point is clear in vol. 3 of *The Rise of the Dutch Republic*, he is writing about a homogeneous "folk;" their rise is inexorable and they can trust one another to fulfill historical contracts. For an excellent discussion of the Bancroft-Motley approach as "whig," "progressive," "idealist," "liberal," or "Germanic," see Harry B. Henderson III, *Versions of the Past: The Historical Imagination in American Fiction* (New York, 1974), chapter 2.

10. Henderson, *Versions of the Past*, p. 23.

11. Bronson Alcott, quoted in "Buckle and Carlyle," in Sargent, ed., *Sketches*, p. 257.
12. "Woman," in Sargent, ed., *Sketches*, p. 43.
13. "Buckle and Carlyle," in ibid., p. 255.
14. Ibid., p. 257.
15. Ibid., p. 257.
16. Ibid., p. 253. (The speaker is William J. Potter.)
17. See Theodore Parker's statement, read aloud at the end of the Radical Club discussion on "Woman," in Sargent, ed., *Sketches*, p. 45.
18. Ibid.
19. Cheney, ed., *Louisa May Alcott*, p. 165.
20. Ibid.
21. Louisa May Alcott, *Little Women*, (Boston, 1868, 1869), chapter 33, "Jo's Journal." References to *Little Women* are cited by chapter numbers and titles which remain consistent in all editions of the novel.
22. Ibid.
23. I do not argue that the Radical Club debates "converted" Louisa Alcott to liberal rationalism. Rather, the debates reflected a general shift in liberal reform ideology within Alcott's "set." She, in turn, presents this shift in *Little Women* and in all her later fiction.
24. Cheney, ed., *Louisa May Alcott*, p. 96.
25. Ibid.
26. Ibid.
27. Ibid., p. 95.
28. Louisa May Alcott, "Happy Women," *The New York Ledger* 24, no. 7 (Apr. 11, 1868). She wrote the article in a very lonely, hardworking period, planning it as she ate a "dilapidated" squash pie, and writing it with the one-hundred dollar bill before her, noting that "liberty is a better husband than love to many of us" (Cheney, ed., *Louisa May Alcott*, p. 162).
29. Cheney, ed., *Louisa May Alcott*, p. 153.
30. Ibid., pp. 152–67. Alcott mentions The Radical Club, The Woman's Club, Emerson, Kate Field, Abby May, Fanny Kemble, etc. during the period she was writing *Little Women*.
31. Ibid.
32. Ibid., p. 165.
33. See Ellen Carol Dubois, *Feminism and Suffrage* (Ithaca, 1978), p. 6.
34. Ibid.
35. Ibid. There is a tendency to view Howe, Stone, and Blackwell as "conservative" feminists because they placed black male suffrage ahead of woman suffrage at this moment. Stanton and Anthony are then viewed as more radical on woman's rights. I would argue that Alcott's position, allied with Howe, Stone, Blackwell and Douglas, was not a betrayal of woman's rights, but a strategic attempt to preserve the liberal reform coalition. That coalition seemed, to Alcott's friends, necessary to democracy in the largest sense.
36. Ibid.
37. Ibid.
38. Louisa May Alcott claimed that the Bellevue Hotel was a bit too sociable for her taste; her sister May, however, enjoyed it thoroughly. See William Leach, (*True Love and Perfect Union: The Feminist Reform of Sex and Society* (New York, 1980), p. 315) for the links between Dio Lewis's hygenic school, the American Social Science Association, and friends and family of Louisa May Alcott, such as Abby May and Caroline Dall.

39. Cheney, ed., *Louisa May Alcott*, p. 162.
40. Ibid., p. 163.
41. Ibid.
42. Ibid., p. 164. Domestic chores remained a problem for the Alcott women. "No girl," Louisa wrote, tersely summarizing the "servant problem" in the Concord household. Admitting that "we don't like the kitchen department, and our tastes and gifts lie in other directions," Louisa knew she had to earn enough to provide domestic "help" for Abba, May, Ann and herself.

Chapter X

1. Louisa May Alcott, *Little Women* (Boston, 1868, 1869), chapter 1, "Playing Pilgrims." References to *Little Women* are cited by chapter numbers and titles which remain consistent in all editions of the novel.
2. Charles Dickens, *Bleak House*, 2 vols. (London, 1854).
3. Ibid.
4. Ibid. Esther's relationship to Charley is crucial to understanding Alcott's version of domestic democracy. Charley is a servant and Esther is a lady; nevertheless, housekeeping duties and mutual nurturance unite them. Esther, "attached to life again" after her near-fatal illness, recalls "the pleasant afternoon when I was raised in bed with pillows for the first time, to enjoy a tea-drinking with Charley!" Charley has taken over Esther's housewifely tasks and the room is "fresh and airy, so spotless and neat," with a pretty tea-table laid by the bedside (II, chapter 15). That relationship occurs between Phoebe and Rose in *Eight Cousins* and *Rose in Bloom* also.
5. Louisa May Alcott, *Little Women*, chapter 42, "All Alone."
6. Ibid.
7. Edna Cheney, ed., *Louisa May Alcott: Life, Letters and Journals* (Boston, 1928), p. 164.
8. Louisa May Alcott, *Little Women*, chapter 11, "Experiments."
9. Ibid.
10. Ibid.
11. Ibid.
12. Ibid.
13. Ibid.
14. Ibid.
15. Ibid.
16. Ibid. Nina Auerbach understands the "primacy of the female family" in the novel "both as moral-emotional magnet and as work of art" (Nina Auerbach, *Communities of Women* [Cambridge, Mass., 1978], pp. 56, 73). She argues, however, that Alcott's female family is a closed circle. I myself think that domestic democracy provides a launching paid for the "little" women's flight into the larger world. They have gained a genuine sense of "power and independence" by combining work outside the home and domestic skills. Only Beth remains at home permanently.
17. Louisa May Alcott, *Little Women*, chapter 2, "Confidential."
18. Ibid., chapter 5, "Being Neighborly."
19. Ibid. Auerbach (*Communities of Women*) is sensitive to the role of Laurie in *Little Women*. Laurie needs the March family's harmony, but in order to gain entrance to the feminist household he must acquire some of the virtues. A

balanced domesticity, Alcott maintains, also depends upon the girls' acquisition of "masculine" courage, independence, and comfortable elegance.

20. Ibid. Anne Hollander notes that "fellowship, insisted on by Jo, appears here
as an American ideal for governing the conduct between sexes;" see Hollander's "Reflections on *Little Women*," *Children's Literature* 28–29.

21. Louisa May Alcott, *Little Women*, chapter 38, "On the Shelf." Meg has already
made the case for true love, telling rich Aunt March, "I shall marry whom I
please, and you can leave your money to anyone you like."

22. Ibid. This scene suggests neither passivity nor female self-sacrifice despite the
claims of Patricia Meyer Spacks in *The Female Imagination* (New York, 1972),
pp. 125–28. She argues that there is "no doubt about which sex really *does
things*" in *Little Women*. According to Spacks, it is men who do things in the
novel; hence, female readers "yearned somehow to be boy and girl simul-
taneously" (p. 120). Jo, Meg, Amy, Beth and Marmee herself are very active
characters, however, arguing for sexually specific but confluent manhood
and womanhood. Alcott argues that both domestic life and public life are in
trouble when women are reared to be passive and men are encouraged to be
aggressive. Coeducation becomes the foundation of sexual equality in
Alcott's later work, allowing both sexes to develop the full range of human
qualities.

23. Louisa May Alcott, *Little Women*, chapter 23, "Aunt March Settles the Question."

24. Ibid., chapter 8, "Jo Meets Appolyon."

25. Ibid., chapter 3, "The Laurence Boy."

26. Ibid., chapter 29, "Calls."

27. Ibid., chapter 39, "Lazy Laurence." Beth's death is not the sentimental artifact
so brilliantly discussed by Ann Douglas in "The Meaning of Little Eva." See
Ann Douglas, *The Feminization of American Culture* (New York, 1972).

28. Ibid., chapter 36, "Beth's Secret."

29. Ibid., chapter 42, "All Alone."

30. Ibid., chapter 24, "Gossip." Douglas (*The Feminization of American Culture*)
notes that "Little Eva's" death is merely decorative. Beth March's death, on
the other hand, provides a rite of passage for Jo, deeply affecting the final
outcome of the novel.

31. Ibid., chapter 35, "Heartache."

32. Ibid., Judith Fetterley sees Jo March's struggle as an inner civil war, a battle
between passivity and sexual rage. See "*Little Women*: Alcott's Civil War,"
Feminist Studies 5 (1979), 369–83.

33. Ibid., chapter 33, "Jo's Journal."

34. Ibid., chapter 46, "Under the Umbrella."

35. Ibid.

36. Ibid.

37. Ibid., chapter 33, "Jo's Journal." See also Sargent, ed., *Sketches*.

38. Ibid.

39. Ibid.

40. Cheney, ed., *Louisa May Alcott* (London, New York, 1957), p. 176.

41. Madeleine B. Stern, *Louisa May Alcott* (London, New York, 1957), p. 176.

42. Louisa May Alcott's Journal, Mar. 16, 1861, Louisa May Alcott, Letters and
Papers at Houghton Library, Harvard University.

43. Louisa May Alcott, *Little Women*, chapter 4, "Burdens." Meg and Jo knit, sew,
cook, clean and garden, in addition to their paid work outside the family
home. The two eldest girls clealy have a major role in caring for their younger
sisters as well.

44. Ibid., chapter 23, "Aunt March Settles the Question."
45. Ibid.
46. Ibid.

Chapter XI

1. Nina Baym, *Woman's Fiction: A Guide to Novels by and about Women in America, 1820–1870* (Ithaca, 1978), pp. 296–99. Baym also assumes that Abba Alcott could not "withstand" the "self-absorbed and unwittingly tyrannical" Bronson, and that as a result all the Alcott daughters were "psychologically scarred " (p. 297). The March family, conversely, represents a sentimental ideal. Even Madeleine Stern greatly suggests that Alcott's success with *Little Women* stopped her pseudonymous, full-blooded tales of passion (Madeleine B. Stein's introduction in *Behind a Mask: The Unknown Thrillers of Louisa May Alcott* (New York, 1975). Stern's biography, *Louisa May Alcott*, however, makes an excellent case for Louisa's growing pleasure in her own success and her widening circle of liberal reformist friends—testimony, I think, to her growing belief in the rationalization of passion.

2. Ann Douglas, *The Feminization of American Culture* (New York, 1972). Douglas includes Louisa May Alcott in the sentimentalist rather than romantic tradition of nineteenth century authors. I am trying to add a third "category" to Douglas' sensitive analysis. Alcott moved from a romantic to a rationalist perspective, though without changing her literary status.

3. Mark Twain's *Tom Sawyer* was published in 1876, *Huckleberry Finn* in 1885.

4. Theodore Parker, sermon, "The Public Function of Woman," rpt. in Theodore Parker, *Sins and Safeguards of Society* (Boston, 1907), pp. 178–206.

5. Louisa May Alcott, *Jo's Boys* (Boston, 1886); idem, *A Garland for Girls* (Boston, 1888).

6. See Harry B. Henderson III, *Versions of the Past: The Historical Imagination in American Fiction* (New York, 1974) for an excellent discussion of holistic and progressive strains that are intertwined in the heroic models of America's historical fiction.

7. Ann Douglas (*The Feminization of American Culture*, p. 87), quotes Harriet Beecher Stowe's novel, *The Pink and White Tyranny* (New York, 1871). While Douglas is generally right about the sentimentalists, I find Alcott fits the liberal pattern of influential, literate reformers described in William Leach, *True Love and Perfect Union: The Feminist Reform of Sex and Society* (New York, 1980). These men and women were initially shaped by Romanticism and then, becoming Rationalists, they often retained many idealist principles in the transformation.

8. Madeleine B. Stern, *Louisa May Alcott* (London, New York, 1957), chapter 10.

9. Moncure Daniel Conway, *The Autobiography of Moncure Daniel Conway*, 2 vols. (Boston, 1904). See I, 10 for details on the *Dial*.

10. Ibid., chapters 19 and 20 for discussions of the Alcott circle and Darwin. See also Rosalind Rosenberg, "The Dissent From Darwin," unpub. Ph. D. thesis, Stanford University, 1974 for the importance of Darwin to the American woman's rights issue after 1809; idem, *Beyond Separate Spheres: Intellectual Roots of Modern Femism* (New Haven, 1981). See also Antoinette Brown Blackwell, *The Sexes Throughout Nature* (New York, 1875).

11. Stern, *Louisa May Alcott*, chapter 10.

12. Ibid.

13. In 1872 Abba Alcott noted in her Diary that Louisa had achieved "literary"

and "practical" power, securing "a maintenance for herself and family, having well invested several thousand before the age of forty." Abigail May Alcott's Memoir, Apr. 20, 1872, at Houghton Library, Harvard University.

14. Stern, *Louisa May Alcott*, chapter 10.
15. Abigail May Alcott's Memoir, Mar. 2, 1868, at Houghton Library, Harvard University.
16. Ibid., Sept. 1867.
17. Ibid.
18. Ednah Cheney, ed., *Louisa May Alcott: Life, Letters and Journals* (Boston, 1928), p. 159.
19. Ibid., p. 173.
20. Louisa May Alcott, *An Old Fashioned Girl* (Boston, 1870), chapter 1, p. 4. All references to the text of *An Old Fashioned Girl* are cited by chapter and page numbers. Chapter numbers remain consistent in all published editions.
21. Ibid., p. 9.
22. Ibid., chapter 8, "The Woman Who Did Not Dare," p. 159. Polly takes the radical step of renting a room of her own "Six Years Afterward." Alcott's point is obvious: Polly is no longer visiting her rich friends; she is a working woman in the second half of the novel.
23. Ibid., chapter 9, "Tom's Success," p. 163.
24. Ibid., p. 164.
25. Ibid., p. 173.
26. Ibid., p. 175.
27. Ibid., chapter 11, "Needles and Tongues," p. 207.
28. Ibid.
29. Ibid., chapter 13, "The Sunny Side," p. 255.
30. Ibid., p. 260.
31. Ibid. This picnic perfectly captures Alcott's notion of feminist abundance, sensible spontaneity and "happy women."
32. Ibid., p. 261.
33. Ibid., p. 257.
34. Ibid., p. 258.
35. Ibid., chapter 3, "Polly's Troubles," p. 42.
36. Epes Sargent, *The Woman Who Dared* (Boston, 1869). William Leach describes Epes Sargent and his brother, John Sargent, a feminist Unitarian minister (*True Love* and *Perfect Union*, pp. 116–18).
37. Louisa May Alcott, *An Old Fashioned Girl*, chapter 19, "Tom's Success," p. 368.
38. Ibid., p. 359.
39. Louisa May Alcott, *Aunt Jo's Scrap Bag* and *Shawl Straps* (Boston, 1872), p. 225 (Scrap Bag, II).
40. Ibid., chapter 2.
41. Ibid., chapter 3.
42. Ibid., chapter 6.
43. Ibid. See also Conway, *The Autobiography*, I.
44. Louisa May Alcott, *Aunt Jo's Scrap Bag* and *Shawl Straps* (Boston, 1872), chapter 3.
45. Ibid.
46. Cheney, ed., *Louisa May Alcott*, p. 213.
47. Ibid. See also Stern, *Louisa May Alcott*, chapter 11.
48. William Taylor Adams [Oliver Optic], *Try Again, or The Trials and Triumph of Harry West* (New York, 1857), p. 11.

49. William Taylor Adams [Oliver Optic], *The Way of the World* (Boston, 1867), p. 47.
50. Ibid., p. 43. Eugene Hungerford's sister, Julia, is described as being "a little disposed to be strong minded." In fact, she had "actually read Locke and Bacon, as well as Scott and Dickens." Adams, like Alcott, wants to restore a mythical equality of opportunity. His world is also one of Yankee homogeneity, but he is not in favor of institutional solutions.
51. Ibid. Adam's ideal restoration of laissez faire nevertheless includes a woman's suffrage plank on the grounds of a well-educated, property-holding electorate. He is for Temperance as well, to insure a sober workforce.
52. Louisa May Alcott, *Little Men: Life at Plumfield with Jo's Boys* (Boston, 1871), chapter 1, "Nat," p. 3. All references to the text of *Little Men* are cited by chapter and page numbers. Chapter numbers remain consistent in all published editions.
53. Ibid., chapter 7, "Naughty Nan," p. 105. Mrs. Aunt Jo's belief in coeducation seems very close to Harriet Martineau's letter to the 1851 Woman's Rights Convention at Worcester, Mass. Printed in *The Liberator*, Nov. 21, 1851, Alcott may well have read it. Martineau was reading Comte at the time and she argued for "one true method in the treatment of either sex, of any color, and under any circumstances—to ascertain what are the powers of that being, to cultivate them to the utmost, and then to see what action they will find for themselves."
54. Ibid., chapter 12, "Huckleberries," p. 205–9. See also Annie Fellows Johnston, *The Little Colonel* (New York, 1896).
55. Sarah Josepha Hale, quoted in Roberts Brothers advertisement for "Louisa May Alcott's Writings," 1888.
56. Louisa May Alcott, *Little Men*, chapter 1, "Nat," p. 5.
57. Ibid., chapter 8, "Pranks and Plays," p. 119–20.
58. Ibid., chapter 21, "Thanksgiving," p. 348.
59. Ibid.
60. Mark Twain, *Innocents Abroad* (New York, 1869). Twain made fun of aristocratic, European antecedents. Alcott was very tempted by the expatriate life; it offered a good deal of freedom for American women artists.
61. Cheney, ed., Louisa May Alcott, p. 267.

Chapter XII

1. Ednah Cheney, ed., *Louisa May Alcott, Life, Letters and Journals* (Boston, 1928), p. 222.
2. Ibid. The series appeared as Louisa May Alcott, "Work, Or Christie's Experiment," *The Christian Union* 6–7 (Dec. 18, 25, 1872; Jan. 1, 8, 15, 22, 29; Feb. 5, 12, 19, 26; Mar. 5, 12, 19, 26; Apr. 2, 9, 16, 23, 30; May 7, 14, 21, 28; and June 4, 11, 18, 1873); rpt. as *Work: A Story of Experience* (Boston, 1873; rpt. New York, 1977).
3. Cheney, ed., *Louisa May Alcott*, p. 225.
4. Ibid., p. 224.
5. Louisa May Alcott, *Work*.
6. Theodore Parker, sermon, "The Public Function of Women;" rpt. in Theodore Parker, *Sins and Safeguards of Society* (Boston, 1907) pp. 178–206. For a contrast to Parker's and Alcott's definition of true womanhood, see Barbara

Welter, "The Cult of True Womanhood, 1820–1860," *American Quarterly* 18 (Summer 1966), 151–75.

7. Moncure Daniel Conway, *The Autobiography of Moncure Daniel Conway*, 2 vols. (Boston, 1904), I, II.

8. Louisa May Alcott, *Aunt Jo's Scrap Bag* and *Shawl Straps* (Boston, 1872), chapter 5.

9. Cheney, ed., *Louisa May Alcott*, p. 220.

10. Louisa May Alcott, *Work*, chapter 1, p. 2.

11. Ibid., chapter 2, p. 14.

12. Ibid., p. 16.

13. Ibid., p. 22.

14. Lucy Maynard Salmon, *Domestic Service* (New York, 1911), p. 148.

15. Ibid., p. 141. Fay Dudden, *Serving Women* (New York, 1983) offers the most recent exploration of domestic servants in nineteenth-century America.

16. Salmon, *Domestic Service*, p. 150. Jean Fagin Yellin forcefully agrees that *Work* should be read as a feminist essay; she also credits Alcott for her "seemingly effortless use of the American vernacular." Yellin, however, finds *Work* lacking an expose of class differences between women (Jean Fagin Yellin, "From Success to Experience: Louisa May Alcott's *Work*," *Massachusetts Review* (Fall 1980), p. 533.

17. Sally Holley to Louisa May Alcott, undated, Alcott-Pratt Collection at Houghton Library, Houghton University.

18. "Marryin' for a livin' " is dismissed with contempt by Cynthie Wilkins, a "clear starcher," in Louisa May Alcott, *Work*, chapter 14, p. 327.

19. Louisa May Alcott, *Work*, chapter 4, p. 81.

20. Theodore Parker, sermon, "On the Labouring Classes;" rpt. in Theodore Parker, *Social Classes in a Republic* (Boston, 1907), p. 54.

21. Cynthie Wilkins uses the imagery of her trade as a laundress. Her satire is sharp, evocative of Carlyle's *Sartor Resartus*, and echoes from Swift's *Tale of the Tub*. Cynthie discovers "how often does the Body appropriate what was meant for the cloth only" (Thomas Carlyle, *Sartor Resartus* [London, 1896], p. 218).
    Louisa read Swift's *Tale of the Tub* and Carlyle; Alcott also wrote a poem about herself as laundress ("Labor: A Song From the Suds," Alcott Family Papers at Houghton Library, Harvard University).

22. Louisa May Alcott, *Work*, chapter 9, p. 204.

23. Louisa May Alcott, *Work*, chapter 19, p, 413, is a prose version of Louisa's memorial poem, "Thoreau's Flute." David Sterling's flute, hung beside the window, is stirred by the wind, carrying a "supernatural" melody to his widow.

24. Ibid., chapter 19, p. 422.

25. Ibid., chapter 20, p. 425.

26. Ibid., p. 428.

27. Ibid., chapter 1, p. 11.

28. Cheney, ed., *Louisa May Alcott*, p. 224.

29. Ibid., p. 225.

30. Review of Louisa May Alcott's *Work* in *The Lakeside Monthly*, copy in Alcott-Pratt Collection at Houghton Library, Harvard University.

31. Review of Louisa May Alcott's *Work* in *Harper's New Monthly Magazine*, 47 (Sept. 1873), pp. 614–15.

32. Miss Phelps, "Address to Working Women," quoted in Rosalyn Baxandall,

Linda Gordon, and Susan Reverby, *America's Working Women: A Documentary History, 1600 to the Present* (New York, 1976). Susan Reverby kindly brought this document to my attention.

33. Louisa May Alcott, *Diana and Persis*, ed. Sarah Elbert (New York, 1978). Original untitled manuscript is listed as "a holograph in Alcott's hand on light blue paper," Alcott-Pratt at Houghton Library, Harvard University.

34. Caroline Ticknor, *May Alcott; A Memoir* (Boston, 1928), p. 105.

35. Ibid., p. 20.

36. Ibid.

37. Ibid., p. 125.

38. Ibid., p. 127.

39. Ibid.

40. Ibid.

41. Ibid., p. 130.

42. Abigail May Alcott, May 1, 1875 [date of copy], Alcott-Pratt Collection at Houghton Library, Harvard University.

43. Ibid.

44. Ibid.

45. Ticknor, *May Alcott*, p. 248.

46. Ibid., p. 248.

47. Ibid., p. 255.

48. Ibid.

49. Ibid., p. 267.

50. Cheney, ed., *Louisa May Alcott*, p. 317.

51. Madeleine B. Stern, *Louisa May Alcott* (London, New York, 1957), p. 275. I am also grateful to Professor Jean Stump, art historian, University of Kansas, for the direct reference to May Alcott's diary entry, Jan. 28, 1879.

52. Louisa May Alcott, *Diana and Persis*. In the spring of 1879, Louisa, missing her sister May, wrote, "No golden-haired, blue-gowned Diana ever appears now; she sits happily sewing baby clothes in Paris" (Cheney, ed., *Louisa May Alcott*, p. 319).

53. Louisa May Alcott, *Diana and Persis*, p. 56.

54. Ibid., p. 64.

55. Ibid., p. 103. In a letter to Marcus and Rebecca Spring, written in Florence during Dec. 1849, Margaret Fuller mentions that she and Count Ossoli call their son "Nino." The full text of that letter and the succeeding one mentioning Mr. and Mrs. William Wetmore Story are rpt. in Franklin Sanborn, *Recollections of Seventy Years*, II (Boston, 1909), pp. 410–11.

56. Ibid.

57. Ibid., p. 127.

58. Ibid., p. 129.

59. Cushman's letters to the Radical Club appear at the end of Mrs. John T. Sargent, ed., *Sketches and Reminiscences of the Radical Club of Chestnut Street, Boston* (Boston, 1880). Louisa wrote to her Aunt Louisa Bond on Sept. 17, 1860, "Saturday we had J. G. Whittier, Charlotte Cushman, Miss Stebbins the sculptress, and Mr. Stuart, conductor of the underground railroad of this charming free country" (Cheney, ed., *Louisa May Alcott*, p. 92).

60. The complete story of "The White Marmorean Flock" remains to be told. Nevertheless, Joseph Leach's *Bright Particular Star: The Life and Times of Charlotte Cushman* (New Haven, London, 1970) is an excellent study. See also Margaret Farrand Thorp, *The Literary Sculptors* (Chapel Hill, 1965); Henry

James, *The William Wetmore Story*, 2 vols. (Edinburgh and London, 1903); Cornelia Curred, *Harriet Hosmer: Letters and Memories* (New York, 1912); and Nathaniel Hawthorne, *The Marble Faun* (Boston, 1860).

61. Daniel Scott Smith, "Family Limitation, Sexual Control, and Domestic Feminism in Victorian America," in *Clio's Consciousness Raised*, ed. Mary Hartman and Lois W. Banner (New York, 1974), p. 121.

62. Ibid., p. 120.

Chapter XIII

1. Rosalind Rosenberg, *Beyond Separate Spheres: Intellectual Roots of Modern Feminism* (New Haven, 1982), xv.

2. Ibid. Rosenberg's chapter, "In the Shadow of Dr. Clarke," graphically details the predicament of Alcott's set.

3. *The Woman's Journal* reported Dr. Clarke's speech in its Dec. 21, 1872 edition. Julia Ward Howe, an editor, then followed with several months coverage of the ensuing debates.

4. Edward Clarke, *Sex in Education: or A Fair Chance for the Girls* (Boston, 1873).

5. Charles Darwin, *The Descent of Man* and *Selection in Relation to Sex*, 2 vols. (London, 1871). For the popular depiction of the Darwinian controversy see issues of *Popular Science Monthly* from the mid-1870s through the 1880s. The social significance of woman's biological specialization is discussed in Charles Rosenberg, *No Other Gods: On Science and American Social Thought* (Baltimore, 1976).

6. Julia Ward Howe, ed., *Sex and Education: A Reply to Dr. Clarke's "Sex in Education"* (Cambridge, Mass., 1874). See also Anna C. Brackett, *The Education of American Girls* (New York, 1874) and Eliza B. Duffey, *No Sex in Education: or An Equal Chance for both Girls and Boys* (Philadelphia, 1874). The latter two books are recommended in Louisa May Alcott *Jo's Boys* (Boston, 1886), Chapter 17, "Among the Maids."

7. Madeleine B. Stern, *Louisa May Alcott* (London, New York, 1957), pp. 236–45. For an excellent description of *St. Nicholas* and the importance of juvenile magazines see Jane Benardette and Phyllis Moe, *Companions of Our Youth: Stories by Women for Young People's Magazines, 1865–1900* (New York, 1980).

8. Ibid. Louisa May Alcott continued to publish in juvenile magazines until the end of her career. Letters to Mary Mapes Dodge, in particular, appear throughout Ednah Cheney, ed., *Louisa May Alcott: Life, Letters and Journals* (Boston, 1928), chapter 11, "Last Years."

9. Louisa May Alcott *Eight Cousins; or, The Aunt-Hill* (Boston, 1890), chapter 2, "The Clan," p. 18.

10. Ibid., chapter 1, "Two Girls," p. 5.

11. Ibid. chapter 16, "Bread and Button-Holes," p. 190.

12. Ibid., chapter 28, "Fashion and Physiology," p. 211.

13. Ibid. chapter 22, "Something to Do," p. 255.

14. Ibid. chapter 24, "Which?" p. 279.

15. Stern, *Louisa May Alcott*, p. 295. In 1862 Frank Sanborn married his cousin, Louisa Augusta Leavitt, after the death of his first wife, Ariana Walker. Ariana, a close friend of Ednah Dow Cheney, was consumptive, dying eight days after her wedding in 1854. Frank and Louisa Sanborn had three sons. Louisa May Alcott maintained close ties with the Sanborns, and included a poem by one of the Sanborn boys in *Under the Lilacs*.

16. Cheney, ed., *Louisa May Alcott*, chapter 10 (Feb. 1875).
17. Helen Wright, "Biographical sketch of Maria Mitchell," ed. E. James *Notable American Women* (Cambridge, Mass., 1971), II, p. 555.
18. Ibid. See also Cheney, ed., *Louisa May Alcott*, chapter 10 (Sept. and Oct. 1875).
19. See Stern, *Louisa May Alcott*, pp. 297–98. Anna Charlotte Lynch Botta was a notable hostess, admired by Emerson, among others, who called her home, "the house of expanding doors." Botta also contributed poetry to *The Democratic Review* and wrote *A Hardbook of Universal Literature* in 1860. She taught for a time at the Brooklyn Academy for Women.
20. Cheney, ed., *Louisa May Alcott*, chapter 10.
21. Louisa May Alcott to Alcott Family, Dec. 25, 1875, in Ibid., pp. 235–39.
22. Louisa May Alcott, *Rose in Bloom* [(Boston, 1876), page references are to 1934 ed.], chapter 1, "Coming Home." This chapter deals with Rose Campbell's adoption of a poor child.
23. Ibid., p. 10.
24. Ibid., p. 11.
25. Ibid.
26. Cheney, ed., *Louisa May Alcott*, p. 284 (Letter to Thomas Niles, Feb. 18, 1881).
27. Barbara Leslie Epstein, *The Politics of Domesticity*, Women Evangelism and Temperance in Nineteenth Century America (Conn., 1981), p. 106.
28. Louisa May Alcott, *Rose in Bloom*, chapter 6, "Polishing Mac," p. 100. Mac is carrying a volume of Thoreau and reading Emerson.
29. Ibid., chapter 18, "Which Was It?," p. 283.
30. Ibid., chapter 16, "Good Works," p. 260.
31. Ibid., chapter 17, "Among the Hay-Cocks," p. 267.
32. See Epstein, *The Politics of Domesticity*, and Ruth Bordin, *Woman and Temperance, The Quest for Power and Liberty*, 1873–1900 (Philadelphia, 1981).
33. Cheney, ed., *Louisa May Alcott*, p. 283.
34. For discussions of the fact that the mean number of children born to a hypothetical woman dropped in Louisa's lifetime from 6.21 to 3.87, see the following: Peter Uhlenberg, "Changing Configurations of the Life Course," ed. Tamara K. Hareven, *Transitions: The Family and the Life Course in Historical Perspective* (New York, 1978); Robert V. Wells, "Family History and Demographic Transition," *Journal of Social History* (Fall 1975), p. 1–19; and Linda Gordon, *Woman's Body, Woman's Right: A Social History of Birth Control Movement and American Society Since 1830* (New York, 1978).
35. See Franklin Sanborn, *Recollections of Seventy Years*, II (Boston, 1909); Franklin Sanborn and William Torrey Harris, *A. Bronson Alcott: His Life and Philosophy*, II (New York, 1893); and Florence Whiting Brown, "Alcott and The Concord School of Philosophy," a paper read at the Concord Antiquarian Society, May 28, 1923. Privately printed, Aug. 1926.
36. See the works cited in the previous note.
37. Sanborn and Harris, *A. Bronson Alcott*, II, p. 622.
38. Ibid. p. 627
39. Ibid. p. 643. Harris praises Bronson Alcott as representative of Anglo-Saxon Protestants. His character, Harris said, was "the ideal of a strong, serious-minded, independent manhood, unswerved by personal interest, thoroughly patriotic and devoted to the public interest." Ibid.
40. Ibid. p. 626
41. Ibid. p. 645. Harris contrasts Bronson's post-war *Tablets* (Boston, 1868) with his earlier works.

42. Cheney, ed., *Louisa May Alcott*, p. 288. See also Stern, *Louisa May Alcott*, chapter 15.

43. Sam B. Warner, Jr., *Streetcar Suburbs: The Process of Growth in Boston, 1870–1900*, (Boston, 1962).

44. Sanborn and Harris, *A. Bronson Alcott*, II, p. 655.

45. Ibid.

46. Maris Vinovskis and Richard M. Bernard, "Beyond Catherine Beecher: Female Education in the Antebellum Period," *Signs: Journal of Womenly Culture and Society* 3 (Summer 1978): 860–86; and Sarah Elbert, "The Changing Education of American Women," *Current History* 70, no. 416 (May 1976): 220–24. "In Massachusetts, by 1860, women comprised 77.8 percent of all public school teachers and this only presaged the feminization of teaching in the twentieth century" (Elbert, p. 223). Thus, the feminization of teaching clearly preceded any large-scale feminist assault on higher education.

47. Louisa May Alcott, *Work: A Story of Experience* (Boston, 1872), chapter 20, p. 427.

48. Cheney, ed., *Louisa May Alcott*, p. 172. In 1869 Louisa began to record the sums given to Samuel E. Sewall to invest for the Alcott family. One year later she mentions $10,000 invested. By 1872 she admitted that the family was "independent." By March 1877, Louisa was able to give Anna Alcott Pratt four thousand dollars from the returns on Vermont and Eastern Railroad Securities toward the purchase of Thoreau House.

49. See Peter N. Carroll and David W. Noble, *The Restless Centuries*, 2nd ed., (New York, 1979), chapter 20, "Peacetime Railroad Empire."

50. Louisa wrote, "The H.H. Book [*Ramona*] is a noble record of the great wrongs of her chosen people, and ought to waken up the sinners to repentance and justice before it is too late. It recalls the old slavery days, only these victims are red instead of black. It will be a disgrace if H.H. gave her work and pity all in vain" (Louisa Alcott to T. Niles, Sept. 18, 1885, in Cheney, ed., *Louisa May Alcott*, p. 301. On the relationship between western expansion, Indian history, and farm agitation see Robert Bartlett, *The New Country: A Social History of the American Frontier* (New York, 1974), Dee Brown, *Bury My Heart at Wounded Knee* (New York 1971); and Helen Hunt Jackson, *A Century of Dishonor* (Boston, 1881).

51. An excellent discussion of this struggle is Dollar, et. al., *America: Changing Times* (New York, 1979), 574–77.

52. Louisa May Alcott, *Jo's Boys* (Boston, 1886), chapter 1, "Ten Years Later," p. 23.

53. Ibid.

54. Ibid., p. 14.

55. Ibid., chapter 17, "Among the Maids," p. 222.

56. Review marked "Jo's Boys and How They Turned Out," copy at Houghton Library, Harvard University.

57. Ibid.

58. Louisa May Alcott, *Little Men: Life at Plumfield with Jo's Boys* (Boston, 1871) chapter 15, "In the Willow," p. 239.

59. Louisa May Alcott, *Jo's Boys*, chapter 17, "Among the Maids," p. 222.

60. Ibid., chapter 1, "Ten Years Later," p. 17.

61. Ibid., chapter 17, "Among the Maids," p. 224.

62. Ibid.

63. Louisa May Alcott, *Little Men*, chapter 19, "John Brooke," p. 301.

64. Louisa May Alcott, *Jo's Boys*, chapter 10, "Demi Settles," p. 150.

65. Ibid., p. 151.
66. Ibid., chapter 19, "White Roses," p. 248.
67. Ibid., chapter 17, "Among the Maids," p. 222.
68. Ibid., chapter 5, "Vacation," p. 89.
69. Ibid., chapter 2, "Parnassus," p. 31.
70. Ibid., chapter 17, "Among the Maids," p. 228–29.
71. Louisa May Alcott, *A Modern Mephistopheles and A Whisper in the Dark* (Boston, 1889), chapter 15.
72. Ibid.
73. Louisa May Alcott, *Jo's Boys*, chapter 7, "The Lion and the Lamb."
74. Ibid., chapter 8, "Josie Plays Mermaid."
75. Ibid., chapter 12, "Dan's Christmas," p. 170.
76. Ibid., pp. 174, 175.
77. Ibid., chapter 20, "Life for Life," p. 257.
78. Ibid., chapter 4, "Dan," p. 67.
79. Ibid., chapter 22, "Positively Last Appearance," p. 285. See also Robert F. Berkhofer Jr., *The White Man's Indian*, (New York 1979), pt. 4.
80. Louisa May Alcott, *Jo's Boys*, chapter 6, "Last Words," p. 98.
81. Ibid.
82. Louisa May Alcott, *Eight Cousins* and idem, *Rose in Bloom*.
83. Louisa May Alcott, "Mountain Laurel and Maidenhair," in *A Garland for Girls* (Boston, 1888), pp. 221–58.
84. Ibid., p. 224.
85. Ibid., p. 221.
86. Ibid., p. 225.
87. Ibid., p. 227.
88. Ibid., p. 241.
89. Ibid., p. 245.
90. Ibid., p. 247.
91. Ibid., p. 247.
92. Ibid., p. 253.
93. Ibid., p. 254.
94. Ibid., pp. 248, 249.
95. Louisa May Alcott, "May Flowers," in *A Garland for Girls*, pp. 1–42. See Barbara Miller Solomon, *Ancestors and Immigrants: A Changing New England Tradition* (Chicago, 1956), for the full significance of Alcott's reassertion of "Pilgrim Fathers."
96. Louisa May Alcott, "Mountain Laurel and Maidenhair," p. 257.
97. Louisa May Alcott, *Little Men*, Chapter 5, "Patty Pans," p. 74.
98. Ibid., p. 77.
99. Louisa May Alcott, "Letty's Tramp," *The Independent* 27, no. 1412 (Dec. 23, 1875); rpt. in *The Women's Journal* 3, no. 5 (Jan. 29, 1876).
100. Ibid.
101. Ibid. Louisa May Alcott, *Rose in Bloom* has Rose investing her wealth in cooperative homes for working women.
102. Quoted in Hugh Hawkins, *Between Havard and America: The Educational Leadership of Charles W. Eliot* (New York, 1972), p. 198.
103. Louisa May Alcott, *Rose in Bloom*, Chapter 1, "Coming Home," p. 9.
104. Louisa May Alcott, *Jo's Boys*, chapter 22, "Positively Last Appearance," p. 284.
105. John Lathrop Motley, *Historic Progress and American Democracy* (New York, 1869), p. 6.

106. Louisa May Alcott, letter to *The Woman's Journal* 14 (Jan. 20, 1883).
107. Cheney, ed., *Louisa May Alcott*, p. 282.
108. Ibid., p. 279.
109. Ibid.
110. Louisa May Alcott, "Preface," to *Prayers by Theodore Parker* (Boston, 1882).
111. Florence Whiting Brown ("Alcott and the Concord School") recalls Bronson Alcott's last sessions and "the days of the long-haired men and the short-haired women who sojourned" in Concord
112. Ibid. The Nonquitt Cottage had no kitchen; a nearby hotel served meals. Alcott reported "Restful days in my little house, which is cool and quiet, and without the curse of a kitchen to spoil it" (Cheney, ed., *Louisa May Alcott*, p. 245).
113. Cheney, ed., *Louisa May Alcott*, p. 306.
114. Ibid.
115. Edward John Waring states that "calomel exercises a powerful beneficial influence" in the treatment of typhus and typhoid fever" (Edward John Waring, *A Manual of Practical Therapeutics* [London, 1854] p. 46.) Calomel is mercurious chloride salt. I am indebted to Professor Sander Kelman, Cornell University, for information on the nineteenth-century use of calomel and also for the modern research on inorganic and organic mercury poisoning (minamata disease).
116. Stern, *Louisa May Alcott*, p. 340.
117. Ibid., p. 340.
118. Louisa May Alcott, *A Modern Mephistopheles and A Whisper in the Dark* (Boston, 1889).
119. Louisa May Alcott, ibid., *A Whispher in the Dark*, p. 337.
120. Ibid., 342.
121. Ibid., 345.
122. Ibid., 349.
123. Ibid., 350.

Index